Refuting the
Anti-Israel Narrative

ALSO BY JEREMY HAVARDI

Projecting Britain at War: The National Character in British World War II Films (McFarland, 2014)

Refuting the Anti-Israel Narrative

A Case for the Historical, Legal and Moral Legitimacy of the Jewish State

JEREMY HAVARDI

McFarland & Company, Inc., Publishers
Jefferson, North Carolina

LIBRARY OF CONGRESS CATALOGUING-IN-PUBLICATION DATA

Names: Havardi, Jeremy, author.
Title: Refuting the anti-Israel narrative : a case for the historical, legal, and moral legitimacy of the Jewish state / Jeremy Havardi.
Description: Jefferson, North Carolina : McFarland & Company, Inc., Publishers, 2016 | Includes bibliographical references and index.
Identifiers: LCCN 2016004834 | ISBN 9780786498819 (softcover : acid free paper) ∞
Subjects: LCSH: Israel—Public opinion. | Israel—Politics and government—Public opinion. | Land settlement—West Bank—Public opinion. | Israel—In mass media. | Arab-Israeli conflict—Influence.
Classification: LCC DS126.5 .H376 2016 | DDC 956.04—dc23
LC record available at http://lccn.loc.gov/2016004834

BRITISH LIBRARY CATALOGUING DATA ARE AVAILABLE

ISBN (print) 978-0-7864-9881-9
ISBN (ebook) 978-1-4766-2297-2

© 2016 Jeremy Havardi. All rights reserved

No part of this book may be reproduced or transmitted in any form or by any means, electronic or mechanical, including photocopying or recording, or by any information storage and retrieval system, without permission in writing from the publisher.

Printed in the United States of America

*McFarland & Company, Inc., Publishers
Box 611, Jefferson, North Carolina 28640
www.mcfarlandpub.com*

To all those in the Middle East who struggle peacefully
for democracy, freedom, human rights
and, above all, the truth

Table of Contents

Preface   1

Introduction: State of Play Today   5

PART I: THE TWISTED NARRATIVE

1. Israel the "Law Breaker": Occupation, Settlements, War and Refugees   19
2. The Calumnies of the Radical Left: Israel as a Genocidal, Racist, Apartheid and Colonialist State   51
3. The Myth of the "All Conquering" Zionist Lobby   73
4. Nailing the Grand Lie: Why Israel Is Not the Cause of Radical Islam's War Against the West   87

PART II: CHANGING THE NARRATIVE

5. The Jewish Historical, Legal and Moral Right to the State of Israel   121
6. The Actual Cause of the 90-Year Conflict: Arab and Palestinian Rejection and Western Appeasement   147
7. Israel Is an Invaluable Asset to the West   189
8. Changing the Narrative: Turning on the Accusers   206

Conclusion   233
Chapter Notes   243
Bibliography   261
Index   267

"For false words are not only evil in themselves,
but they infect the soul with evil."
—Plato, *Phaedo*

"Everyone is entitled to his own opinion,
but not to his own facts"
—Daniel Patrick Moynihan

Preface

We live in an era shaped by a postmodern attitude towards truth and reality. For many, the age-old requirement to check viewpoints against evidence and logic is an anachronism. Instead, subjectivity and personal feelings have taken over as the arbiters of truth; literally anything goes in judging the validity of opinions. After all, who is to judge what is true and false when truth is merely an "instrument of power" (Michel Foucault), when Western intellectual progress is merely imperialist oppression, when all forms of authority are suspect and when individual views matter more than facts and logic?

At the same time we live in an era of conspiracy theory with an instant readiness to seize upon criticisms of the establishment. The Internet has become a prime source for disseminating contrarian perspectives that are designed to shake up the received wisdom about our world. Crackpots and fantasists lend weight to unorthodox opinions, which are then instantly seized upon by an army of devotees. We are awash with what Damien Thomson has called "counterknowledge," which he defines as "misinformation packaged to look like fact." So ubiquitous is counterknowledge that Thomson warns that the "twenty first century is facing a pandemic of credulous thinking."[1]

The combination of these perspectives, with their cavalier attitude towards truth, has led to an avalanche of ill-founded ideas that are passed off as the received wisdom about the world. The 9/11 truth movement, Holocaust denial, Diana conspiracy theories, the Da Vinci code, and the belief in a global Illuminati are just a few of the more modern examples.[2] All are characterized by a belief that the truth has been hidden from us by a set of sinister forces beyond our control, but all involve an equally sinister twisting of the evidence. Moreover, the twin ideologies of Third Worldism and political correctness, which hold sway throughout much of academia, have corrupted debates on race, nationhood and identity. Western ideals have come under relentless assault as a result.

These currents of thought have certainly influenced discussions of the Middle East, at both popular and academic levels. It is common for Israel to be pictured as the primary cause of the region's troubles and as an international pariah deserving isolation and disdain. She has been accused of fomenting violence, terrorism and global crises to serve her own interests. As a result, she has become a pantomime villain par excellence, held to blame for many of the world's ills.

This book is an attempt to question much of this received wisdom. It exposes the falsifications, distortions and ignorance that lie behind the "anti–Israel narrative" and suggests how the picture they offer fails to add up when stacked against logic and evidence. The truth about Israel and the wider Middle East has been twisted out of all recognition, and this volume sets the record straight. This subject is increasingly relevant despite the focus of scrutiny in the Middle East shifting in recent years. Recent convulsions in the region, including the Arab Spring, the ouster of the Muslim Brotherhood, the rise of the Islamic State and the Iranian nuclear threat, have removed some focus from Israel's relations with its neighbors. But the area of Israel and the disputed territories remains one of the most sensitive conflict zones anywhere on earth, and resolving the conflict is of perennial concern to policy makers.

This is certainly not the first book to challenge the prevailing narrative of the Arab-Israeli conflict. I owe a debt to Alan Dershowitz, whose books *The Case for Israel* and *The Case Against Israel's Enemies* have been influential. Robin Shepherd's *A State Beyond the Pale* has extensively analyzed the mainstreaming of an anti–Israeli discourse in European circles. I should also mention Mitchell Bard's *Myths and Facts*, which offers a detailed rebuttal to many of the egregious falsifications about the conflict. But this book goes further than the others insofar as it does four things: it identifies the main themes in the anti–Israel narrative; it exposes their inherent falsity using evidence and logic; it substitutes an alternative, pro–Israel narrative; and, finally, it attacks Israel's critics by exposing their hypocrisy and double standards.

My own interest in this subject is longstanding. I have been arguing Israel's case since the tender age of 16, when the Arab-Israeli issue came under discussion during A-Level English lessons. Perry Keenlyside, my English literature teacher at Haberdashers Aske's, liked to debate politics with his students prior to delving into a passage of Chaucer or Shakespeare. Israel was one of those subjects that produced the liveliest discussions, inevitable perhaps in a school where more than a third of the students were Jewish.

At Bristol University I helped organize an Israel stall for a huge event called One World Day, covered by the local media. I have a vivid recollection of warmly greeting the representative of Egypt and of being snubbed by a Palestinian stall-holder. Then there were meetings of the Socialist Workers Party, in which the Middle East was a subject of frequent debate. The mere mention of Israel or America left young hotheads frothing at the mouth in indignation. Their worldview was a simplistic one: these bastions of Western power were pariah states, international outliers that needed to be isolated and brought to an end. In the years since, little has changed.

After the shocking events of September 11, 2001, I made a conscious decision to challenge the myths, lies and falsifications in the Western press. Writing letters to newspapers became an almost daily obsession, particularly during the troubled times of the second intifada. I became a journalist in my early 30s, and letters soon gave way to feature-length articles, opinion pieces and book reviews. I interviewed activists on both sides, as well as politicians, ambassadors and academics. This book builds upon the arguments put forward over many years.

This volume should appeal to a variety of audiences. First, it should interest university students reading modern history or politics, particularly those pursuing Middle East studies who seek an alternative to the Arabist narrative so prevalent within academia. Second, it contains arguments and rebuttals that can be used by pro–Israel advocates to put forward their case. Last, it is aimed at all those who question the received wisdom about Israel and the Middle East and who maintain an interest in this most complex, longstanding and seemingly unsolvable conflict.

Some acknowledgments are due. To carry out research, I used the excellent facilities at the British Library to search through the archives of British newspapers, particularly those relating to the 1948 war. I would also like to thank the staff there for their unstinting help in tracking down much-needed articles. I also want to thank the following for their very useful comments on different chapters of the book: Professor Brad Blitz of Middlesex University for his insightful comments on refugee law; Professor Denis McEoin and Professor Alan Johnson for their insightful comments on the anti–Israel narrative; Omar Madhloom of De Montfort University for his observations on radicalization and radical Islam; Professor Eric Moonman for his comments on the Israel lobby; Robin Shepherd for his views on Europe's anti–Israel derangement; and Sebastian Steinfeld for his expert comments on international law relating to the conflict. Despite all the help I received, I naturally take full responsibility for any errors in the text.

Introduction: State of Play Today

Today Israel finds herself condemned in the international court of public opinion. She stands accused of crimes and misdemeanors that are wholly without parallel in the modern world. She has been labeled a pariah nation, an apartheid regime, a strategic liability and even a genocidal state. She has been likened to the vilest regimes in human history and blamed for fomenting political conflict, wars and economic crises around the globe. The accepted wisdom among many of the West's policy makers, political academics and media elites is that Israel's actions are the primary cause of instability in the Middle East.

At the UN she is routinely singled out for condemnation. The founding philosophy of the state of Israel, Zionism, has been described as racist and colonialist, and more resolutions have been passed against the Jewish state than against any other country. It is now commonplace to see debates on university campuses that question whether the country has a right to exist. Conspiracy theories suggest that Israel actively manipulates Western governments for her own sinister ends, forcing them to genuflect before the terrifying power of pro-Israel lobbies and invoking the specter of malevolent Jewish power. Quite simply, no other nation on earth has been subjected to such a systematic and relentless assault on her legitimacy.

In recent years, when Israelis have been forced to defend themselves against terrorist provocation in Lebanon and Gaza, there has been an orchestrated outpouring of rage around the world. Anti-Israel rallies have attracted tens of thousands of people in major cities, with many carrying banners calling for Israel's destruction. Some of these banners have included explicit calls for the murder of Jews while Israel's victims have been likened to those persecuted in the Holocaust. Their rage has been fuelled by media coverage of Israeli actions that often portrays a hapless Palestinian David suffering from the blows of an Israeli Goliath. Israel is perceived as the regional bully, pumped up with Western money to pursue an expansionist and oppressive foreign policy. Little or no coverage is given to the actions and ideologies of terror groups attacking Israel, or to the alternative military options that Israel could be expected to take. Israel's wars, unlike those of other Western democracies, automatically result in one-sided international enquiries and fact-finding missions.

Aside from environmentalism, anti-Israel activism is surely the fashionable cause of the modern world. It has helped to spawn a vocal campaign of demonization against the Jewish state, symbolized in particular by the demand for boycotts, divestment and sanctions against Israel. This was a key demand made at the notorious Durban conference in 2001, an anti-racist gathering that was rapidly transformed into an anti-Semitic hate-fest. The advocates of the BDS (boycotts, divestment and sanctions) campaign frequently liken Israel to apartheid South Africa and seek the same pariah status for the Jewish state. Israel apartheid week is now a commonplace in leading Western universities and speakers are invited to demonize the country with incendiary rhetoric.

In recent years, there have been calls to boycott a variety of Israeli products and institutions, ranging from the country's trade unions, academics, theater groups, sports teams, philharmonic orchestra and even her principal language, Hebrew. In 2014, a Jewish Film Institute was asked to renounce links with the Israeli embassy before it could showcase its work in a London theater. An Israeli dance company was banned from the Edinburgh festival and a recent performance of the Israeli Philharmonic Orchestra was aggressively disrupted. A number of Israeli academics and diplomats have been effectively barred from speaking on Western campuses. The BDS movement has been at the forefront of this anti–Zionist campaign, mobilizing "progressive" forces in Western culture and academia to isolate Israel in every sphere of public life. They seek to entrench the belief that Israel is a rank outsider to the global community, an affront to the civilized community of nations and the ultimate rogue entity. This is not about upholding Palestinian human rights but about traducing Israel's global reputation.

While countless thousands march regularly in support of "Palestine," there are dozens of other human rights causes that receive much less attention among the intelligentsia. Few march in Western capitals for the long-suffering Shia in Saudi Arabia, for the stateless Kurds, for Tibetans living under repressive Chinese occupation, for North Koreans languishing in prison camps or for the cause of women or gays in Iran. The abuses of Burma, Cuba, Syria and many an African dictatorship rarely bring the masses to the streets of Western countries. By the same token, the appalling discrimination meted out to Palestinians by Arab countries such as Kuwait and Lebanon is met with stony silence on the part of those claiming to be their greatest champions. While Israeli military campaigns automatically lead to international investigation and censure, other democracies routinely get a free pass. The hypocrisy is truly breathtaking.

Perhaps it is little surprise that, according to the Peace Index, 56 percent of Jewish Israelis believe that "the whole world is against us."[1] More than three-quarters think that, regardless of what Israel does or how many concessions are made on the Palestinian issue, the world will continue to chastise their country. More than half of Israelis think the country is partly or wholly isolated in the global community. This is less a state of paranoia than an accurate reflection of current global trends. A poll commissioned by the European Commission in 2011, surveying 7,500 people across 15 European countries, showed that Israel was believed to be the biggest threat to world peace, ahead of Iran and North Korea. In 2011, there was a major poll conducted by the University of Bielefeld on behalf of the German Friedrich Ebert Foundation. In each of 7 countries, 1,000 citizens aged over 16 were asked whether Israel was carrying out a war of extermination against the Palestinians; 42 percent of UK citizens agreed along with 48 percent of Germans, 38 percent of Italians, 39 percent of Dutch and 63 percent of Poles. In other words, Israel was being compared to Nazi Germany, the worst foe of the Jewish nation. According to the results of a survey commissioned by the *Daily Telegraph* in 2005, Israel was in the top 5 "least democratic countries" and one of the 5 "least deserving of international respect."[2]

As Manfred Gerstenfeld points out, this and other polling data indicates the extent to which "demonization and negative views of Israel have permeated mainstream European society."[3] Such polling data provides the most compelling evidence of how ordinary people have bought into an agenda of anti-Israeli delegitimization. With Islamism on the rise and with increasingly vocal Muslim minorities flexing their muscles in Europe, such antipathy to the Jewish state looks set to continue. Yet rather incredibly, it has been claimed that the Zionist narrative has "virtually canonical (fixed, and revered) status, enjoying some of the privileges one associates only with 'sacred texts.'"[4] The claim is breathtaking in its naivety.

David or Goliath?

Yet still some argue that, for all this relentless demonization, Israel remains the regional superpower and the Goliath of the Middle East, meaning that she has little to fear from this global diplomatic assault. There is some truth in the notion that Israel is stronger today than ever before. There are longstanding ties between the Jewish state and some of the most powerful countries in the world, among them the United States, Germany, Canada, the UK, and India. The leaders of those nations make public visits to Israel and make no secret of their support for the burgeoning links between their respective countries. Today, those ties are being cemented by a number of factors, including growing trade, as well as cooperation in the fields of intelligence, science, technology and defense. Israel has improved relations considerably with Russia, a remarkable turnaround from the old Cold War days when the Soviet Union was a formidable diplomatic adversary.

Since 1994, Israel has enjoyed diplomatic relations with Vatican City, following a period of 20 years in which Catholic-Jewish relations warmed under Pope John Paul II. She has diplomatic relations with 159 nations, and over 80 percent of the world's countries recognize the Jewish state. Even at the UN, scene of so much relentless hostility, there is the odd sign to warm the optimist. Israel has recently won a number of posts at the UN on various committees, including one on disarmament. In 2014, the Israeli ambassador to the UN, Ron Prosor, was unanimously chosen by 170 members to chair the elections for the UN human rights committee.

For many years, Israel has not been menaced by the threat of war with Arab states. Egypt and Jordan are allies, albeit in a cold peace, Syria remains gripped by the specter of civil war and Iraq is convulsed by its potential breakup. The old adage that "my enemy's enemy is my friend" has potentially brought Israel closer to countries such as Jordan, Saudi Arabia and some of the Persian Gulf states, given their shared anxiety about a nuclear Iran and the terrifying prospect of a regional Shiite insurgency. Diplomatic contacts exist (at an unofficial level) with a number of these countries, though normalization remains a long way off.

Israel has also enjoyed one of the fastest growth rates of any economy in the world in recent years. A survey carried out by Bloomberg in 2013 found that the shekel was the strongest of 31 main currencies around the globe in the first quarter of that year.[5] Three years earlier, the country formally acceded to the Organization for Economic Co-operation and Development (OECD).

In recent years Israeli trade with both China and India has burgeoned. In 2012–13 alone, Israel's bilateral trade with India soared to $6 billion with Israel emerging as India's second-largest supplier of arms.[6] China recently signed two agreements with Israel to link the port of Eilat to its Mediterranean ports at Ashdod and Haifa, providing an alternative land-based route for shipping to the Suez Canal. With the discovery of natural gas off its Mediterranean coastline, Israel is set to become energy independent and could even become a net exporter of gas.[7] It may also be on its way to water independence, given how much of the country's demand for water is met by water desalination and recycling. As of January 2015, unemployment stood at just 5.6 percent, despite a significant gap between rich and poor.[8] Its prowess in science is such that in January 2014, Israel was invited to become CERN's 21st member.[9]

When one takes into account Israel's scientific and technological prowess, its capacity for entrepreneurship and innovation, the formidable power of its military and world-renowned intelligence operations, the success of its leading universities, hospitals and research centers and, above all, the unyielding resilience and patriotism of its population in the face of adversity, it is easy to appreciate the major strengths that will allow Israel to survive and flourish in the coming decades.

But Israel also has significant weaknesses. Today, the country is surrounded by a variety of unappeasable enemies that seek her outright destruction. Unlike in the 1960s and 1970s, that threat does not emanate primarily from secular Arab regimes. It comes today from the Islamic Republic of Iran, one of the world's leading sponsors of terror and a potential nuclear weapons state. Iran is a revolutionary Islamist state, animated by a genocidal anti–Zionism and anti-Semitism, whose leaders have long issued blood-curdling rhetoric about wiping Israel off the map.

In Gaza, Hamas has launched a decade-long attritional war designed to drive communities from southern Israel and terrorize the rest of the population. Gaza also hosts a number of other more extreme Salafist groups. In Lebanon, the Iran-backed Hezbollah possesses a vast arsenal of weapons, which are capable of hitting every city in Israel.[10] The Sinai Peninsula is a hotbed of extremist groups that have received weapons from abroad.[11] The Islamic Republic, formerly ISIL, perhaps the most repugnant manifestation of Sunni jihadism yet seen, has taken over parts of Iraq and Syria. Further afield, support for the anti–Semitic Muslim Brotherhood is strong in many Middle East countries. Add to this Israel's tiny size, only slightly bigger than New Jersey or Wales, and her consequent lack of strategic depth, and one can understand the persistent anxieties that Israelis have about their security. Certainly Israel is vastly stronger than these forces, but she faces a far-from-benign environment.

Israel is also hopelessly outnumbered in international forums. At the UN General Assembly and in the Human Rights Council, anti–Israel resolutions are practically certain to pass, given the membership of those bodies. Arab states outnumber Israel by 22 to 1 and, in respect of the Organization of Islamic Conference, by 57 to 1. Muslim minorities vastly outnumber Jewish communities across Europe and are growing in other Western nations. Many countries in Europe have chosen to appease these populations and their frequently hostile rhetoric towards Israel. They continue to be dependent on Arab oil imports. With such formidable demographic and economic weapons, the Arab and Islamic world today possesses tremendous political clout to pressure Israel indirectly, and pro–Israel governments more directly, and to delegitimize the Jewish state in all the forums of public opinion. Such pressure may also come from policy elites, academics and champions of the human rights industry that buy into an anti–Israeli narrative. For these reasons, Israel can be regarded as the regional underdog, the Jewish David to the Islamic Goliath.[12]

This book will essentially argue that the anti–Israel narrative is pervasive among Western elites. It will show that there are a number of themes that typify the hostility, misunderstanding and sheer ignorance foundational to this narrative. It will also argue for a correction, a change of perspective, a kind of detoxification of the mind if you will. In arguing that this narrative is widespread in the West, I am not suggesting that it is the only narrative. There are a significant number of conservative news forums, Web sites, newspapers and think tanks in which this narrative receives short shrift and in which Israeli actions are understood and praised. But as these Western advocates for Israel are swimming against an entrenched perspective in policy, media and academic circles, their views cannot be said to predominate.

Why the Hostility?

This book scarcely touches on the reasons for the obsessive hostility towards Israel, and explaining them is naturally as controversial as the conflict itself. But some points are clear. The hysteria that Israel generates reflects far more than the brutality and intensity of the conflict purely in terms of casualty count. From 1967 to 2006, some 6,187 Palestinians were killed by Israel, and a huge number were terrorists, not civilians.[13] This is a small fraction of the number killed in many other contemporary conflicts. Nor can it reflect the (contested) charge of occupation. If occupation of Muslims was a main source of anger, why is there no anger stirred against Muslim-majority countries such as Turkey and Iraq, which have blocked the creation of "Kurdistan," or Syria for its occupation of Lebanese people, or Sudan's occupation of Darfur? There is clearly a special quality in a non–Muslim, American-backed nation occupying what is perceived to be Muslim land. One is entitled to ask for the source of such obsessive and frenzied hostility to Israel, and at least four explanations can be given.

First, since the 1960s, the Arab states have used their vast financial muscle to infiltrate the centers of global influence and power. With the help of poisonous Soviet propaganda, these states used the United Nations as their prime forum to pass endless anti–Israeli resolutions. The most obvious manifestation of their efforts was the passage of UN Resolution 3379, equating Zionism with racism. For four decades, Saudi petrodollars have flowed around the world, funding the erection of mosques, schools, student bodies and madrasahs, all of which promulgate the fiery, puritanical message of Wahhabism. The Wahhabi sect is virulently anti–Christian, anti–Semitic and anti–Zionist, and from Pakistan to Egypt, and Luton to Los Angeles, millions of minds have come into contact with the radical and radicalizing messages of the Saudi religious establishment. Anti–Israel sentiment is a natural consequence.

Arab petrodollars have also been used to purchase influence within academic circles. Vast donations have created Middle East Studies departments on both sides of the Atlantic, allowing sympathetic academics to promote an Arabist agenda in which Israel is deemed to be the prime barrier to regional peace. Ephraim Karsh talks of how Middle East studies have "increasingly fallen under the sway of Arabists and their disciples (i.e., veterans of institutions dealing with the region, such as the Department of State, oil companies, economic/financial organizations, etc.) and/or scholars of Arab descent" and of how "Arab oil producing countries have been penetrating the foremost Western universities and academic publishing houses by subsidizing publications and extending generous grants," the results being that they "exercise a lasting control, however indirect"[14] on these institutions. To take just one case, the London School of Economics accepted money from the regime of Muammar Gaddafi before awarding a rather dubious doctorate to Saif Gaddafi.[15] Other recipients of Saudi money include Oxford and Cambridge universities, while Durham received Iranian cash.

One of the most frequently cited scholars on Middle East affairs, Georgetown University's John Esposito (whose institute has been funded by the Saudis), has long been at pains to downplay the influence of radical Islam and to stress the "Islamophobic" nature of the media that reports on it. A similar message was promoted by the even more influential writer Edward Said. In the 1970s, he startled Western academia with his book *Orientalism*, the main thesis of which was that virtually any Western perspective on Islam, the Orient or the Arab world was automatically racist, colonialist and intellectually bankrupt. This region, he argued, had suffered under the hammer blow of Western colonial intervention and its Arab population, particularly the Palestinians, were victims of untrammeled First World aggression. Said's thesis proved to be remarkably influential in Western academia and provided a paradigm-shifting frame of reference for any "progressive" discussion of the Middle East.

The second explanation is that Israel is hated because of anti–Semitism. Without doubt, the global pathological virus of Jew hatred has mutated since World War II, transforming a detestation of "world Jewry" into a fiery rejection of the Jewish state. A pathology as old as anti–Semitism has a perennial power to excite the imagination, and many today use the Middle East conflict as a cover for bigotry and prejudice. One only has to digest the language of the debate to notice the recognizable tropes of anti–Semitism.

One of the most familiar charges against the Jews was that they were to blame for their own suffering, usually on the basis of some perceived fault of character. This gave a free pass to those who perpetrated evil crimes against them, transferring blame to the Jewish victims. For today's demonizers, the Jewishness of Israel is the country's major fault of character and helps explain why it is hated and attacked by its "innocent" enemies. References to the "chosen" can be found in anti–Israeli literature with attempts to link Israeli "misdeeds" to a primitive but ancient Jewish lust for revenge. These explanations try to root Zionism's alleged excess in perennial Jewish character.

Whereas once Jews were pictured as part of a diabolical clique conspiring to take over the world, now Zionist lobbies are accused of the same thing, using their financial muscle to sway foreign governments to their will. An age-old conspiracy theory attacking Jews as the center of international influence has been updated, though the word "Zionist" has replaced "Jew." In centuries past, anti–Semites repeatedly demonized Jews by likening them to child murderers who killed youngsters for their own diabolical and twisted purposes. Today, the Jewish nation is likened to the demonic, child-killing state of Nazi Germany in a bizarre form of Holocaust inversion. Finally, the longstanding charge of divided loyalties, the idea that Jews cannot be loyal, patriotic citizens because of their preferred clan loyalty, has resurfaced with venom. Now it is their Zionist affiliation that suggests a divided loyalty.

But while anti–Semitism cannot be discounted, it is not the principal driver of this relentless frenzy of hostility. The central reason why Israel is so hated is that she has come to symbolize everything that progressive elites dislike, namely Western values. For many decades, the ideology of Third Worldism has seeped into the leftist vernacular. This postulates a state of mutual antagonism between the rich, powerful First World and a long-suffering, victim-centered Third World. The West has been conceived of as an immoral political entity bringing endless suffering and exploitation to the indigenous cultures of the Third World. By contrast, those in the Third World have been depicted as soldiers in the global resistance to colonialism and tyranny. Members of this Third World are pictured as romantic rebels rightly demanding the support of Western progressives. For many, the enemy-in-chief of the First World is the USA.

How does Israel fit into this picture? She is an economically successful and highly democratic state that truly embodies First World, Western ideals. Indeed, the country is a stunning advertisement for how Western values can transform a nation. She is also a valuable ally of the United States that does not apologize for using force in its own defense, including against a perceived Third World minority (the Palestinians). In its desire to champion "romantic rebels," today's left-liberal alliance sees Palestinians as the vanguard for undermining the perceived excesses and brutality of the "arrogant" West. For them, Israel is a hated symbol of colonialism and exploitation, while the Palestinian underdogs are "the Vietcong of the Middle East."[16] The New Left, which has come to "regard race as a more salient axis of oppression than class, views the Palestinians 'as the new proletariat.'"[17]

Much of this reflects a political strategy adopted by the Palestinians under Soviet sponsorship. In the early 1960s, the PLO adopted the language of the freedom fighter and of the liberation struggle. Instead of talking about the destruction of Israel and the Jews, which strongly reflected the pro–Nazi sentiments of past leaders (the mufti, Ahmed Shuqiary), now Fatah and the PLO spoke about a people's "struggle against oppression" and their "search for freedom." This was deliberately modeled on the kind of revolutionary leftist language being used by Third World liberation movements, whether in Cuba, Vietnam or Africa. Suddenly the war against Israel was no longer about a vast Arab bloc seeking to wipe out a tiny neighbor. Now it was about a beleaguered Palestinian people desperate to regain their homeland from the clutches of a colonial oppressor. The Palestinians started to abandon hope in Israel's military overthrow. Instead, in a reversal of Von Clausewitz's formula, they turned diplomacy into "war by other means."

Today, Israel is particularly estranged from European "progressives" in virtue of embodying national culture and tradition. She is a *Jewish* nation-state, one imbued with preserving the values and ideals of one people rather than being a culture-free zone. Her population insists on reviving a national ideal, using a long-dead language to imbue the character of its society. Its dominant Jewish perspective is a source of pride, not shame. For many Europeans, these features of ethnic nationalism are a throwback to the past, a symbol of discord and instability that feels distinctly pre-modern.

Being a progressive and enlightened European today means embracing the fashionable ideals of multiculturalism and transnational identity. It means that one should reject a primary attachment to nation-states or any adherence to ethnic or cultural exclusivism. In a world mired in moral relativism, the idea of defending the West is deemed arrogant, racist and discriminatory. A thriving Israel discredits the contemporary fashion for universalized, postnational identities and arouses the admiration of those who remain skeptical about the EU's multiculturalist agenda.[18] In sum, we can see why the campaign of delegitimizing Israel is impervious to facts and rational discussion—it is part of a revolutionary, anti–Western ideology.

All these reasons account for Western hostility, but there is a fourth reason that is rooted in the Middle East. Why are so many in the Arab world enraged by a Jewish state in their midst and by Zionism? Here it is not enough to cite an obvious answer, namely that Israel has defeated Arab states in the past, or that it continues to kill fellow Arabs in violent conflict. Hostility to Israel has been encouraged by regimes for reasons of political self-interest, namely to distract the highly discontented masses from their domestic concerns. Such hatred is welcomed, both because it removes anger directed towards them and also externalizes the cause of their suffering. If Israel is to blame for poverty, corruption, repression and disorder, then there is no need for internal policy change. As long as the Zionist hand is at work, the populace has no need to turn against its rulers. The tidal wave of anger gives Arab despots a degree of popularity and credibility that can help shore up their regimes. For this reason Barry Rubin once described anti–Zionism as "the opiate of the Arab world" and as "an addiction that could not be broken but that provided false satisfaction and distraction to the masses."[19]

Of course, the Arab Spring has shown the limits of this diversion tactic as one Arab state after another (Tunisia, Egypt, Libya, Yemen, Syria) has experienced the convulsion of mass discontent and violent, bloody civil war. But the externalization of the region's turmoil, with state rulers using their powers over national media to blame Zionism and America for all their people's problems, has continued to prevent the proper re-appraisal that is necessary to transform the region root and branch. Such a re-appraisal, if it ever happens, would identify a plethora of reasons why the Middle East lags so spectacularly behind every region on earth (excepting perhaps sub–Saharan Africa). They would include the existence of repressive dictatorships, the corruption and nepotism of the Arab political class, the lack of basic freedoms, stagnant economies and the failure to create knowledge-based societies. The Palestinian journalist Khaled Abu Toameh is right when he says: "The real threat to peace in the Middle East is the absence of freedom, democracy and transparency in the Arab and Islamic world."[20]

Quite simply, a successful Israel helps to demolish the lazy argument that the Middle East is just a poor region from which little of significance can be expected. She is a tiny nation, half of whose land is desert, and with few natural resources to speak of. Despite this, she has won more Nobel Prizes per capita than almost all major nations on earth and has made a plethora of scientific, technological and cultural contributions to Western society. It is a truly incredible feat. Israel, a successful and dynamic economy and an oasis of democracy and liberty, represents a standing rebuke to the leaders of authoritarian, poverty-stricken societies. If Israelis can make great advances in science, medicine and education, why can't the Arab peoples? If Israel can hold free and fair elections, have an uncensored press, tolerate sexual differences, elect women leaders and operate a judiciary that stands up to its government, why are such glittering prizes not available across the region?

Blaming Israel for every fault in the Arab world is, as one Egyptian writer puts it, "the logic of the weak, who seek a peg on which to hang all their mistakes in order to evade a true confrontation with reality."[21] The peoples of the Middle East are desperate to exchange freedom and openness for autocracy and stagnation. They need to escape the endemic trap of tyranny, illiberalism, and underachievement rather than imbibe yet more anti–Israeli propaganda.

Not Black and White

While this book adopts a pro–Israeli position, it does not attempt to cast all Israelis as angels and their detractors as demons. Such a view would be absurdly simplistic and one-sided. The complexity of the world requires not so much a black-and-white approach as one with shades of grey and chiaroscuro. One can accept this book's basic premises while also believing that Israel should be subjected to fair and reasonable criticism as is appropriate for any nation state under the rule of law; indeed no democracy could thrive without it. Far from being without sin Israel is, to paraphrase King Lear, "more sinned against than sinning." There are certain areas where criticism is legitimate.

SETTLEMENTS

In particular, one can have certain reservations about aspects of settlement policy since 1967. Certainly, a great deal of nonsense has been talked about how settlements are the prime impediment to peace in the region and how they are illegal, and both these myths are exposed in Chapter 1. It is also undoubtedly true that settlement numbers have grown the more that Palestinians have rejected peace overtures, and this can be seen as a deterrent to further rejectionism. The more they waste time rejecting initiatives, the more settlements will expand.

But the experience of the Gaza pullout in 2005 did show that uprooting settlers for the sake of peace was a complicated and painful affair. The disengagement required the services of thousands of soldiers, some of whom came under attack from more hard-line settlers. Increasing the number of settlers living on land that Israel does not intend to retain appears to be a self-defeating strategy. In recent decades, Israel would have helped its cause by clearly preventing settlement growth in those areas that were likely to become part of a Palestinian state and redirecting that growth to areas that were certain to be annexed to Israel. This would have sent out a clear message that expanding settlements, legal in any case, was doing no fundamental harm to the cause of a peaceful Palestinian state. Announcing settlement expansion in the wake of a terror attack appears to be part of a retaliatory, tit-for-tat strategy, a punishment for poor behavior rather than a carefully thought-out policy. In addition, "price tag" attacks, which involve vandalizing neighboring Palestinian villages whenever an illegal Israeli outpost is removed, have rightly merited censure across the Israeli political spectrum.[22]

Settlements are championed by religious political parties that often wield disproportionate influence within the Israeli political system. As a result, these kingmakers hold the balance of power in Israel's various coalitions, giving them power to impose a sometimes divisive religious agenda on the majority and exacerbating the deep fissure that exists between the religious and the secular in the country. Among the issues that divide opinion are the exemption from military service granted to ultra-orthodox students and the extensive welfare payments given to their families. But the problem of allowing small parties to dictate a political agenda has beset several countries that adhere to proportional representation. In the most recent election in 2015, the threshold for attaining representation in the Knesset was raised to 3.25 percent, and this has reduced the chance for tiny parties to gain a political foothold. But ultimately, religious parties maintain a strong political influence and, in the long term, the tension between secular and religious forces will provide the state with considerable challenges.

Much criticism from progressive Israelis centers on areas of discrimination affecting the Israeli Arab population. There would appear to be some truth to the claim. The Or Commission (2003) found that "the state did not do enough to grant equality to its Arab citizens and to eliminate discrimination and deprivation." The government, it recommended, had to achieve "genuine equality for the Arab citizens of the state."[23] A quick look at some socio-economic data suggests some forms of inequality.

Health

Israeli Jews have a higher life expectancy and lower infant mortality than their Arab counterparts. For Israeli Jews as of 2010, the figures are 83.9 years for women and 80.7 for men. Among Israeli Arabs the number is 80.9 for women and 76.5 for men.[24] In the Jewish population, the infant mortality rate for 2011 was 2.6 per 1,000 live births, and 6.4 per 1,000 live births in the Arab population, though some figures put the Arab rate higher.[25] There are significant discrepancies between Israeli Arabs and Jews in terms of death from heart disease and cerebrovascular events and the incidence of breast cancer and diabetes. These outcomes are often related to the lower socio-economic position of Israeli Arabs.

Despite the disparities, Israeli Arabs generally have a long life expectancy, indeed one year higher than U.S. citizens and very significantly higher than the rest of the Arab world.[26] Arab infant mortality figures are greater, in part because babies in the Arab population are more likely to suffer from congenital defects and diseases, owing to more first-cousin marriages, and to the fact that there is less likelihood of a termination for cultural reasons. Arab women tend to have children when very young, often below the age of 20, adding to the complications in pregnancy.[27] In particular, the Bedouin suffer from a variety of birth defects and hereditary diseases that have a strong impact on figures for infant mortality.[28] But Arab figures are still considerably lower than for other First World countries.[29]

There are also a variety of factors to take into account to explain discrepancies in health between Jewish and Arab citizens, among them socio-economic status, education, heredity and lifestyle choice. But culture too may play a role. To take one example, researchers from the Hebrew University Hadassah School of Public Health in Jerusalem found that Jewish heart patients were several times more likely to undergo cardiac rehabilitation than Arab patients (61 to 17.2 percent). This was despite the fact that in the research, Arabs suffered from the same cardiac event and were treated in the same hospital as Israeli Jews, indicating that a cultural factor may have been at work.

Rates of breast cancer are also higher among Israeli Arabs than Jews, but this is not the result of unequal treatment. Included in Israel's health service basket is a mammogram for the early detection of breast cancer from the age of 50, and once a year at 40 for women with a family history of breast cancer. However, the median age for the incidence of breast cancer is lower in the Arab than Jewish sector (51.6 to 62.7). Clearly, the health service needs to adapt to the differentiated needs of the Arab sector, but this is not an issue of unequal service provision.[30]

Education

Another area of concern is education. A U.S. State Department report published in 2014 noted, "Resources devoted to education in Arabic were inferior to those devoted to education in Hebrew in the public education system," and said that on average the state spent, per student, "24,800 NIS ($7,050) at government secular Jewish high schools, and 21,100 NIS ($5,990) at Arab high schools."[31] Class sizes are lower in Jewish areas at elementary level compared to Arabs (24.6 students to 29) and at high schools (27.6 students in Jewish areas to 30.5 in Arab.)[32] There is also a significant disparity in the numbers of Arab and Jews obtaining doctorates.

Yet while class sizes are lower and years in education higher among Israeli Jews than Arabs, it is also true that significant advances have been made over the last half decade to equalize opportunities. Amnon Rubinstein, a professor of law, has written that the "disparity in education subsidies has in recent years substantially decreased ... today the ratio is 1.1 to 1."[33] Interestingly, the Israel Democracy Institute has estimated that over the last seven decades, there has been a ninefold increase in the average number of years of schooling for Israeli Arabs, an incredible increase by any standard.[34] These results are very significant and offer the promising prospect that educational gaps will narrow between the Jewish and Arab communities.

Employment and Per Capita Income

Unemployment in Israel for the first quarter of 2014 does show an overall national rate of 5.9 percent but a higher rate for Israeli Arabs (7.8 percent, and 9.6 percent for Arab women).[35] A recent U.S. State Department has noted that Arabs are discriminated against in hiring practices as the lack of military service has rendered them "ineligible to work in companies with defense contracts or in security-related fields."[36] Access to prestigious professions can be hard too, with some surveys indicating that employers discriminate against Israeli Arabs, ultra-orthodox Jews and Israelis of Ethiopian descent.[37]

Yet Israel has also taken steps to narrow Arab unemployment, including the opening of 21 job centers in Arab areas. The Tel Aviv Stock Exchange has also created a program that is designed to boost the listings of Arab companies and create greater prosperity for Arabs and non–Arabs alike.[38] Even though Arabs are underrepresented in the civil service, there has been a dramatic increase, with the Arab share of its workforce rising from 2 percent in 2007 to 7.8 percent by 2014.[39]

There is also an alternative form of national service that Israeli Arabs are taking part in, allowing them the opportunity to assist their community and provide services to Arab areas. They are eligible for the same financial benefits as military veterans. The number of Arabs volunteering for national service went up from 240 in 2005 to 1,473 in 2010.[40]

Another way to measure possible inequalities in the labor market is by analyzing wages. According to the Israeli "Income Survey of 2011," produced by the Central Bureau of Statistics, "the average salary for the entire population of Israeli Arab males was 50.2 percent of the mean for the entire population of Jewish males" and "Arab females earned only 28 percent of the salaries of Jewish females."[41] Given that Arab households are bigger than Jewish ones in Israel, this will translate into a much lower per capita income.

However, there are several factors that underlie wage disparity, other than simply endemic ethnic or racial discrimination. For one thing, there are more Jewish women in employment than Arab women, something that significantly impacts on wage levels.[42] Another factor is the generally lower median age of Israeli Arabs (19) as compared to Israeli Jews (31). This means that there are more young Arabs in the workforce who, in turn, have a lower earning potential. Age structure and economic inequality have been found to be related in the United States too, where black and Hispanic Americans, whose median age is lower than white Americans, earn less than their white counterparts on average.[43] When one factors into the higher educational achievement of Israeli Jews (already noted), it is clear that discrimination plays only a limited role in explaining these figures.

It is worth bearing in mind that not all Arabs face economic difficulties. As Joshua Muravchik points out, Christian Arabs are considerably better off than their Muslim counterparts. He notes that for Muslim Arabs, "their scores on measures of education, income, and the like, resemble those of Israel's secular Jews, while those of Muslim Arabs approximate those of ultra-Orthodox Jews." Both these groups place great value on religious observance and having large families rather than on material comforts and high wages. As Muravchik concludes: "Poverty and income inequality in Israel can be explained to a great extent by lifestyle choices rather than lack of opportunity."[44] Another salient point in discussing wage differentials is that Israeli Arabs are being compared to an ethnic group (i.e., Jews) who tend to outperform all other groups in every Western country in which they reside.[45] In the United States, their per capita income is estimated at twice that of non–Jews, with significant discrepancies noted in European countries too. The discrepancies between Arabs and Jews in Israel are also replicated outside the country where the two communities live.[46]

In 2015, the government announced that a 15 billion shekel fund would develop infrastructure, industry, education and healthcare in Arab areas of Israel. Economic development grants have also been authorized for Druze councils and for Bedouins. Clearly, more needs to be done to equalize socio-economic opportunities for Israeli Arabs, as well as other minorities, but few could doubt that the state is moving in the right direction.

Institutional Racism

Many critics within Israel also point to a level of institutional anti–Arab racism within sections of Israeli society. Every so often, research polls indicate that a substantial number of Israelis hold negative views towards Arabs. In 2007, the Association for Civil Rights in Israel reported an increase in anti–Arab views and a 26 percent increase in anti–Arab racist incidents. The report quoted polls that suggested 50 percent of Jewish Israelis do not believe Arab citizens of Israel should have equal rights, 55 percent said they wanted the government to encourage Arab emigration from Israel, and nearly 75 percent of Jewish youths said Arabs were less intelligent and less clean than Jews.[47]

It should be pointed out that polls are notoriously unreliable and depend on the type of questions posed by researchers. Furthermore, a survey carried out in 2012 by the Index of Arab-Jewish relations in Israel (which interviewed 700 Jewish and 700 Arab citizens) suggests that there is a greater tolerance towards the Arab community. Three-quarters of Jews surveyed agreed that Arabs should have "full citizenship rights" and "recognized the collective rights of the Arabs to separate religion, culture and education." A majority (58.3 percent) "agreed that the state has to accord Arabs the powers of self-administration of their religious, cultural and educational institutions." Compared to a decade ago, nearly 10 percent more Israeli Jews "were also ready to accept Arab citizens as neighbours," though still not a majority.[48]

Occasionally there is incitement from the country's most senior rabbis. Ovadiah Yosef, leader of the Shas party, was slammed by the ADL after he said in a sermon, "Goyim were born only to serve us. Without that, they have no place in the world; only to serve the People of Israel."[49] A group of prominent rabbis, including the chief rabbi of Safed, also stirred controversy when they urged Jews not to rent or sell apartments to non–Jews, including Arabs.[50] They also called for the ostracizing of any Jew who committed such an act. In another example, in

2009 Rabbi Yitzhak Shapira stirred controversy with a book *Torat Hamelech*, which dealt with how Jews could treat gentiles during a time of war. It provided justification for how gentile children could become legitimate targets in warfare on the basis of deterring a future threat.[51]

It is not hard to see how a climate of hostility is created by such remarks, with consequent attacks on Israeli Arabs by extremists. Such attitudes are indefensible and need to be challenged through all the organs of civil society. Some will argue understandably that such bigoted attitudes are symptomatic of the country's ongoing struggle against Arab incitement and terrorism. Israel has experienced over six decades of unremitting hostility from her Arab neighbors, including a decade of suicide bombings from Palestinian terror groups. It should not be surprising if this has created a climate in which anti–Arab attitudes have proliferated. But even then, such vitriol usually leads to a chorus of disapproval from much of the Israeli political and religious establishment, making it abundantly obvious that such attitudes do not go unchallenged. Ultimately, tackling societal racism in Israel, as in every other country, is a long-term project requiring education, integration and law enforcement.

One final egregious myth should be tackled, namely that Israel sells land only to its Jewish citizens. On the contrary, 80.4 percent of Israeli land is government-owned while another 13.1 percent is owned by the Jewish National Fund. The remainder (6.5 percent) is owned privately by Jews and non–Jews. The Israel Lands Authority administers 93.5 percent of land, and this is not sold either to Jews or to non–Jews. Instead it is leased out on an equal basis. There is therefore no official discrimination against Arab citizens in terms of Israeli land law.[52]

Occupation

Frequent criticism is also made of Israel's human rights record in the West Bank. The Israeli measures that are usually singled out for opprobrium include the security barrier, built in 2002, that separates the West Bank from pre–1967 Israel (Israel behind the green line), the demolition of Palestinian houses by the Israeli security services, the military checkpoints that exist throughout the West Bank and the occasional military operations against targets in the territories.

Israel's record in the disputed territories has been far from perfect. As reported in the Israeli media, human rights violations have occurred and innocent people have suffered over the decades. The checkpoints, curfews and security barrier do cause considerable inconvenience, financial hardship and sometimes humiliation for Palestinian civilians. It would be wrong to minimize the impact of these measures on the lives of ordinary people.

That said, these measures are employed only because there is an ongoing and serious security threat to the Jewish state. Israel has to balance human rights with security and is hardly alone in that regard. Were the terrorist threat to disappear, the lives of Palestinians (and Israelis) would be much freer. This has been shown in Northern Ireland with a moderate political settlement consequent on the decommissioning of weapons and removal of the terrorist threat. Thus, direct comparisons between Israel and other democracies are somewhat facile in this respect. The true comparison is with other democracies that are forced to fight asymmetric wars with their neighbors and that are hedged in by hostile enemies on all sides. Israel's record in war often compares very favorably with other democracies in terms of the civilian casualty count.

There is an imperative today for Israel to solve its conflict with the Palestinians, using all the resources at its disposal. There is a consensus for the country to share some of the land between the Mediterranean and the Jordan River, disengaging from the West Bank and its inhabitants. There is a correct recognition that the Palestinians deserve a better future and must escape from the trap of victimhood imposed on them by their leaders for seven decades. They are clearly not about to depart *en masse* from the West Bank to Jordan or any other Arab country. That the Palestinian leadership, both Fatah and Hamas, constitutes the principal impediment to a solution doesn't change this equation. That said, it is incumbent on the international community to recognize the grave risks that Israel is making, and has long made, to achieve a genuine peace. They must identify the correct stumbling blocks to any solution and act upon such knowledge.

Sources

In choosing sources for the first four chapters, I deliberately ignore those from the Islamic world and concentrate on ones produced in the West, mainly Europe and the United States. Today the Arab and Muslim nations are the epicenter of hatred towards the Jewish state, with bilious commentary that poisons their political culture. Contempt for the Jewish state exists at a profound level in Egypt, Syria, Lebanon, Libya, Iran, Jordan and Saudi Arabia, as well as Muslim countries outside the region. It would hardly come as a surprise if the Middle East was also the locus of virulent anti–Israel activity, and such documentation has been done many times in any case. So I concentrate on Western nations whose founding values of tolerance and rationality are a paean to the enlightenment—though not when it comes to Israel.

Bias

It is standard practice at this point to identify biases. The conclusions of this book do point in a direction that is more favorable to Israel, though without adopting a black-and-white approach. However, it does not follow that this book's conclusions are automatically untrustworthy or methodologically suspect. Bias is more than merely adopting a position that happens to favor one group over another. It is the idea that one is closed minded towards alternative viewpoints, and that facts, evidence and information are either ignored or viewed through a distorted lens. It is closer to bigotry than favoritism. In this book, criticisms of Israel, far from being ignored, are closely examined and ruthlessly dissected using historical evidence, logic and legal reasoning.

To be unbiased is also not the same as being balanced, at least if a balanced argument implies that competing narratives must have equal credence. According to a standard argument, it would be unbalanced (and biased) to conclude that Israel was largely in the right or the Palestinians mainly in the wrong. But truth is never a compromise between the views of two sides, and to think otherwise is to commit the fallacy of the golden mean. What is necessary is to put forward the Palestinian case and see how well it stands up to rigorous intellectual scrutiny. The judgment about whether both sides have been fairly represented is left up to the reader.

PART I: THE TWISTED NARRATIVE

1. Israel the "Law Breaker": Occupation, Settlements, War and Refugees

There is a joke right now that, despite its levity, reveals much about how the world sees Israel. An Israeli tourist, excited by his first visit to the USA, is being questioned at La Guardia airport. As he eyes the visitor, a somewhat officious member of the security staff asks for his nationality. "Israeli," comes the reply. The security guard follows up with "Occupation?" "No, just visiting," he is told.

Today, much enlightened opinion around the world believes that it is only by ending the Israeli occupation of territory seized in 1967, and the "siege" of Gaza, that peace may finally be achieved in the Middle East. According to this Arabist view, the Arab/Palestinian-Israeli conflict lies at the root of the conflict between the Jewish state and the many groups and nations that oppose it. Thus it is only by placing concerted pressure on a "reluctant" Israeli government that a change of policy and attitude can come about. Others argue that the occupation lies at the heart of all regional disputes and conflicts and acts as a recruiting sergeant for wider discontent in the Arab and Muslim world. As we will discuss in Chapter 4, this supposedly makes Israel a strategic liability for the West by its perceived refusal to compromise with the Palestinians. Ending the occupation is thus seen as the precondition for regional peace and stability.

The occupation is viewed by many as a violation of international law for allegedly contradicting UN resolutions 242 and 338, as well as a host of other Security Council resolutions. It is therefore commonplace to hear the West Bank described as "illegally occupied territory" by Western politicians, NGOs and media pundits, especially in Europe. Israel, it is claimed, must vacate these territories if she is to have peace, recognition and an end to terror. This view, which receives a sympathetic hearing in policy and media circles across Europe, the UK and in the U.S. State Department, represents a significant victory for the Palestinian national movement, represented today by Fatah, the PA and Hamas. Together with their Arab backers and much of mainstream Western opinion, they have effectively placed the onus for conflict resolution on Israel and given a free pass to the Palestinian movement.

To take one example, in a speech to the Knesset in 2008, Nicholas Sarkozy spoke about how there could not be peace "without a border negotiated on the basis of the 1967 agreement and exchanges of territory making it possible to build two viable States." An editorial in *Le Monde* from 2001 similarly stated, "The precondition for any future peacemaking is now no less than Israel's unilateral withdrawal from the occupied territories."[1] The position in some

European legislatures today is to back the Palestinian bid for unilateral recognition proposed by Mahmoud Abbas, whereas the EU position is to back this through negotiation. Recently the British Parliament voted to recognize "Palestine," and this followed a similar move by the Swedish Parliament. Warnings were sounded from a number of quarters that Israel could not afford to ignore such a sea change in opinion.[2] In particular, there was the palpable threat of EU sanctions against Israel in the event that progress was not made to end the occupation. Some warnings even came from friendly states. Angela Merkel chided Netanyahu in 2011, saying: "You haven't made a single step to advance peace."[3]

Recent American presidents, including George W. Bush, Jimmy Carter and Barack Obama, have also called for Israel to end the occupation of the West Bank as part of a negotiated settlement, sometimes downplaying the significance of other factors, such as Palestinian maximalism and incitement. Some influential voices within the American media go further. The editor of the *New Yorker*, David Remnick, recently described the occupation as "illegal, inhumane, and inconsistent with Jewish values," as did Tom Friedman.[4] Michael Gove sums up the issue well. The principle that Israel must cede land to its unforgiving enemies has become a "fixed assumption of Western diplomacy and a given among Western commentators."[5]

Gaza too is described as being under illegal Israeli control. Typical is a report from Amnesty International that declared that Israel, post-disengagement, was "the occupying power in the Gaza Strip" and that "the Israeli army has retained effective control over the Gaza Strip."[6] Amnesty is not alone in this view. Human Rights Watch has said, "Even though Israel unilaterally withdrew its troops and settlements from Gaza in 2005, it continues to have obligations as an occupying power in Gaza."[7] Many other human rights organizations and NGOs echo such views.

Israel's blockade of the strip, imposed after the Hamas coup of 2007, is frequently blasted as a counterproductive and inhumane way to treat Gaza's residents. For Ireland's foreign minister, Michael Martin, the blockade was "inhumane and unacceptable."[8] For William Hague, it was "unacceptable and unsustainable" and "restrictions on Gaza" had to be "lifted."[9] These views were echoed by Harriet Harman. The EU commissioner for humanitarian aid, Kristalina Georgieva, called in 2011 for the "immediate, sustained and unconditional opening of crossings for the flow of humanitarian aid, commercial goods and persons" and said that Gaza's humanitarian crisis was "artificially created because of the blockade." In effect, Israel had created conditions for its own lack of security.[10]

Chris Patten, a former EU commissioner for the UK, said that the blockade policy was a "terrible failure—immoral, illegal and ineffective" and one that "deliberately triggered an economic and social crisis which has many humanitarian consequences."[11] A more recent declaration from the meeting of the European Union and the League of Arab States stated that ministers were concerned "at the grave humanitarian situation in the Gaza Strip largely caused by the closure imposed by the Occupying Power."[12]

Highlighting the economic crisis in Gaza is one of the chief weapons of today's anti-Israel movement. Israel is accused of laying siege to the tiny Palestinian enclave and using the tactics of medieval warfare to isolate, enslave and decimate its beleaguered residents. In a statement issued in January 2009, War on Want blamed Israel for fomenting a "humanitarian crisis for the 1.5 million people trapped there." It went on: "The root cause of the humanitarian crisis in Gaza is Israel's illegal occupation, which has raised poverty among ordinary Palestinians to the levels of sub-Saharan Africa."[13]

Johann Hari, prior to his exit in disgrace from the *Independent*, wrote a piece on Gaza that purported to reveal a deliberate policy of imprisonment by Israel: "The Gaza Strip is smaller than the Isle of Wight but it is crammed with 1.5 million people who can never leave. They live out their lives on top of each other, jobless and hungry, in vast, sagging tower blocks. From the top floor, you can often see the borders of their world: the Mediterranean, and Israeli barbed wire."[14]

Owen Jones, who enjoys deriding Britain's rich and powerful in the same publication, weighed in with his own critique. During Israel's operation to silence Hamas rocket fire in 2012, he declared on the television show *Question Time*: "What people on earth would tolerate a siege which stops basic supplies getting in [and] a 45 year old occupation, a brutal occupation at that."

The views of these figures and organizations might evoke little surprise, given that they are associated with British left wing tendencies. Yet similar sentiments can be found in the political mainstream too. Today, few Europeans are more mainstream than David Cameron. Yet in a speech to Turkish businessmen in 2010, the prime minister described Gaza as nothing less than a "prison camp" and added that the "Israeli attack on the Gaza flotilla was completely unacceptable." Earlier in the House of Commons, he had told MPs, "We are not going to sort out the problem of the Middle East peace process while there is, effectively, a giant open prison in Gaza."[15] The Holy See went much further in the opprobrium heaped on the Jewish state. In 2009, the Pope's justice minister, Renato Martino, described conditions in Gaza as resembling "a big concentration camp."[16] Not surprisingly, there are more vituperative voices within the UN.

The status of the Golan Heights, captured from Syria in the Six-Day War and subsequently annexed by Israel, differs from the West Bank and Gaza in that it does not contain a restive Palestinian population. Nonetheless, Israeli governments have shown a willingness to return this territory subject to a peace agreement with Syria.

Settlements as Illegal and a Barrier to Peace

The purported status of the West Bank in international law influences perceptions of Jewish settlements. These are widely viewed in Europe (and Britain) as illegal in international law. A more common position in the United States is to regard them as illegitimate and a significant hindrance to a permanent accord. They are commonly viewed as an attempt to create "facts on the ground" and to seize vital areas of land, effectively prejudging the outcome of any peace talks between the two sides. At various times between 2009 and 2013, Palestinian leader Mahmoud Abbas called for a permanent halt to all settlement building before any resumption of peace talks, a stance encouraged, at least in part, by the Obama administration.

His condemnation of settlement expansion is echoed frequently by European leaders, U.S. presidents and the heads of major international organizations. Following the breakdown of talks sponsored by John Kerry over a nine-month period in 2013–14, the secretary of state derided settlement expansion as the sticking point between the two sides. "In the afternoon when they [the sides] were about to maybe get there, 700 settlement units were announced in Jerusalem and, poof, that was sort of the moment."[17]

At a recent AIPAC conference in Washington, Hilary Clinton said: "We do not accept the legitimacy of continued settlement activity. We believe their continued expansion is corrosive not only to peace efforts and the two-state solution, but to Israel's future itself."[18] One of her predecessors, Colin Powell, declared in 2002, "Something has to be done about the problem of the settlements, the settlements continue to grow and continue to expand."[19] Another predecessor, James A. Baker, said in 1991 that there was no "bigger obstacle to peace than settlement activity that continues not only unabated but at an enhanced pace."[20]

Such views are *de rigueur* across Europe. In 2010, a number of former European leaders wrote to Herman van Rompuy, the president of the European Council, expressing their concern that no negotiated outcome to the Israeli/Palestinian conflict was in sight. In particular, they pointed to "developments on the ground, primarily Israel's continuation of settlement activity in the Occupied Palestinian Territory" that in their view posed "an existential threat to the prospects of establishing a sovereign, contiguous and viable Palestinian state also embracing Gaza, and therefore pose a commensurate threat to a two-state solution to the conflict."[21]

More recently, a number of British PMs have made an issue of ending settlement activity in the West Bank. In the 1980s, Margaret Thatcher was disturbed by Menachem Begin's belief in settlement expansion, arguing that it could "kill the whole process of the search for a comprehensive settlement in the Middle East."[22] In a meeting with President Giscard in 1979, she added: "All our efforts to convince Mr. Begin that his West Bank policy was absurd, and that there should not be Israeli settlements on the West Bank, had failed to move him."[23]

In a press conference with the Palestinian prime minister, Salaam Fayyad, Gordon Brown declared: "Everybody now sees the contours of what a two-state solution would look like.... One of the blockages to that is clearly the settlement issue."[24] His views have been echoed by David Cameron. In 2012, in a meeting with Mahmoud Abbas, he said: "Time, in some ways, is running out for the two-state solution, unless we can push forward now, because otherwise the facts on the ground will make it more and more difficult, which is why the settlement issue remains so important."[25] His deputy PM, Nick Clegg, was more forthright. The expansion of settlements constituted "an act of deliberate vandalism to the basic premise on which negotiations have taken place for years and years and years."[26]

For good measure, in November 2012, Conservative Foreign Secretary William Hague said that the expansion of settlements constituted the "single biggest factor in removing the time and opportunity to create such a two-state solution."[27]

These views can be found from within the most influential shaper of public opinion in the UK, the BBC. Here is a section from Middle East editor Jeremy Bowen's much-criticized piece on the Six-Day War: "Israel has settled around 450,000 people on land occupied in 1967, in defiance of almost all countries' interpretation of international law except its own."[28] In the same article, he goes on to say that for the Palestinians, "The settlements are a catastrophe, made worse every day by the fact that they are expanding fast."

Bowen clearly believes that settlement expansion is the prime barrier to a breakthrough between the warring sides. "Israel," he says elsewhere, "continues to pour concrete and blast roads through the rocky hills and valleys of the parts of the occupied territories that it wants to incorporate permanently into an enlarged Jewish homeland.... If the settlements stay against the will of the Palestinian people, along with the security perimeters and access roads and military patrols that go with them, it is hard to see how there can be anything like peace."[29]

Such views are not confined necessarily to political institutions with a left-of-center leaning. They also appear in sections of the British media that are more traditionally favorable to Israel. In an article focusing on the Israeli/Palestinian negotiations instigated by John Kerry, the *Telegraph*'s David Blair wrote thus: "Today, 325,000 Jewish settlers live in the West Bank and another 190,000 in East Jerusalem, according to B'tselem, an Israeli human rights group. As a result, no viable Palestinian state could emerge in the cracks and gaps between the settlements and their web of access roads."[30]

He is supported in his view by the "paleo-conservative" journalist Peter Oborne, who wrote: "If he [Netanyahu] is allowed to go ahead with the latest plans for settlement construction, all hopes of Middle East peace will vanish and die."[31] Thus the major stumbling blocks to a peace between Israelis and Palestinians are seen to be the "illegal" occupation of the West Bank and Gaza and continued settlement activity. Israel's critics contend that Israel has become a lawless state, arrogantly disregarding her obligations under international law and thumbing her nose at the court of world opinion. Not surprisingly, this view is echoed at the UN, where Navi Pillay said that settlement activity violated "the entire spectrum of Palestinians' social, cultural, civil and political rights."[32]

The Charge of Disproportionate Force and Targeting Civilians

During recent years, Israel has also been accused of violating two cardinal principles of the laws of war and international humanitarian war: the principle of proportionality and the principle of distinction. The first refers to the level of force involved in military operations. Israel is regularly accused of using excessive or disproportionate force against her enemies. In an almost knee-jerk reaction to every Israeli use of force, Western leaders, while supporting the country's right to self-defense, have consistently slammed the level of force involved. They are partly motivated by casualty counts in recent wars that show far more Palestinian than Israeli deaths. In Operation Cast Lead, 13 Israelis were killed to at least 1,166 Palestinians, a ratio of 1 to 90. The ration was lower in the 2006 Lebanon war, in which over 160 Israelis died to some 1,500 Lebanese and Hezbollah. The implication is that if only the casualty count was equal, no such charge would apply.

At the height of the second intifada in 2000, Human Rights Watch claimed to have documented "repeated excessive use of lethal force against unarmed Palestinian demonstrators, who posed no imminent danger of death or serious injury to security forces or to others."[33]

Writing in the *Telegraph* in 2006 at the height of the war in Lebanon, William Hague said, "In some instances, such as attacks on the Lebanese army or on parts of the civil infrastructure, Israeli actions have been disproportionate, and our Foreign Office should not be afraid to say so."[34] In a conversation with the author in 2010, Hague reiterated the charge, though he claimed that it was not applicable to Operation Cast Lead as the country was "under fire" in 2009.[35] Such criticisms were voiced elsewhere. French president Chirac condemned a "totally disproportionate" Israeli attack, while Finland's government condemned her "disproportionate use of force." Senator Chuck Hagel said that Israel was guilty of "systematic destruction" in Lebanon.[36] The charge of disproportionality was again raised in November 2006 when the five main political groupings in the European Parliament condemned Israeli actions in Gaza and Beit Hanoun.[37]

During Operation Cast Lead, the EU condemned "the disproportionate use of force"[38] as early as December 27, 2008, while the Turkish premier, Tayyip Erdogan, declared that Israel had created a "a human tragedy" through the use of "excessive force."[39] During the same conflict, UN Secretary General Ban Ki-Moon's spokesmen declared that while he acknowledged Israel's security concerns regarding the continued firing of rockets from Gaza, he condemned the "excessive use of force leading to the killing and injuring of civilians."[40] The Polish foreign ministry, while condemning rocket attacks, could "find no justification for the scale of military operation taken in response by the Israeli side."[41] For his part, Spain's foreign minister, Miguel Angel Moratinos, condemned Hamas for "launching rocket attacks"[42] but also "the Israeli Armed Forces' disproportionate retaliation." The charge of using disproportionate force also became a key finding in the UN-sponsored Goldstone report of 2009.

After Israel seized control of the Turkish vessel *Mavi Marmara* in 2010, the Belgian foreign minister described the action as "disproportionate." Nicholas Sarkozy again condemned what he called "the disproportionate use of force,"[43] words also used by Angela Merkel's office and the Irish Taoiseach. For the Portuguese foreign ministry, Israel was responsible for an "excessive use of force against civilian targets,"[44] while David Cameron called the action "completely unacceptable."[45]

During the escalation in Gaza in November 2012, India's external affairs minister, Salman Khurshid declared that "the disproportionate use of force" in Gaza was "unacceptable" and decried the "tragic escalation of violence that cost the loss of some innocent lives, particularly women and children."[46]

The same accusations surfaced repeatedly during Operation Protective Edge, Israel's response to rocket fire and tunneling by Hamas. In a short piece in the *Guardian*, Owen Jones decried the BBC's lack of balance. He objected to a headline stating that Israel was "under renewed Hamas attack," saying that it was "as perverse as Mike Tyson punching a toddler, followed by a headline claiming that the child spat at him." This was because Israel, "a military superpower," was being pitted against Gazans with "almost entirely ineffective missiles."[47] There was an outrageous cartoon in the *Independent* by Dave Brown, purporting to show Israeli jets pounding Gaza while evoking a Biblical verse from Leviticus. The suggestion was that Israel was exacting disproportionate and inhuman revenge for Palestinian wrongs.[48] At the UN, Ban Ki Moon condemned Palestinian rocket fire but added this warning to Israel: "The excessive use of force and endangering of civilian lives are also intolerable."[49] Similar sentiments were expressed by a number of world leaders and diplomats, including the leaders of Belgium, Spain, New Zealand and a host of South American nations.

Allied to this charge is the allegation that Israel has deliberately targeted civilians in conflict zones, a violation of the principle of distinction. Statistics are frequently produced that appear to show that the prime victims of any Israeli assault are non-combatants, usually women and children. Israel often stands accused of showing a reckless disregard for the rights and lives of civilians who live in combat zones, and breaching the most fundamental laws of war. Thus in one of his columns for the *Independent*, Johann Hari slammed Israel's hypocrisy in condemning rocket attacks while it "has been terrorising civilians as a matter of state policy."[50] Nor is this allegation merely the favored charge of the left. The mainstream and much-read *Financial Times* has often accused Israel of "collective punishment" and acting illegally to harm civilians.[51] For author Michael Morpurgo, the IDF shoots children "like a video game."[52]

The coverage of the case of Mohammed Al Dura, a 12-year-old Palestinian boy reported to have been shot by Israeli forces in 2000, revealed the same willingness to accuse Israel of targeting an unarmed child. Despite news outlets, which included ABC, Timeout, Agence France-Presse and the BBC relying on footage from one cameraman from France 2, few appeared to doubt where the blame lay. Charles Enderlin of *France 2* said that the boy had been "cut down by Israeli fire." For ABC's Gillian Findlay, Al Dura had been killed "under Israeli fire." For Lee Hockstander of the *Washington Post*, "the Palestinian youths were no match for the well armed Israeli troops," among whom was a "12 year old boy." The Associated Press reported too that Al Dura had been "caught in the crossfire." For Time.com, Al Dura did "everything in his power to shrink his slender frame behind that of his cowering father" but pleas for "Israeli soldiers to cease fire" were "answered with a fusillade of bullets." *The Guardian* reported that Israeli gunners "from their concrete fortress ... inflicted the death that has become the symbol of these days of blood and rage."[53] These accounts fed into a narrative in which an innocent Palestinian child was targeted and killed by merciless and murderous Israeli soldiers. As the *Atlantic* commented, the image of al Dura had become "the Pieta of the Arab world."[54]

This charge of targeting civilians has been repeated many times since. In 2002, the IDF was widely believed to have perpetrated a "massacre" in Jenin by killing some 500 people and showing wanton disregard for the lives of the residents. During the Lebanon war of 2006, Israel was accused by Human Rights Watch of a "consistent failure to distinguish combatants and civilians," this being tantamount to a "war crime."[55] Following the 2009 Gaza war, Israel was accused in the Goldstone Report of deliberately targeting civilians. Judge Goldstone, who later recanted some of his accusations, observed that the Israeli action constituted "a deliberately disproportionate attack designed to punish, humiliate and terrorize a civilian population."[56]

In an article published during the same offensive, War on Want, a charity with a long record of anti–Israel hostility, characterized the Jewish state's policy towards Gaza in the previous year and a half: "This attack marked the culmination of a policy of collective punishment and killing practised by Israel against the people of Gaza over the past 18 months. Israel has imposed an illegal state of siege on Gaza and created a devastating humanitarian crisis for the 1.5 million people trapped there."[57] The implication was that Israel was engaged in a systematic policy of "collective punishment," affecting the entire civilian population. Amnesty International, too, characterizes Israel's Gaza policy as one of collective punishment designed to enforce military occupation and control.

Cycle of Violence

Israel is often described as being engaged in a "cycle of violence" with Hamas, Fatah and Hezbollah. A typical example is an opinion piece in the influential *Economist* magazine from 2001. The article, titled "Breaking the Cycle," described a visit to Middle Eastern capitals made by Tony Blair as part of an effort to create a global response to 9/11. But set against his visit, the piece noted that Israelis and Palestinians were "still locked in a cycle of violence and retaliation" from which a ceasefire was desperately needed.[58] In a speech at the UN General Assembly, which had been convened to discuss the Israeli-Palestinian conflict, French president Sarkozy warned that a veto against the Palestinian bid for statehood "risked engendering a cycle of violence in the Middle East."[59]

The BBC too has been fond of this description. On its learning zone website we learn how "a cycle of violence has now evolved as suicide bombers and retaliation attacks take place."[60] Other mainstream broadcasters are hardly immune to this type of thinking. A CNN report in 2002 described a series of killings by both Israel and Palestinian terror groups as part of "a 17-month cycle of violence [that] continued unabated."[61] A year later, as the intifada continued, Palestinians killed a 7-year-old child on an Israeli highway and murdered an Israeli in his grocery store. Reuters headlined its report: "Israeli Girl Killed, Fueling Cycle of Violence," before commenting that this crime was typical of "tit-for-tat Israel-Palestinian attacks."[62] The Canadian organization Rights and Democracy, commenting on suicide bombings and the Israeli responses, said that there were "victims on both sides (in quite unequal numbers we should emphasize)."[63] For journalist David Gelernter, the cycle of violence was akin to nothing more than a "tiresome Punch and Judy show."[64]

During a series of rocket attacks from Gaza in 2012, which led to Israeli counterterrorist responses, the British publication the *News* wrote: "Tit-for-tat attacks began on Friday after Israel killed Zuhair al-Qaisi, the head of the militant Popular Resistance Committees, in a targeted airstrike, prompting Palestinians, led by the militant group Islamic Jihad, to fire hundreds of rockets into southern Israel. Israel responded with further airstrikes."[65]

The notion of tit-for-tat behavior featured in a report that appeared in *Time World* titled: "The Problem of Gaza: An Endless Cycle of Violence." Within was the following sentence: "As thousands of Hamas rockets rained down on Israel, parallel Israeli strikes have led to the deaths of more than 130 Gazans over the span of less than a week (five Israelis have been slain by Hamas rocket fire)."[66]

Following the slaying of five residents of the Itamar settlement, one of whom was a three-month-old baby, the *LA Times* saw fit to run an editorial titled: "The Tragedy of an Israeli Family's Slaying in the West Bank, and Israel's Response to It, Are Part of a Continuing Cycle of Violence." It went on to talk about how one of the "most depressing characteristics of the dysfunctional Palestinian-Israeli relationship" was "the self-destructive tit-for-tat mentality that often seems designed to keep the conflict alive rather than to end it."[67]

During Operation Protective Edge, the overwhelming response from world leaders was to lament the "escalation of violence." Many world leaders called on Israel and Hamas to accept an immediate and unconditional ceasefire, treating both parties as if they were on an equivalent moral plane.

A related argument is that terrorism inevitably arises from the experience of living under occupation. Palestinians certainly do face the daily difficulties of checkpoints and the security barrier, as well as economic hardship and the experience of corruption under Palestinian rule. Terrorism is seen as a regrettable but nonetheless entirely rational, as well as *inevitable*, response. It is the daily cry of despair from a beleaguered people who see little other option but to lash out at their tormentors.

The Right of Return

Israel has also been accused of fundamentally breaching international law and refugee law by denying the global Palestinian population the "right of return" to the Jewish state. As we will see in Chapter 6, it has become an article of faith among even the most moderate Palestinian leaders that in any future peace agreement, Israel must accept the return into their country of potentially millions of Palestinians now living across the region. According to the Global Policy Forum, "Their right of return is clearly and unambiguously guaranteed by international law."[68] A recent report from Christian Aid states, "For Palestinian refugees, the individual and collective inalienable right of return cannot be negotiated away."[69] A number of prominent academics working in refugee law, including refugee expert, Professor Susan Akram, argue that Israel's continuing refusal to allow millions of Palestinians to return to Israel is also a serious violation of international law.

Why the Occupation Is Not the Prime Cause of the Conflict

At the outset, there is a difference between two positions: (1) the view criticizing Israeli policy in the West Bank and expressing a desire for change (i.e., to create a Palestinian state through Israeli disengagement) provided that such a state is peaceful and not compromised by terrorism, anti–Semitism or any of the other ills that plague the region; and (2) the view that Israel's partial control of the West Bank is illegal and constitutes the *primary* impediment to achieving a lasting solution to the conflict. For many years, a majority in Israel has accepted the moral and political case for a two-state solution. They reason that in the long term, both peoples must live with each other, and they cannot do so in one state without each violating the other's right to self-determination. The case for creating a peaceful, democratic and demilitarized Palestinian state through negotiations conducted in good faith has been made repeatedly and receives a consistent level of support in Israel.

But it is striking how much of the Western narrative is so heavily tilted towards the second viewpoint. When the West Bank is described in the Western media, the implications are (1) that it is being held by a belligerent power in defiance of international law, and (2) that this defiant occupation is the *primary* issue that fuels the ongoing conflict.

Firstly, what exactly is the current status of the "West Bank"? Here one can start with the internationally recognized framework that defines occupation, namely the Hague Convention: "Article 42: Territory is considered occupied when it is actually placed under the authority of the hostile army. The occupation extends only to the territory where such authority has been established and can be exercised."[70] One should also look to article 2 of part 1 of the Fourth Geneva Convention (1949). Here it is stated that the convention applies to "all cases of declared war or of any other armed conflict which may arise between two or more of the High Contracting Parties."

From these articles, it is clear that there are several preconditions for an area to be described as occupied. The area has to be under the control of another army in order for authority to be exercised. That army, in other words, must be able to exercise authority over the territory in question to the exclusion of the displaced sovereign. The occupying forces must have substituted their power for that of the previous government or regime, which implies boots on the ground.[71] Occupation also implies that the area is held with the purpose of returning it to the prior sovereign. Occupation is seen under international law as a temporary state, subject to the territory being returned to the rightful owner (the prior and ejected sovereign) at a later date.

There is little doubt that Israel maintains effective control of large parts of the West Bank. Under the terms of the Oslo Accords, the West Bank was divided into three areas (areas A, B and C). In Area A, largely consisting of the seven main Palestinian cities of Hebron, Ramallah, Jenin, Jericho, Tulkarem, Bethlehem and Nablus, the Palestinian Authority has maximal control, effectively a form of autonomy with considerable powers of local government. In Area C, Israeli military control is maximal. Yoram Dinstein argues that despite these consensual arrangements, Palestinians in the West Bank remain "subject to overall Israeli belligerent occupation."[72] This is because, as Dinstein points out, an occupying power "may equally allow a new local government—with a wide array of powers—to be installed during the occupation."[73]

The Israeli Supreme Court has agreed. It has affirmed on several occasions that the West Bank is "held by the State of Israel in belligerent occupation" and that the laws of such occupation (including the Hague Conventions and the Fourth Geneva Protocol from 1949) apply to its administration.[74] They have rejected the argument that occupation law does not apply because in conquering the West Bank in the Six-Day War, Israel crossed no internationally recognized *border*, merely a ceasefire line from the 1948–49 war, meaning that the West Bank was not legally or rightfully "the territory of another state."[75] It can still be an occupation without a prior legal sovereign. It has also been deemed irrelevant that one of the parties to resolving the current dispute (the Palestinians) is a non-state entity.[76]

Israelis have also argued that the West Bank was part of the land that had been earmarked under international law for a Jewish national home. As we shall see in Chapter 5, this is a factually and historically valid claim. Yet Israel has never annexed the West Bank and it is not a part of Israel proper. Israeli civilian law does not apply in the territory, that is to the Palestinian population. It can also quite legitimately be described as disputed territory, characterized by a "sovereignty gap" with overlapping claims by both the government of Israel and the Palestinians, the latter claiming a right of self-determination. It seems perfectly legitimate to talk of the West Bank as both "occupied and disputed."[77]

But though the West Bank can be described as occupied, this does not represent any breach of international law. During a time of armed conflict, countries will shift their borders and often try to seize enemy territory for a given period of time. Examples from the twentieth century are legion. After the conclusion of the Second World War, Allied forces occupied both Germany and Japan for a number of years, prior to the creation of democratic and peaceful postwar governments. Similarly, after the First World War, there was an allied army of occupation in the German Rhineland, designed to last for 15 years though it was terminated in 1930. Few doubt the justice or wisdom of these occupations and few continue to malign the occupying forces for the effective control they established in those countries. Nor is there anything inherently illegal in the decision to maintain an occupation following a war. As one legal expert on the laws of occupation notes, "Resolution 1483 (2006) of the United Nations (UN) Security Council makes a matter-of-fact reference to the takeover of Iraq by occupying powers," something that ought to indicate the non-illegality of such a process.[78]

Status of Gaza

What about the legal status of Gaza? Israel patrols Gaza's territorial waters and maintains a naval blockade on Gaza. It is argued that this contravenes Article 1(1) of the Geneva Convention on the Territorial Sea and the Contiguous Zone, which states, "The sovereignty of a State extends, beyond its land territory and its internal waters, to a belt of sea adjacent to its coast, described as the territorial sea." Israel also has exclusive control of Gaza's air space and, together with Egypt, maintains border restrictions that control the entry crossings into the territory.

But none of this is equivalent to occupation. Since 2005, there has been no Israeli military or civilian presence in Gaza; instead it is Hamas that is the territory's sovereign. Israel therefore lacks effective control of the territory. As Tristan Ferraro, legal advisor to the International Red Cross, has observed: "In general, the obligations and rights conferred upon the Occupying Power by IHL require, to be given effect, its physical presence in the occupied territory." He goes on: "Occupation and its related element of effective control cannot in principle be established and maintained solely by exercising power from beyond the boundaries of the occupied territory.... How could an occupant discharge its obligation to maintain law and order without being present in occupied territory."[79] Occupation requires setting up an administration to ensure that the occupant can discharge its obligations. A similar point is made by the Oxford Manual of Naval War, which states, "Occupation of maritime territory ... exists only when there is at the same time an occupation of continental territory, by either a naval or a military force."[80]

It is equally true that Gaza is a *hostile* territory. Since 2005, when the last Israeli solider left Gaza to its new rulers (the PA until the 2007 coup), thousands of rockets and mortars have been fired from the territory on to Israeli towns and cities. The total barrage exceeds 15,000 and the vast majority of these have been fired since 2005. These indiscriminate and unprovoked attacks have killed more than 20 people, mostly civilians, and injured 1,700 others. Nearly one million Israelis live in areas that have come under sustained missile attack. The town most affected is Sderot, which is close to the border with Gaza. Thousands of its residents have fled and schools, shops and businesses have been closed on a regular basis. The inhabitants have a mere 15 seconds to find nearby shelter while Palestinian missiles are flying over. According to one study, three-quarters of Sderot's children aged 4–18 suffer from post-traumatic stress, including sleeping disorders and severe anxiety.[81]

Under article 51 of the UN Charter, Israel is fully entitled to defend herself, if need be, by preventing the airspace and sea around that hostile state from being used to stage further attacks. This is applicable regardless of whether Gaza is a state or a non-state. In essence, a blockade is a perfectly lawful means of exercising self-defense under article 51 of the UN Charter. In particular, it prevents the smuggling of arms that could be used to target Israeli civilians.

That this is not a gratuitous act of punishment can be shown by the fact that naval vessels carrying weapons have indeed been intercepted prior to unloading in Gaza. In 2002, Israeli commandos intercepted the *Karine A*, a cargo ship that was found to have dozens of tons of weapons bound for Gaza.[82] Concealed anti-ship missiles that were bound for Gaza were also discovered aboard a German-owned vessel, the *Victoria*, in 2011.[83] It was feared that these could be a strategic game changer if put into the hands of the Islamist group. In each case, the weapons originated from Iran, which, for years, had been the chief weapons supplier to Hamas. For as long as the Islamic Republic remains in a state of *de facto* war with Israel, the fear is that it will continue to supply lethal arms to its Palestinian ally. Hence the blockade is in place for good reason.

The aim of the blockade is military; i.e., to curtail the military and terrorist objectives of Hamas and other jihadist groups, and not to punish Gaza's civilians. Thus Israel does not block the flow of humanitarian aid or items that could not be used to produce military hardware. Crucially, there seems to be no nonviolent alternative that Israel could take to counter the threat. In 2011, the UN Palmer report found that the naval blockade of Gaza was legal, given the range of security threats that Israel faced.[84]

The argument that the Israeli blockade of Gaza constitutes an effective occupation is simply without legal foundation. It has more in common with the U.S. quarantine imposed on Cuba in 1962, which was not referred to as an occupation. Indeed, that blockade was imposed before a single one of the lethal nuclear weapons stocked in Cuba had been fired on a U.S. city. Similarly, Britain in World War I did not occupy Germany, despite the naval blockade it imposed, nor did the Allies occupy France just before D-Day by virtue of controlling the entirety of French airspace. If control of Gaza's borders were deemed to constitute occupation, Egypt too would be accused of occupying Gaza, yet she isn't.

There is, similarly, nothing surprising about the Israeli control of Gaza's airspace. This measure is designed to prevent the planes of another hostile nation (such as Syria and Iran) from launching a surprise attack on the Jewish state. The possibility of an air attack constitutes a military threat, and a blockade is a legitimate instrument designed to counter that threat, there being little viable non-military alternative. In any case, these arrangements should come as little surprise to the Palestinians. They were spelled out in Article XII(1) of Oslo II, where it was clearly stated, "Israel shall ... carry the responsibility for defense against external threats ... from the sea and from the air ... and will have all the powers to take the steps necessary to meet this responsibility."

The Main Cause of the Conflict

In any case, the claim that the occupation of the West Bank is the main cause of this conflict is politically dubious. From 1948 to 1967, the West Bank and the Gaza Strip were occupied by (respectively) Jordan and Egypt following the 1948 Arab-Israeli war. Geographically, these were the same territories that came under Israeli occupation following the 1967 war and (excepting Gaza) that remain under Israeli control today.[85] During these 19 years, no one complained about an Arab occupation of "Palestinian" land. It is true that the Arab League regarded the Jordanian annexation as illegal and refused to recognize it. But no resolutions were passed at the UN calling for an end to an "illegal" occupation. Neither Jordan nor Egypt came under intense international pressure to change the status quo and create a new Arab state called Palestine. Such pressure was only exerted on Israel following its control of these territories. This is a mistake made in a spectacularly ill-informed diatribe by Timothy Shanahan that supports Palestinian terrorism. In the essay he writes, "Terrorist attacks could yet succeed in securing for Palestinians much of the land seized from them in 1967."[86] The Palestinians were not the sovereign power in 1967, nor are they mentioned in Resolution 242.

More importantly, if the occupation is the sole cause of conflict, one must ask why Israel failed to enjoy peace between 1948 and 1967, why she was forced to fight major wars in 1948 and 1956, and why she has had to defend herself against a relentless tide of terror attacks from the 1920s onwards. If the occupation of these territories was the sole or even the main cause of the conflict between Israel and its neighbors, it is a puzzle that the PLO, which constantly claimed it was seeking a state in these territories, was formed in 1964 and not after 1967. It came into being a full three years before the start of Israel's occupation.

The argument also ignores the fact that Israel offered to create a Palestinian state in the territory of the West Bank in the peace talks of 2000–1 under Ehud Barak and in 2008 under the prime-ministership of Ehud Barak (see Chapter 6). On both occasions the Palestinian leadership decisively rejected the Israeli overtures. As we shall see later on, this was not the first time that Zionist leaders had offered "land for peace" and not the first time that the Palestinian leaders had rejected it. Clearly Israel has been willing to trade land rather than hold on to it in perpetuity, and this is as true of the West Bank as it is of other areas of disputed territory. Does this make Israel's current occupation illegal or illegitimate as so often claimed? To answer this, we need to understand something about the Six-Day War. (The case for Israel's having superior legal claim to be the area's sovereign, based on the prior League of Nations Covenant from 1922, will be dealt with in Chapter 5.)

Six-Day War

Israel came to occupy Gaza and the West Bank following the Six-Day War in June 1967, the background to which is crucial to evaluating Israel's subsequent actions. Far from being an imperialist war designed to enlarge the borders of the Jewish state, this was a war of self-defense by Israel in response to Arab aggression. The *casus belli* was a decision by Egyptian leader Nasser to mass his troops in the Sinai Peninsula and force the UN Emergency Force to withdraw from the area, as well as his decision to close the Straits of Tiran to Israeli shipping. The UNEF had been stationed in the Sinai as a buffer as part of an agreement to end the Suez war. Israel had previously declared that it considered the closure of this important international waterway to be an act of war. Nasser's actions were a clear breach of international agreements.

As Egypt, Syria and Jordan massed their troops on Israel's borders, it was clear that these Arab nations were planning a war of extermination. Nasser declared that this war's objective would be "Israel's destruction." Egypt planned to massacre the civilian population of Tel Aviv and their soldiers were equipped with poison gas. Seized Jordanian documents revealed plans for the capture of Jewish villages near the Jerusalem corridor and the massacre of their inhabitants. Iraq's PM predicted that after a successful Arab invasion, there would be "practically no Jewish survivors," while Hafiz al Assad of Syria exhorted his soldiers to "pave the Arab roads with the skulls of Jews."[87] Ahmed Shuqairy, the head of the PLO, had vowed to "wipe Israel off the face of the map," adding ominously, "No Jew will remain alive."[88] Such genocidal rhetoric led many Israelis to fear a second Holocaust. Trenches were built in civilian areas, gas masks were distributed and graves were dug in the lead-up to the war.[89]

In the end, Israel decided to launch a preemptive strike against the air forces of Egypt, Syria and Iraq, providing the Jewish state with air superiority for the rest of the war. Far from being an act of aggression, this action was undertaken because it was militarily necessary, in order to prevent a genocidal assault by the country's enemies. Being militarily necessary, it was valid in international law.

In general, international law prohibits the "use of force against the territorial integrity or political independence of any state" under article 2 (4) of the UN Charter. However, under article 51 of the charter, exception is given for the use of force in self-defense: "Nothing in the present Charter shall impair the inherent right of individual or collective self-defence if an armed attack occurs against a Member of the United Nations, until the Security Council has taken measures necessary to maintain international peace and security." Any sovereign UN member state is thus perfectly entitled to defend itself from attack by another state.

The problem here is that, barring the aggressive acts of the Arab countries, the first shots were fired by Israel. Israel acted first, in anticipation of its enemies' collective aggression, by launching a series of preemptive strikes. Some have argued that there is no scope in international law for anticipatory self-defense or preemptive action.

But this is somewhat unrealistic. A state that was unable to defend itself until an enemy attacked might find that its civil and military infrastructure was damaged beyond recognition. If it faced imminent destruction as a result, the whole notion of self-defense under article 51 would be robbed of any value. As President Kennedy said in 1962 during the Cuban Missile Crisis: "We no longer live in a world where only the actual firing of weapons represents a sufficient challenge to a nation's security to constitute maximum peril."[90] Put another way, "the right of self defence is not an entirely passive right."[91]

More recently, the Bush administration in 2002 acknowledged the following:

> For centuries, international law recognized that nations need not suffer an attack before they can lawfully take action to defend themselves against forces that present an imminent danger of attack. Legal scholars and international jurists often conditioned the legitimacy of preemption on the existence of an imminent threat—most often a visible mobilization of armies, navies, and air forces preparing to attack. We must adapt the concept of imminent threat to the capabilities and objectives of today's adversaries.[92]

Preemption can be justified if it is "a response to an impending unjustified attack."[93] The test under international law for the preemptive use of force is one of necessity. There must be a "credible, imminent threat" and there must have been an "exhaustion of peaceful remedies." Naturally this begs the question of what is meant by imminence, a somewhat elusive term. One leading test case much cited by scholars is the *Caroline* incident.

In 1837 British troops attacked the ship *Caroline*, which was carrying supplies to Canadian rebels. These rebels, led by William Lyon Mackenzie, were seeking a Canadian Republic and had fled to the Canadian side of the Niagra River. They were given money and arms via the *Caroline* from sympathizers. One night a British force from Canada entered the United States and attacked the *Caroline*, a move that caused outrage among American politicians. According to U.S. secretary of state Daniel Webster, the action could only be a justifiable form of self-defense if the need for action was "instant, overwhelming" and left "no choice of means, and no moment for deliberation." That key principle from the *Caroline* case has been recognized as the vital component of self-defense, arguably of a legal right to preemptive defense.[94]

Expanding on when preemption becomes a legitimate tool for warfare, philosopher Michael Walzer in *Just and Unjust Wars* offers three criteria. He writes that there must be "a manifest intent to injure," "a degree of active preparation that makes that intent a positive danger," and finally a "general situation in which waiting, or doing anything other than fighting, greatly magnifies the risk."[95]

Using these criteria, it is clear, first, that the incendiary threats of extermination from several Arab leaders in 1967 created an intent to injure. Second, the decision to close the

Straits of Tiran followed by the expulsion of UN troops from Sinai and finally massing troops on Israel's borders constituted active preparation. Third and above all, the Israelis were entitled to believe, together with outsiders, that inaction would have magnified the risk of destruction. Thus Ted Honderich is completely wrong when he describes Israel's actions in the Six-Day War as "less a pre-emptive attack by the Israelis" and more "aggression by way of a pretence of believing something about an imminent attack."[96]

The Palestinians, ignoring the context of the Six-Day War, nonetheless insist that UN Security Council resolution 242 makes the *continuing* occupation illegal. They further claim that Israel must surrender this land unilaterally under the terms of this resolution as the West Bank is designated as the future Palestinian state. This claim is belied by the specific wording of the resolution.

Security Council Resolution 242 emphasizes the "inadmissibility of the acquisition of territory by war" and also calls for the "establishment of a just and lasting peace in the Middle East" based on "withdrawal of Israel armed forces from territories occupied in the recent conflict" and the "termination of all claims or states of belligerency and respect for and acknowledgement of the sovereignty, territorial integrity and political independence of every state in the area and their right to live in peace within secure and recognized boundaries free from threats or acts of force." It also affirms the necessity for "guaranteeing freedom of navigation through international waterways," achieving "a just settlement of the refugee problem" and "guaranteeing the territorial inviolability and political independence of every State in the area."

Already it should be clear that nothing in this resolution demands a *unilateral* Israeli withdrawal from the West Bank. For such a withdrawal is inextricably linked to the need for a "just and lasting peace" and that necessitates Israel's acquiring "secure and recognized boundaries free from threats or acts of force." In other words, Israel is not required to act alone but to negotiate a political settlement with her neighbors. No just and lasting peace can be made without reference to the regional actors, and today that includes the PA. As the Jerusalem Centre for Public Affairs puts it, "the provision on the establishment of 'secure and recognized boundaries' proves that the implementation of the resolution required a prior agreement between the parties."[97] There are only multilateral obligations in resolution 242.

Crucially, this resolution was passed under chapter 6 of the UN Charter, not chapter 7. Unlike chapter 7 resolutions, which deal with "threats to the peace, breaches of the peace, and acts of aggression," chapter 6 resolutions are non-binding in nature. They are more in the form of recommendations of an advisory nature and, as such, may be indicative of state practice. As spelled out in article 33 (ch. 6), "the parties to any dispute, the continuance of which is likely to endanger the maintenance of international peace and security, shall, first of all, seek a solution by negotiation, enquiry, mediation, conciliation, arbitration, judicial settlement, resort to regional agencies or arrangements, or other peaceful means of their own choice." This is precisely the process that Israel underwent with Egypt and Jordan. In the former case, bilateral negotiations between Israel and Egypt led to the Camp David accords in 1978 and the withdrawal from Sinai Desert (90 percent of the occupied territories). By contrast, chapter 7 resolutions require countries to comply with the directives that are set forth, deliberately allowing no room for negotiation or conciliation.[98]

Nor does resolution 242 imply that there is anything illegal about the Israeli occupation. While it is deemed inadmissible to "acquire" land in war, it is not inadmissible or illegal to occupy it during an armed conflict or prior to a post-conflict negotiated settlement. Were it to be otherwise, then any state acting in self-defense following armed aggression from a neighboring state would have to return to the *status quo ante* at the cessation of hostilities, an absurd and unworkable proposition. This position is supported in a speech given by Lyndon Johnson on 18 June 1967. In it he said: "There are some who have urged, as a single, simple solution, an immediate return to the situation as it was on June 4. As our distinguished and able Ambassador, Mr. Arthur Goldberg, has already said, this is not a prescription for peace but for renewed hostilities."[99]

One can also turn to the 1970 UN General Assembly "Declaration on Principles of International Law concerning Friendly Relations and Cooperation among States," which upheld the legality of military occupation provided the force used to establish it was not in contravention of the UN Charter. Similarly, despite the bias of the ICJ, its former president, Rosalyn Higgins, has stated, "There is nothing in either the Charter or general international law which leads one to suppose that military occupation pending a peace treaty is illegal."[100]

Another misconception is that resolution 242 calls for Israel to return *all* of the West Bank to Arab control. The wording of resolution 242 is clear: Israel should return "territories" rather than "the territories" captured in 1967, allowing for the kind of political leeway that would enable Israel to live in "secure and defensible borders." In fact in 1967, Israel did not have borders as such. It merely had armistice demarcation lines resulting from the various armistice agreements that Israel signed with its Arab neighbors at the end of the first Arab-Israeli war in 1949. These were transitional lines whose purpose was to "delineate the lines beyond which the armed forces of the respective Parties shall not move" (Israel-Jordan armistice agreement, Article VI [9]). Permanent ones would have to be negotiated as part of a peace agreement. They left Israel a mere 9 miles wide at its narrowest point and left the country intensely vulnerable to attack from a neighboring state. Resolution 242 was designed to rectify that.

The view that Israel was not required under international law to withdraw from the entire West Bank was confirmed by George Brown, British foreign secretary in 1967, on January 19, 1970:

> The phrasing of the Resolution was very carefully worked out, and it was a difficult and complicated exercise to get it accepted by the UN Security Council. I formulated the Security Council Resolution. Before we submitted it to the Council, we showed it to Arab leaders. The proposal said "Israel will withdraw from territories that were occupied," and not from "the" territories, which means that Israel will not withdraw from all the territories.[101]

Above and beyond these points there is another crucial one. The West Bank was seized by Israel following a war of aggression by a hostile Arab state. In general, aggressors should not expect to regain land that they lost as a result of their belligerent actions. A reversion to the *status quo ante* is immoral, for what would deter a state's leaders from further hostile acts if they had nothing to lose? If there were automatic protection for warlike nations whose wars of aggression had resulted in defeat, it would give a green light to militarism and undermine the interests of peace-minded nations. So when it is claimed that Israel must relinquish the West Bank without preconditions, this goes beyond the requirements of international law and arguably of international morality too.

In addition, it is a myth that the Israeli withdrawal from land is a *sine qua non* of peace. In 2005, Israel made the painful concession of withdrawing from the Gaza Strip and uprooting the area's Jewish settlers. The Palestinians had the chance to prove their honorable intentions, build a viable mini-state and demonstrate that they could be trusted with further acquisitions of land. The net result was a Hamas government that facilitated a huge increase in rocket and missile attacks on southern Israel. Not that this should have come as any surprise. A poll of Palestinians in 2004, conducted by the Development Studies Programme at Birzeit University, showed majority support (61 percent) for continuing terror attacks from Gaza if the Israelis withdrew. Among those surveyed, support for violence was higher among those living in Gaza.[102] Similarly, when Israel withdrew unilaterally from Lebanon in 2000, Hezbollah built up a formidable arsenal of missiles in clear defiance of international law. Withdrawal simply created a vacuum that was exploited by the most radical actors in the region, both Iranian allies. So Israelis naturally ask what would happen if there were to be a withdrawal from the strategically more vital West Bank.

Why Settlements Are Not Illegal or the Prime Cause of the Conflict

The construction of Jewish settlements in the West Bank has certainly proven to be a controversial issue, both within Israel and around the world. It has led to accusations that Israeli governments are not sincere about making territorial compromises with the PA. It has created a perception that these governments merely pay lip service to the peace process, helping to undermine it by "creating facts on the ground." In addition, the extension of settlements following a Palestinian atrocity has fuelled the belief that Israel is acting in a retaliatory and short-sighted manner, rather than in its own long-term interests.

It would have been better if, in recent years, Israeli governments had clearly stipulated that settlements would only be built in areas that would never form part of a Palestinian state. In areas to be annexed to Israel, growth could occur without limit.[103] By failing to provide long-term clarity, they have played into the hands of Palestinian extremists who are desperate to provide cover for their own inaction in the peace process. Sensing all this, most Israelis seem prepared to make serious compromises on this issue in order to create a long-term peace settlement. But the questionable wisdom of establishing settlements should not blind us to the modern realities of the Middle East and the real causes of the current impasse.

First, one should deal with the claim that settlements are illegal under international law. This rests on an interpretation of the Fourth Geneva Convention (1949), which was set up "for the Protection of Civilian Persons in Time of War." Article 49 states: "The Occupying Power shall not deport or transfer parts of its own civilian population into the territory it occupies." The argument goes that Israel, as the occupying power, has indeed "transferred" parts of its civilian population into the occupied territory contrary to the Fourth Geneva Convention and is thus in breach of international law.

The claim of illegality rests on a dubious interpretation of the word "transfer" in article 49. According to the official commentary produced in 1958 by the International Committee of the Red Cross, the article was intended to "prevent a practice adopted during the Second World War by certain Powers, which transferred portions of their own population to occupied territory for political and racial reasons or ... to colonize those territories." They made it clear that such transfers both "worsened the economic situation of the native population and endangered their separate existence as a race." Similarly, Morris Abram, who helped to draft the Fourth Geneva Convention, stated that the convention was designed to cover "the forcible transfer, deportation or resettlement of large numbers of people."[104]

During the war, tens of millions of people from different racial and national groups were forcibly deported, transferred and displaced, among them Soviets, Poles and Germans. Transfer implies some measure of coercion by the occupying power. As David Matas observes, transfer is something *done* to people whereas settlement is something that people have chosen to do.[105] This much is clear from the rest of article 49, which deals exclusively with coercive actions undertaken by an occupying state, such as evacuations, detentions or deportations of "protected persons." It would be a little strange if this fairly unambiguous meaning was radically different in the last sentence of the article.[106]

But there is no evidence that settlers were forced into the West Bank or that they would be forced to remain under future Palestinian sovereignty. They have moved there as a choice, not as a result of unlawful government pressure. Israeli governments have allowed such volunteers to settle and buy land that is not privately owned. In some cases, the settlers are simply regaining land from which they were dispossessed by Jordan. Nor is it the case that the entire West Bank is being "colonized." As discussed in Chapter 2, Israel is an unusual colonizer insofar as the majority of land seized in 1967 and later settled upon (Sinai and Gaza) has been returned.

More importantly, thanks to the Oslo agreements of the 1990s, the Palestinian authority has agreed that settlements remain one of a number of issues to be discussed in the Permanent Status negotiations. The 1995 Interim Agreement, agreed by the PA (and by much of the rest of the international community) divided the West Bank into areas A, B and C, the latter territory being solely under Israeli jurisdiction. Part of that agreement stipulated that Israel would have responsibility for settlements in Area C. Thus when the PA claims that settlements are an obstacle to peace, they are forgetting their own prior consent to them being a core issue for negotiation.

Politically, the issues are even more clear cut. For starters, the settlements made their mark from 1967 onwards (and only expanded after the mid–1970s), and the conflict predated this period considerably. It is widely assumed that in any peace settlement with the Palestinians, the major settlement blocks will be incorporated into Israel proper, with the Palestinians being given land swaps for compensation. This formula is one that even the PA appears to have acknowledged, and it is reflected in the Clinton parameters. From this point of view, the settlements are not an insurmountable barrier to an eventual peace settlement.

In the past, Israel had withdrawn settlers from territory that has been handed back in exchange for peace. Thus as part of the peace agreement with Egypt, Israel evacuated settlements in Yamit in the Sinai. More to the point, since the late 1990s, the amount of land that has been offered for a Palestinian state has increased, despite the burgeoning settlement population in the territories. Thus some thirty-five years after the first settlement was created, Ehud Barak was offering the most generous terms of statehood to a Palestinian leader since 1947. Eight years later, there was an even more generous peace agreement under Ehud Olmert despite Jewish population growth in the West Bank. Settlements do not stand in the way of a comprehensive peace agreement, were there the will to reach one. They are instead used as an excuse for failing to reach a peace settlement, particularly by those who are too timid to castigate the Palestinian leadership. The Palestinian Authority is all too well aware of this, which is why it has little incentive to make breakthrough compromises.

That settlements are not the prime factor in the Arab-Israeli conflict was demonstrated dramatically in 2005 during Israel's pullout from the Gaza Strip. In painful scenes, the IDF uprooted some 9,000 Jewish civilians who had been living in Gaza and relocated them to other areas within Israel. An ostensible source of conflict between Israel and the PA had been removed for the sake of peace. Yet over the next few years, a number of Palestinian rejectionist groups (Hamas, the popular resistance committees, the Palestine Islamic Jihad) fired well over 10,000 missiles into sovereign Israeli territory, keeping close to one million Israelis in underground shelters and disrupting life across the south of the country. The ending of settlements in Gaza has, if anything, correlated with an upsurge of terror.

In addition, in 2010 at the behest of the American government, Benjamin Netanyahu's government froze settlement activity for ten months in order to facilitate a dialogue with the PA. Yet for the vast majority of that time, Abbas refused to sit down with his Israeli counterpart. With the prime impediment to peace taken out of the equation, there was virtually no willingness by the Palestinian leader to engage in potentially fruitful dialogue. That is surely telling. Settlements must stop being used as a catch-all explanation for the moribund peace process. They are a symptom of the conflict, and a highly surmountable one.

Finally, there appears to be a significant discrepancy in how the international community, especially the EU, deals with settlements in Israel and other countries. Recent guidelines issued by the European Commission have indicated that there should be no funding of activities by private entities across the green line and that grants to Israel should not be spent in the West Bank. They also maintain that there should be labeling of settlement products, a consequence of non-recognition. The EU, unlike the United States, excludes from preferential customs treatment any products made in the West Bank.

Morocco has occupied Western Sahara for some four decades and has moved 350,000 civilians into the area. Western Sahara is considered occupied territory, and the Security Council has demanded the withdrawal of Moroccan forces. This has not stopped the EU from signing an agreement with Morocco (the 2013 Protocol to the Fisheries Partnership Agreement) that allows it to import fish from all areas where Morocco "exercises its jurisdiction," with the explicit understanding that this applies to Western Sahara. The commission rejected those voices, arguing that this was a violation of international law. The EU also provides Morocco with funding to the tune of hundreds of millions of euros with no requirement to avoid such money's reaching Western Sahara. The United States also now authorizes foreign aid to Morocco, with an understanding that this will not exclude the contested region. The EU has also resisted attempts to issue the labeling of products from Western Sahara. The justification given, namely that Western Sahara is not occupied, stands at odds with widespread legal and academic opinion.

Turkey occupied Northern Cyprus in 1974 and in 1983 declared the Turkish Republic of Northern Cyprus to be independent. The UN refuses to recognize this state, whose formation has been declared illegal. Turkish settlers have moved to Northern Cyprus over many years and now form a significant percentage of the population. Yet as Professor Eugene Kontorovich states, the EU has not asked European companies to desist from commercial activities with Turkish firms who are involved with the occupation of northern Cyprus. The EU provides a significant level of foreign aid to Turkey but, as with Morocco, makes no attempt to demand that it does not reach occupied territory. Indeed it gives direct funding to the Turkish Cypriot community in Turkish-occupied territory. It thus funds the occupation and helps cement Turkey's settlement enterprise. However, Cyprus is required to certify products from TRNC that are exported through Turkey, a demand that effectively outlaws such exports to the EU.

Nonetheless these two cases show very clearly that the attitude towards Israeli settlements in respect of commercial activities is inconsistent with state practice elsewhere.[107]

Does Israel Employ Disproportionate Force and Target Civilians?

The frequent accusations of disproportionality reflect the prevailing lens through which this conflict is seen: one in which a group of desperate, beleaguered victims fighting for their national rights are pitted against an oppressive, imperialist conqueror. Israel is the Goliath to the Palestinian David, a reversal of the pre–1967 paradigm. The disparity in casualty count is taken without qualification as evidence of Israeli wrongdoing and international lawbreaking.

But this view fails to take into account the relevant legal background, as well as the notion of military necessity in wartime. The principle of proportionality states quite simply that while no country is obliged to avoid killing any civilians in war, the loss of civilian life (or injury to civilians or damage to civilian objects) must not be "excessive in relation to the concrete and direct military advantage anticipated."[108] Put in other terms, a state is allowed to use only as much force as is *necessary* to achieve a specific military gain, and anything in excess of this is to be regarded as disproportionate.

On the face of it, an operation to destroy a minor weapons dump in a city center would not require the destruction of the city center. Such a use of force would be excessive, the thousands of civilian casualties being too high a price to pay for a relatively minor military advantage. On the other hand, if the target was an enemy's command and control center or a major weapons base, a greater level of force might be justified, even if this led to a significant number of civilian deaths.

In carrying out military actions against military targets, the preferred course of action is the one with the minimal impact on civilian lives. A state should weigh up alternative courses of action and choose that which, consistent with its military objectives, is likely to kill or maim the fewest civilians.

What also matters is not the outcome of the attack but the "initial expectation and anticipation."[109] The protocol talks about the expected civilian casualties that will ensue from any attack, as the attacker is unlikely to have certain knowledge of the outcome. This partly reflects the "fog of war," the way in which a battle can destroy situational awareness for those engaged in it. As Yoram Dinstein states, how one stacks up the anticipated loss of civilian casualties against military advantage is not an "exact science." Subjectivity will creep into any calculation, for there is no objective calculus by which to make these judgments. But the principle seems clear enough. Finally, assessments of proportionality must be made in relation to a "given attack" rather than on a "cumulative basis."[110]

Thus in making any judgment about excessive force one must haven a proper understanding of the context: (1) a viable assessment of the threat being faced; (2) the nature of the military operation(s) envisioned, and (3) an assessment of the alternative courses of action, including non-action.

1. One should start with the level of threat faced. During Operation Protection Edge in 2014, Hamas fired thousands of rockets over Israeli civilian areas. Israel's civilian infrastructure and its Iron Dome succeeded in providing protection to the population, and the death toll was mercifully low. Nonetheless, these rockets were capable of killing thousands of Israeli civilians at random and without discrimination. Life in many civilian areas was disrupted and economic activity halted. During the war, some rockets were fired towards Ben-Gurion Airport, causing an international panic and the disruption of tourism for some days. Hamas also built a vast tunnel infrastructure that, according to reports, was going to be used to carry out a huge terror attack killing thousands of Israeli civilians. Hamas also attempted seaborne landings in an attempt to claim a mass killing. In the 2006 war with Hezbollah, the terrorist group fired thousands of rockets at Israel's northern cities, causing one million people to flee their homes and severely disrupting civilian life. The terror threat faced by Israel in recent wars has not been negligible, therefore. It constitutes a major and continuous form of terrorism perpetrated by genocidal enemies against Israel's civilian population.

2. So how should Israel have proportionately responded to such a threat? Operations were needed to remove the growing threat of missiles and tunnels, permanently if need be, using a variety of means. These included targeted air strikes and the use of ground forces. Nor did the fact that the main threat came from missiles and tunnels mean that these alone could be targeted. Israel was entitled to neutralize Hamas' command and control centers, its weapons stores, its military leaders and any other military facility. It was entitled to strike at the terrorists firing the weapons, carry out targeted assassinations and destroy terrorist infrastructure. To quote Israeli law professor Yoram Dinstein, in a war like Protective Edge, it was legitimate to fight "to the last bunker of the enemy dictator."

Proportionality here does not require an equal death toll on both sides or that the weapons used must be of identical force. The fact that Israeli fatalities are low does not reduce the military necessity of eliminating the threat. As famed jurist, Alan Dershowitz, points out: "Proportion must be defined by reference to the threat posed by the enemy and not by the harm it has produced."[iii] Proportionality of force is not equality of force. If it were, then it would be impossible to fight any war against terrorists like Hamas. Israel would be unable to achieve victory or even long-term deterrence, and would instead create a situation of permanent stalemate. Indeed the current global pressure on Israel to limit its force to a more "proportional" level is indeed leading to a situation of attritional stalemate, one in which Hamas feels emboldened, every couple of years, to force an improvement in its standing by orchestrated violence. The global outrage from many quarters at Israeli militarism has given Hamas a perverse incentive to continue attacks on Israeli targets.

3. Accepting that military force has to be used, Israel is obliged to choose that option which is likely to lead to the least projected number of civilian casualties. She should therefore consider a range of alternative actions prior to launching an operation. If an option existed to remove the threat of Hamas rocket launchers and tunnels in Gaza without harming any civilians, that option would clearly have been preferable to the one that Israel chose. To ignore such an alternative would invite the charge of disproportionality.

Unfortunately, no such alternative was available. Certainly sitting back and allowing the country to come under rocket and tunnel attack was a non-option, and something acknowledged by many world leaders during the wars of 2008–9, 2012 and 2014. Moreover, Israel could not solely rely on the Iron Dome; effective as it was, its interception rate was never 100 percent. Military operations had to be undertaken against a terrorist infrastructure embedded in a civilian area. To take effective measures, sustained action was needed and civilian casualties (largely owing to the widespread and illegal use of human shields by Hamas) were inevitable. Kneejerk critics of Israeli actions conveniently overlook these facts.

So in general, there was an acute threat to Israeli civilians that required the use of force in a series of operations, provided that the targets were military and that no alternatives entailing less suffering were viable. This is the context in which each and every Israeli action can be judged in regard to the principle of proportionality. Clearly, where there are allegations that certain operations involved more force than necessary, that there was indiscriminate or unnecessary destruction of civilian property, these require an extensive and detailed investigation. All the factors above must be taken into account, together with an understanding of the "fog of war" and the difficulties of fighting in war zones where sudden decisions might need to be made by commanders on the spot. Accusations of disproportionality can be hard to sustain under these circumstances.

Principle of Distinction

Israel has officially observed the principle of distinction. This prohibits intentional attacks on noncombatants or threats of violence designed to spread terror.[112] The intended targets of attacks must be military ones. As per article 51 of protocol 1 to the Geneva Convention, "the civilian population as such, as well as individual civilians, shall not be the object of attack." In addition, "indiscriminate attacks are prohibited." It follows from what was previously said that intention is critical. The mere killing of civilians is not a war crime; only the targeting of civilians *as* civilians is. Similarly, the mere fact that a civilian population may feel terrorized does not imply guilt on the attacking party, for a military attack may have *unintended* effects on civilians. What matters is the intention behind the attack. Thus, Bomber Harris' aerial bombardment of German cities in 1942–45, like the Blitz of 1940, was a breach of international humanitarian law because his policy was designed to make the enemy population submit to the will of the Allies. By contrast, the attack by coalition forces on the Amiriyah bunker during the first Gulf War, in which hundreds of civilians were killed, cannot be considered indiscriminate or a violation of the principle of distinction, though its legal status remains questionable. Forces undertook the operation in good faith and on the basis of intelligence that suggested it was a command and control center.

The evidence points to Israel aiming at legitimate, non-civilian targets and doing all it can to distinguish between protected persons and enemy combatants. Like all Western armies, the IDF operates according to a strict moral and legal code, and any infringements of that code must be investigated swiftly. One part of that code involves doing everything possible to avoid harming civilians or noncombatants: "The IDF servicemen and women will use their weapons and force only for the purpose of their mission, only to the necessary extent and will maintain their humanity even during combat."[113]

This ethos is reflected in the extensive measures undertaken by Israel to minimize civilian casualties. Firstly, the IDF has given advance warnings to civilians in war zones. Prior to Operation Cast Lead, the IDF carried out a series of unprecedented measures. They distributed leaflets to civilians in Gaza telling them to leave the conflict zone. (In 2006, leaflets had also been dropped on suburbs of Beirut, prior to the IAF's bombing.) They gave advance warnings on Palestinian radio and television after breaking into their broadcasts. They also left a recorded message on some 160,000 phones. Finally, they fired noisy nonlethal weapons onto the roofs of buildings used by terrorists, telling them (and the terrorists) that an attack was coming.[114] Such warnings are intended to allow civilians to reach safety before their locality is attacked. Even the UN has acknowledged that these measures were carried out.[115]

But once combat commenced, the Israeli air force used precision guided weapons to hit their targets and employed unmanned aerial drones as an integral part of its intelligence gathering and remote operating capability. Among the IAF's smart weapons is the Delilah missile, a cruise missile capable of changing course at the last minute if it is about to hit civilians.[116] They also used artillery shells in the heat of combat, weapons that are of lower precision but that are designed to counter more immediate threats. (Compare all this with the 1999 ballistic missile attack launched on Grozny market by Russian forces, in which hundreds of civilians were killed or injured because the weapons were not targeted on the terrorists in a discriminate manner.)

After witnessing Israeli measures in Operation Cast Lead, Colonel Richard Kemp, former commander of the British army in Afghanistan, was led to declare: "During operation Cast Lead, the Israeli Defense Forces did more to safeguard the rights of civilians in the combat zones than any other army in the history of warfare." He has gone on to say that, according to the UN's own figures, "the ratio of civilian to combatant deaths in Gaza was by far the lowest in any asymmetric conflict in the history of warfare."[117] He came to this conclusion after examining the statistics for the civilian-combatant ratio in a number of modern asymmetric conflicts. This measures the ratio of civilian deaths to the combatants killed. The average ratio is 3:1 (three civilians to one combatant killed), which is the approximate ratio in the war in Afghanistan. The figure is estimated to be 4:1 in Iraq and Kosovo and could well be far higher in the Chechnya conflict. In Gaza, it was less than 1:1.

True, this was not the conclusion of the UN Goldstone Report, which investigated Cast Lead in 2009. In Operation Cast Lead, Israel claimed that it had killed approximately 700 combatants, i.e., Hamas terrorists, half of those killed. The Goldstone Report, which quoted statistics from anti–Israeli NGOs, instead claimed that less than one in five of those killed was a combatant. But confirmation of Israel's claims came ironically from Hamas. Fathi Hamad, the Hamas interior minister, admitted the following: "It is a fact that on the first day of the war Israel struck police headquarters and killed 250 members of Hamas and the various factions, in addition to the 200–300 operatives from the al-Qassam Brigades. In addition, 150 security personnel were killed, and the rest were from people." In other words, some 700 people (half those killed) were indeed combatants.[118]

In recent conflicts in Gaza, the West Bank and in southern Lebanon, Israel has targeted terrorist infrastructure, including individual terrorists and their leaders, missile batteries, command and control centers and the buildings and vehicles from which terrorists are operating. Inevitably civilians have died in these operations, but that does not prove that they have been the *intended* object of these operations, that they have been *targeted*. Naturally, suspicions that individual soldiers have violated this code must be investigated by the appropriate authorities. But the automatic assumption by some that the IDF has targeted civilians simply because some happen to die is wide of the mark.

In any case, the civilian casualties in Israel's recent asymmetric wars owe a great deal to her enemies' extensive use of human shields, a further violation of international law. There is ample evidence that both Hamas and Hezbullah have stockpiled and fired weapons from mosques, schools, hospitals and the rooftops of houses. Weapons have also been fired from UN compounds and ambulances seized for military purposes. Women and children have been forced to climb onto the roofs of houses in order to deter Israel from attacking the buildings. During Operation Protective Edge, rockets were found in three UNRWA schools and an UNRWA health clinic was booby-trapped.

Proof comes from what Israel's enemies themselves say. Hezbollah's Hassan Nasrallah admitted before the 2006 war that his fighters "live in their houses, in their schools, in their mosques, in their churches, in their fields, in their farms, and in their factories."[119] In February 2008, Hamas representative Fathi Hamad had this to say in the Palestinian Legislative Council: "For the Palestinian people death became an industry, at which women excel and so do all people on this land: the elderly excel, the Jihad fighters excel, and the children excel. Accordingly [Palestinians] created a human shield of women, children, the elderly and the Jihad fighters against the Zionist bombing machine, as if they were saying to the Zionist enemy: We desire death as you desire life."[120]

During Operation Protective Edge, Sami Abu Zuhri, a Hamas spokesman, used Al Aqsa-TV to tell the population not to heed Israeli warnings to leave their houses. He went on to say: "Our noble, Jihad-fighting people, who defend their rights and their homes with their bare chests and their blood. The policy of people confronting the Israeli warplanes with their bare chests in order to protect their homes has proven effective against the occupation.... We in Hamas call upon our people to adopt this policy, in order to protect the Palestinian homes."

Nor is such an egregious violation of the laws of war confined to these groups. There is ample evidence that the Taliban has been using human shields in Afghanistan. According to one Afghan general, speaking in 2010: "The enemy is fighting from compounds where soldiers can very clearly see women or children on the roof or in a second-floor or third-floor window."[121]

A joint U.S.–Afghan investigation in 2009 into deaths in an Afghan village found that "Taliban fighters deliberately forced villagers into houses from which they then attacked ANSF [Afghan security forces] and Coalition forces."[122] In other Middle Eastern conflict zones, from Saddam's Iraq in the first Gulf War to Syria in 2012, human shields have become a ubiquitous feature of modern warfare. It is a weapon of choice used by Islamists to defame Western countries in the eyes of public opinion. Academic Anthony Cordesman was right when he warned that terrorists fighting Western forces in asymmetric warfare had learned to "steadily improve their ability to use civilians to hide, to deter attack, to exploit the political impact of strikes, and to exaggerate damage and killings."[123]

Article 51(7) of the Fourth Geneva Convention clearly states: "The presence or movements of the civilian population or individual civilians shall not be used to render certain points or areas immune from military operations, in particular attempts to shield military objectives from attacks or to shield, favour or impede military operations." Civilians are "protected persons" who cannot be used to create military advantages for one side. When civilian casualties ensue, it is the belligerent power using human shields that takes responsibility. This also extends to civilian infrastructure such as schools, hospitals, and mosques. Thus Hamas and Hezbollah *have* violated international law and committed war crimes.

It is naturally a tragedy that any civilians have been killed or injured in Gaza, the West Bank and Lebanon, just as it is a tragedy that civilians have perished in any war zone. But that is no reason to single out Israel for special treatment. Her army has shown more care for non-combatants than many of its Western counterparts, and its record in avoiding harm to civilians is exemplary. It should be one of the last Western democracies to be condemned, not the first.

Targeted Killings

It is often argued that while Israel's military operations in war zones are not breaches of law, the state's policy of targeted killings (or extrajudicial killings) is. Targeted killings have been defined as the "premeditated, preemptive and intentional killing of an individual ... known or believed to represent a present and/or future threat to the safety and security of a state through affiliation with terrorist groups or individuals."[124] It is crucial to differentiate this type of action from a straightforward assassination. The latter is a tactic designed to eliminate a given enemy on ideological or political grounds. By contrast, the former involves the crucial element of "anticipatory self-defence" in which a state acts preemptively to eliminate terrorists before they can carry out harmful actions against that state's citizens. It is a state-planned and -executed killing. Kofi Annan would have spoken for many in declaring Israeli actions "contrary to international law."[125] The exact legal position on this issue is hard to ascertain, but what is certain is that states other than Israel carry out the same policy. The United States has been using drone strikes to kill leading terror operatives in Yemen, Afghanistan and elsewhere without anything like the equivalent outcry. State practice suggests that this type of warfare is being legitimized by stealth.

Such preemptive strikes have become a much more accepted tool of counter-terrorism in the aftermath of 9/11. As President Bush outlined in a speech at West Point in 2002: "Our security will require all Americans to be forward looking and resolute, to be ready for preemptive action when necessary to defend our liberty and to defend our lives."[126] Hence the focus of U.S. counter-terrorism in recent years has been the use of extrajudicial drone strikes against al-Qaeda targets in Pakistan, Yemen and elsewhere.

A set of conditions for justifying the use of this policy is now suggested. Firstly, the principle of distinction is key, namely that the person being targeted is an enemy combatant and not a civilian. Even though civilians may have repugnant views, including the fact that they justify the use of terrorism against civilians, this can be no justification for their killing. By contrast, combatants cannot be blameless for hostile acts that affect another state.

Secondly, and even more importantly, that terrorist must be about to commit a hostile act. It is not enough that they committed such an act in the past, for then the targeted killing would be motivated more by revenge than self-defense. One could apply the *Caroline* test (that the need for action is "instant, overwhelming, leaves no choice of means, and no moment for deliberation"). As philosopher Daniel Statman puts it, "The crucial condition that must be satisfied to justify killing human beings in self-defense is that they are morally responsible for some grave threat whose neutralization is the end in mind."[127]

Thirdly, the killing must be proportional so that no greater evil is committed by the targeted killing than would have occurred in its absence. Thus if is known or strongly suspected that the targeted killing would be likely to spark a regional conflagration, its justification would be called into question.

Fourthly, there must be no legal means of intercepting the individual prior to the attack being carried out; i.e., there is no means of arrest available in whichever jurisdiction the terrorist finds himself in. Finally, the justification for any specific targeted killing will surely decrease the more there is collateral damage as a result of any strike. Israel's killing of Salah Shehade on 23 July 2002 resulted in the deaths of 14 civilian bystanders, owing to the size of the bomb that was used. The action was understandably criticized, including in Israel.

One recent example of a targeted killing was the assassination of Mahmoud al-Mabhouh in 2010, an act widely attributed to Mossad. Al-Mabhouh was a senior Palestinian figure within Hamas who was engaged in smuggling Iranian weapons to Gaza via Sudan and Egypt. In a carefully coordinated operation, more than two dozen agents using doctored passports converged on a hotel in Dubai where al-Mabhouh was staying and killed him. Al-Mabhouh was dressed in civilian clothing at the time of his death, looking indistinguishable from other hotel residents. Does that mean he was illegally assassinated?

For starters, the principle of distinction was upheld in this case. Though dressed in civilian clothes, al-Mabhouh was an enemy combatant, both because he was a senior Hamas military commander and a founder of the military affiliate of Hamas and because he was trying to bring lethal weapons into Gaza from another hostile state. These weapons were designed to kill and maim Israeli civilians or soldiers. Even though al-Mabhouh was involved in the killing and abduction of two Israeli soldiers in 1989, that event was not the trigger for his killing. The pretext was the threat he posed to Israelis in 2010 as a current Hamas leader. The killing was proportional because it saved lives and involved only the killing of one individual who was at the heart of the operations against Israel. It would have been practically impossible for Israel to rely on Dubai to arrest al-Mabhouh.

Given the absence of judicial process, and the grave and imminent threat to civilians, the use of targeted killings was an entirely legitimate example of counter-terrorism. No doubt if the operation had resulted in the deaths of innocent bystanders, this would have raised questions about its overall justification. But only al-Mahbouh was killed in this operation. Though the killing of this individual outside of Israel is technically a violation of another state's sovereignty, it can be justified as a last-ditch measure of self-defense.

Of course, there is a question as to the tactical astuteness of such a policy in the medium term. Against Islamist terror groups, such as al-Qaeda, which can rely on a large pool of recruits who are not deterred by facing death at the hands of an enemy, the policy may be ineffective. In addition, capturing terrorists is often preferable to killing them because under interrogation, they can provide an intelligence bonanza, giving invaluable insights into terrorist groups' operational capabilities and future plans. But the legality of such operations should not be called into question.

Why There Is No "Cycle of Violence" Between Israel and the Palestinians

From some of the points just mentioned it is clear why there is no "cycle of violence" in this conflict. In essence, this term implies a strong form of legal and moral equivalence between terrorism and the response to it. The Palestinians attack an Israeli target, then (inevitably) Israel responds, followed by a Palestinian revenge attack, and so on. There is no moral difference between the Palestinian action, whether it be the kidnapping of a soldier on Israeli territory or a suicide bombing in a crowded marketplace, and the Israeli military's response. A further implication is also that Israel's actions are counterproductive because they provide fuel to the terrorists for further attacks. Before continuing, it would be helpful to define exactly what terrorism is. A useful definition has been provided by political philosopher Michael Walzer: "The deliberate killing of innocent people, at random, in order to spread fear through a whole population and force the hand of its political leaders."[128]

Violence has always been intrinsic to terrorism, as today's generation of terrorists aim to kill and maim the maximum number of civilians, including children. The more civilian deaths, the more successful the terror attack. As one writer notes, "For terrorists, the killing of non combatants is not a regrettable by-product or side-effect"; it is a "distinct form of belligerency characterized by the deliberate targeting of civilians as a method of spreading outright fear amongst a population."[129] The violence is also indiscriminate insofar as its victims come from every walk of life, every age group and potentially any nationality.

Crucially, the actions of terrorist groups are "designed to have far-reaching psychological effects beyond the immediate victim(s) or object of the terrorist attack."[130] While they engage in many criminal acts, such as murder, rape and forgery, they do not aim just to kill, rape and forge. They aim to coercively change entire societies by inducing panic and terror within that society, effectively sapping the will of government or society to pursue whichever policy the terrorists dislike. They aim to kill some and cow the rest.

Palestinian attacks against Israelis certainly qualify under Walzer's definition. In the last 20 years in particular, suicide bombers have targeted Israelis at nightclubs, restaurants, market places and on the country's public transport system. These are all places frequented typically by civilians. As one scholar of terror notes, the victims are ones who typically pose "no threat to the common good of Palestinians."[131] By contrast, Israel does not aim to kill civilians by going after terrorists, though sadly, civilians are sometimes killed in its military operations. Those who plot bloodshed are the target.

Thus any attempt to equate Israel's self-defense operations designed to *minimize* harm to her civilians and the acts of terror designed to *maximize* harm to Israeli civilians is morally obnoxious. No equivalence would ever be made between the criminal act of murder and the legitimate act of national self-defense, or between the violent vigilante and the law enforcement agent. Similarly, there is a world of difference between a legally constituted state using all its powers of self-defense and the actions of internationally proscribed terror organizations. The implication of blurring this distinction is that one would have to liken the U.S. war against al-Qaeda to the attack on the Twin Towers, or drone attacks to suicide bombings.

The argument that Palestinian terrorism is the inevitable response of a beleaguered people is equally misguided. There is nothing inevitable about detonating a bomb in a crowded market or flying a plane into a building. No external grievance compels these actions or coerces the individuals concerned. They are the choices of the groups that order them and no doubt, a cost-benefit calculation is made about whether this tactic will reap dividends or enhance the group's credibility. Other choices include nonviolent resistance, as advocated by Gandhi and Martin Luther King, and the targeting of military establishments rather than civilians.

The best response would have been to accept an offer of statehood made on several occasions since 1937. Moreover, if terrorism were the inevitable response to occupation, tyranny and injustice, it is strange that we see no Tibetan suicide bombers laying waste to Chinese civilians. After all, their occupation has lasted since 1950 and came about because of Chinese imperial designs rather than because of an act of self-defense. The Tibetans have also never been offered the chance of statehood. With these very real grievances, they have resorted to nonviolent protest.

A final implication of believing in a cycle of violence is that reduced military responses by Israel might take the sting out of Palestinian violence. But this is not borne out by recent history. A decade studying al-Qaeda should show that it is only when Western forces took the fight to the terrorists in Afghanistan and elsewhere that the network suffered crippling defeats. Since the 9/11 attacks, many of its leaders have been killed and its terrorist bases destroyed after the West's determined military onslaught. By contrast, the hesitant and weak-willed responses to al-Qaeda attacks in the mid–1990s, including the withdrawal from Somalia, persuaded Bin Laden that the American superpower was tottering on its legs and on the brink of defeat, paving the way for 9/11. Israeli inaction may therefore provide even further fuel for terrorism, as the groups involved sense their enemy's weakness and lack of resolve.

The Right of Return

In regard to the right of return, the first question one must ask is how many Palestinian refugees there actually are. The Survey on Palestinian Refugees and Internally Displaced Persons claims there is a global population of 9.7 million Palestinians, some 7 million of whom are refugees or internally displaced. Reportedly, the refugee figure includes "6.8 million of the original 1948 refugee population."[132] Firstly, only a small fraction of those claiming to be refugees can be truly considered to be such, with the vast majority being the descendants (children, grandchildren and great-grandchildren) of those who left Palestine in 1947–9. It is unprecedented for such rights to be claimed by the descendants of refugees, as opposed to those who have genuine grounds for compensation and restitution.

The 1951 Convention Relating to the Status of Refugees offers the following definition of a refugee: "Any person who: (2) owing to well-founded fear of being persecuted for reasons of race, religion, nationality, membership of a particular social group or political opinion, is outside the country of his nationality and is unable or, owing to such fear, is unwilling to avail himself of the protection of that country; or who, not having a nationality and being outside the country of his former habitual residence, is unable or, owing to such fear, is unwilling to return to it."

This refers to people outside the country of their nationality, not their descendants. Yet Arab States were able to acquire a special exclusion for Palestinian refugees: "This Convention shall not apply to persons who are at present receiving from organs or agencies of the United Nations other than the United Nations High Commissioner for Refugees Protection and assistance."[133]

Thus according to UNRWA: "A Palestinian refugee is a person whose normal residence was Palestine for a minimum of two years preceding the conflict in 1948, and who, as a result of this conflict, lost both his home and his means of livelihood and took refuge in one of the countries where UNRWA provides relief. Refugees within this definition and the direct descendants of such refugees are eligible for Agency assistance if they are: registered with UNRWA; living in the area of UNRWA operations; and in need."[134]

At the outset, it will strike any fair-minded observer as odd that an exception was created in how to define a political refugee. As Sol Stern points out, "No other refugees in the world had a special UN agency (UNRWA) looking after their welfare for six decades and indulging their fantasies of return."[135]

In any case, one cannot even rely on this agency's figures for its bizarre counting of refugees. UNRWA registration figures are based on information voluntarily supplied by refugees primarily for the purpose of obtaining access to agency services; hence, the information cannot be considered statistically valid demographic data. The number of registered refugees present in the agency's area of operations is almost certainly less that the population recorded. Thus a perverse incentive has been created to falsely claim food and other vital resources.

David Matas rightly points out that the Palestinian right of return is a misnomer, given that it is applied to a vast number of people who have not actually set foot in Israel.[136] The fair and objective definition of a refugee found in the Convention Relating to the Status of Refugees should be applied to the Palestinians. Until then, such a blatant discrepancy should be seen for the politically motivated anomaly that it is.

Resolution 194

Yet it is argued that the right of return is a recognized right of Palestinian refugees and that its denial is tantamount to a violation of international law. Some specifically cite resolution 194, passed in December 1948. Paragraph 11 resolved the following: "That the refugees wishing to return to their homes and live at peace with their neighbours should be permitted to do so at the earliest practicable date" and that "compensation should be paid for the property of those choosing not to return."[137]

Several points are in order. Firstly, there is no explicit reference to Arab refugees, so this can be taken to mean both Arab and Jewish refugees from the war of 1947–8. Second, this General Assembly resolution was a non-binding one, which could only suggest rather than require action by the parties involved. This is reflected in its language. It says that refugees "should" be permitted to return home if they so wished. The word *should* has a hortatory or moralistic quality, exhorting rather than demanding action. It is simply wrong to argue that the UN gave the Palestinians some absolute, unconditional right of return to their place of origin simply because of subsequent (wholly biased) UN resolutions. The conditional language of the original resolution is unambiguous.

More fundamentally, the resolution stipulated that the refugees had to "live in peace with their neighbors." Yet there is evidence that this condition would not be met. Contemporary Arab spokesmen predicted that the returning refugees would be the vanguard of a renewed assault on the Jewish state. Typical was the view expressed by Salah al-Din in 1949: "In demanding the return of the Palestinian refugees the Arabs mean their return as masters, not slaves, or to put it more clearly—the intention is the extermination of Israel."[138] According to *Al Siyyad* on 6 April 1950, the returning refugees would form "a powerful fifth column for the day of revenge and reckoning."[139]

There is also no right of return because an equal emphasis is placed on repatriation, resettlement and the payment of compensation on an equal footing. Thus Resolution 393 of 1950 stated, "The reintegration of the refugees into the economic life of the Near East, either by repatriation or resettlement is essential ... for the realization of conditions of peace and stability in the area." Resolution 513 also speaks of "reintegration either by repatriation or resettlement." Also, no party is named as being responsible for compensating the refugees who had lost property, meaning that responsibility could devolve on both Israeli and Arab shoulders.

Lastly, it should not be forgotten that a number of Arab states (Egypt, Iraq, Lebanon, Saudi Arabia, Syria and Yemen) voted against resolution 194, which lacked any binding legal force in any case. No doubt this was because the resolution failed to establish any unequivocal right of return.

Over time, instead of allowing for the resettlement of Palestinian refugees as recommended by UN resolutions, the Arab states kept them in squalid refugee camps, ensuring that a permanent state of hostility with Israel would be maintained. It is little wonder that Ralph Galloway, a former director of UN Aid in Jordan, once said that the Arab states were refusing to "solve the refugee problem" in order to "keep it as an open sore, as an affront to the United Nations and as a weapon against Israel."[140]

It is true that later General Assembly resolutions reaffirmed Resolution 194 and gave it a new and binding quality. To take one example, United Nations General Assembly Resolution 3236 "reaffirms also the inalienable right of the Palestinians to return to their homes and property from which they have been displaced and uprooted, and calls for their return." Resolution 194 was reaffirmed until recently on a yearly basis, and according to Susan Akram, "no other Resolution in the history of the United Nations reflects such repeated, overwhelming, decades long international consensus as Resolution 194."[141] However, this is a specious argument. Subsequent highly politicized attempts to correct the meaning of a resolution cannot undo its original intent, which was in any case to merely recommend a course of action during the Arab-Israel war of 1948–9.

UDHR

Others cite the Universal Declaration of Human Rights. In Article 13 (2), it is stated, "Everyone has the right to leave any country, including his own, and to return to his country." The Palestinians are deemed to have been denied rights under the UDHR in view of Israel's refusal to allow them a right of return. Yet the declaration, while an undoubtedly important one, is not generally considered to be legally binding on its signatories. In any case, according to Alexander Safian, the reference to return was meant to "underscore the right to leave" and was "aimed at governments that, in effect, imprisoned certain subgroups of their nationals by preventing them from leaving—Jews in Eastern Europe or the Soviet Union, for example." The sponsor of this clause explained that the phrase "and to return to his country" was only inserted to assure that "the right to leave a country ... would be strengthened by the assurance of the right to return."[142]

In addition, there is an issue about whether Israel is the Palestinians' "own country." Those Palestinian Arabs who became refugees as a result of the 1948 war were resident in Palestine, prior to Israel's creation. They were never Israeli citizens, arbitrarily deprived of their citizenship, but rather citizens of mandatory Palestine, a political entity that no longer exists. To defeat this argument, it is claimed that Israel is today the country of the Palestinians because it is the country with which they have genuine and effective links, an attachment that is then inculcated in the descendants of the original refugees.

Case law suggests otherwise. A test for nationality was provided in the famous Nottebohm case of 1955. Friedrich Nottebohm was a German citizen who lived in Guatemala from 1905 to 1943. During this time he retained his German citizenship and his family ties with the country. Shortly after the start of World War II, he applied for citizenship of Lichtenstein, despite having no links with the country and having no intention to leave Guatemala. Nottebohm was granted citizenship of Lichtenstein and made a brief visit to the country. However, he was barred from returning to Guatemala in 1943 as he was deemed to be a German citizen, and was extradited to the United States instead where he spent some time in an internment camp.

Lichtenstein subsequently brought a case against Guatemala before the ICJ, insisting that by refusing Nottebohm entry, seizing his property and extraditing him, they had breached international law. The court dismissed the case, arguing that Guatemala could not be compelled to accept the conferral of nationality by Lichtenstein. Nottebohm never intended to reside in Liechtenstein and had no business or family connections there. He had also not severed his previous ties to Germany. In effect, his change of nationality was a mere convenience, a subterfuge, brought about by the war.

Specific criteria for nationality were invoked in *Nottebohm* to decide what constituted genuine and effective links to a country. They included tests concerning habitual residence, whether the country was the center of a person's interests, family ties, participation in public life, attachment shown for a country and inculcation of patriotism in a person's children. On these criteria, Israel is not the country of the Palestinians, if the matter is viewed objectively. The vast majority have never lived in Israel and do not share a cultural affinity with the state. Their families live outside the country and they do not participate in its public life. The state with which they have the strongest links is a putative Palestinian state, a state in the making. Thus the optimal solution to the predicament of Palestinian statelessness is "not nationality in a state in whose territory ancestors have lived, but rather nationality in the state where the descendants have been born."[143]

ICCPR

In addition, the International Covenant on Civil and Political Rights is often cited as providing a legal basis for a right of return. Article 12 (4) states, "No one shall be arbitrarily deprived of the right to enter his own country." A country is a person's own country when, because of the special ties with that country, he cannot be considered an alien. As regards the International Covenant, the diplomat and legal scholar Stig Jagerskiold once said that the right to enter one's country was "intended to apply to individuals asserting an individual right." He added that there was "no intention here to address the claims of masses of people who have been displaced as a by-product of war or by political transfers of territory or population, such as the relocation of ethnic Germans from Eastern Europe during and after the Second World War, the flight of the Palestinians from what became Israel, or the movement of Jews from the Arab countries."[144] Thus this important document appears to offer no legal support for the idea of a right of return.

Sometimes Resolution 242 is invoked as justification for an alleged right of return. But the wording of the resolution suggests otherwise. It affirms the necessity of "achieving a just settlement of the refugee problem" but does not mention the Palestinians specifically or any specific solution. In any event, the overall context of the resolution is one that calls for a bilateral Israeli-Arab negotiation. Coming under chapter 6, it does not make any demands on Israel.

The right of return should also be seen within its correct historical context. The Palestinian Arab leadership rejected the two-state formula proposed by the General Assembly. They then launched a war of aggression against the Jewish inhabitants of Palestine, designed to snuff out a Jewish state. During the course of that war, both Arabs and Jews became refugees, in the former case, from mandatory Palestine, and in the latter case, both from that territory and from several Arab states. Israel gave citizenship to Jewish refugees whereas Arabs were on purpose denied integration in most Arab countries (except Jordan) in order to prevent any possible accommodation with Israel.

Wars then, as now, involve population exchanges between combatant nations, and the usual pattern is for each side to absorb co-nationals from enemy territory. After the Second World War, millions of Germans were transferred from Poland, Czechoslovakia and Hungary and had to be absorbed by the West German government. The Great Powers did not demur. The Arab states largely refused to absorb Palestinian refugees, whereas Israel absorbed its Jewish refugees. But in any case, it beggars belief that any civilian population displaced in a war of aggression that it started, or which was commenced on its behalf, should be allowed to return to the territory that it was unable to conquer, and which it would still like to conquer. Yet today, this remains the position of mainstream Palestinian leaders (see Chapter 6).

Quite obviously, no Israeli government could countenance the return of 5–6 million Palestinians, never mind that the majority had never lived in the land and thus had no physical connection with it, because it would spell the end of Israel as a Jewish state. The country would quickly have an Arab majority and its Jewish minority would be subject to the vagaries of dhimmitude. Any treaty providing for a right of return today would instantly void the Jewish right to self-determination and is therefore a non-starter.

Undoubtedly, the failure to resolve the Palestinian refugee crisis has had damaging repercussions. It has "contributed to Palestinian feelings of dejection and despair as second and third generations were born into statelessness, without authentic or effective political leadership, dependent on the machinations of cynical or bombastic politicians."[145] The solution for genuine Palestinian refugees could be either a return to Israel or some form of monetary compensation for their lost property. But for their descendants who are stateless, it is either absorption into their host countries (Jordan, Lebanon and elsewhere) or repatriation to their own state, whose creation has been delayed due to Palestinian rejectionism.

2. The Calumnies of the Radical Left: Israel as a Genocidal, Racist, Apartheid and Colonialist State

The criticisms of Israeli policy in the West Bank are amenable to an open debate. Though they are often misguided and historically and legally illiterate, they do not necessarily represent an attempt to delegitimize the Jewish state. The future of the territory and the fate of settlements, together with Israel's military options during war, are the subject of intense and vigorous debate within the Israeli press and among the wider population. Moreover, there is a consensus within Israel that, under the right circumstances, the country should accept a two-state solution and the removal of some settlements if it will bring a long-term peace deal with the Palestinians. The disagreement centers more on why this conflict persists and on how barriers to resolving it can be overcome, than on the need for compromise and dialogue.

There is, however, a wholly different set of allegations that derive from the worldview of the radical left but that are increasingly entering mainstream political discourse. In an attempt to destroy Israel's international image and reduce it to pariah status, some have leveled a series of outrageous accusations against the Jewish state. The country has been openly compared to Nazi Germany, with its politicians likened to the SS. The country stands accused of genocide, apartheid, ethnic cleansing and colonialism, the most odious crimes against humanity in the modern age. This is nothing less than an attempt to traduce Israel's reputation and image in the eyes of "right thinking" people and to suggest that the state is an outcast among the nations.

Israel as a Genocidal and Nazi State

Historically, the comparison between Israel and the Nazis was a key feature of Soviet Cold War propaganda. Numerous articles in the Soviet press denounced Zionism and Israeli leaders in the most venomous tones. Cartoons routinely depicted leading Israelis as the "heirs to Hitler" and of imbibing Nazi race-hate theory, comparing Israel policy towards the Arabs with the Final Solution. Relying on the fictitious claims of the *Protocols*, Soviet commentators alleged the existence of a vast global Zionist conspiracy that helped control the spread of Western imperialism and capitalism. Both Zionism and Judaism were condemned as racist ideologies. Another vile slander, often repeated in the Arab world, was the notion that the Zionists either ignored or collaborated in the slaughter of millions of their co-religionists during the war.¹ (The culmination of decades of virulent Soviet propaganda was the UN Resolution that condemned Zionism as racism.) Britain's Trotskyist papers, such as *Socialist Worker*, *Labour Review* and *News Line*, echoed Moscow's hate-filled diatribes, particularly during the 1982 Lebanon War when cartoonists depicted Israeli leaders wearing SS uniforms.²

Such grotesque vilification has not been lost on today's more militant *gauchistes*. When the celebrated Portuguese novelist Jose Saramago visited Yasser Arafat's compound in Ramallah, at the time under Israeli siege, he described the situation he observed as "a crime comparable to Auschwitz." When he was asked by an Israeli journalist to point out the gas chambers, he replied "Not here yet."³

In an article for the *Independent*, columnist Yasmin Alibai-Brown made similar allusions to the Holocaust. Decrying the policy of "brutal ethnic cleansing" that she believed to have characterized the 2009 war in Gaza, she asked, "How many Palestinian Anne Franks did the Israelis murder, maim or turn mad?" In the same article she said the 1,200 Gazans who died in Cast Lead were "slaughtered like animals in an abattoir."⁴

Veteran anti-apartheid campaigner Ronnie Kasrils has also made repeated comparisons between Israel and Nazi Germany by accusing the former of propagating a "pathological racist ideology," the same one that "fuelled Hitler's war lust and implementation of the Holocaust." In a speech from 2009, he made allusions to the Holocaust in his condemnation of Operation Cast Lead: "How do we evaluate the inhumanity of dropping bombs and blazing white phosphorous on civilian populations, burning people alive, gassing them in a Gaza ghetto under relentless siege with no place to run or hide." In a roll call of twentieth century atrocities, he listed "Deir Yassin" and "Sabra and Shatilla" with "Lidice" and "the Warsaw Ghetto." The "perpetrators of the slaughter in Gaza are the off-spring of Holocaust victims," and they are, he declared, "behaving like Nazis." Genocide was clearly Israel's ultimate aim, according to Kasrils, for the Palestinians will soon be "targeted to go the way of the extinct peoples of the former colonial era."⁵

Elsewhere John Pilger has described Israel's war in Gaza in 2009 as a "Holocaust denied" and that it followed a genocidal plan, laid down in 1948, for the "extinction of the indigenous people." He describes Israeli policy towards Gaza as if it were a record of collective atrocity: "enforced starvation," "denial of humanitarian aid," "piracy of life-giving resources such as fuel and water," "the systematic destruction of infrastructure and the killing and maiming of the civilian population" and says that this meets "the international standard of the Genocide Convention." This, he declares, is a "holocaust-in-the-making." He alludes to the Holocaust in his description of the security barrier as a means of "imprisonment of Palestinians behind a ghetto wall" which has turned the West Bank and Gaza into "effectively a concentration camp."⁶

Referring to Israel's 1982 war in Lebanon against the PLO, Noam Chomsky wrote that if the Syrians had conquered Israel in the same way, "Few would have hesitated to recall the Nazi monsters."⁷ He also repeatedly refers to the existence of Israeli "concentration camps." Elsewhere: "How sickeningly appropriate, then, that just as Europeans and North Americans looked the other way when the Nazis were perpetrating the Holocaust, the Arabs are finding a way to do nothing as the Israelis slaughter Palestinian children."⁸

In a poem he wrote for the *Observer* called "Killed in the Crossfire," the academic and poet Tom Paulin talked of Palestinians being "gunned down by the Zionist SS."⁹ In another interview in 2002 with *Al-Ahram* he expressed his "hatred" for Israeli settlers, who he described as "Nazis, racists." These settlers, he added, "should be shot dead."¹⁰ The noted philosopher Slavoj Žižek said that the description of the Gaza Strip as "the greatest concentration camp in the world" had come "dangerously close to truth" and that Israeli settlement policies would eventually make the West Bank "Palestinian-frei."[11]

These sentiments are not confined to the far left. In 2001, Erkki Tuomioja, the Finnish foreign minister, said he was "appalled" by Israel's policy to "crush, humiliate, subjugate and impoverish the Palestinians." He went on: "It is rather shocking that some people advocate towards the Palestinians the same kind of policy as they themselves were victim to in the 1930s."[12]

Many have chosen to compare Gaza to the Warsaw Ghetto. The UN special rapporteur for the Palestinian territories, Richard Falk, has openly compared conditions in Gaza to the Warsaw Ghetto. Speaking during Operation Cast Lead, he said, "To lock people into a war zone is something that evokes the worst kind of international memories of the Warsaw Ghetto, and sieges that occur unintentionally during a period of wartime."[13]

The former Labour MP, Oona King, wrote of how Israel's founding fathers "could surely not imagine the irony facing Israel today: in escaping the ashes of the Holocaust, they have incarcerated another people in a hell similar in its nature—though not its extent—to the Warsaw ghetto." She reinforced the comparison by describing Gaza as a "Palestinian ghetto" in which "residents are sealed off and live under curfew; the authorities view torture as acceptable and use collective punishment as a means of control; soldiers drive families from their homes, confiscate property and demolish neighbourhoods."[14] During the 2014 Operation Protective Edge, former UK deputy prime minister Lord Prescott joined in with this Holocaust analogy by likening Gaza to a "concentration camp."[15]

Added to this are determined attempts to hijack Britain's Holocaust Memorial Day in order to make a political statement. In 2013, Liberal Democrat MP David Ward caused outrage with remarks posted on his blog. He expressed sadness that the Jews, "who suffered unbelievable levels of persecution during the Holocaust" could "within a few years of liberation" go on to inflict "atrocities on Palestinians in the new State of Israel and continue to do so on a daily basis in the West Bank and Gaza."[16]

His belief in collective responsibility, blaming Jews for Israel's actions, sparked widespread anger. Lee Jasper, a race-relations activist and candidate for the Respect party, exploited the commemoration to launch his own spiteful attack. Israel, he declared, had "failed to learn the lessons of its own tragic history having evolved into a racist oppressor." He added: "Israel has ... allowed itself to turn into the very thing that it despises the most, a political ideology that seeks to oppress people on the basis of race or religion."[17]

For several years, the Muslim Council of Britain boycotted Holocaust Memorial Day, citing the failure to remember other purported victims of genocide. In particular, it said that the commemoration excluded and ignored "the ongoing genocide and violation of human rights in the occupied Palestinian territories." Indeed, there is no Holocaust iconography too sensitive for these critics. So in an article called "Dark Echoes of the Holocaust" written for the *Daily Record*, George Galloway drew attention to claims that the body parts of Palestinian prisoners had been harvested by Israeli doctors without their families' consent. For this Galloway accused those responsible of "playing mini–Mengele on Palestinian prisoners in Israeli jails."[18]

Shamefully, the site of Yad Vashem, Israel's national memorial to the victims of the Holocaust, has come under attack. Daniel McGowan, a former professor of economics in New

York, lamented that the museum overlooked the site of Deir Yassin, the town that came under attack by Irgun forces in 1948: "To build a Holocaust museum within sight of this crime while totally brushing it off is unconscionable. To continue to show indifference towards Deir Yassin, while standing in front of it, is hateful." The equivalence continues: "For Jews to recognize Deir Yassin and for Palestinians to recognize the victimisation of Jews in the Holocaust are steps towards recognizing the humanity and suffering of both people."[19]

Even Holocaust denial has been hijacked. Denying the Palestinian narrative has been described by some as "Naqba denial," and one commentator says it is "as pernicious as Holocaust revisionism."[20] One university professor has even gone as far as saying, "The heritage of the victims of the Holocaust belongs to the Palestinian people. The state of Israel has no (legitimate) claim to the heritage of the Holocaust."[21] Another academic has written: "Today, the Palestinians are the heirs of the Jewish sufferings, the sufferings of Treblinka, Dachau and Auschwitz. The Jews were the direct victims of Nazism. The world recently discovered that the Palestinians were the Nazis' indirect victims."[22]

Some argue that Israel cynically exploits the memory of the Holocaust in order to justify its present behavior. At the height of Operation Cast Lead, the Labour MP, Gerald Kaufman, directly compared Israel's actions in Gaza to those of Nazi Germany. Citing the murder of his grandmother at the hands of the Nazis in the Second World War, he told MPs: "My grandmother did not die to provide cover for Israeli soldiers murdering Palestinian grandmothers in Gaza." He declared that Israel's government was "ruthlessly and cynically" exploiting "guilt among gentiles over the slaughter of Jews in the Holocaust as justification for their murder of Palestinians."[23]

This is a major theme in the writings of Norman Finkelstein, an academic and the son of Holocaust survivors. In his book *The Holocaust Industry*, Finkelstein argues that the memory of the Holocaust has been systematically exploited by leading members of the American Jewish establishment in order to promote the interests of Israel. He also accuses this Jewish establishment of exaggerating the number of Holocaust survivors and using this to blackmail European governments. In his words: "Since the late 1960s, there has developed a kind of Holocaust industry which has made a cult of the Nazi Holocaust. And the purpose of this industry is, in my view, ethnic aggrandisement—in particular, to deflect criticism of the State of Israel and to deflect criticism of Jews generally."[24]

Some go further and actually question the reality of the Holocaust. The Israeli author Gilad Atzmon has written this about the Holocaust: "When I was young and naive I was also somehow convinced that what they told us about our 'collective' Jewish past really happened. I believed it all, the Kingdom of David, Massada, and then the Holocaust: the soap, the lampshade, the death march, the six million." He goes on to write: "It took me many years to understand that the Holocaust, the core belief of the contemporary Jewish faith, was not at all an historical narrative for historical narratives do not need the protection of the law and politicians." As a result, the Holocaust "became the new Western religion … the most sinister religion known to man."[25] The aim of this Holocaust analogy is to vilify Israel, demean Jewish suffering and suggest that today it is Palestinians, not Jews or Israelis, who are deserving of victim status.

Allied to the accusation of being a genocidal state is the charge that Israel is an ethnic cleanser, both of its own Arab population and the Palestinians. In an article entitled "Is Israel a Democracy or an Ethnocracy?" Ben White asserts that Israel "was founded on the basis of ethnic cleansing and mass land expropriation" and that "the only reason there is a 'Jewish majority' is because of the historic fact of the forced exclusion of Palestinians from their homes and lands."[26]

Ken Livingstone has long made the same charge. In an article written in the *Guardian* in 2005, the former London mayor talked of how Israel's expansion "included ethnic cleansing" and of how "Palestinians who had lived in that land for centuries were driven out by systematic violence and terror aimed at ethnically cleansing what became a large part of the Israeli state."[27]

For good measure, Ilan Pappe is at hand to detail systematically this apparent policy of ethnic cleansing at Israel's inception. Israel's founding year involved nothing less, he says, than "the expulsion, direct and indirect, of some 750,000 Palestinians, the systematic destruction of more than 400 villages and scores of urban neighbourhoods, as well as the perpetration of some 40 massacres of unarmed Palestinians."[28]

Israel as an Inherently Racist State

Even if anti–Israel critics do not use the "Nazi" label they will often characterize the Jewish state as an inherently racist entity. The accusation was made most notoriously at the UN when, in 1975, the General Assembly adopted resolution 3379, which stated, "Zionism is a form of racism and racial discrimination." It came about because of a concerted effort by an Arab/Muslim/Third World bloc within the UN to delegitimize the Jewish state in the aftermath of defeat in the Yom Kippur war. In 1991, the General Assembly rescinded the resolution, but the damage had already been done to Israel's reputation. In 2001, the United Nations World Conference against Racism, held in Durban, South Africa, singled out Israel for calumny, condemning its policies as racist and calling the country an apartheid state. Many on the left have seized on the UN resolution as evidence of what they perceive to be Israel's racist character.

No writer has pursued this idea with greater tenacity than Noam Chomsky, the grandfather of the anti–Israel movement. He has long argued that the very idea of a Jewish state is beyond the pale because such a state is inherently racist, unequal and discriminatory. "Embodied in the political institutions of a Jewish state," he argues, are "concepts of purity of nation and race" that can prove quite ugly.[29] "In a Jewish state," he writes elsewhere, "there can be no full recognition of basic human rights.... Such limitations are inherent in the concept of a Jewish state that also contains non–Jewish citizens."[30] In a 2004 interview with Jennifer Bleyer published in *The Ugly Planet*, Chomsky stated: "It ends up that about 90% of the land [in Israel] is reserved for people of Jewish race, religion and origin. If 90% of the land in the United States were reserved for people of white, Christian race, religion and origin, I'd be opposed. So would the ADL. We should accept universal values."[31]

Ben White echoes these sentiments when he quotes Oren Yiftachel: "Despite declaring the regime as democratic, ethnicity (and not territorial citizenship) is the main determinant of the allocation of rights, powers, and resource ... [and] the logic of ethnic segregation is diffused into the social and political system."[32] Thus it is hardly surprising that the radically anti–Israeli historian, Ilan Pappe, has talked of "the de–Zionisation of Israel" as an essential "pre-condition for peace."[33]

Judith Butler is another who argues that there is something constitutionally unsound in Israel as a Jewish state. In her book *Parting Ways*, she makes a connection between Zionism's "hegemonic control" over Jewishness and the "colonial subjugation [it] has implied for the Palestinian people." She argues that it is only by "an end to political Zionism, understood as the insistence on grounding the State of Israel on principles of Jewish sovereignty" that the region can come to realize "broader principles of justice."

She argues that somehow Zionism has hijacked the true meaning of Jewishness and that, in its essence, the ethos and values of the faith must include "cohabitation as a norm of sociality" and "ethical relationality," understood as a non-insular way of reaching out to the non–Jew, both of which would serve as a basis for "a critique of nationalist modes of state violence that sustain the occupation, land confiscation, and the political imprisonment and exile of Palestinians."[34] Her interpretation of cohabitation is heavily influenced by the writings of Hannah Arendt, another critic of Zionism, who inveighed against nation states as a means for creating conditions of statelessness given their need to maintain national-ethnic homogeneity.

One aspect of Israel's constitution that is most reviled is the right of return, which guarantees that a Jew from any part of the world can become a citizen of Israel.[35] For many, such an arrangement smacks of ethnocentric racism, both by privileging one group of people but also because it denies the same right of return to Palestinian refugees. For Ben White, this piece of statute among others has "shaped an institutionalised regime of ethno-religious discrimination by extending Israel's 'frontiers' to include every Jew in the world (as a potential citizen), at the same time as explicitly excluding expelled Palestinians."[36] Judith Butler's critique of the right of return is couched as a critique of a wider issue: "It would be unjust for any state to insist on one religious and ethnic group maintaining a demographic majority to create differential levels of citizenship for majority and minority populations."[37]

The Guardian's Seumas Milne offers a similar analysis: "Those who insist there can be no questioning of the legitimacy of the state in its current form—with discriminatory laws giving a 'right of return' to Jews from anywhere in the world, while denying it to Palestinians expelled by force—are scarcely taking a stand against racism, but rather the opposite."[38]

It is sometimes claimed that Zionism is a form of crude ethnic nationalism and, as such, a racist and illegitimate form of self-determination. This is the argument put forward by Michael Neumann in *The Case Against Israel*. He writes: "Advocating the assignment of territory and political power according to ethnicity" is tantamount to "advocating the political supremacy of an ethnic group." He then goes on to give a roll call of failed attempts at self-determination that supposedly illustrate his point, ranging from Yugoslavia and Rwanda to Turkey and Algeria. "At best," he declares, "the self-determination of peoples has been a smokescreen for bitter religious or class warfare" and tends to the production of "racially pure enclaves." A division of the world into ethnically distinct states can only be achieved, he says, "by continued purification campaigns and the suppression of ethnic minorities." He applies this critique to Zionism, which, far from being a Wilsonian dream, was a crude form of ethnic nationalism in which non–Jews would be forced to live "at the good pleasure of the Jews."[39] Tony Judt makes the same point. Israel, he says, "is an oddity among modern nations … because it is a Jewish state in which one community, Jews, is set above others, in an age when that sort of state has no place."[40]

The notion that the Jewish state grants rights on an ethnocentric basis leads the writer Joel Kovel to decry Zionism's "racist character." He goes on: "What are we to call a project which, though it boasts of being a 'democracy,' reserves 92% of its land for Jewish people? Where one who converts to Judaism or has a Jewish great-grandmother is automatically given full rights to the land while those others whose families merely happened to have lived there for centuries are at best second-class and landless?"[41]

In his autobiography, Ken Livingstone tries to explain why Zionist leaders in 1948 engaged in "ethnic cleansing" on the grounds that "Zionism was conceived at a time when the concept of racial superiority was normal" and it was "born in a world where belief in race and blood was deep-rooted."[42]

In explaining Israel's supposedly racist character, some writers have attempted to delve into the Jewish faith and its "discriminatory" character. Thus Naomi Klein once titled a lengthy essay: "What Israel Has Become: Racism and Misogyny at the Core of Its Being." She starts her piece by decrying Jewish education, which she describes as "an education of fear." "From early primary school we are thought that Jews have always been persecuted and hated; that Israel exists for a reason: because nobody else would take us, because they will come again." From there, she talks of how "Jews made the shift from victims to victimizers with terrifying ease." The main instrument of this victimization is the army where young Jewish men "are taught the siege mentality and to hate Arabs." Israeli men, she continues, "reach maturity by brutalizing and degrading Palestinians, particularly Palestinian women." She ends: "So long as Israel continues to usurp Palestine, it will be a country with racism and misogyny at the core of its being."[43]

The most virulent attempt to link Jewish cultural values with alleged Israeli misdeeds can be found in Jostein Gaardner's infamous opinion piece "God's Chosen People." The famous Norwegian writer invoked the concept of the "chosen people" as a stick with which to attack Israeli policy. He believed that Israelis saw themselves as morally superior, possessing a divine mandate to launch blows at their racially "inferior" cousins: "We don't believe in the notion of God's Chosen People. We laugh at this people's capriciousness and weep at its misdeeds. To act as God's Chosen People is not only stupid and arrogant, but a crime against humanity. We call it racism." In sanctimonious fashion he intoned, "We do not believe in divine promises as a justification for occupation and apartheid. We laugh uneasily at those who still believe that the god of flora, fauna and the galaxies has selected one people in particular as his favourite and given it silly, stone tablets, burning bushes and a license to kill." Judaism is characterized as a faith animated by retribution and outright belligerence, unlike Christianity, which is marked by "compassion and forgiveness."

Gaardner's op-ed goes on to say that Israelis were animated by "blood vengeance" that was based on the principle of "an eye for an eye," stating that many Israelis supported their county's military actions "in the same manner they once cheered the plagues of the Lord as 'fitting punishment' for the people of Egypt." The ancient notion of a Jewish lust for revenge created a state based on an "archaic national and warlike religion." The article became increasingly hysterical in tone. He wrote that Israel, with its "disgusting weapons," had "massacred its own legitimacy," had "raped the recognition of the world" and was, in its current form, "history." At one point he accuses some Israelis of seeking "a final solution" to the Palestinian problem.[44]

Another mainstream columnist, the *Independent's* Deborah Orr, who once derided Israel as a "shitty" country, echoed Gaardner's vilification. When Israel decided to release more than 1,000 Palestinians in return for a kidnapped Israeli soldier, Gilad Schalit, Orr commented as follows: "There is something abject in their eagerness to accept a transfer that tacitly acknowledges what so many Zionists believe—that the lives of the chosen ... are of hugely greater consequence than those of their unfortunate neighbours."[45] *The Independent* decided to apologize after receiving complaints.

A similar argument was made by Tariq Ali in 2006 during the height of the Lebanon war. He decried many elements of "hubris" in the Jewish state, including "a belief in its racial superiority," and used this to explain why "the loss of many civilian lives in Gaza and Lebanon matters less than the capture or death of a single Israeli soldier."[46]

But perhaps their comments were mild compared to those of fellow columnist Yasmin Alibhai-Brown. Nearing the end of the Gaza war she wrote: "Shocking are the mathematical calculations of revenge for Jewish lives cruelly cut down and the differential values placed on deaths. Kill the kids before they grow, is that it?" She goes on to write, "The abused have become righteous abusers" who "avenge themselves for the Holocaust on people who had nothing to do with the six million dead."[47] Righteous abusers who *avenge* themselves? She cannot conceive how the Jewish state can defend itself robustly without invoking some notion of anti–Arab hatred, hence her comment in the same article that the "moral health of Israel" is at risk because of "pathological" racist attitudes towards Arabs.

The same alleged linkage between modern-day Israeli policy and Biblical values was made by Jose Saramago. The Portuguese novelist is one who sees in modern Israel's war against Palestinians an expression of Biblical blood lust and Jewish fidelity to a tradition of revenge. He wrote these lines in *El Pais* in 2002:

> The blond David of yesteryear surveys from a helicopter the occupied Palestinian lands and fires missiles at unarmed innocents; the delicate David of yore mans the most powerful tanks in the world and flattens and blows up what he finds in his tread; the lyrical David who sang praise to Bathsheba, incarnated today in the gargantuan figure of a war criminal named Ariel Sharon, hurls the "poetic" message that first it is necessary to finish off the Palestinians in order later to negotiate with those who remain.

He thus inverts the true story of David and Goliath, a story of underdog triumph against the powerful, into a story of Israeli ingenuity facing off against powerless Palestinians. David is now an Israeli "Superman" whose blondness has echoes of the master race. And the reason for David's oppression of his enemies is that he is "intoxicated mentally by the messianic dream of a Greater Israel." The Jewish David has become "contaminated by the monstrous and rooted 'certitude' that in this catastrophic and absurd world there exists a people chosen by God and that, consequently, all the actions of an obsessive, psychological and pathologically exclusivist racism are justified." Like Shylock demanding his pound of flesh, "Israel seizes hold of the terrible words of God in Deuteronomy: 'Vengeance is mine, and I will be repaid.'"[48]

A similar linkage between purported Biblical vengeance and Israeli behavior can be found in a recent book by Israeli academic Marcelo Svirsky. He writes: "Consuming the last drops of holocaustic fuel, it runs on air like a maniac. It fires missiles and bombs at civilian populations, it destroys homes and erects separation walls everywhere, as if to say 'I will take you all with me' in a Samson venture: 'Let me die with the Philistines.'"[49]

The idea that alleged Israeli abuses stem from religious vindictiveness, specifically Talmudic prescriptions, can also be found in the writings of Israel Shahak, a notorious recycler of anti–Semitic canards whose writings are now found on many neo–Nazi and Islamist Web sites.

A final disturbing attempt to demonize the Jewish state has come from Sabeel, a radical Christian theology outreach center in Jerusalem. Its founder, Naim Ateek, has invoked the ancient charge of deicide, likening the suffering of Palestinians at the hands of Jews to that of the Biblical Christ. In his Easter message of 2001, he declared, "The suffering of Jesus Christ at the hands of evil political and religious powers two thousand years ago is lived out again in Palestine." Jesus, he says, "is the powerless Palestinian humiliated at a checkpoint, the woman trying to get through to the hospital for treatment, the young man whose dignity is trampled." He added: "It seems to many of us that Jesus is on the cross again with thousands of crucified Palestinians around." He likens Palestine to "one huge Golgotha" suffering under the daily operation of "the Israeli government crucifixion system."[50] In a few sentences, Ateek has restated the long-repudiated charge that Jews killed Jesus, but has put this into a modern context.

Amid such demonization, it follows naturally that some will personify Israel in the vilest terms. For the Stop the War coalition, Israel's policy was akin to the "sadism" of American exceptionalism and "legitimized by righteousness."[51] Elsewhere, Michael Neumann says, "Israel stands out among other unpleasant nations in the depth of its commitment to gratuitous violence and nastiness." He goes on: "This you expect to find among skinheads rather than nations."[52] In July 2013, the German newspaper *Süddeutsche Zeitung* depicted Israel as a hideous Moloch, utilizing the kind of images that were commonplace in Nazi Germany. On the far right, Israel is described as a "sadist, sociopath Jewish state,"[53] while for Gideon Levy, the country's population are in a state of "psychosis."[54]

For the chairman of Amnesty's Finnish division, Israel is a "scum country"[55] and for veteran Israel-basher Alexei Sayle, Israel has become "the Jimmy Saville of nation states."[56] When Israel intercepted the Mavi Marmara in 2010, a *Guardian* editorial likened Israel's actions to those of "Somali pirates."[57] Finally, Johann Hari could not even think of modern Israel without the "smell of shit," a reference to raw sewage that he claimed was being pumped across Palestine.[58] The same linkage was also made by Deborah Orr and Daniel Bernard. Comparing whole countries to monsters, sadists, pedophiles and excrement is rare in international politics. For much of the left, and in regard to Israel, it is a common feature of such discourse.

Israel as a Colonialist Power

For others, Israel is a classic product of colonialist thinking, an offshoot of a late nineteenth century European mindset that believes in domination over an oppressed and indigenous people. The state, according to this critique, is a throwback to a past age when liberal values were being trumped by imperialist dogma. In recent decades, this venomous charge has become the shrill cry of numerous academics on the hard left. In 1973, the French Marxist Maxime Rodinson's book *Israel: A Colonial Settler State?* argued that Israeli statehood was the "culmination of a process that fits perfectly into the great European-American movement of expansion in the 19th and 20th centuries." Was its aim "to settle new inhabitants among other peoples or to dominate them economically and politically"?[59]

Naturally, these critiques have been given rocket fuel at the U.N. General Assembly. As early as 1973, the body denounced in no uncertain terms a purported "collusion between Portuguese colonialism, apartheid and Zionism."[60]

Ronnie Kasrils declared Israel "guilty of an illegal and immoral colonial project" and cited a report by South Africa's Human Sciences Research Council confirming that "the everyday structural racism and oppression imposed by Israel constitutes a regime of apartheid and settler colonialism."[61] For the late Tony Judt, Israel was guilty of importing a "late–19th-century separatist project into a world that has moved on, a world of individual rights, open frontiers and international law." Such a state "in which Jews and the Jewish religion have exclusive privileges from which non–Jewish citizens are forever excluded" is an "anachronism" and a "dysfunctional one."[62]

Israel's settlement policy has frequently been labeled colonialist, or settler-colonialist. Thus Rafael Reuveny writes that "the Israeli control since 1967 of the West Bank and (until recently) the Gaza Strip is essentially colonialism" and the Jewish state is "the last colonialist." He argues that the administration in the Territories exhibits "standard colonial attributes," which include, among other things, "segregation of settlers and Palestinians; settlers interacting with natives only economically; settler business based on cheap local land, labor, and subsidized water; settlers and other Israelis looking down on Palestinians; Palestinians requiring Israeli permissions for daily affairs; hostility and violence between settlers and natives; and settlers taking the law into their hands, grabbing local lands, uprooting olive trees." Reuveny adds, "Like its colonial counterparts, Israel has not invested in the Palestinian economy, which has remained highly underdeveloped."[63]

The journalist Nir Rosen agrees with this assessment, viewing Israel as the "world's last colonialist state"; one that, like other such states, uses its own civilians strategically to "claim land and dispossess the native population, be they Indians in North America or Palestinians in what is now Israel and the Occupied Territories."[64]

Comparisons of Israel with other colonialist states come naturally to others. Writing in the *Progressive* in 2000, Matthew Rothschild declared that Israel was like "the Brits in India, the Belgians in the Congo, and the French in Algeria" before adding that Palestine was "the colonized" to Israel "the colonialist." Some BDS advocates reject the idea of Israeli/Palestinian dialogue because it "avoids acknowledgement of the basic colonizer-colonized relationship."[65]

For Ilan Pappe, Israel's whole founding reflected the colonialist interests of others. He thus writes: "The colonisation of Palestine fitted well the interests and policies of the British Empire on the eve of the First World War."[66]

With colonialism comes the charge of having expansionist aims. Thus Noam Chomsky pictures the early Zionists as intent on a regional policy of expansionism. One of the constant themes in Ben-Gurion's tenure as prime minister, he said, was regional hegemony so that Israel would come to conquer "southern Lebanon, southern Syria, today's Jordan, all of cis-Jordan [Palestine], and the Sinai." The Zionists would be in command "from the Nile to Iraq."[67] Israel's long-term goals, he says, might be "a return to something like the system of the Ottoman Empire." But these expansionist aims are to be explained by the inherent nature of Israeli aggression, the country's "Samson complex" and its desire to be an "Israeli Sparta."[68] Such colonialism thus purportedly reflects a founding philosophy in which a desire for regional domination is central.

Israel as an Apartheid State

Closely connected to this calumny is the accusation that Israel is akin to apartheid South Africa. Comparisons with the racist regime in Pretoria are now routine and are accepted as a template for understanding Israeli-Palestinian relations. The aim is to make the world think that Israel is an illegitimate nation that acts in a constitutionally racist manner towards its non–Jewish inhabitants. As such, it does not deserve to exist in its current form.

In 2001, the Durban Conference declared that Israel was "a racist, apartheid state." Its brand of apartheid was described as "a crime against humanity" and one "characterized by separation and segregation, dispossession, restricted land access, denationalization, 'bantustanization' and inhumane acts." Not surprisingly, both the former and current UN special reporters for Palestine, John Dugard and Richard Falk, have openly compared Israel to South Africa, with the latter also evoking the charge of systematic genocide. At the annual session of the UN International Conference of civil society in support of the Palestinian people, there was a call "for the perpetrators of the crime of apartheid being committed in the Occupied Palestinian Territories to finally be brought to justice."

Advocates of this comparison are actively engaging in a sustained campaign of boycott, divestment and sanctions. The allegation is multifaceted and draws upon many of the themes already cited: that Israel reserves rights only for Jews, that there are roads in the West Bank only for Jews, that there is segregation across Israel and that Israeli Arabs are less than full citizens because they are not compelled to do army service. More often, the position of Palestinians in both Gaza and the West Bank is likened to that of blacks in apartheid South Africa. For many in BDS, such as Ronnie Kasrils, Israeli "apartheid" is worse than that practiced in South Africa.[69]

In a recent article in the *Guardian*, Israeli political scientist Meron Benvenisti, a former deputy mayor of Jerusalem, described Ariel Sharon's withdrawal from Gaza as a "bantustan plan for an apartheid Israel." He described the withdrawal as a form of "conceptual transfer" that represented the "confinement of one and a half million people in a huge holding pen." He compared the plan to the South African attempt to create "homelands for the blacks," which was an attempt to "confer legitimacy on the expulsion of black people, and their uprooting." He talks of the separation wall built in the West Bank as a means of "imprisoning three million Palestinians in bantustans" and a "means to oppress and dominate."[70]

Another individual adding rocket fuel to this bigoted assault on Israel is Archbishop Desmond Tutu. Tutu, a Nobel Prize–winning figure in the struggle against apartheid, has argued that the position of the Palestinians is akin to that of black people in apartheid South Africa. In an op-ed written for the *Boston Globe* in August 2007, Tutu wrote: "What do I see and hear in the Holy Land? Some people cannot move freely from one place to another. A wall separates them from their families and from their incomes. They are arbitrarily demeaned at checkpoints and unnecessarily beleaguered by capricious applications of bureaucratic red tape. I have to tell the truth: I am reminded of the yoke of oppression that was once our burden in South Africa."[71] Tutu has also argued that people in the United States are scared to condemn Israel "because the Jewish lobby is powerful—very powerful."[72]

The most virulent attacks on Israel as an apartheid state have come from Ronnie Kasrils. In a speech in 2009 at an Israel apartheid week event, Kasrils quoted former South African prime minister Dr. Hendrik Verwoerd, who stated that Israel was an apartheid state. Kasrils agreed with the statement and characterized Israel as a state "based on racial ethnicity" where Jews in Israel possessed "exclusive citizenship." He regarded Israeli policy after 1967 as one of creating "miniscule Bantustans" in the West Bank and Gaza as a means of enclosing "Palestinians in their own ghettoised prisons." South African bantustans were "uncannily comparable to the derisory, ever shrinking pieces of ground Israel is consigning to the Palestinians." Kasrils went on to say, "In its conduct and methods of repression, Israel increasingly came to resemble more and more apartheid South Africa at its zenith—even surpassing its brutality, house demolitions, removal of communities, targeted assassinations, massacres, imprisonment and torture of its opponents."[73] Kasrils has not been alone in believing that Israel is somehow worse than the apartheid regime in Pretoria.

Jimmy Carter made a similar point. Israeli behavior in the occupied territories, he wrote, including "a rigid system of required passes and strict segregation between Palestine's citizens and Jewish settlers in the West Bank" as well as "an enormous imprisonment wall," was "more oppressive than what black people lived under in South Africa during apartheid."[74]

The "enormous imprisonment wall" that Carter refers to is the security barrier that Israel has erected close to the green line in the West Bank. More often, it is referred to as an "apartheid wall" that "illegally" sneaks into the occupied territory in an effort to implement *de facto* the annexation of Palestinian land.

In his recent book *Goliath*, American journalist Max Blumenthal spoke of how the "ascent of a rightist-dominated Likud faction signalled a collective vote in favour of stripping away whatever remained of the country's democratic patina … all in order to consolidate a system of open apartheid." Alluding to Israel as a semi-totalitarian state, he talked of how the results of the 2010 elections (68 of whose 120 MKs were described as being "members of extreme right-wing parties") showed a population that had been "heavily indoctrinated" and with "little patience left for the complications of democracy."[75]

Others make the claim that if Israel is not yet an apartheid state, it very soon will be. Here is a short passage from John Mearsheimer: "Israel is not going to allow the Palestinians to have a real state of their own in Gaza and the West Bank…. Instead, those territories will be formally incorporated into a Greater Israel, which will be a full-blown Apartheid state bearing a marked resemblance to white-ruled South Africa."[76] This view is predicated on the assumption that Israel will apply her law across the West Bank and then deny Palestinians the vote, a position that is not advocated by any mainstream political party in Israel.

These are the central diatribes about Israel that emanate from today's radical left but which are starting to filter through to more mainstream thinking.

Why Israel Is Not a Genocidal State

The starting point for assessing whether Israel is a genocidal state is the 1948 UN Convention on the prevention and punishment of genocide.[77] According to article 2, genocide is defined as a series of acts that are committed with the "intent to destroy, in whole or in part, a national, ethnical, racial or religious group." These acts include "killing members of the group," "causing serious bodily or mental harm to members of the group," "deliberately inflicting on the group conditions of life calculated to bring about its physical destruction in whole or in part," "imposing measures intended to prevent births within the group" and "forcibly transferring children of the group to another group." It is important to recognize that genocide, according to this definition, involves intention and act. Simply killing members of a particular ethnic or racial group is not per se genocidal; killing those people *because* they belong to that group, and with an intention to destroy that group, most certainly is.[78]

The most infamous examples of genocide have occurred in the twentieth century, most notably the attempt by Nazi Germany, with the help of its collaborationist allies, to implement the Final Solution from 1939 to 1945. The Holocaust was an attempt to eradicate the biological basis of European Jewry and render the Continent "Judenfrei." It was an industrial genocide, carried out with a terrifying level of organization, efficiency and precision and employing the instruments of science for destructive purposes. It followed several years in which the Nazis had vilified, demeaned and delegitimized German Jews, stripping them of all civic rights and excluding them from public life. Jews were openly compared to traitors, parasites and vermin and blamed for Germany's social and economic woes. They were repeatedly threatened with destruction.

A more recent example of systematic genocide occurred in Rwanda. Between April and July 1994, some 800,000 members of the Tutsi minority were slaughtered by militias and civilians from the dominant Hutu tribe. The genocide had been planned by members of the Akazu, a group of Hutu extremists who sought to create a Tutsi-free Rwanda, with many enjoying positions of power and influence at the heart of government. The killing spree of Tutsis, and moderate Hutus, was endorsed enthusiastically by the government, the military and the media. Hate speech against the Tutsi population became the norm, with the Hutu radio station, HTLM, likening Tutsis to cockroaches and broadcasting malicious rumors about them. This was regarded as a key factor in persuading ordinary civilians to take part in the genocide. Nor was this a spontaneous outpouring of hatred by one faction against another. The plan for a genocide of Tutsis had been openly discussed in cabinet meetings for several years before the killings started. Just as Germany sought to inculcate Nazi values among German youth, ensuring their loyalty to the regime at the expense of their families, so too the Rwandan government manipulated family ties to create killing squads (the Interahamwe) to enable a more efficient form of mass killing. The elements of government planning, demonization, systematic preparation and eventual slaughter make this a typical modern genocide.

Applied to the conflict between Israel and the Palestinians, it is immediately apparent that the charge of genocide is at the same time obscene and absurd. The Nazi Judeocide destroyed two-thirds of European Jewry, reducing a prewar population of 9 million people to some 3 million. In Poland, Germany, Austria, Czechoslovakia, Lithuania and a number of other countries, only a small remnant of the country's Jews survived the extermination process. By contrast, the Palestinian population has significantly increased since 1948. According to the Palestinian Central Bureau of Statistics, the Palestinian population in the West Bank stood at 690,000 in 1967. In 2010, the figure was 2.52 million, an increase of 265 percent. In 1970 there were an estimated 340,000 Palestinians in Gaza but by 2010, this figure had risen to 1.6 million. There are reasons to doubt the modern figures, but even if they are exaggerated, they give a clear enough picture of overall population increase in both areas. So in terms of simple demography, the comparison with either of the genocides discussed is absurd. Populations subjected to a sustained policy of mass extermination do not increase in number during their experience of genocide. The Palestinian experience has not involved the slaughter of a nation.

Now look at the simple numbers of those killed in this supposed Israeli genocide. According to historian Ahron Bregman, from 1967 to 2006, some 6,187 Palestinians were killed by Israel during a number of high-intensity conflicts.[79] Moreover, that figure would have to come down enormously if one calculated the number of Palestinians civilians killed, rather than combatant deaths. If the number of civilian deaths was a more realistic 5,000 over a 40-year period, this would represent some 34 Palestinians killed for every 100 days of the conflict. By contrast, some 800,000 Tutsis were killed in the 100 days of the Rwandan genocide, while nearly 3,000 Jews on average were being massacred by the Nazis for every day of the Second World War. It is not that one should discount these 5,000 deaths, for every civilian who dies represents a human tragedy. But the figures must be put into perspective. Given that Israel's supposed genocide has taken place over nearly half a century, it can only be counted as a most spectacular failure.

In any case, Israel has its own Palestinian population, namely some 1.6 million Arab citizens. How can it be that Israel has a political blue print for the eradication of Palestinian Arabs while turning other Arabs who are ethnically indistinguishable into its own citizens? Why the discrepancy in treatment? Those who draw the insidious analogy between Israel and Nazi Germany would have to imagine a situation where Nazi Germany had Jewish judges on its supreme court, where Jews and non–Jews voted on equal terms, where both groups mingled freely on buses, restaurants and universities, where German NGOs defended Jewish rights against the state with legal immunity, where laws against incitement were enforced and where all of the above was set against a backdrop of continuous Jewish terrorism designed to destroy the German state. Citing these simple facts is enough to render the comparison absurd.

But the most fundamental obscenity in this argument is that it ignores the question of intention and motivation. Remember that what is crucial to genocide as defined by the 1948 UN Convention is the intention to eradicate a people or race. A simple glance at the Arab-Israeli conflict shows that while there have been Palestinian civilian casualties at every stage, these have not resulted from premeditation or design. Rather, as we have shown, there have been repeated attempts by Israel to limit noncombatant deaths. Certainly with the vast array of military power at her disposal, Israel could have achieved precisely what these detractors accuse her of doing.

By contrast, had the Arab states succeeded in the wars of 1948 or 1967, the Jewish population of Israel would most certainly have faced destruction, if the rhetoric of Arab leaders is anything to go by. The charters and statements made by Israel's modern enemies, including Hamas, Fatah, Hezbollah and Iran, indicate a similar virulent strain of intense Judaeophobia (see Chapter 4). One can only imagine the horrors that would await Israel's Jews in the event that these groups succeeded in defeating Israel. Then we would see something far more akin to massacres and ethnic cleansing.

Given how absurd it is to charge Israel with genocide, some resort to a more watered-down allegation. They say that Israel is attempting to destroy the Palestinian economy and lower Palestinian living standards in a form of slow genocide. This is purportedly a policy of mass murder by stealth, of using Israel's vast economic resources to undermine and eventually strangle ordinary Palestinian life until it becomes impossible for people to live.

But this is an equally specious argument. Indeed, if one looks at the West Bank Palestinian Arabs under the period of direct Israeli rule (1967 to 1994), one sees a very different picture. From 1967, Israel invested considerable resources to improve the infrastructure of the West Bank, spending hundreds of millions of dollars to improve roads, the sewer system, and electrical and water facilities. This meant that by 1986, over 90 percent of the population in the West Bank and Gaza had electricity around the clock, as compared to one in five in

1967; 85 percent had running water in dwellings, as compared to 16 percent in 1967; and 83.5 percent had electric or gas ranges for cooking, as compared to 4 percent in 1967. During the 1970s, the West Bank economy was the fourth fastest growing in the world, ahead of Singapore, Korea and Hong Kong. This was largely due to the close links between the Palestinian and Israeli economies.

Israeli rule provided a range of economic and social benefits. The number of Palestinians working in Israel rose from "zero in 1967 to 66,000 in 1975 and 109,000 by 1986, accounting for 35 percent of the employed population of the West Bank and 45 percent in Gaza." Access to the Israeli medical system improved living standards too. From 1968 to 2000, Palestinian infant mortality fell from 60 to 15 per 1,000 live births. Killer diseases such as polio, whooping cough, tetanus and measles were eradicated as Israel opened 100 clinics and offered comprehensive medical insurance.[80] Life expectancy for Palestinians increased from 48 in 1967 to 72 in 2000. Illiteracy rates also nosedived, dropping to 14 percent of adults over the age of 15. Israel opened 8 universities in the territories (6 in the West Bank and 2 in Gaza) and oversaw the expansion of Palestinian newspapers from 1 (1967) to 40 (1994).[81] Needless to say, the Palestinians of the West Bank and Gaza also enjoyed a range of political freedoms that they had previously been denied by Jordan and Egypt respectively.

It is undeniable that as violence has intensified, Palestinians have faced closures, checkpoints, restrictions and arrests. The First Intifada certainly caused a disruption in educational provision, as universities and schools that were thought to be a hotbed of radicalism were closed down for periods of time. Between 1994 and 1996, the government of Rabin and Peres imposed closures and stopped the movement of workers into Israel in an attempt to stem terrorism. This led to a rise in Palestinian unemployment. However, as terrorism fell, there was a decrease in closures under the Netanyahu administration, and unemployment subsequently halved.[82] The point is that Israel's direct rule led, in general, to an improvement rather than a deterioration in the social and economic life of the Arab inhabitants. When there was a stable political environment, Israeli rule benefited its inhabitants, and in times of violence, there was an economic decline. Charges of slow genocide are thus misguided and highly malicious.

When people describe Israel as a genocidal state, they engage in a perverse form of vilification. They suggest that Israel is the ultimate pariah state that can have no place in the civilized community of nations. After all, a state that mandates the deliberate slaughter of innocents is an abomination; it is morally beyond the pale. The insidious genocide comparison is an attempt to even up the score between the Nazis and the Jews by suggesting that the victims have now become the victimizers. Such an obscene view may be designed to assuage European guilt for the Holocaust, but all it does is mock and trivialize the suffering of six million victims of German genocide, and indirectly the victims of every other genocide. It could even be described as a form of Holocaust denial, in that the Palestinians are now deemed to be the victims deserving of sympathy, not the Jews.

Is the Zionist Project for Jewish Self-Determination Inherently Racist?

In essence, Zionism is a movement for Jews to "attain political independence and instigate a national renaissance of the Jewish people."[83] It is the national homeland for the Jewish people, the place in which they exercise national self-determination and express their culture, language and heritage most fully. It is not to be identified with any specific Israeli policy or the words of any Israeli leader. It is not identical to the "occupation" or the settlement movement either.

National self-determination is a fundamental right enshrined in international law. In article 1 of the UN Charter, it is clearly stated that the development of "friendly relations among nations" is based on "respect for the principle of equal rights and self-determination of people." The 1966 International Covenant on Civil and Political Rights also calls on all states to "promote the realization of the right of self-determination" by which people can "freely determine their political status and freely pursue their economic, social and cultural development."[84] The concept is anti-imperialistic in nature and affirms that a group defining themselves as a nation has the right to determine its destiny and control its own social and economic affairs, rather than be ruled over by an alien government. No one would suggest that the movements for Belgian or Croatian or Tibetan self-determination were inherently racist simply because they promoted the interests of those cultural or ethnic groups. The same applies to Zionism, the movement for the national self-determination of the Jewish people in their ancestral land.

Of course, there is one sense in which Zionism differs from many other movements for self-determination: it has been dependent on migration. Unlike most other movements asserting national independence, this one required the "ingathering" of Jews from countries around the world, rather than relying purely on the existing community in Israel. That in itself does not delegitimize the Jewish state. It is purely due to historical circumstances, often tragic ones, that the majority of Jews were dispersed around the world and that the only way for them to activate their claim to self-determination was through emigration. Thus to deny them that right purely because of their dispersal is tantamount to an attack on the very notion of Jewish self-determination, period. It would have been almost impossible for Israel to prosper without large scale Jewish emigration from the Diaspora.

So why is there a furor? For many critics, the idea that a state would grant exclusive rights to people based on their religious or ethnic character smacks of ethnocentrism, a pre-modern notion at odds with a modern belief in equality and universal values. Israel, so it is claimed, gives Jews exclusive rights by being labeled "the Jewish state," even though more than 20 percent of its citizens are non–Jewish. Worse, they say, it gives priority to Jews through the right of return, which allows someone with even one Jewish grandparent to automatically immigrate to the country. No such ease of entry applies to non–Jews, particularly the Palestinian Arabs.

Certainly, Israeli nationality has been defined by reference to one religion: Judaism. The defining cultural characteristics of the state are Jewish (the flag, the national anthem, official holidays, the majority language). Immigration laws (the law of return) also favor one ethnic group as well. The 5 July 1950 Law of Return stated, "Every Jew has the right to immigrate to the country" unless that person was "engaged in an activity directed against the Jewish people" or could "endanger public health" or security.

But at the same time, Israel is a state of all its citizens. Jew, Arab and Christian are equal under the law and fundamental rights do not depend on ethnicity, race or religion. Non-Jews in Israel are not politically or economically disadvantaged just because they live in a state with a Jewish national character. The Declaration of Independence stated that Israel would ensure "complete equality of social and political rights to all its inhabitants irrespective of religion, race or sex." Civil rights are upheld in the country's Basic Laws.

But there is a fundamental inconsistency here. Those who condemn a "Jewish state" as inherently racist have seemingly few reservations about the dozens of countries with similar national characteristics. Countries in Europe such as France, Germany and Romania have long been established on national lines and define themselves by reference to Christian tradition, heritage or symbolism. As Daniel Gordis points out in *The Promise of Israel*, a number of European constitutions "give a unique place to individual religions," among which are the constitutions of Norway and Denmark, which make the Evangelical-Lutheran religion the established or official church of those countries.

In similar fashion, some South American countries have declared that Roman Catholicism is the state's official religion. Israel is therefore not unique in putting religion or ethnicity "at the core of its self definition."[85] The same applies to a number of Middle Eastern nations that are imbued with a staunchly "Arab" or "Islamic" character and heritage. The move to create a Palestinian state, even one devoid of Jewish inhabitants, is apparently morally unproblematic, yet Zionism, the founding philosophy of Jewish nationhood, is inherently illegitimate.

Nor is it the case, as Michael Neumann argues, that the Jewish state is one "in which one race is guaranteed supremacy" or one where Jewish inhabitants force non–Jews to live at the mercy of their Jewish overlords.[86] It does not follow that because a Jewish state had been set up, it will automatically distinguish between its Jewish and non–Jewish citizens. It is a *Jewish and democratic* state, not one that is engaged in a campaign to purify its population to achieve an ethnic majority.

Moreover, Israel is not the only county in the world with a right of return. Dozens of nations, including France, Germany, China and the UK, have enacted similar legislation, offering preferential arrangements to their nationals abroad to return to their "national" home. Thus any person of German ethnic origin can automatically be granted citizenship no matter where they were previously living. As Lord Hailsham once wrote, "All the great nations of the earth have what the Jews call a Diaspora," and such communities are owed "special and residual obligation(s)" by the host nation.[87] Israel has extended that special obligation to Jews, their spouses and the children and grandchildren of Jews, in keeping with the state's constitutional arrangements. While this may be wider than the equivalent rights of return elsewhere, it is not a racist arrangement. Indeed it is no more racist than the idea of a nation-state that constitutionally defines itself as a state for a specified people.

It is equally specious to interpret the Biblical notion of a "chosen people" as evidence of Israel's constitutional racism. Indeed this is to radically misunderstand the concept. Most denominations within Judaism today would regard chosenness as a form of obligation rather than a mark of superiority. According to Jewish tradition, God chose Abraham and his nation so that they could spread the concept of monotheism to the rest of idol-worshipping mankind. Another tradition has it that Jews were chosen to spread the Torah (the first five books of the Old Testament) and its ethical precepts to the world. With these precious gifts, they are enjoined to be "a kingdom of priests and a holy nation" or, in the words of the prophet Isaiah, "a light unto the nations." This implies a strict moral duty to propagate their ethical and theological code to the benefit of all mankind. Thus the idea of a chosen people implies not Jewish superiority but the superiority of Judaistic morality and monotheism. Indeed far from bestowing some special benefit, it is arguably a burden that Jews must carry throughout their lives. Hence this famous verse in the book of Amos: "You alone have I singled out of all the families of the earth. That is why I call you to account for all your iniquities" (Amos 3:2).

Furthermore, the accusation that "chosenhood" connotes a Jewish belief in racial superiority directly contradicts a core belief in Jewish ethics, namely that all people are entitled to justice on an equal and non-arbitrary basis. Dan Cohn-Sherbok comments on this aspect of Judaic law: "On the basis of the biblical view that everyone is created in the image of God, the Torah declares that false and irrelevant distinctions must not be introduced to disqualify human beings from the right to justice."[88] The righteous of all nations are believed to have a share in the world to come. Being chosen imparts no special rights.

It has been argued that "Zionism's claims to exclusive Jewish title to the 'land of Israel' are constantly predicated on the basis of the Bible, particularly of the narratives of the promise of land to Abraham and his descendants."[89] This is certainly true for many orthodox Zionists. They will quote Biblical verses to support Israeli policies, and base their justification for Jewish statehood on divine promises. But none of this is true for the vast majority of secular Zionists. Certainly they may look to the Bible for references to Jewish history and civilization, but their worldview is grounded empirically, in political rights, international law and history. The narrative of Exodus, whether believed or not, is not the primary foundation for Jewish rights in the Holy Land.

Why Israel Is Not a Colonialist State

Colonialism usually involves a dominant power's annexing foreign territories and then settling its own citizens in them as part of a long-term land grab. To take the most familiar example, throughout the nineteenth century, millions of Britons left their mother country and chose to make new lives in various far-flung regions of the Empire. Often they went in search of new economic opportunities, appalled by the poverty they encountered back home and hopeful of a better life abroad. They were often enticed by the raw materials on offer, whether it was gold in the Transvaal or rubber in Nigeria. Sometimes they were looking for positions of governance or administration in underdeveloped regions, anxious to impart the wonders of commerce, civilization and Christianity to "backward" natives. But for all the benefits brought by imperialism, these colonialists represented an Anglo-Saxon intrusion in a foreign land. The colonialists were using force to claim the soil of others.

Taking these factors into account, it is clear that Israel cannot be accused of being an outpost of colonialism. For starters, the Jewish pioneers did not arrive in Palestine at the behest of any foreign power; they fled from other countries in which they had been experiencing relentless persecution, such as Tsarist Russia. They wanted to be free of foreign interference, controlling their own destiny rather than being beholden to any overseas despot. In no way were they the agents of hostile powers. This is especially true of Britain, which has been accused of being the colonial puppet master masterminding Zionist impulses in Palestine. One would be hard pressed to understand why there was so much friction between the mandate power and the Zionist movement, particularly at times of unrest (1920–1, 1929), during 1939 following the White Paper and in the three years after the war. British officials were consistently accused of having Arabist sympathies and undermining rather than helping the Jews of Palestine. It undercuts the colonialist thesis rather badly.

More importantly, the Zionists were returning to a land with which they already had an intimate historical association. As Dershowitz pointed out, the Zionists did not import the names of their home cities in Palestine. Unlike the Puritan settlers in the seventeenth century who lit up the east coast with the new settlement of New York, the Zionists did not create a New Vilnius, New Warsaw or New Petrograd in Palestine. Zionists were not trying to replicate their home nations so much as rebuild the Jewish national home. That was why the preamble to the 1922 League of Nations mandate for Palestine specifically recognized "the historical connection of the Jewish people with Palestine" as well as "the grounds for reconstituting their national home in that country."

This also applies in many cases to the settler movement. Today, less than 1,000 Jews live in Hebron's old quarter, surrounded by a vastly larger Arab population of over 160,000. This town had a thriving Jewish population until 1929, when dozens were massacred in the Arab revolt. The same holds true for other settlers, including those Jewish inhabitants of East Jerusalem regarded as illegal occupiers of Palestinian land. However, there is an emerging consensus in Israel that this historical right does not justify the permanent retention of all settlements. No doubt, some settlements in the West Bank will be abandoned in the event of a peace accord with the Palestinians, just as they were in Gaza and Sinai. Quite simply, the price to be paid for living under Palestinian rule will be too high.

While the territories acquired in European colonial conquests were enticing because of their raw materials, Palestine held out no such prospects. There were no gold mines, diamond mines or palm oil. It was a land infested with swamps and malaria, and the Jewish arrivals had to carry out back-breaking work in order to reclaim it. Economic gain was not the main driver of the Zionist enterprise, either then or now. In addition, they did not seize the land by illegal conquest. It was acquired through legal purchase, often at inflated prices from absentee landlords. One cannot say the same about British India or the Belgian Congo.

Similarly, the boundaries of the Jewish state were established not by some pre-modern right of conquest but by the dictates of international law. Both the League of Nations and the United Nations confirmed these boundaries, though final and definitive ones remain to be negotiated as part of a peace settlement. Additionally, Israel's expansion from the UN's proposed boundaries in 1947 came about only because the state was attacked both by Arabs within Israel and, later, by surrounding Arab states. In other words, Israel enlarged her frontiers in a war of self-defense, not a war of territorial conquest.

This explains why Israel has returned land captured in previous wars. Thus in 1957, Israel returned the Sinai Peninsula to Egypt following the Suez War of 1956. In the Camp David accords, Israel again returned the whole of Sinai to Egyptian control, some 90 percent of the land captured in the 1967 war. In 1994, Israel also returned land to Jordan in the peace treaty signed by both countries. Again in 2000, Israel unilaterally vacated the security zone in Lebanon after sporadic forays into Lebanese territory. Israel withdrew from Gaza in 2005 and, twice since 2000, has offered near total disengagement from the West Bank, only for those offers to be comprehensively rebuffed by the PLO. This is hardly textbook expansionist behavior.

Moreover, during the wars of 1967 and 1982, Israel could have seized control of far more territory than she eventually controlled. If she really had a Sparta or Samson complex, this could have been achieved without any difficulty, given the bewildering level of her military superiority compared to that of her neighbors. But she chose not to because her main war aims were not territorial or expansionist but defensive (to defeat the Egyptian, Syrian and Jordanian threats to her borders and to defeat the PLO).

Why Israel Is Not an Apartheid State

To show how inappropriate it is to label Israel as an apartheid state, we need to remind ourselves what is meant by apartheid. The policy was specifically defined in the 1973 UN Convention on the Suppression and Punishment of the Crime of Apartheid as "inhuman acts committed for the purpose of establishing and maintaining domination by one racial group of persons over any other racial group of persons and systematically oppressing them." Among the acts that constitute the crime of apartheid are "murder, torture, inhuman treatment and arbitrary arrest of members of a racial group; deliberate imposition on a racial group of living conditions calculated to cause its physical destruction; legislative measures that discriminate in the political, social, economic and cultural fields; measures that divide the population along racial lines by the creation of separate residential areas for racial groups; the prohibition of interracial marriages; and the persecution of persons opposed to apartheid."[90] An updated definition was given in the Rome Statute of the International Criminal Court where apartheid was defined as "inhumane acts committed in the context of an institutionalized regime of systematic oppression and domination by one racial group over any other racial group committed with the intention of maintaining that regime."

Even though both definitions were designed to have general application, they were modeled on the apartheid policies of the South African state between 1948 and 1994. Apartheid refers to the policy of racial discrimination and segregation enforced on the black majority of South Africa by white minority rule over a 46-year period. Under the system of extensive racial classification put in place, black people were denied voting rights and political citizenship. Black people could not marry white people under the Prohibition of Mixed Marriages Act 1949 and the Immorality Act 1950. The Reservation of Separate Amenities Act of 1953 institutionalized racial segregation by reserving municipal areas for certain races. Beaches, buses, hospitals and schools were among some of the premises and services separated on racial lines and signs in public areas indicated that they were for "whites only." As defined by the 1965 International Convention on the Elimination of All Forms of Racial Discrimination, apartheid involved "governmental policies based on racial superiority or hatred." It resulted from a form of *constitutional* as opposed to *institutional* racism.

There is a stark contrast when you examine the lives of Israeli Arabs. They enjoy an array of political and economic rights similar to those in comparable democracies. They are citizens of the state, able to choose their political representatives on an equal basis to the country's Jewish citizens. These rights are guaranteed under the Basic Laws. As a result, a number of Arab political parties are represented in the Knesset, among them the United Arab list and the left wing Jewish-Arab party, Hadash. Their representatives can (and do) freely criticize the policies of Israeli governments.

Israel has had an acting Arab president,[91] while Israeli Arabs have been represented in the Cabinet, the civil service and in the Supreme Court. One judge, George Karra, was the presiding judge in the trial of former Israeli president Moshe Katsav in 2010. In recent years, members of the Arab and Druze communities have served as diplomats as well as in the army and police service. No laws in Israel ban sexual relationships between Jews and non-Jews, though such marriages are not performed in Israel for religious, rather than racial, reasons. Jews and Arabs attend schools and universities together, work and receive treatment in the same hospitals, frequent the same restaurants and use buses and public facilities on an equal basis. Arabic is Israel's second official language, and Arabic newspapers and media outlets serve the population. In addition, the "Ya Salam" program, rolled out in 2010, introduced an Arabic language requirement for fifth and sixth graders in 170 schools in northern Israel. It allows Jewish schoolchildren to learn Arabic language and culture from Arab teachers, itself a valuable way to close the gaps between the two communities.

The key point is that the upholding of individual and community rights for Israeli minorities derives from actions of the state. The country's Basic Laws guarantee equality to all regardless of their religion, race, sex or ethnicity. In 1978 the Supreme Court stated that the prohibition of discrimination on the grounds of race, religion, nationality or beliefs was a key constitutional principle. It is a crime under Israeli law for any public body to discriminate on the basis of either race or religion.[92] In 2000, another law outlawed discrimination in the registration of students by government and local authorities or educational institutions. Incitement too is a criminal offence in Israel. Quite obviously, there was no such comparable set of laws in apartheid South Africa to protect the black majority.

Some have accused Israel of apartheid because "only Jews serve in the Israeli army" and only they are entitled to receive military benefits. This is incorrect. Israeli Arabs can and do serve in the Israeli army, often with distinction. The point is that they are not *forced* to do this, as they are not subject, for security reasons, to compulsory military service. Those Israeli Arabs that do serve in the army voluntarily receive the same military benefits as their Israeli Jewish counterparts. In addition, there has been a huge increase in the number of Arab citizens undertaking civilian national service as an alternative to military enlistment.[93]

As a result, Israel's Arabs have a generally favorable impression of the country. According to the 2012 Index of Jewish-Arab Relations, 60 percent regard Israel as their homeland and 71 percent describe it as a good place to live. Another report indicates that nine tenths of Israeli Arabs believe that their future lies in the Jewish state. It is hard to imagine these figures being replicated in apartheid South Africa.[94]

While the apartheid label does not apply to Israel's Arab population, some believe it accurately describes Israel's treatment of Palestinians. It is pointed out, for example, that Palestinians cannot vote in Israel despite the IDF's presence in the West Bank. They face restrictions and inconvenience, such as roadblocks and checkpoints, when they want to enter Israel or move around the West Bank. They also cannot access certain roads in the territory, as these are allegedly Jewish only roads. Finally, Israel's security barrier is often referred to as an apartheid wall that sneaks into Palestinian land and undermines their economy.

An important question should be asked at this stage. If Israel within the pre-1967 lines does not resemble an apartheid state and is characterized by being a constitutionally liberal, democratic, tolerant and open society, why would such a state choose to contradict these values in 22 percent of the land it controlled? It really makes no sense for a genuinely racist state to be so selective in its application of racism. Clearly it is the different and special circumstances pertaining to the West Bank that help to explain the differential treatment of Arabs on either side of the 1967 lines.

For starters, Palestinians are not citizens of Israel, and this fact, rather than a racial bar, explains why they do not vote in Israel. The Palestinian Authority has responsibility for the civic and economic life of the West Bank's Arab population and it organizes elections for its population, just as Gaza's political affairs are controlled by Hamas.

The military restrictions, regrettable as they are for innocent Palestinians, exist for one sole purpose: the protection of Israeli civilians. They have been put in place because many hundreds of Israelis were murdered in a sustained wave of suicide bombings since the start of the Second Intifada. The security measures have dramatically reduced the number of successful terrorist outrages, though it has not stopped the glorification of terror by the Palestinian leadership. Moreover, Israeli Arabs can also access the "Israel only roads" in the West Bank; they are not designed to be used by Jews alone.

It is particularly egregious to describe the separation fence as a symbol of apartheid. A barrier that ensures that terrorist threats can be contained more easily is not an institutionalized form of racial discrimination. If so, then India would have to be an apartheid state because its leaders have built a 460-mile fence in the contested region of Kashmir for security purposes. So too Saudi Arabia, which has built fences against both Yemen and Iraq to prevent terrorist attacks from these countries. From 1980 to 1987 Morocco built a 2,700-kilometer barrier in Western Sahara to prevent attacks by the Front Polisario. China has built a barrier against Hong Kong, Pakistan against Afghanistan, Greece against Turkey and the United States against Mexico, to name just a few examples. Yet Israel's separation barrier is somehow *sui generis*, a unique example of discrimination.

Finally, it should be noted that Palestinians living in the West Bank (and other territories) have long been afforded the opportunity to petition Israel's Supreme Court.[95] There have been many hundreds of such petitions and, according to Yoram Dinstein, a study of cases over a ten-year period (1986–95), including out-of-court settlements, reveals that "the majority of Palestinian petitioners actually obtained at least partial redress by filing a petition." The mere threat to petition, Dinstein adds, exerts a "chilling effect on the military government."[96]

As stated in the introduction, it is true that the Arab community still faces some discrimination and inequality in Israel. Arabs are underrepresented in the Israeli university system, both as students and as academics, and are disproportionately represented among the poorer and unemployed classes of Israeli society. Arab villages in the country have received less funding than their Jewish counterparts, and Arab towns face difficulties in regard to infrastructure, housing and access to municipal services. But the state is working to reduce these gaps and improve the prospects for all the country's minorities. Such a Herculean effort would be impossible in a state that was committed to maintaining the exclusive rights of one group.

While discrimination affects Israeli Arabs, it is essentially *de facto* and not *de jure*. As in nearly every country in the world where such discrimination occurs, it is an institutional rather than a constitutional problem and one that ultimately derives from a complex range of factors. One can only hope that in years to come, the progressive reach of government policies and changing social attitudes will lead to a more integrated Arab population. But right now, Israeli Arabs enjoy a range of political benefits not found elsewhere in the Arab world. In essence, the comparison of Israel and South Africa is as intellectually baseless as it is morally offensive. It shows contempt, not only for Israelis, but for the millions of black people who experienced decades of legally sanctioned degradation under apartheid.

3. The Myth of the "All Conquering" Zionist Lobby

In 2002, an article appeared in the *New Statesman* under the heading "A Kosher Conspiracy." Emblazoned on the front cover was a particularly striking but equally chilling image—a Star of David piercing a Union Jack. In the article Denis Sewell wrote: "That there is a Zionist lobby and that it is rich, potent and effective goes largely unquestioned on the left. Big Jewry, like big tobacco, is seen as one of life's givens. According to this view, Israel has the British media pretty well sewn up." He concluded, however, that though such a lobby did exist, the Zionist lobby were "a clueless bunch."[1] After some heated objections, an editorial in the *New Statesman* apologized for the cover, while insisting that the publication would continue to speak out against Israeli policy.

A year earlier, just days after the 9/11 attacks, journalist Richard Ingrams warned that there was a "reluctance throughout the media to contemplate the Israeli factor" that lay behind the attacks. The reason for this silence was due to "pressure from the Israel lobby in this country" which has made "even normally outspoken journalists ... reluctant to refer to such matters."[2] He was backed a year later by John Pilger, who lamented the BBC's failure to show his documentary, *Palestine Is Still the Issue*, saying that the organization "would never have dared to incur the wrath of one of the most influential lobbies in this country." For Pilger, the pro–Israel lobby "intimidates journalists to ensure that most coverage remains biased in its favour."[3]

The notion that "Big Jewry" or "Big Zion" had the media "sewn up" was beginning to become more fashionable among the chattering classes at this time. For years, Soviet propaganda had been obsessing over the existence of a powerful Jewish/Zionist lobby secretly pulling the strings of Western foreign policy and subverting Western interests for Israeli gains. According to this twisted conspiracy theory, Western governments were the hapless victims of the lobby, with gentile politicians unable to contend with the Zionists' financial muscle and influence. The Jewish/Zionist lobby, a veritable Fifth Column, was likened to a dangerous "octopus," a malign influence exercising an omnipotent control of Western foreign policy. Such diabolical imagery, replete with anti–Semitic references, could have come straight from the *Protocols of the Elders of Zion*. In slightly subtler form, the *New Statesman* was echoing this charge for a British audience.

It was inevitable that the Holocaust had to feature in this conspiratorial cacophony. In 2010, Gretta Duisenberg, the widow of the first president of the European Central Bank, decried how "Holland's powerful Jewish lobby [was] playing on the country's sense of guilt over the Holocaust." Her words triggered a storm of protest. After commenting in 2005 that she wanted to collect six million signatures for a pro–Palestinian petition, she said that she hoped "the Jews realize they can't take over the south of Amsterdam the same way they took over the West Bank."[4]

Some British politicians too were seduced. Veteran Labour MP Tom Dalyell warned that Tony Blair was being unduly influenced by a "cabal of Jewish advisers" in forming his Middle East policy towards Iraq, Syria and Iran.[5] Chief among this cabal was Blair's Middle East envoy, Lord Levy. In 2006 Chris Davies, a Liberal Democrat MEP, warned he would "denounce the influence of the Jewish lobby that seems to have far too great a say over the political decision-making process in many countries."[6] In the same year, a veteran pro–Palestinian campaigner, Baroness Jenny Tonge, declared: "The pro–Israeli lobby has got its grips on the Western world, its financial grips. I think they've probably got a grip on our party."[7] Her party leader condemned this remark, together with an earlier assertion that she would consider becoming a suicide bomber if she had been Palestinian.[8]

Shortly before the 2010 election, Labour MP Martin Linton declared that there were "long tentacles of Israel in this country who are funding election campaigns and putting money into the British political system for their own ends."[9] His fellow Labour MP, Gerald Kaufmann, was simultaneously claiming that "right wing Jewish millionaires" owned large parts of the Conservative Party. As recently as 2012, Labour MP Jeremy Corbyn was calling for a "public inquiry" into the influence on government of "pro–Israel lobbying groups."[10] And Corbyn's view was shared by fellow Labour MP and former home secretary Jack Straw. At a panel event in Westminster, he was reported to have claimed that groups like AIPAC had "unlimited" funds that were used to "control and divert American policy in the region."[11]

Such insidious allegations of Israeli/Jewish power don't just emerge from within left-liberal parties. Arabist Conservative MP and former government minister Sir Alan Duncan launched a scathing attack on Israel and the Israel lobby in a speech to the Royal United Services in October 2014. He said that there were rules in the UK that "political funding should not come from another country or from citizens of another country, or be unduly in hock to another country." This rule, he added, "seems to apply to every country except when it comes from Israel." He added in a follow-up interview that everyone knew that "the United States is in hock to a very powerful financial lobby which dominates its politics."[12]

These claims were aired in 2009 by Peter Oborne, a respected mainstream journalist, who argued that "the presence of an Israel lobby as a factor in British public life [had been] systematically ignored in British reporting." In the documentary he produced, he said that the lobby group Conservative Friends of Israel was "beyond doubt the best connected, and probably the best funded, of all Westminster lobbying groups." He added: "Eighty percent of Conservative MPs are members. The leader of the Conservative Party is often expected to appear at their events, while the shadow foreign secretary and his team are subjected to persistent pressure by the CFI." He quoted Michael Mates, a member of the Intelligence and Security Committee and former Northern Ireland minister, who told the documentary that "the pro–Israel lobby in our body politic is the most powerful political lobby. There's nothing to touch them." Mates added: "I think their lobbying is done very discreetly, in very high places, which may be why it is so effective."[13]

As evidence of the purported power of this lobby, Oborne looked at a dinner held by Conservative Friends of Israel some months after the Gaza war. Oborne was "astonished" that David Cameron made no reference to Gaza at the dinner and that he went out of his way to praise Israel for helping to "protect innocent life." The subtext was obvious—the CFI had managed to subvert Cameron's political instincts by offering financial inducements to keep him quiet. In his documentary, Oborne tried to provide "proof" of how this determined lobby foisted itself on the BBC, bombarding it with evidence of anti–Israel bias and forcing it to investigate such esteemed personalities as Jeremy Bowen and Orla Guerin. Oborne was particularly scathing about the purported McCarthyite tactics of the lobby, silencing criticism of Israel by "coordinated campaigns and denunciation." Many people, he declared, "just don't want to speak out about the Israel lobby." Yet like Sewell, Oborne was forced to conclude that the power of the lobby may be less influential than some think. For he declared that, in reference to CFI, "any effort to portray either William Hague or David Cameron merely as a passive instrument of the pro–Israel lobby is wide of the mark."[14] Many would have doubted the latter remark.

A former BBC Middle East correspondent, Tim Llewellyn, has also recently alluded to the idea that the pro–Israel lobby has battered down the defenses of British broadcasting in a relentless effort to pursue Israel's cause. In a book launch hosted by Middle East Monitor in October 2012, he declared that the "higher level of pro–Israel Zionists" were "scattered at strategic points throughout the British establishment, throughout British business and among the people whose voices are respected." He described Zionist propaganda as, at times, "extremely intense," "bitter," "angry" and "violent" and said that it is something that "the suits at the BBC find very hard to resist." The result is that the BBC and ITV have engaged in "a kind of self-censorship."[15]

Perhaps no single article on the Israel lobby has had such influence as that by two American academics, Stephen Walt and John Mearsheimer. Mearsheimer and Walt speak of "the unmatched power of the Israel Lobby." The lobby, which is described as the second most powerful in Washington, is incredibly effective in Congress, where Israel "is virtually immune from criticism." This is described as "remarkable" as "Congress rarely shies away from contentious issues," but "where Israel is concerned, however, potential critics fall silent." The leading organization within the lobby, AIPAC, is said to have a "stranglehold" on Congress and is described as a "de facto agent for a foreign government." But that is not all. According to Mearsheimer and Walt, because Jewish voters have influence on presidential elections, the lobby "also has significant leverage over the executive branch."[16] Such is the power of the Jewish lobby, particularly as represented by neo-conservative friends of Israel, that they were able to persuade America to attack Iraq in 2003 because the threat from Iraq was purportedly a threat mainly to Israel.

The authors argue that were it not for groups like AIPAC, America would be holding Israel more at arm's length and that its stance might be more even-handed in the region. As it is, the authors decry the lobby's ability to sway U.S. foreign interests in such a strongly pro–Israel position. They picture the lobby as a political parasite, eating away at the goodwill that might otherwise emanate from the Arab and Muslim world, as well as from domestic Muslim constituencies.

They also argue that supporting Israel does not serve U.S. interests because the Jewish state is not a loyal ally, as "Israeli officials frequently ignore US requests and renege on promises" as well as offering "sensitive military technology to potential rivals like China." "Thanks to the Lobby," they argue, "the United States has become the de facto enabler of Israeli expansion in the Occupied Territories, making it complicit in the crimes perpetrated against the Palestinians. This situation undercuts Washington's efforts to promote democracy abroad and makes it look hypocritical when it presses other states to respect human rights." The authors decry the extent and nature of U.S. aid to Israel, some $3 billion a year. Israel, say the authors, "is the only recipient that does not have to account for how the aid is spent," which means that the money can be "used for purposes the US opposes, such as building settlements on the West Bank."[17] At least one former presidential candidate, Pat Buchanan, has described Capitol Hill as "Israeli occupied territory."[18]

Is the Pro-Israel Lobby All-Powerful?

When assessing claims about the pro–Israel lobby, one must separate three different propositions. The first is that there exist well-financed and influential lobbies, both in the United States and the UK, that actively support and promote Israel and Israeli policy. The second is that these lobbies manage to stifle criticism of Israel and ensure that Israel's interests predominate in American and British foreign policy-making. In other words, the Israel lobbies somehow steamroller opposition to the Jewish state and force the "puppet" governments in London and Washington to do their bidding. These governments are thus pictured as the hapless victims of a conspiracy whose tentacles stretch outwards from Jerusalem. The third proposition is that when these lobbies are successful, it is automatically to the detriment of the governments concerned. The assumption is that adopting a pro–Israeli position is automatically harmful to national interests and that alliances in the Arab and Islamic world would serve those interests better. The first claim is largely true, the second extremely questionable and the third, to be fully discussed in Chapter 7, unquestionably false.

THE LOBBY

First, it is true that there are British and American pro–Israel lobbies that possess significant political and economic clout. Chief among them is the America Israel Public Affairs Committee (AIPAC). AIPAC, which has a $60+ million budget raised from private donations, has been described by the *New York Times* as "the most important organization affecting America's relationship with Israel." It is true that AIPAC is a well-organized, grassroots advocacy organization that enjoys a great deal of support from across the political spectrum. American presidents, both Republican and Democrat, address AIPAC conferences each year, as do a variety of other senior American politicians. AIPAC's position is to support a compromise two-state solution between Israelis and Palestinians and to urge the resumption of peace talks between the sides. AIPAC also supports the suspension of aid to the PA (for as long as it violates commitments to negotiation) and sanctions against Hezbollah and Iran.

Some allege that groups such as AIPAC use their considerable financial muscle to extract pro–Israeli positions from U.S. politicians. There is no doubt that support for Israel is particularly widespread in America, both in Congress and among the wider public. At a congressional level, support is expressed in a number of ways, most particularly in the annual financial aid given to the Jewish state. Over the last 35 years, Israel has received some $3 billion a year in grants, though some three-quarters of that aid must be spent on American defense equipment and training.[19]

Support is also expressed through enacting pieces of legislation that support Israeli policy positions. It was Congress that passed the Jackson-Vanik Amendment in 1974, making U.S.–Soviet trade relations dependent on Soviet goodwill towards that country's beleaguered Jewish community, and other potential emigrants. Within the last five years, Congress has passed bills demanding the release of Gilad Schalit, a bill urging the EU to recognize Hezbollah as a terrorist organization, a bill to rescind the Goldstone report and several bills that recognize Israel's right to self-defense in the face of a terrorist threat. One of the most famous examples of congressional support came in 1995 when both houses of Congress passed the Jerusalem Embassy Act. This provided for the United States to move its embassy to Jerusalem no later than 1999. However, successive governments have resisted any such move, seeing the vote as an encroachment on executive powers.

Saying all this is relatively uncontroversial. American politics plays host to a vast number of lobbying groups all jostling for influence on the public stage and all hoping to be persuasive at the highest levels of government. One of the most well-known and most powerful in Washington is the gun lobby, represented by the National Rifle Association, while the oil lobby is represented by industry giants such as Exxon Mobil. The hugely deserved victories of the African American civil rights movement might well have been delayed without the influential role of the NAACP.

The Saudi lobby, in all its guises (former American ambassadors to Arab countries, other career diplomats, Saudi ambassadors, and influential academics) clearly plays an important role in the political debate.

Westminster too plays host to a large number of special interest groups, NGOs and lobbies. The interests represented include business (CBI), the environment (Greenpeace), human rights (Amnesty and Liberty) and animal rights (RSCPA). None of these lobbies "controls" government policy on the respective areas of policy to which these groups are devoted. Influence is one thing; control is another.

In Britain, a number of organizations promote and extol the Anglo-Israel relationship, among them the Zionist Federation, BICOM and Conservative Friends of Israel (CFI). Some 80 percent of Conservative MPs are believed to be members of CFI, though the vast majority of these MPs are not Jewish. The historian Robert Rhodes James described CFI as "the largest organization in Western Europe dedicated to the cause of the people of Israel."[20] CFI says that it "campaigns hard for Tory candidates in target seats, and works to ensure that Israel's case is fairly represented in Parliament." Its twin aims are "supporting Israel and promoting Conservatism."[21] The Labour and Liberal Democrat parties also have friends of Israel groups that claim a certain number of MPs, including members of the shadow cabinet. However, the second notion, namely that the Israel lobby exercises a bewitching, almost quasi-omnipotent, level of influence in Washington or London, is far-fetched in the extreme.

Omnipotent Lobby?

Taking the United States as a starting point, the Walt/Mearsheimer thesis is particularly flawed. It ignores all those times when American governments have failed to kowtow to America's Israel lobby or to the pro–Israel views held by the majority of American citizens. As Professor Organski observes in his book *The $36 Billion Bargain,* successive U.S. administrations provided negligible economic and military support for Israel from 1948 to 1970. When Israel was established in 1948, U.S. arms to Israel had been embargoed. This was because some of the leading figures in the Truman administration, such as Secretary of State George Marshall and Secretary of Defense James Forrestal, believed that presidential support for the new state would cripple America's economic relations with the Arab world. There was no bilateral or multilateral formal alliance for the same reason. The United States could not be persuaded to pressure Arab states to drop the economic boycott of Israel, nor could any Israel lobby prevent Washington from condemning Israel's retaliatory raids across the armistice lines.

In the 1950s, Eisenhower and his secretary of state, John Foster Dulles, consistently adopted a hardline Arabist approach to Israel. The United States had offered to sell arms to the Egyptian Free Officers regime in 1952, though this foundered on the method of payment offered to Washington. Israeli orders for spare parts were also stopped as part of a bid to shore up support in the Arab world. Later Eisenhower denounced Israel's capture of the Sinai Peninsula during the Suez crisis and threatened to cut all economic aid and impose economic sanctions unless the country withdrew. Had this threat involved a Security Council resolution, Israel would have been unable to trade with other countries.[22] His administration's hostility only began to dissipate following the 1958 Jordan crisis.

While the United States did provide financial support for Israel from early on, the level of assistance was paltry at first. In 1952 and 1953, American aid for Israel amounted to a total of $137.3 million, and this was reduced to $24 million in 1955, a tiny fraction of that year's foreign aid budget. Far from the United States supplying Israel with its military needs, it was France that became Israel's chief arms supplier in the 1950s. Washington's chief allies in the region during this period were Iraq, Iran and Turkey.

It would take another decade and the administrations of Kennedy and Johnson for there to be a greater level of warmth between Washington and Jerusalem. Under two successive Democrat administrations, military assistance was provided. In 1962 Kennedy sold HAWK anti-aircraft missiles to Israel, overruling the State Department, while under Johnson, Israel received 50 Phantom jets in 1968. Yet it was not until the early 1970s under the Republican administration of Richard Nixon that Israel became the largest recipient of U.S. aid and military supplies.[23] In 1970–74, Nixon came to see unequivocal support for Israel as axiomatic, despite also reaching out to moderate Arab regimes. This was manifested particularly in the arms lift during the Yom Kippur War. Thus whereas from 1946 to 1971, the United States provided Israel with $1.5 billion as part of a foreign assistance program, that figure increased to $100 billion over the next 30 years.[24]

Why for the first 10 years of Israel's existence were two American administrations either so lukewarm or hostile to Israel, given the staunch support of U.S. Jews for the new state? Why did it take until 1967 for a real improvement in relations and some 25 years for an American president (Richard Nixon) to provide Israel with the extensive military support she had for so long craved?

The simple answer in both cases is that the support, or lack of it, reflected what the foreign policy elites perceived to be in the national interest. For most of the 1950s, the Eisenhower administration viewed Israel as a strategic liability and sought to build relations with Arab states in order to deter Soviet influence in the region. As Safran explains, "Bringing the Middle East into the Western defence system required, among other things, courting the Arab countries and drawing them into the Western camp."[25] The strategic importance of oil, a commodity in which Israel was naturally lacking, was also being recognized at this stage.

Under Kennedy, relations improved somewhat, and in his drive for a regional balance of power that pleased all sides, room was made for Israel in America's strategic worldview. When the Yemen war started, Israel was viewed as a counterweight to Nasser's overweening influence and hegemonic ambitions, and it made sense to increase arms sales and aid. Israel's victory in 1967, preventing a victorious Nasser from sweeping away pro–American Arab regimes and denting Soviet confidence, impressed the U.S. administration, as American and Israeli interests now appeared more closely intertwined. The Phantom jets sold by Johnson countered the Soviet decision to rebuild the Egyptian and Syrian arsenals.[26]

In 1970 the Jordanian Civil War occurred, with Syrian troops supporting the PLO. Viewed as another example of Soviet-inspired meddling, this situation was viewed with apprehension in Washington. Quite simply, the overthrow of King Hussein's regime would put in jeopardy other oil-rich and nominally pro–Western nations and make a regional conflagration more likely. Israel's role as a buffer in that crisis was further evidence of the country's strategic importance in the region.[27] Nixon's decision to airlift weapons to Israel in the 1973 war was a matter of following the national interest. In the view of Nixon and Kissinger, it was better to have a U.S. ally defeating Soviet-supported radical states, thus dealing a severe blow to the USSR's regional ambitions. Moreover, it was clear that no Arab state would be able to contribute effectively to the defense of American interests in the Middle East.[28] More importantly, by supporting Israeli retention of the assets of 1967, pending a peace negotiation, America was making itself the indispensable guarantor for Arab states that wanted to regain their territory, Egypt especially. For without U.S. pressure on Israel, there would be no change. American national interests were key here.

Relations between Israel and the Reagan administration were in many ways very strong in the 1980s. Yet even here, the Israel lobby was powerless to influence Washington on every occasion. For one thing, the lobby was unable to contain the vast multi-billion-dollar arms trade between Washington and the Saudis. In particular, it argued without success against the sale of AWACS radar planes to the desert kingdom in 1981, much to Begin's personal chagrin. But as Reagan pointed out rather provocatively: "American security interests must remain our internal responsibility. It is not the business of other nations to make American foreign policy."[29]

Reagan imposed a temporary embargo on aircraft shipments to Israel after the 1981 bombing of the Osiraq reactor. Reagan provoked further Israeli outrage when he attended a commemoration at a German cemetery at Bitburg in 1985. It was intended as a gesture of reconciliation with the West German government, but it transpired that former SS officers were buried there. Despite lobbying from Jewish groups, the president decided that national interests dictated he should attend. The Arabist administration of George H. W. Bush threatened to withhold $10 billion in loan guarantees to Israel unless the Shamir government attended a peace conference in Madrid. This was despite the government of Yitzhak Shamir acceding to an American request not to retaliate after Iraq's scud missile attacks in 1991.

Conspiracy theories about the overreaching nature of Zionist power reached their apotheosis under the presidency of George W. Bush. Mearsheimer and Walt blame the Iraq War on an unaccountable cabal of neo-con advisors who were busy promoting Israeli and not American interests. But the idea that the decision to invade Iraq was carried out purely because of pressure from the Israel lobby smacks of the worst kind of conspiracy thinking. What it suggests is that the Bush's administration key decision makers, including President Bush, Dick Cheney, Donald Rumsfeld and Condoleeza Rice (all non–Jews) were somehow pressured into taking their country into war, not because they sensed any compelling national security need, but because they were hoodwinked by emissaries of a foreign power.

Reading through Bob Woodward's excellent account of the run-up to the Iraq war, one senses that the administration, after 9/11, did indeed put an early plan into place for defeating Saddam Hussein. Fundamentally they came to believe that his removal would serve vital American interests. These included ridding the region of an authoritarian dictator, removing the threat (as they saw it) of his weapons of mass destruction and spreading democracy throughout the region. But there is strong evidence that Bush's invasion was carried out in spite of, rather than because of, Israeli opinion in 2003. At the time, the Israeli government saw not Iraq but Iran as the primary threat to regional stability.

A former Bush administration official, Lawrence Wilkerson, who was chief of staff for Colin Powell, remembered the Israeli message to Bush in 2002: "If you are going to destabilize the balance of power, do it against the main enemy." He went on to describe this warning as "pervasive" in Israel's communications with the administration, and said that it was communicated by "a wide range of Israeli sources, including political figures, intelligence and private citizens."[30] The idea that Israel was "behind the Iraq war" understates the independent resolve of the Bush administration and the objections that were emanating from Jerusalem.

In addition, while Bush was well-disposed towards Israel, he was not averse to taking a range of punitive measures against Israeli governments. In the early part of his presidency, America protested the use of U.S.–made helicopters that were being used for targeted killings and imposed an embargo on spare parts. A minor crisis in relations occurred over the proposed sale of arms to China, which led to an embargo on spare parts for U.S.–made helicopters; this was lifted after 9/11. It was also under Bush in 2007 that an infamous National Intelligence Estimate report effectively downplayed the Iranian nuclear threat, much to the chagrin of Israeli leaders. Bush also refused to bomb suspected nuclear sites in Syria, leaving Israel to undertake the operation.

The Obama administration has pressured Israel over settlement activity and called for restraint during Israel's wars in Gaza. They have also defied many Israeli government requests to release Jonathan Pollard, a naval intelligence analyst who passed classified information illegally to Israel. Enormous tension has been created over whether to attack Iran's nuclear installations, with Jerusalem's requests for more forceful action often hitting a brick wall. Such calls have been consistently impeded, under the presidencies of both George W. Bush and President Obama.

Quite simply, if the Mearsheimer and Walt analysis were valid, Israel would have got its way on all these occasions. If the Israel lobby has such awe-inspiring omnipotence, how can one explain the appointment of officials like secretary of state James Baker and national security advisors Brent Scowcroft and Zbigniew Brzezinski?[31] Their agenda has been, at the very least, unsympathetic to Israel and, at worst, downright hostile.

It is often claimed that the pro–Israel lobby forces a reflexive level of U.S. support at the UN, in particular the use of the American veto against anti–Israeli resolutions. Yet it was also not until 1972 that America first vetoed a UN Security Council resolution that was critical of Israel. Furthermore, American support for Israel in the Security Council is far from guaranteed anyway. From 1973 to 2000, America used its veto on 35 percent of occasions, effectively endorsing anti–Israel resolutions through support or abstention nearly two-thirds of the time.[32]

Quite simply, American interests don't start and end with the state of Israel. The country's strategic interests, as discussed in Chapter 7, include the need to secure cheap oil supplies, thus requiring the United States to keep on friendly terms with a number of autocratic regimes, principally the Saudis. They need to station troops in friendly countries, hence the ties to countries such as Bahrain, which hosts the Fifth Fleet. They have a range of economic, military and diplomatic interests that ground their presence across the region and that make them particularly sensitive to the concerns of their Arab allies. Support for Israel, as we shall see, is not carried out at the expense of those interests.

The common view of Uncle Sam as a blind guarantor of Israeli aspirations is highly incorrect. The misconception lies in failing to realize that American foreign policy, like that in Britain, is a tug of war between competing institutions and interests: between the president and elected politicians in Congress, who have an eye on domestic politics, and State Department diplomats with their global perspective. The latter have often had extensive experience in the Arab world, a world "where Israel is not on top of the popularity list."[33] It is hardly surprising if they are generating policy positions that are in accord with some of the deeply held assumptions within that world, namely that concessions must be wrung from Israeli administrations as a precondition for a regional peace.

Some agree that the lobby is a less important aspect of organized Jewish power and that what matters is electoral politics. For example, seasoned observers know that America's Jewish constituency represents a highly valued prize in American politics. It has been said, with good reason, that "the clout that Jewish Americans exercise in American politics is far incommensurate with their population."[34] A simple glance at the relevant statistics provides powerful evidence for this view. American Jews make up from 1.75 to 2.5 percent of the population, according to most opinion polls. Nonetheless, they make up a higher proportion (at least 4 percent) of the electorate. This is partly due to voting habits (they are more likely to vote than non–Jews) and registration (a greater percentage of Jews are registered to vote than non–Jews).

Where American Jews live is also significant from an electoral point of view. Most U.S. Jews live in nine key states (New York, New Jersey, Florida, Massachusetts, Maryland, Connecticut, California, Pennsylvania and Illinois), which cast nearly 40 percent of electoral votes (202 out of 535) in the Electoral College. In some recent elections, most notably in 1992, the Jewish vote has had a demonstrable impact on the outcome. This was largely because far more Jews voted Democrat than the general population, making up one-fourth of Clinton's margin of victory. His appeal to Jewish voters appears to have paid dividends, as did Clinton's appeal to women and ethnic minority voters. In other elections, such as Roosevelt's fourth-term triumph in 1944, the Jewish swing vote was also deemed highly significant. Taken together, these electoral statistics explain the well-targeted campaigns aimed at trying to win over Jewish voters, a feature of every election in U.S. politics for several decades.[35]

But if this electorally based Zionist "lobby" had a veto on American Middle East policy, if it was purely the result of electoral arithmetic, would we not expect to see huge differences between Republican and Democratic administrations on Israel? It is hardly a secret that American Jews have overwhelmingly voted Democrat for the last century. To prove the point, one need only consult the relevant voting figures. In 1968, the Jewish vote went overwhelmingly to Democrat Humphrey (81 percent) rather than Republican Nixon (17 percent), and earlier in 1960, the margin against Nixon had been even bigger (82 to 18 percent). In 1984, the Democratic Walter Mondale won 67 percent of the Jewish vote as compared to 33 percent for Reagan.[36] In 2000, the Jewish vote swung heavily to the Democrats' Al Gore and away from Republican George W. Bush (79 percent to 19 percent), while in the 2008 election, Obama won the Jewish vote by a very significant margin (78 percent to 22 percent). Yet three of the most pro–Israel presidents in history have been Republican (Nixon, Reagan and George W. Bush), while some of those who have been most criticized for their policy positions have been Democrat (Carter, Obama).

While it is true that Carter, Johnson and Clinton felt a religious attachment to Israel, that was equally true of Republicans Reagan and George W. Bush. Moreover, it was only under a Republican president that the strategic alliance between Israel and the United States really took off in the 1970s. For many, Reagan is regarded as the most pro–Israel president of the lot while Obama is seen as innately hostile to Israel. So whether Jews vote Democrat or Republican does not appear to be a critical factor in levels of presidential support for Israel.

If presidents are not thus swayed, is this not true of the Senate? Is senatorial support for Israel predicated on the fear of being ousted by Jewish voters in an election? That this is not so straightforward was revealed in an extensive study carried out by a revered political scientist, Professor Abramo Organski. He firstly calculated the size of American constituencies, ranking them in terms of the relative size of their Jewish population. He then examined the "mean support" for Israel shown by senators in those constituencies, as indicated by how they voted on Israel-related bills over the period 1969 to 1982. In 114 constituencies with less than 1 percent Jews, senators supported Israel on roughly 63 percent of occasions. At a 2–3 percent Jewish population, support rose to nearly 79 percent; at 3–4 percent of Jews, senatorial support for Israel exceeded 90 percent, and it reached 98 percent where Jews formed 5–6 percent of the population. Ostensibly, this would appear to show that senatorial support was closely tied to Jewish demography and possibly fear of losing votes in forthcoming elections.

But as Organski argues, there are plenty of examples where senators voted overwhelmingly to endorse Israeli positions despite having virtually no Jews in their constituency. In the case of Alabama, Jews formed only 0.2 percent of the population during those years, yet Senator John Sparkman voted in a pro–Israeli fashion on 85 percent of occasions. Senator Frank Church voted for Israel on a total of 96.6 percent of occasions, yet only 0.1 percent of his constituency was Jewish. There are many other glaring examples. As Organski concludes: "Such evidence clearly indicates that there is something else going on in the dynamic of support for Israel."[37] Quite simply, there was no guaranteed correlation existing between the likelihood of Jews swinging votes and voting patterns on Israeli matters, at least during the period surveyed.[38]

The same is true when it comes to the issue of money. It is alleged that even if Jews overwhelmingly vote Democrat in national elections, even if in many constituencies their influence is tiny, their money is not. Without doubt, there are many Jewish donors who make substantial financial donations to their chosen political parties and causes. Another study in Organski's invaluable book shows clearly that the level of senatorial support for Israel (between 1970 and 1982) increases immeasurably with the greater levels of financial contribution received from Jewish donors. The higher the contribution, the more likely the senator is to be favorably disposed to Israel in voting terms. But this does not prove that money "buys" votes; far from it. It is equally plausible to argue that the money follows those senators who have already shown themselves to be consistently pro–Israel. In other words, it is the "result, not the cause of what senators do."[39] The simple reason is to ensure that those senators remain in power because they have proven themselves to be consistent supporters of the Israeli cause. This is particularly significant when they have attained positions of influence and power.

Thus it makes sense that Senator Church (mentioned above) received a significant level of financial contributions from Jewish sources. Not only was he a Democrat who adopted a pro–Israeli line, he was the second-ranking Democrat in the Foreign Relations Committee. It was worth paying to ensure that he remained in power. Having said all this, it does not pay to overestimate financial contributions from pro–Israel groups or individual donors. According to Mitchell Bard, the pro–Israel "lobby," in terms of individual, PAC and soft money contributions to national candidates made between 1990 and 2006, rank 41st out of 80 "donor industries," the largest of which are the trade associations, labor unions and doctors.[40]

The demolition job on the purported demonic power of the pro–Israel lobby is even more straightforward when applied to British institutions.[41] Just as American governments fail to kowtow to AIPAC, so too British governments frequently act independently of the wishes of the Conservative and Labour Friends of Israel, BICOM or the Zionist Federation.

To take one prominent example, in 1973, Ted Heath's Conservative government placed an embargo on all the combatant nations during the Yom Kippur War. This gravely affected Israel at the time, as the Arab states were being resupplied by the Soviet Union. Margaret Thatcher was very much a friend of Israel and of Jewish communities around the world. But that did not translate into uncritical acceptance of all Israeli policies. When she met Menachem Begin in 1979, she railed against his policy of settlement construction and found it "unrealistic." She pressed for increasing recognition of the PLO and publicly attacked the 1981 strike against the Osiraq reactor, describing it as a "grave breach of international law."[42] Her belief in Palestinian self-determination did not go down well with leaders such as Begin and Shamir.

Vigorous public criticism of settlements has been echoed by other leaders and ministers, particularly under the relatively friendly administrations of Tony Blair and Gordon Brown. Brown, a member of Labour Friends of Israel, was noted for his romantic attachment to the Jewish state. Yet that did not stop him from visiting Israel and demanding an immediate "settlement freeze" or declaring: "Settlement expansion has made peace harder to achieve."[43]

No British pro–Israel lobby stopped David Cameron from calling Gaza a "prison camp," from demanding a ceasefire during Operation Cast Lead or from his controversial decision to step down as patron of the JNF. No amount of lobbying has altered a strong Arabist leaning in the Foreign and Commonwealth Office, which has, among other things, prevented the queen of England from visiting Israel for over 60 years. For that matter, the Labour Friends of Israel failed to prevent the parliamentary party from passing a resolution to unilaterally recognize "Palestine" in 2014. Indeed LFI specifically supports a negotiated, two-state solution to the conflict, hardly evidence of a right-wing, anti-establishment agenda.

Yes, many prime ministers and their governments have recognized and celebrated the alliance with Israel. But this hardly translates into a blank check for Israeli policies or a blanket refusal to articulate differences over policy.

Peter Oborne's documentary featured an interview with the *Guardian*'s editor, Peter Kellner. During the interview, Kellner complained about the persistence with which pro–Israel lobbies challenged the paper's editorial guideline on the conflict. His views are echoed in comments from current editor, Alan Rusbridger, who has complained of an "unparalleled, utterly disproportionate, cynical and quite ugly" response by pro–Israel supporters to the *Guardian*'s Middle East coverage.[44]

What neither man seems to realize is that there might actually be good reason for such determined lobbying. In recent years, the *Guardian* has become the publication par excellence for disseminating virulent anti–Israeli propaganda. The *Guardian*'s contributors, particularly in "Comment Is Free," rarely hold back when publishing vitriolic assaults on the Jewish state.

In July 2000, the *Guardian* published two extracts from Norman Finkelstein's *Holocaust Industry*, something that led to a stern response from Jonathan Freedland. In November of the same year, the paper published a piece by Jemima Khan in which the campaigner spoke of the U.S. media and Hollywood being "largely controlled by the Jews." She went on: "Driving to pick up my son from school yesterday, I was horrified to see a freshly painted red sign on a wall: 'Kill all Jews. Jihad.'" And a statement has just been issued from a London-based Islamist group that, "All Jews and Americans have now become targets in the Muslim lands as a result of American policy. Abhorrent as this kind of extremism may be, it is a direct result of what Muslims see as gross injustice, due to overwhelming Jewish influence in US politics and the media."[45]

In other words, the murderous and pathological rage of Jew-haters was really being fuelled by irresponsibly powerful American Jews and their "distorted" perception of Israeli policy. Blaming and smearing the victim doesn't come close to describing how callous this statement is. In January 2001, the paper published an article by Muslim journalist Faisal Bodi titled "Israel Simply Has No Right to Exist." In the piece, Bodi made the astonishing and wholly misguided claim that a "biblical promise is Israel's only claim to legitimacy" and that there could be no moral or legal entitlement of the Jews to their state.[46]

The paper has given op-ed space to Ismail Haniyeh, the Hamas prime minister, despite the organization that he heads promulgating a medieval level of anti–Semitism and homophobia. It has also published the cartoons of Carlos Latuff, a Brazilian artist who regularly compares Israel to Nazi Germany.

With articles like this, and far worse, is it any wonder that the paper receives a regular torrent of criticism from its pro–Israel readers? Moreover, the strenuous efforts of the Israel lobby have hardly succeeded in stopping inaccurate and dishonest reporting in the *Independent*, the *Financial Times* or the *New Statesman*. None of these publications' editors feel cowed when they parrot the Arabist line that Israel is the main cause of regional instability and conflict.

Oborne claims to have proof of how this determined lobby foists itself on the BBC, bombarding it with evidence of anti–Israel bias and forcing it to investigate such esteemed personalities as Jeremy Bowen and Orla Guerin. But the implicit charge that this pressure is unwarranted is undermined by the fact that Oborne fails to investigate the bias in the first place. In other words, his guiding assumption is that the BBC is, as it claims to be, completely neutral and impartial.

The documentary failed to mention the anti–Israeli and pro–Palestinian viewpoint that is found all too often in BBC reports, despite lobbying by supporters of Israel. During Israel's wars in 2002, 2006 and 2009 against the Palestinian terror machine, the BBC beamed images from the conflict zone that gave the clear impression that Israel had used excessive force to achieve its objectives. These images invariably showed the results of an Israeli action, featuring an array of dead bodies, flattened houses or apartment blocks, scorched cars and bloodied victims (including women and children) receiving urgent medical help. The implication was that Israel had been engaged in a wanton display of destructive behavior, targeting innocent civilians in a reckless killing spree. No context was offered about what precipitated the Israeli measures.

Another clear example of Arabist bias included the listing of East Jerusalem as the capital of Palestine on a Web page dedicated to Olympic athletes in 2012. No capital was given for Israel. After Israeli objections, West Jerusalem was described as the Israeli "seat of government" with the stipulation that "most foreign embassies are located in Tel Aviv."[47] In 2004 the BBC's Jerusalem correspondent, Barbara Plett, broadcast that she "started to cry" when a dying Arafat left his Ramallah compound for hospital treatment. The BBC upheld complaints that her comments were a breach of impartiality. The BBC has also been accused of downplaying the anti–Semitism of Hamas and offering an unbalanced analysis of Israeli policy in the West Bank. The BBC has fought against public demands to reveal the contents of the 2004 Balen Report, which is "said to contain scathing criticism of the BBC" and its coverage of the Arab-Israeli conflict.[48]

In the absence of the Balen Report, the best people to ask about issues of bias and impartiality within the BBC are those that used to work within the organization. Andrew Marr has said: "The BBC is not impartial or neutral. It's a publicly funded, urban organization with an abnormally large number of young people, ethnic minorities and gay people."[49]

Peter Sissons is one of the most celebrated BBC journalists of his generation. He has written of how "the most popular and widely read newspapers at the BBC are *The Guardian* and *The Independent*." He continues: "Producers refer to them routinely for the line to take on running stories, and for inspiration on which items to cover. In the later stages of my career, I lost count of the number of times I asked a producer for a brief on a story, only to be handed a copy of the *Guardian* and told 'it's all in there.'"[50]

Michael Buerk, another former BBC superstar, has twisted in the knife even further with some trenchant analysis in *Standpoint*: "What the BBC regards as normal and abnormal," he said, "what is moderate or extreme, where the centre of gravity of an issue lies, are conditioned by the common set of assumptions held by the people who work for it."[51] When America is depicted as an avaricious imperialist nation responsible for the world's ills, when Israel is viewed as a regional hegemon that mercilessly attacks innocent Palestinians, when Conservative values are described as "right wing" or "extreme," these are sentiments that come straight from *Comment Is Free*.

Another institution much maligned for its pervasive anti–Israel bias, the Foreign and Commonwealth Office, has also managed to avoid being manipulated by the "sinister cabal" of zealous Zionist lobbyists. The FCO has long been accused, and not unfairly, of adopting an Arabist stance at Israel's expense. During the early 1950s, a major bone of contention was the refusal of successive British governments, acting under FO advice, to sell major arms to Israel. While the official reason given was that it was necessary to avoid inflaming regional tensions, Britain's Arab countries continued to receive significant supplies.

In 1956 the Foreign Office rejected an Israeli request to join the Commonwealth, as such a move would have met with deep Arab suspicion. Contrary to the views of Israeli governments and lobbyists, the FCO favored Israel's withdrawal to the pre–1967 lines even as the state's Arab neighbors refused to recognize her existence. In part, this was designed to separate Arab countries, such as Egypt, from their Soviet ally, though dependence on Arab oil was no doubt an important consideration too. In the 1980s, there would be growing tension between the FCO and successive Israeli governments as a result of the Lebanon War, the growth of settlements and the refusal to withdraw from the West Bank. This would continue in succeeding decades, particularly when Likud governments were in power, the center left Labour being more amendable to Foreign Office thinking.

Put very simply the Foreign Office, for most of the last 65 years, has consistently prioritized the interests of Arab countries over Israeli ones. Many explanations have been put forward for this imbalance, ranging from a fondness for Arab nationalism to visceral anti–Semitism to a longstanding dislike of Zionism dating back to the mandate era. But the simplest explanation is that the FCO has come to believe that British commercial and political interests in the Middle East are better upheld by being more closely aligned with, and sensitive to, the interests of the Arab world than the Jewish state. Among those interests are, hardly surprisingly, the flow of oil and the growing arms trade with Arab countries. As Israel's policies towards the Palestinians and her neighbors have met with deep resistance and hostility from her Arab neighbors, this has shaped the Foreign Office's attitudes towards Israel. This no doubt also explains why Queen Elizabeth has never visited Israel despite accepting the hospitality of many undemocratic regimes. The Palace has been careful to emphasize that the two visits to Israel by members of the Royal Family were made in a private and not official capacity.

All of this flies in the face of the argument that the pro–Israel lobby has some demonic power to manipulate those with responsibility for shaping British foreign policy. Western governments kowtow to their own agendas, and they are not unquestionably Israeli ones.

4. Nailing the Grand Lie: Why Israel Is Not the Cause of Radical Islam's War Against the West

In 2001 at a party hosted by Conrad Black, Daniel Bernard, a senior French diplomat in the foreign ministry, was reported to have said: "All the current troubles in the world are because of that shitty little country Israel. Why should we be in danger of World War Three because of these people?"[1] His words were highly revealing. He believed that Israel had become such a liability and regional menace that it was likely to cause an imminent conflict with global repercussions.[2] Bernard's comments have since resonated with a left-of-center commentariat for whom Western self-loathing seems to come quite naturally. These commentators have persuaded themselves that Israel's alleged misdeeds are at the heart of the Islamic rage against the West and that Zionist "excesses" must be curbed to diminish the threat from international terrorism.

Polly Toynbee is typical. She has written of Israel as a progenitor of worldwide terrorism. Palestine, she has declared, is "the rallying cry for the terrorism that hurled itself at the World Trade Center." She went on: "Once secure as the West's best friend, overnight Israel's failure to make peace has turned into a lethal liability."[3] She has been joined in her view by Caroline Lucas, leader of Britain's Green Party, who commented about how grievances over Palestine were at the heart of the Mumbai attacks in 2008. She said: "I think that the situation in Palestine for example, with the ongoing Israeli occupation with the absolute strangulation of Gaza with this siege on Gaza—essentially this economic blockade—is really feeding so much anger right across the world and it means that there is more of a fertile breeding ground then for extremists to flourish."[4]

Elsewhere Robert Fisk has directly linked British foreign policy with Islamist terror: "The only way to protect ourselves from the real violence which may—and probably will— be visited upon us, is to deal, morally, with courage and with justice, with the tragedy of Lebanon and 'Palestine' and Iraq and Afghanistan. And this we will not do."[5] Such sentiments find ready acceptance among the great and the good at the BBC. Thus John Simpson, their world affairs editor, has argued that the only method for "defeating political violence" was "reducing the causes of discontent," implying a change in Western foreign policy.[6]

During a speech in the House of Lords during the Strategic Defence and Security Review, Liberal Democrat Jenny Tonge talked of how the "treatment of Palestinians by Israel" was "the root cause of terrorism worldwide." She added that she felt "sorry for the people of Israel" as "their government's policies have made that country the cause of a lot of the world's problems, yet now they are seen as the remedy and the base for the West to fight back."[7] And in the *Guardian* on 22 August 2005, Madeleine Bunting wrote, "The main inspiration for British Muslim extremists is not their local mosques but television footage of Palestine and Iraq," implying that it was "our" foreign policy that was aggravating the radicals.[8]

The argument that the Israel-Palestinian conflict is fuelling Islamic rage across the Middle East can also be found in British high political circles. On several occasions, Tony Blair has talked of the need to resolve the conflict in an effort to weaken al-Qaeda's recruitment drive among Muslims. One of his first meetings after 9/11 was with Yasser Arafat, despite the fact that the Palestinian leader was in the midst of a campaign of terror against Israelis. In an article for an Iranian newspaper in 2001, Blair's foreign secretary Jack Straw wrote: "One of the factors that helps breed terrorism is the anger which many people in this region feel at events over the years in Palestine."[9] His comments caused outrage in Israel, and Straw did not ingratiate himself to the Israelis when he added a comment about the root causes of Palestinian terror: "There is an obvious need to understand the environment in which terrorism breeds. That is why the whole of the international community is so concerned to see a lasting peace in the Middle East."[10]

According to CNN's European political editor, both Blair and Bush believed at the time that this was "the key to ending much Arab resentment against the United States. America is often seen as too much on the side of Israel."[11]

Nor is the Foreign and Commonwealth Office immune to such thinking. According to a report produced by the FCO and submitted to the British cabinet in May 2004, some 1 percent of the British Muslim population were potential terrorists or terrorist supporters. The report talked about how the anger of British Muslims was being stirred up by "a perception of 'double standards' in British foreign policy, where democracy is preached but oppression of the ummah [the nation of believers] is practiced or tolerated, e.g., Palestine, Iraq, Afghanistan, Kashmir, Chechnya."[12]

It is important to remember that these sentiments come from figures who operate within mainstream political environments. Hardened champions of the left, such as John Pilger, have been even less nuanced and more vocal in their denunciation. Thus Pilger wrote in 2004: "The Zionist state remains the cause of more regional grievance and sheer terror than all the Muslim states combined."[13] Of course, it is hardly surprising that Ken Livingstone, former mayor of London, has voiced identical sentiments. In 2005, he spoke of how the policies of successive Israeli governments were "fuelling anger and violence across the world. For a mayor of London not to speak out against such injustice would not only be wrong—but would also ignore the threat it poses to the security of all Londoners."[14] The "security of all Londoners"? He also said that Israel was "a threat to all of us" because its "abuse of the human rights of the Palestinians … raises the temperature of the Middle East to a boiling point."[15]

Such sentiments have also found support from across the pond. During the 9/11 Commission hearings, FBI Special Agent James Fitzgerald said that al-Qaeda had attacked the United States because they felt "a sense of outrage against the United States." He went on: "They identify with the Palestinian problem, they identify with people who oppose repressive regimes, and I believe they tend to focus their anger on the United States."[16]

For Noam Chomsky, Bin Laden's terror campaign was a form of outrage for "long-standing US support for Israel's brutal military occupation" as well as U.S. support for Israeli policies and "the decade-long US–British assault against the civilian population of Iraq."[17] Radical that he is, Chomsky remains one of America's most influential public intellectuals.

According to Chas Freeman, a former U.S. ambassador to Saudi Arabia, Americans have suffered from terrorism because of the U.S.–Israeli strategic alliance. Speaking in 2006, he declared: "We have paid heavily and often in treasure in the past for our unflinching support and unstinting subsidies of Israel's approach to managing its relations with the Arabs. Five years ago we began to pay with the blood of our citizens here at home. We are now paying with the lives of our soldiers, sailors, airmen and marines on battlefields in several regions of the realm of Islam."[18]

In an influential essay published prior to the Iraq war, Michael Ignatieff wrote that if the United States abandoned the Palestinians "to face Israeli tanks and helicopter gunships," it would be "a virtual guarantee of unending Islamic wrath against the United States." He went on: "Now, with every day that American power appears complicit in Israeli attacks that kill civilians in the West Bank and in Gaza, and with the Arab nations giving their tacit support to Palestinian suicide bombers, the imperial guarantor finds itself dragged into a regional conflict that is one long haemorrhage of its diplomatic and military authority." In the same vein he argued that if America helped the Palestinians to achieve a state, it would not win over those "who hate America for what it is" but it would "address the rage of those who hate it for what it does."[19]

No sooner had the 9/11 attacks occurred than Susan Sontag wrote: "Where is the acknowledgment that this was not a 'cowardly' attack on 'civilization' or 'liberty' or 'humanity' or 'the free world' but an attack on the world's self-proclaimed superpower, undertaken as a consequence of specific American alliances and actions."[20] Her sentiments were echoed by Karl Lamers, the foreign policy spokesman for the CDU/CSU group in the German Parliament. He said, "I claim that September 11th is only the most radical expression of the revolt against Western dominance, embodied above all by the United States."[21]

Islamism denial, the tendency to blame the violence of Islamist radicals on external grievances, can also be found in the writings of Elizabeth Barlow from the University of Michigan: "Violence in the contemporary Muslim world is best explained not by religion, but as resistance to the violence of domination and, in Israel-Palestine, also of occupation."[22]

Mearsheimer and Walt concur with the view that Israeli policy is fuelling Islamist aggression against the West, making Israel a strategic liability. They dismiss the idea that the Jewish state serves Western strategic interests in the war on terror. For these authors, she is "a liability in the war on terror and the broader effort to deal with rogue states." That the United States has a "terrorism problem" is "in good part because it is so closely allied with Israel, not the other way round." Supporting the country, they say, "increases the terrorist danger that all states face—including America's European allies," because it "gives extremists a powerful recruiting tool, increases the pool of potential terrorists and sympathisers, and contributes to Islamic radicalism in Europe and Asia." They go further: "There is no question that many al-Qaida leaders, including Osama bin Laden, are motivated by Israel's presence in Jerusalem and the plight of the Palestinians. Unconditional support for Israel makes it easier for extremists to rally popular support and to attract recruits."[23]

One other person who seems to have imbibed this narrative is current U.S. secretary of state, John Kerry. He appeared to suggest that resolving the Arab-Israeli conflict would arrest the growth of Islamic State in Iraq and Syria. At least that is what he implied in a set of extraordinary comments in October 2014 when he spoke at a ceremony to mark Eid. Kerry called for a two-state solution to be implemented with haste before adding: "As I went around and met with people in the course of our discussions about the [ISIS] coalition, there wasn't a leader I met with in the region who didn't raise with me spontaneously the need to try to get peace between Israel and the Palestinians, because it was a cause of recruitment and of street anger and agitation."[24] His implication was that the failure to create a Palestinian state, or to end Israeli control of the West Bank, was causing a surge in recruitment to IS. That some of the representatives were from countries that had financed ISIL seemed to be lost on him.

These analyses, which come from highly influential opinion-formers in Western countries, all assume the same thing. Their assumption is that the West has brought militant Islamist wrath upon itself, that it is a form of understandable retribution for past misdeeds and ongoing injustices being meted out to Muslims round the world. In other words, the Islamist war upon the West is being generated by injustices for which our own governments bear considerable responsibility. Chief among these injustices is support for Israel and the failure to provide a lasting territorial solution to the conflict. As the Arab scholar of jihadism, Walid Phares, has put it: "The intellectual spokespersons of the Arab and Muslim world on both sides of the international divide [have] developed a single dominant paradigm, ignoring opposing views.... These elites claimed that the sole crisis in the Middle East was the Arab-Israel conflict, and that all other problems were caused by it and would find their way to resolution only with the end of the Palestinian-Israeli quagmire."[25]

What gave these analyses intellectual rocket fuel was a stubborn refusal to identify the religious-ideological roots of Islamist terror. Almost as soon as the planes had struck their targets on September 11, world statesmen went out of their way to distance the terrorists from the faith they professed to follow. Some months after the attacks, President Bush declared that the terrorists who had struck on September 11 were practicing "a fringe form of Islamic extremism" which was a perversion of "the peaceful teachings of Islam." The terrorists, he declared, were "traitors to their own faith."[26]

In a visit to a Muslim center a few days after the attacks he went further. He said that the acts of violence against innocents "violate the fundamental tenets of the Islamic faith" and that the "face of terror is not the true face of Islam.... Islam is peace."[27] For Colin Powell, these acts "should not be seen as something done by Arabs or Islamics; it is something that was done by terrorists."[28] The attempt to distance religion or religious ideology from terror was also made succinctly by Deputy Secretary Paul Wolfowitz, who told Americans, "Our enemy is terrorism, not Islam."[29]

Under the Obama administration, there has been a concerted effort to avoid terms like "Islamist" or "Islamic terrorist" or anything implying a connection between Islam and the global terror threat. When Major Nidal Hasan opened fire at the Fort Hood military base in 2009, killing 13 people while screaming "*Allahu Akhbar*," his acts were labeled "workplace violence" rather than theologically inspired terror. The FBI made no connection to his extremist Islamic beliefs. When a Nigerian man with links to Yemeni terrorists, Umar Farouk Abdulmutallab, tried to blow up a plane over Detroit in 2009, Obama referred to the perpetrator as "an isolated extremist."[30] Distancing Islam from terror has come naturally to a former director of the CIA, John Brennan, who argued that "there is nothing, absolutely nothing, holy or pure or legitimate or Islamic about murdering innocent men, women and children."[31]

When the U.S. ambassador to Libya, Chris Stevens, was murdered in Benghazi, the administration blamed people who had released a 14-minute video on YouTube. Even more bewildering was the sheer ignorance shown by Lieutenant General James Clapper, who in 2011 testified to Congress that the Muslim Brotherhood was "a very heterogeneous group, largely secular, which has eschewed violence and has decried Al Qaeda as a perversion of Islam."[32] Describing a militantly Islamist group that has spawned terror organizations like al-Qaeda as "secular" represents bewildering ignorance. As Michael Widlansky put it, such an analysis "cannot be classified as intelligence, but only as an insult to intelligence."[33] This denial in the United States also extends to the American military.[34]

In Britain, a touchstone for European liberal opinion, there was an especial outbreak of political correctness immediately after the 7 July 2005 attacks. Imams immediately denounced the attacks as "unIslamic," while the deputy commissioner of the Metropolitan Police, Brian Paddick, told an audience, "Islam and terrorists are two words that do not go together."[35] Similar sentiments were emanating from sections of the Church of England. "There is one small practical thing that we can all do. We can name the people who did these things as criminals or terrorists. We must not name them as Muslims."[36]

In the aftermath of the attempted bombings in London and Glasgow in 2007, there were reports that the government was dropping any reference to "Islamic terror," stressing instead the "criminality" of "terrorists." Following the murder of Drummer Lee Rigby on the streets of Woolwich in 2013, David Cameron went out of his way to distance Islam from the terrorist attack. This attack, he said, was "a betrayal of Islam."[37] So too did Boris Johnson, who declared: "This is not a question now of blaming the religion of Islam."[38] In 2014, the Islamism denial simply continued. In response to the attack on the Westgate shopping center in Nairobi by Islamists, David Cameron was led to assert that the attackers "do it in the name of terror, violence and extremism" and "don't represent Islam or Muslims."[39] He has been on record as saying that the Islamic State has "nothing to do with the great religion of Islam, a religion of peace."[40]

There was similar myopia following the 2014 Islamist assault on the offices of *Charlie Hebdo* in Paris. Ban Ki Moon explained that the tragic events had nothing to do with religion, claiming that "this is not … a war against religion or between religions…. This is a purely unacceptable terrorist attack—criminality."[41] France's president François Hollande said that the *Charlie Hebdo* fanatics had "nothing to do with Islam," while in the *Daily Mail*, Piers Morgan wrote that the perpetrators were "not 'real' Muslims" and that this was "not a religious war."[42]

Exposing the Fallacy

The notion that Israeli foreign policy, or that of the West towards the Islamic world, is primarily to blame for Islamist aggression is a fallacy. Undoubtedly, Western countries have occasionally pursued some unwise policies towards Muslim states. These have resulted in needless suffering, the death and maiming of innocent people and possibly the exploitation of resources. United States support for regimes in the Middle East, such as Egypt, Saudi Arabia, Iran under the Shah and the Gulf States has also sat uneasily with the image of that nation as a protector of liberal and democratic values. But this is still far removed from the simplistic causal claim that "bad" foreign policy has *inevitably* spurred the Islamist war against the West.

For one thing, there are many ways to deal with grievances arising from what is perceived to be unjust foreign policy. One is to engage in democratic protest, doing everything from lobbying MPs to taking part in peaceful protests against the said policy. Most Muslims, together with members of other aggrieved groups, have resorted to just these legal and peaceful means of dissent. Violence remains a last resort, albeit one that is highly morally compromised. Even here there are various categories of violence, ranging from attacks on property to violence perpetrated against the military to attacks on noncombatants. Yet for today's Islamists, such brutal methods have become the option of first resort, especially terrorist outrages in which civilians are the primary target.

In addition, Islamists choose to ignore all those cases where Western foreign policy has benefited Muslims worldwide. Whether in Kosovo, Kuwait or Mali, there have been many Western interventions that have averted Muslim suffering. Yet because Islamists believe in a black-and-white view that pits secular, Western forces against those of the Muslim world (the house of non–Islam versus the house of Islam), such instances are erased from the record.

Moreover, there are also plenty of cases where Muslims have been killing Muslims on a vastly larger scale than in conflicts with the West. According to UN estimates, some 250,000 Syrians have been slaughtered in the country's protracted civil war in the last 5 years. The Islamic State (ISIL), which has declared a Caliphate in Iraq and Syria, has been busy beheading their Muslim opponents. Previously, Islamist terrorists killed tens of thousands of Muslim Iraqis in a vast number of suicide bombings. Syria killed between 20,000 and 40,000 people in Hama in 1982, and Jordan killed several thousand Muslims in the 1970 Black September crackdown. Indeed, the majority of those killed in Islamist attacks in the Middle East have been Muslim. More to the point, Islamists have to be blind to the suffering inflicted on non–Muslims. To take some salient examples, Iran has long persecuted the small and beleaguered Ba'hai community. Some 400,000 Sudanese are estimated to have been killed in Darfur during the recent genocide by the Sudanese government. The Bodo inhabitants of Takimari in Northeast India have been ethnically cleansed by Muslims. The Berbers, Copts and Assyrians have also suffered under Islamic rule.

Also, whenever Muslims suffer at the hands of Western countries, whether due to war, counter terrorism or incarceration, it is automatically assumed to be the fault of the Western "infidels." All crimes and aggression carried out by Muslims are excused, and always interpreted through the lens of the dichotomously opposed forces at the heart of the Islamist worldview. Thus there cannot be legitimate Western self-defense against Islamist aggression. If Muslim terrorists are killed in Yemen, Afghanistan, Iraq or Somalia, they are always victims of Western aggression, even if they struck first. If Muslims are jailed because of their involvement in a terrorist plot, they are presumed innocent because it is secular non–Muslims who have jailed them. One key principle here is *Unsur Akhaka Zaaliman Kana am Mazluma* (Back up your brother, as oppressor or as an oppressed).[43] This means that whoever was in a conflict with a Muslim was a *kafir*, regardless of the conflict.

Ultimately, all that matters, in the words of one theorist, is "the metanarrative of Muslim suffering" and, one could add, "victimhood."[44] Or as columnist David Aaronovitch has stated, "anything that conflicts with the Grievance is discounted, and anything that contributes to it is emphasised."[45] This metanarrative is hardly conveyed through any intellectual or rational process. Instead, would-be jihadists are introduced to disturbing, violent images of Muslim suffering, or purported suffering, through the electronic media, ones that "project the militant notion of the ummah" and that encourage watchers to "imagine themselves and those they watch as part of the same community." One could term this "cyberjihad."[46] Such images are not mediated by any context nor do they encourage reflection, debate or discussion. What is created is a kind of "virtual community" in which considerations of local identity or space become irrelevant. As one researcher into militant jihad writes: "Footage of conflict is taken to demonstrate the existence of a battle waged by the West against Muslims, and the appropriate response of some righteous believers."[47]

Finally, many of these figures are familiar with the Islamic notion of *taqiyya*, the idea that Muslims can legitimately conceal their beliefs and deceive others if circumstances require it. Nowadays, radicals use *taqiyya* to promote the view that terrorism is a cry of despair from the anguished and the aggrieved, a device for fighting back against the perceived wickedness of Western foreign policy. In other words, they tell Western sources what they want to hear, such is the deep Western obsession with viewing Middle Eastern terror through the monocausal lens of the Arab-Israeli conflict. For all these reasons, the notion that Western foreign policy, whether in Iraq, Afghanistan, Kosovo or Israel, drives the Islamist assault on the West is utterly simplistic.

Deeper Roots of the Fallacy

The accusation that Israel is fuelling Islamist rage across the world is deeply flawed on other, more fundamental grounds. Firstly, it fails to take into account the deep ideological roots of radical Islam, which predate the 1967 occupation and even the birth of Israel in 1948. Secondly, it misunderstands the ideological focus of jihadism, which is the restoration of the Caliphate and the cultural subjugation of "infidels," rather than opposition to Israeli policy per se. Thirdly, it fails to appreciate that where Islamists do oppose Israel, their objections are to the very existence of a Jewish state; further, that this is driven by a centuries-long hatred and distrust of Jewry, some of it rooted in Islam's holy texts but with little attention paid to more positive references. Nothing Israel does can diminish this hatred because the Jewish state is hated for what it *is*, not what it *does*. Finally, it wrongly assumes that Israel's peace overtures would lessen terrorism when, in reality, they might actually increase them.

A qualification: It is worth stressing at the outset that radical or jihadist Islam is not the faith of the majority of Muslims worldwide. Most Muslims, according to many opinion polls, do not believe that their religion enjoins them to engage in a cosmic battle against the "unbelievers" or murder "infidels" to achieve political domination. Within the West, most Muslims are law-abiding and peaceful, conceiving of their faith as a means of spiritual nourishment.

Neither are Islam and Islamism quite the same thing. Islamism is a revolutionary political movement with ambitions to create a Muslim theocratic empire, rather than a vehicle for spiritual fulfillment. Like every faith, Islam's holy scriptures are capable of multiple interpretations, and religious radicals often distort Islamic concepts for their own ends. Islamism is a plausible interpretation of the faith, but not the only one. Yet it is equally true that Islamism derives much of its inspiration from aspects of mainstream Islam. Traditionally, Muslims are taught to regard Islam as God's final and perfect revelation to the world, superseding the earlier monotheistic faiths. This has encouraged a literalist approach to the holy texts that decries any attempt at reinterpretation or pragmatism. In effect, modern Islam is in the same dogmatic and obscurantist state as was Christendom prior to the Reformation. As a result, Muslim majority countries treat critics of Islam as apostates to be punished.

Within Islam there is no traditional separation between church and state as there is within the Judaeo-Christian tradition. In early Islam, Muslims formed both a political and religious community and Muhammad was head of state. There was no clash between emperor and divinity. This lack of church-state separation gives impetus to jihadists who reject democracy and seek to apply Sharia law to every social, economic and political question.

When extremists talk of the Dar-al-Islam and the Dar-al-Harb (House of Islam and House of War), they also reflect centuries-old Muslim tradition. According to that tradition, the world is divided into two houses, one ruled by Muslims and applying Muslim law and the other ruled by non–Muslims. A battle will be waged against the infidels until they accept Muslim rule and submission.

That battle or war against the unbelievers can be understood by the word *jihad*. In the encyclopedia of Islam, Emile Tyan defines jihad as consisting of "military action with the object of the expansion of Islam." Bernard Lewis too writes: "For most of the recorded history of Islam, from the lifetime of the Prophet Muhammed onward, the word jihad was used in a primary military sense."[48]

There are those who argue that jihad primarily connotes a struggle for spiritual self-improvement and overcoming base urges. Many interpret jihad in this way, especially Sufis, but for many others, the word has retained its martial connotations. Moreover, jihad is not a new concept but "is present from the beginning of Islamic history—in scripture, in the life of the Prophet, and in the actions of his companions and immediate successors."[49] After all, Muhammad was a warrior prophet who carved out the beginnings of an enormous empire ruled by his faith. He argued that God's message was for all mankind and that those who had accepted Islam had to strive to spread the faith across the globe, converting and subjugating all those who came in their path.[50] Islam remains a universalizing faith with a mission to spread the faith and convert people to the "true cause," by persuasion or force. The subjugation of and battle against "infidels" appear frequently in the Qu'ran.

There are, however, important obligations in waging a jihadist war. These include treating prisoners well and avoiding the killing of noncombatants (women and children), both of which are routinely ignored by today's jihadists. Jihad can also only be declared by legitimate political authorities rather than by individuals. But at the same time, the ill treatment of women, homosexuals and non–Muslims under Islamist rule reflects the Sharia with its endorsement of discrimination and inequality for these groups.

To claim, as many do, that jihadist militants bear *no* relation to Islam and do not arise from within Muslim civilization is a bare-faced lie. To argue that they and they alone represent either Islam or all Muslims is equally false. Islamism and Islam may not be identical, but the former undoubtedly arises from the latter, and there are points of agreement.

It is equally true that the global jihadist movement predates the war on terror, 9/11, George Bush and the Israeli occupation. As a movement, al-Qaeda was formed in the aftermath of the Soviet defeat in Afghanistan and as a response to Saudi Arabia's decision to allow American forces on its soil prior to the First Gulf War. But it also has very deep roots in the writings and actions of a number of important Muslim thinkers.

Historical Roots of Islamism

To get to the historical roots of this extremist ideology, we must start by looking at the medieval godfather of militant Islam, the Sunni scholar Sheikh Ibn Taymiyyah. Taymiyyah's age was one of great spiritual and political upheaval. In 1258, the Abbasid Empire was defeated by the invading Mongol armies, leading to the capture of Baghdad and the defeat of the Caliphate. After centuries in which Islam had enjoyed a political ascendancy, this event caused a profound degree of soul searching for Muslims, just as much as would the subsequent abandonment of the Caliphate seven centuries later.

Taymiyyah's answer to this loss of power was intimately connected to his conservative religious views. He belonged to the most extreme of Islam's four legal schools, the Hanbali School. Hanbalis rejected any innovative or modernizing tendencies in the faith and sought a return to the Islam of the 7th century. Taymiyyah believed that Muslims had lost the purity of the original faith and that only a return to the religion of Muhammad and his earliest followers (the caliphs) offered any hope for an Islamic revival. Ibn Taymiyyah sought to purge the faith of any beliefs or customs that had been introduced after the 7th century and particularly rejected the worship of saints and prophets, which he considered to violate the idea of God's unity.

He also adopted an extremely literal approach to the Koran, interpreting metaphorical references to God's "hand, feet, shin, and face" in an anthropomorphic sense. Like later radicals, he divided the world into the Dar-al-Islam and the Dar-al-Harb (world of Islam and the world of war). When the Mongols had converted to Sunni Islam, Taymiyyah declared them non–Muslims and apostates for not implementing Sharia law, and called upon other Muslims to wage war against them. He also interpreted jihad in literal terms as an "unrelenting struggle against all who stood in the way of Islam's destiny."[51] In his view, jihad against the disbelievers was the finest and noblest of actions, implying devotion to God. According to his intolerant, literalist worldview, disbelievers included infidels such as Christians and Muslims who had abandoned the purity of their faith.

One of Taymiyyah's admirers was a Saudi educator and writer called Muhammad bin Abdul Wahhab. Wahhab was born in the Nejd (part of what is now Saudi Arabia) in 1702 or 1703 and was educated in Medina before spending several years teaching in what is now Iraq and Iran. Wahhab developed an uncompromisingly conservative and literal interpretation of Islamic teaching. His new theology was called *ad Dawa lil Tawhid* (the Call to Unity).

He sought to purify the religion by going back to what he considered its original teachings and principles. The most important of these principles was *tawhid*, the oneness of God. Like the Islamists who would come after him, Wahhab believed that the doctrine of tawhid had been abused and misunderstood by the Muslim community. In Wahhab's eyes, the doctrine of the oneness of God implied that God alone could rule on earth and that he could have no partners in lawmaking. Thus human society had to be ruled on the basis of God's law, the Sharia, and any man-made laws were invalid. To alter the Sharia meant setting oneself up as a rival to God, and this was equivalent to apostasy. Wahhab's followers thus called themselves *Salafis* or *Muwahidun*, meaning "those who advocate oneness." In declaring there to be but one true interpretation of the faith, he actively rejected all forms of innovation (*bidat*).

Wahhab had little time for dissenters, branding them heretics guilty of *shirk* (polytheism). The only way to punish Muslims who deviated from Wahhabi practices was to launch a jihad against them that would end in their deaths. Thus as with Taymiyyah, a jihad to defend the community could be nothing other than a violent struggle against those opposing his brand of conservative Islam.[52]

In the eighteenth and nineteenth centuries Wahhabis did just this, launching a bloody campaign against Sufis and Shiites, which led to the capture of Karbala in Iraq in 1802 and Mecca in 1803. The Shiites, with their veneration of Muhammad's brother-in-law, Ali, were seen as heretical polytheists (*mushrikin*) worthy of extermination. The very same anti–Shiite tendencies within modern Sunni-led terrorism explain why so many Shiite shrines and communities have come under attack within the last decade. But Wahhab also condemned as un–Islamic many Sunni practices and beliefs, such as visiting the graves of holy men, celebrating the Prophet's birthday and making votive offerings.

The extremism of the Wahhabis has obvious repercussions when discussing relations between Islam and the West. Far from Saudi radicalism being a response to the encroachment of European imperialists, it had an internal spiritual dimension. It emerged from a barren expanse of central Arabia where Europeans were invisible and at a time when the USA had yet to be formed.

In 1744, Wahhab forged an alliance with Muhammad ibn Saud (a desert warrior and later founder of the House of Saud), creating a remarkable partnership of politics and faith that continues to this day. In the early twentieth century, the Wahhabis maintained an alliance with the House of Saud by helping Abd al-Aziz ibn-Saud recapture Riyadh and found the state of Saudi Arabia in 1932. The Wahhabis then formed a further pact with the Saud dynasty. In return for legitimizing the rule of the House of Saud, the Wahhabi *ulama* (religious establishment) "exercised a monopoly over educational and religious policies," which ensured that Saudis "learned, and followed, Wahhabi principles and values."[53] The eighteenth century Wahhab could be regarded, then, as the founding father of radical Islamic ideology.

But Islamism, as a specific political movement, was very much a product of modernity. Though it drew upon a vernacular of Islamic medievalism, it was primarily a twentieth century phenomenon inspired by the revolutionary élan of modern totalitarianism. Its two principal ideologues were both Egyptian—Hasan Al Banna and Sayyid Qutb. Both produced a revolutionary doctrine that would shake Islamic politics to its foundations.

The first two decades of the twentieth century were marked by a crisis of identity within the Muslim world. During the First World War, the Ottoman Empire, Europe's sick man, had finally tottered to extinction after the collective strains of the war. After the defeat of the Ottoman Empire, Turkey's founder and first modern ruler, Kemal Ataturk, extinguished the Islamic Caliphate, the religious state that traditionally symbolized Muslim spiritual and political unity. For many later Islamists, this represented "the mother of all crimes."[54] It was, as Loretta Napoleon puts it, an event that "carved deep scars in the identity and self-esteem of the Muslim population."[55]

Arab peoples, including Egyptians, now found themselves under the control of European powers whose decisions were guiding the destinies of the Muslim world. In fact, as Bernard Lewis argues, the post–World War I collapse was the culmination of a centuries-long process involving the retreat of Muslim power in the face of Western economic and technological advances. A mood of Arab hostility to and rejection of the West was "surely due to a feeling of humiliation—a growing awareness, among the heirs of an old, proud, and long dominant civilization, of having been overtaken, overborne, and overwhelmed by those whom they regarded as their inferiors."[56]

The feeling of Muslim powerlessness in the face of these arbitrary decisions only compounded the sense of agony. The ensuing march of secularization and the end of the Caliphate led to a great deal of Muslim soul-searching. For many, these changes symbolized the profound need for adaptation and modernization, with Kemal Ataturk's secular reforms a model for the kind of transformation that was necessary. But not all Muslims saw things this way. In the face of these sudden social shocks some saw only chaos and destabilization. What grew was a "perception that the public world [had] gone awry" and that behind this confusion lay "a great spiritual and moral conflict."[57]

This led to a belief that mighty cosmic forces were tearing apart the Muslim world, in turn providing fertile ground for conspiracy theories. The prize villain was Western modernity, the process by which once-traditional societies, anchored in the simple pieties of faith and family, were now beset by rapid economic change, individualism and cosmopolitan culture. For a new generation of Muslim thinkers, the sudden advance of cultural and economic change, accompanied by the erosion of Muslim power, bred intense resentment, frustration, fear and helplessness. They felt that the Muslim world was under siege and no longer the master of its own destiny. Such beliefs were profoundly alienating and traumatic and still cause angst today, as the impact of globalization reaches across the globe.

This intellectual vanguard offered a prescription for the Muslim world's ills. They came to believe that the collapse of Islamic power mirrored a loss of faith and that only a return to the guiding principles of premodern Islam would restore lost glories. Like the other (modern) totalitarian movements of that era, Islamist fundamentalism sought to reassert a beleaguered tradition in the face of the relentless onrush of modernity. And this vanguard would "become foot soldiers in an army whose goal [was] the wholesale destruction of what the movement [considered] a despoiled present."[58]

Thus Islamism emerged as a curious mixture of medievalism and modernity. On the one hand, its advocates expressed contempt for what they saw as a spiritually empty and rootless cosmopolitanism. They sought to remake the world by a reversion to premodern, illiberal Islam. But on the other hand, as John Gray points out, their desire to purify humanity through violence was a modern obsession, a utopian ideal that animated the fascists, Nazis and communists of our own era. One such Islamist was Hassan al-Banna. Al-Banna was born in Egypt in 1906 and educated in Cairo, where he took up a post as a teacher. He lived through the tumult of the 1919 Egyptian revolution, a nationalist revolt against British rule, which may have inclined him from an early age to dedicate himself to religious revivalism. During his years in Cairo, he also witnessed at first hand the ubiquitous penetration of materialistic, Western influences. Egypt was gradually opening up to modernity, with women taking off their headscarves and leading scholars embracing liberal currents of thought. He came to regard secularization and the West's liberal tendencies as corrupt and decadent, believing that they had caused the decline of the Islamic world. In his own words:

> A wave of dissolution, which undermined all firm beliefs, was engulfing Egypt in the name of intellectual emancipation. This trend attacked the morals, deeds and virtues under the pretext of personal freedom. Nothing could stand against this powerful and tyrannical stream of disbelief and permissiveness that was sweeping our country.... I saw the social life of the beloved Egyptian people, oscillating between her dear and precious Islam which she had inherited, defended, lived with during fourteen centuries, and this severe Western invasion which was armed and equipped with all destructive influences of money, wealth, prestige, ostentation, power and means of propaganda.[59]

In 1928 he set up a religious revivalist society, al-Ikhwan al-Muslimeen (Society of the Muslim Brothers), known by the more familiar English name "the Muslim Brotherhood." It aimed to counter the march of Western ideas in the Islamic world and restore the lost

Caliphate. But it also had a populist orientation, as al-Banna argued that Egypt's official religious establishment lacked the zeal and piety of the masses.[60] By the end of the 1930s the society had attracted over 200,000 members and had branches across Egypt. This staggering success was due, in large part, to the organizational skills of al-Banna. He built up a mass movement among peasants, workers and professionals, using a variety of social, economic and political issues to attract their interest.

Al-Banna ultimately sought to replace the pro–British Egyptian government with one based on implementing Islamic law. He also vehemently attacked the corruption, nepotism and elitism in Egyptian political circles and sought to replace political parties with an overarching representative body that could rule the entire nation more justly. Their articulation of lower middle class grievances and strong anti-colonialism won them many converts. But it was al-Banna's uncompromisingly militant cult of jihad that would mark out the Brotherhood as a subversive influence. It brought the organization into conflict with the monarchy and in 1948, following rumors of a coup, Prime Minister Nuqrashi Pasha disbanded it. Following Pasha's assassination later that year, al-Banna was himself gunned down and killed in February 1949, almost certainly by government agents. However, the Muslim Brotherhood survived the loss of their founder and in the 1950s, branches opened up in Jordan, Egypt and Syria.

One of its most influential members was an Egyptian writer and intellectual called Sayyid Qutb. Qutb is often regarded as the true godfather of the Islamist movement and the inspiration for al-Qaeda. He is perhaps the most influential advocate of jihadist warfare in the modern era.

Like al-Banna, Qutb was born in Egypt in 1906. He moved later to Cairo, where he received a Western education before he began his career as a teacher in the Ministry of Public Instruction. His life would be transformed by an extended visit to the United States from 1948 to 1950. He had been sent by the Egyptian government to study the American education system and spent time in New York, Washington and Colorado. Much of what he saw there repelled him. He railed against the country's rampant postwar materialism, its lack of cultural enrichment and the spiritual void at the heart of American religious life. What he despised was the idea of America: "A rootless, cosmopolitan, superficial, trivial, materialistic, racially mixed, fashion-addicted civilization."[61]

One example that struck him was the time that American householders spent cultivating their lawns. The cultivation of gardens was, for Qutb, merely another manifestation of the selfish individualism that prevented spiritual growth. He also exhibited an obsessive dislike of American sexual liberalism. He attended a church service in Greenly, Colorado, and wrote of its "seductive atmosphere" where the hall "swarmed with legs," where "lips met lips" and "where the atmosphere was full of love."[62] He thought of churches as centers of entertainment and sexual playgrounds. The American woman was, for Qutb, a primitive seductress who exploited her body parts to entice males and whose bestial appetites were far removed from austere Islamic ideals.

Upon his return to Egypt in 1950, Qutb became the foremost spokesman for the Muslim Brotherhood. He was now convinced that the Muslim world was in danger of cultural implosion and that to survive, it had to embrace a rigid Islamic code devoid of Western influences. He threw his support behind Gamal Nasser's nationalist coup and fully expected the implementation of Islamic law to follow. However, Qutb and the Brotherhood were to be sorely disappointed. Nasser's secular pan–Arab nationalism had little room for Islamic rule, and Qutb and the other Islamists soon turned against him. During a severe crackdown on the Muslim Brotherhood, Qutb was arrested and imprisoned. He spent more than a decade in confinement, witnessing the worst features of Nasser's totalitarian state. He viewed Nasser as an "iniquitous prince ... who governed an empire according to his own caprice."[63]

Later he was hanged after being accused of plotting to overthrow the government, his execution making him a *shahid* (martyr) in the eyes of his followers. Qutb's death was to galvanize the Muslim Brotherhood in Egypt and elsewhere, while his voluminous writings were to exercise a bewitching influence over later Islamists. One of Qutb's followers, Ayman al-Zawahiri, would later join Osama Bin Laden and form the al-Qaeda network.

During the next thirty years, there was a fusion of Muslim Brotherhood ideology and Wahhabism. Saudi universities such as the Islamic University of Medina gave jobs to members of the Brotherhood, who were in exile after being expelled by Egypt, while Saudi petrodollars, in their billions, were used to fund the establishment of organizations such as the World Muslim League and the World Assembly for Muslim Youth (WAMY). These foundations helped to promote the global jihad, providing a source of funding as well as ideological justification.

After Saudi Arabia and Egypt, Pakistan has become the third epicenter of revolutionary Islamism. Its most influential advocate was Abul Ala Mawdudi, born in 1903 in the region of Hyderabad in what was then British India. In 1941 he founded a radical Islamist party called Jamaat-i-Islami, and for the next thirty years until the onset of ill health, he was its guiding chief. Like Wahhab, al-Banna and Qutb, Mawdudi's thought was dedicated to the proposition that Western influences were harming Muslim minds and that a pure Islamic faith alone provided an all-encompassing solution to life's problems. His political party was dedicated to establishing an Islamic state in Pakistan and thus stood in opposition to successive, non–Islamist governments in the country.

For Mawdudi, a truly Islamic state was based on Sharia law and its sphere of influence was all-encompassing. There was no meaningful distinction between private and public. Islamic law would determine all domestic laws, the rights and duties of citizens, social relationships and international affairs—there was no issue on which it could not pass judgment. Islamic democracy was thus diametrically opposed to the type of democracy found in the secular West, or the governments found in the Muslim world. Mawdudi was often arrested and imprisoned and narrowly escaped capital punishment for one of his writings. By the time he died in 1979, ironically in the "heathen" United States, his influence had become global.

Osama Bin Laden remains the most infamous cult figure in the history of modern jihadism. His terror assaults against the United States and the years spent dodging his pursuers have given him near legendary status among millions of disillusioned Arabs. But despite his enormous stature there is no formal body of doctrine called Bin Ladenism, merely a set of statements, interviews and declarations given to the Arab media. From these we can build up a clear sense of how he viewed the world and what he sought to achieve.

Like al-Banna, Qutb and Wahhab, Bin Laden perceived the Muslim world to be in a tragic state of decline, having been weakened and humiliated by the "infidel" West. He made frequent reference to the eighty years of pain since the end of the Caliphate in 1924 and the state of Muslim countries that he believed were suffering under the weight of Western imperialism, as well as pro–Western corrupt autocrats.

In a message he addressed to Saudi clerics, he spoke of the "degradation and corruption" to which the "Islamic umma [had] sunk," and the "feebleness and cowardice" of many of its scholars. This came about, he believed, because of their "neglect of religion and weakness of faith." He was writing in the aftermath of Saudi Arabia's decision to allow U.S. troops onto Saudi soil in 1990, prior to the First Gulf War. This was the pivotal event for Bin Laden's war against America. He described the Saudi decision as a "calamity unprecedented in the history of our umma" and likened U.S. forces to a "Crusader invasion."[64]

In his 1996 Declaration of Jihad, he referred to the American presence in Saudi Arabia as "the greatest disaster to befall the Muslims since the death of the Prophet Muhammad." In the same statement, he also lamented the kingdom's economic mismanagement (accusing them of handing over their oil) and the arrest of religious figures, both of which had "desecrated its legitimacy." In 1997, he called the Saudi regime a "branch" of the United States and as a result, his main problem was "the U.S. government."[65]

In numerous statements, he made reference to how Muslims worldwide were the victims of Western (Judaeo-Christian) "aggression," whether in Israel, Chechnya, Kashmir, Iraq or Lebanon. Whenever Muslims died in those places, he sniffed a conspiracy by the "Crusader alliance" to attack the innocent and crush and subjugate Islam. He saw the 2003 war against Saddam Hussein as a "Crusader war" directed "against the people of Islam." Later he declared that Bush and Blair wanted to "annihilate Islam" and "change the region's ideology" by targeting "60 states."[66]

The central theme was that the *umma*, the world of Islam, was in mortal peril from the designs of a purported American-Jewish imperialistic plot, which he linked to the medieval Crusades. All Muslim suffering was blamed on Western plotting and scheming, though any Western intervention to defend Muslims was all too conveniently airbrushed from the record.

The armies of the Americans and their allies must, he said, "leave all the territory of Islam" and cease supporting "corrupt leaders in our countries." This would bring about the "removal of the man-made laws that America had forced on its collaborators in the region" and the reestablishment of the "righteous caliphate." For in his view, the "great deterioration in all walks of life" that beset the Arab world happened because people lacked "the correct and comprehensive understanding of the religion of Islam." This religion, he went on to say, was about more than prayer and fasting. It encompassed "all the affairs of life, including the religious and the worldly, such as economic, military and political affairs."[67] Bin Laden promised a "cure" for Arab humiliation, though he sidestepped the fact that his proposed solution of Islamist rule under the Caliphate would bring in its wake far greater abuses of human rights. For as one scholar puts it: "Extremists do call for the destruction of the autocratic, sometimes secular regimes that govern much of the Middle East, but their concern is not primarily about ineffective rule (on which they could scarcely improve) or human rights (which, after all, they have no desire to offer) but with creating a society capable of fighting off modernity's insults."[68]

Yet in his call to the Americans in 2002, Bin Laden also condemned a lifestyle that he depicted as debauched and immoral. He specifically demanded that America abandon the separation of church and state, the practice of usury, the tolerance for gambling and drugs and its liberal attitude towards sexuality.[69] In short, he was calling for America to become an Islamic state ruled by Sharia law. But his main focus was on forcing the United States out of the Arab and Muslim world in order to facilitate a takeover by his revolutionary, global Islamist movement. The short-term grievances that he wanted rectified (U.S. troops in Saudi Arabia, and Israel's "crimes") were only mentioned because they stood in the way of a totalitarian caliphate.

All the ideologists mentioned so far come from the majority Sunni branch of Islam. But Shiite Islam has not been immune to the influence of radical Islamism and is represented today by the Islamic Republic of Iran, founded in 1979. The Islamic Republic, like the Sudanese dictatorship, the Saudi state or Afghanistan under the Taliban, can be thought of as Islamism *made flesh*. Prior to 1979, Islamist radicals could only harbor dreams of bringing down "infidel" states and replacing secular constitutions with Islamic ones. They aspired to lead their fellow Muslims out of "ignorance" and "darkness" and into a new promised land of religious purity. But with powerful Western backed autocrats holding sway in Cairo and Baghdad, such dreams appeared unrealistic, almost fantastical.

But in 1979, Ayatollah Khomeini seized control of the Iranian state during a time of revolutionary opposition to the Shah. He soon set about creating a new Iranian state whose constitution and guiding principles would be based on (Shiite) Islamic principles. Khomeini was the revolution's inspiring figure, its intellectual mentor and chief interpreter. But he also appointed a master of Islamic religious law (Wilayat-al-Faqih) and an elite group of conservative clerics to help guide the affairs of state. This blueprint for theocratic government had already been spelled out in Khomeini's book *Islamic Government* (1971). In this influential volume Khomeini argued that God had sent Islam to be implemented and thus required an Islamic government on earth. The best people to implement this vision were the *ulama* or guardians. To create a true Islamic government, it was necessary to frame laws on the Sharia and that this required a jurist (*faqih*) to provide guardianship over society.

This neo–Platonic theory was called the "guardianship of the jurist" (*velayat-e faqih*). Laws would not be made in a democratic manner because this would involve man legislating for his fellow man. Nor could the Shah be relied on to defend Islam. Indeed Khomeini referred to the Shah as a "corrupter of the earth" and "a false god," invoking the kind of language used to refer to the enemies of the Twelfth Imam. He projected himself to the nation as a messianic figure at the head of a populist but authoritarian theocracy. All in all, this would ensure that the Islamic Republic would become a formidable bastion of clerical rule as well as a global power base for Shia Islam. But Khomeini's revolution was not a specifically Shia one, even though, as Vali Nasr points out, he succeeded "in wrapping [the] regime in Shia symbolism and Shia stories." Nasr continues, he also "wanted to be accepted as the leader of the Muslim world, period."[70] Many in the Sunni world, however, did not accept Khomeini as the spearhead of Islamic revivalism. Thus he appealed to issues that united all Muslims, such as the battle against the Jewish state and anti–Americanism. Despite the deep ideological differences between the various branches of Sunni and Shia Islamism, both denominations embraced a form of reactionary, totalitarian Islam that was inherently anti–Western in its leanings.

All these theoreticians of jihad were the vanguard of a revolutionary movement that promised to restore Islam's past glorifies and reverse its decline. They had a seemingly irresistible appeal for the masses, casting a spell over their followers with their conspiratorial worldviews and their all-too-believable narratives. What made them so seductive was the sheer simplicity of their vision. Their writings featured a Manichean cast of heroes and villains, of rapacious Westerners and deceitful Jews who were bringing about Islam's collective downfall. The West was the ultimate "out group" that could be blamed for the loss of Muslim identity, the turbulence of socio-economic change and the humiliating loss of power. But as well as offering a diagnosis of the Muslim world's current ailments, these authors provided the prescription: Islam would again become a potent force if only its followers could return to a premodern existence.

The Islamists' Central Demand Is to Recreate an Anti-Western Caliphate

It follows from the above that the ideology of radical Islam is not centered on the Palestinian issue or any one specific grievance with Western foreign policy. Its primary emphasis is on rescuing Islam, and the global Muslim community generally, from the perceived harmful effects of Westernization, modernization and secularism.

Islamism is best thought of as a revolutionary political program for the forcible remaking of societies on an Islamic model. It is a revolutionary ideology in that it seeks to purge existing societies, especially Muslim majority ones, of what are perceived to be corrupt, decadent and immoral influences, replacing them with societies ruled by Islamic (Sharia) law. In their remaking, Islam will hold the answer to every conceivable social, political or economic issue that arises between humans. Islamists reject the Western model for society, which incorporates some sacrosanct values: a fundamental division between state and church, individual freedom, democracy, religious tolerance and freedom of expression, equality between those of different sexual orientations and equality for non–Muslims. Islamism is thus anti–Western, antidemocratic, authoritarian, racist, homophobic and sexist to the core.[71]

To justify their objectives, Islamists believe that the Islamic world is in a state of perpetual war from the *kuffar* or "unbeliever" and that unless militant jihadist warfare is conducted against non–Islamists, Islam will be permanently undermined from without and from within. The apostate states, initially in Muslim lands, but also in the West, must therefore be defeated and replaced with a single and unified Muslim state, the restored Caliphate, ruled by Sharia law and answerable to the Islamic divinity alone. As Walid Phares puts it, "The jihadists not only believe in the continuous existence of a civilization as a real political entity, but are also committed to removing any obstruction to its revival, including 21 Arab governments and more than 50 Muslim states—all of which are to be subsumed under the caliphate."[72]

Islamism in Detail

Islamists fundamentally believe in the supremacy of the Koran as a complete and infallible guide for human existence. Accepting the literal truth and perfection of the Koran (and *hadiths*), the Islamists claim that Islam provides a complete system of morality, justice and governance for all human societies and reject every other ideology or belief system as invalid. Islamists believe that the only valid rules for governing society are the Islamic Sharia laws, which are "as accurate and true as any of the laws known as the 'laws of nature.'"[73]

In an interview with Al Jazeera in 1998, Bin Laden called on all Muslims to "contemplate God's book," adding, "Our remedy is the Koran and the traditions of the prophet."[74] Another Islamist, Abu Hamza, has declared that the Koran is "like a manual for a machine" that dictates what man can and cannot do.[75] For many Muslims, the Koran has a mainly personal and spiritual significance, which should not mandate what goes on in the public sphere. The Islamists reject any such distinction, believing that the Koran binds man in every respect, whether in his private or public life. Qutb understood this when he wrote: "Islam has a mandate to order the whole of human life."[76] He railed against what he called the "hideous schizophrenia" of Western societies in which religion had been relegated to the private sphere of life and not allowed to influence public policy. These societies represent "an alien and threatening culture that must be ruthlessly resisted and vanquished."[77]

God's Unity Contradicts Man-Made Rule

Islamists adopt the mainstream belief in the absolute oneness of God (*tawhid*). God alone is sovereign and deserves worship, a belief that is also part of the declaration of belief (*shahada*). But it is the implications of *tawhid* that set Islamists apart from other Muslims. If God alone is sovereign and perfect, then only his immutable rules and laws can legitimately govern all of humanity. For the jihadists, Islam is a complete system for ruling man on earth. Given that it contains God's final revelation, it can have no equal and cannot be contained by a superior system. It implies that Muslims cannot live in a society in which Islam is not the guiding belief system, and Muslims cannot be ruled by non–Muslims. As Sheikh al Qaradawi has summed it up: "If the Islamic truth is one how can there be more than one truth among Muslims?"[78]

This means that Islamists are bound to reject almost every political settlement that exists in the world, for they are all based on the rule of man by man. In democracies or autocracies, humans have set themselves up as "national leaders" governing society while those countries' judiciaries apply laws that have been framed by the people. For Islamists, man-made rule is akin to apostasy, a rejection of God's right to rule man in accordance with the Koran. All man-made laws are considered a form of polytheism (*shirk*), a negation of God's right to rule his creation without partners. Qutb summed up this aspect of Islamist belief very clearly: "Any system in which the final decisions are referred to human beings, and in which the sources of all authority are human, deifies human beings by designating others than God as lords over men."[79]

For Mawdudi, "It is God and not man whose will is the primary source of law in a Muslim society." The belief in *tawhid* (unity of God) "negates the concept of the legal and political independence of human beings, individually or collectively."[80] Thus he regards the "domination of man over man" as a "root cause of all evil and mischief."[81] He added that human societies had to "surrender all rights of overlordship, legislation and exercising of authority over others" and that no individual had the right to "pass orders and make commands on his own right" and, furthermore, that "no one ought to accept the obligation to carry out such commands and obey such orders."[82]

The Islamist Umar Bakri Mohammad has declared that backing political parties in a democratic system is "*haram*," or forbidden. For Bin Laden, "a ruler's enacting legislation contrary to God's will" is "a greater atheism." Indeed legislation about what is and isn't allowed is "a type of worship."[83]

While not negating the role of leaders in society, it restricts their scope to merely implementing the Sharia law and Koranic injunctions. As Kramer points out in his exposition of the Islamist world view, "The shar'ia, as a perfect law, cannot be abrogated or altered, and certainly not by the shifting moods of an electorate."[84] Put simply, Islamists believe that their faith can legislate for every aspect of human life and thus there can be no schism between the private and the public life.

One should not be fooled by the fact that the Islamists occasionally use democratic means to gain power. Here they are embracing the methods of democratic populism in order to destroy the system from within, a means-end approach that is familiar to all those who have studied the early years of the Nazi party. For all their impressive grassroots mobilization in the Egyptian elections of 2012, the Muslim Brotherhood's central aim was unchanged: The gradual establishment of Sharia-based, Taliban-style government, denying rights to the Copts and other minorities, as part of a master plan to recreate the Caliphate.[85]

Overturn Apostate Societies

But Islamists go beyond this simple rejection of man-made law. While non–Muslims are automatically "apostates" for rejecting Islam, so too are Muslims who live under any political system that incorporates man-made rule and legislation. Qutb, Mawdudi and others then draw a radical conclusion. If human societies are based on the denial of God's sovereignty, those societies are practicing a form of apostasy and have to be forcibly reformed until God's laws prevail. In other words, a vanguard of true believers is needed to overturn existing societies and set up proper Islamic states ruled not by national leaders but by God's injunctions.

In his book *Milestones* Qutb argues, "The Muslim community has been extinct for a few centuries" as a result of not living under Sharia law, and it has thus reverted to a pre–Islamic state of *Jahiliyyah* (the state of ignorance of the guidance from God). If Muslims venerated "anyone who serves someone other than God" then they were "outside God's religion, although he may claim to profess this religion."[86] As no state in the Muslim world has implemented Sharia law in accordance with Islamist precepts, there have been no "Muslim" countries as such. For Qutb, even Muslims who lived under apostate regimes had ceased to be Muslims.

From this observation Qutb argued that it was possible to declare fellow Muslims as unbelievers who practiced *shirk*, or polytheism. This revolutionary conclusion explains why Islamic extremists have shown no compunction in ordering attacks in Islamic countries where the majority of victims are their co-religionists.[87] In one example, during the Algerian Civil War, the armed wing of the Islamic Salvation Front (the Armed Islamic Group or GIA) slaughtered tens of thousands of Algerian civilians in a terrible series of massacres, sometimes going from village to village and wiping out the inhabitants. With good reason, the Conservative politician Michael Gove has described Islamists as "a self conscious vanguard who look down on other Muslims and consider the majority of their co-religionists as sunk in barbarity or error."[88]

Like any true revolutionary of the modern era, Qutb has identified a state of social degradation and alienation and the cause of this state of affairs (turning away from the true faith, under secular influence). But he also makes clear that words alone are insufficient for the battle. The elimination of the *jahili* societies cannot be done "through sermons and discourse."[89] It requires a committed vanguard of true believers who are ready to lead a movement for revivalist Islam.

Yet the battle to establish Islamic law is not confined to Muslim countries or those with a Muslim majority. Islamists believe that ultimately their faith must conquer the globe and form the ideological underpinning of all societies.⁹⁰ Thus militant Muslims believe it is justified to attack the *kuffar* (unbeliever) even if they are not attacked first. They justify an offensive jihad because they believe they are merely following a divine command to spread the faith by the sword until God's laws reign supreme and his oneness is recognized by all his creatures. This was a central part of Bin Laden's motivation for declaring war on the United States in 1996.⁹¹ Qutb argues that an offensive or militant jihad against the "unbelievers" is necessary because "those who have usurped the authority of God" will not "give up their power" without a fight.⁹²

REJECTION OF ALL WESTERN VALUES

From these precepts, Islamists draw a range of startling conclusions about the West. Western societies believe in a fundamental division between state and church. The state's remit and powers are restricted to matters of the public sphere and there is no interference in the private realm. The state does not dictate matters of religion and conscience, which are left to the individual's own choosing. There are some significant freedoms that flow from this basic philosophy. Yet Islamists utterly reject the notion of a secular state or any separation between state and church. If Islam offers a complete philosophy for humanity, there are no questions which it cannot settle and no issues on which it cannot legislate.

Any liberal society must uphold the sacrosanct freedoms of expression, action and belief. Islamists reject all these freedoms when their expression clashes with the Islamists' own interpretation of Islam. Freedom is often derided as a license for immoral and exploitative behavior. Thus Hizb al-Tahrir derides liberal notions of freedom as "the freedom of fornification, sexual perversion, immorality, drinking alcohol, and other diseases."⁹³ Mawdudi argued that the denial of freedom would save people from "that satanic flood of female liberty and license which threatens to destroy civilization."⁹⁴ This is reminiscent of Qutb's scornful observations of the "vixen" American female. The Taliban produced a series of rules for dress and behavior that clashed with Western notions of freedom of choice. Women were required to wear a long veil (*Burqa*) covering them from head to toe (women could be whipped for not complying); there was a ban on the wearing of cosmetics or laughing loudly, a ban on listening to music or watching television and videos, and a ban on kite flying. Instead, as Qutb put it, true freedom could only be tasted in "obedience to the divine law."⁹⁵ The mufti of Jerusalem also loathed the whole basis of Western civilization and sought to combat all its manifestations, including female equality, sexual liberalism, freedom of thought and places of entertainment such as cinemas and theaters.⁹⁶

Individuals cannot be allowed to express beliefs that are un–Islamic, because this is deemed to be a contradiction of divine sovereignty and a form of *kufr* (unbelief). Thus academic freedom is unknown in Islamist societies, as it was also unknown in other modern totalitarian societies. All academic research in an Islamist state must conform to the precepts of traditional Islam, and if academics dare to challenge the holy writ or Sharia law, they would become *murtadd* (apostates). Islamism makes no allowance for free intellectual enquiry, since all education must be based on and conform to the precepts of traditional Islam.

Religious equality between all faiths (and none) is also anathema for supporters of radical Islam. Jews and Christians must accept domination under Muslim rule while for Hindus, the options narrow to conversion or death. Islamists make clear their vehement opinions about non-Islamic belief systems, as in this statement by Abu Hamza: "Only the most ignorant and animal minded individuals would insist that prophet killers (Jews) and Jesus worshippers (Christians) deserve the same right as us."[97] But Islamist societies are just as restrictive when it comes to the rights of a Muslim majority. If a Muslim wishes to change religion, this is considered a form of apostasy and the punishment is death or forcible recantation. As Lewis explains in his discussion of traditional Islamic and Islamist societies: "The Muslim who abandons his faith is ... not only a renegade; he is a traitor, and the law insists that he must be punished as such. The jurists agreed on the need to execute the apostate individual."[98] Partly for this reason, Islamists reject the concept of international law as a man-made instrument for governing humanity. They also condemn the UN Declaration of Universal Rights, which safeguards many of the liberal freedoms mentioned above, including "the freedom to choose one's religion and one's spouse."[99]

By now it should be abundantly clear why Islamist extremists have targeted both the USA and its pro–Western Arab allies in the Middle East (principally Israel, Jordan, Egypt and Saudi Arabia). In the Islamist worldview the world is divided between supporters of truth (*al-Haqq*) and the enemy of truth, falsehood (*batil*). There can be no accord between the two systems, as Qutb argued in *Milestones*: "Islam cannot accept or agree to a situation which is half–Islam and half–Jahiliyyah.... The mixing and co-existence of the truth and falsehood is impossible."[100] Non-Muslims, particularly those in the West, are deemed to be unbelievers, and it is in the nature of unbelievers, Islamists claim, that they inevitably oppose Islam and hate all Muslims.

For most Islamists, the arch-unbelievers are the Jews and Christians, ignoring the fact that these people are described in the Koran as "the people of the book." Qutb traced the purported enmity of the Christians and Jews to the 7th century, arguing that their "deviance" and "sinfulness" caused them to reject Muhammad's revelation.[101] Qutb weaves an elaborate historical narrative in which Western powers, principally the grand Satan (the USA), Europe, Israel and the Jews in general, together with their associated allies, are engaged in a ceaseless and protracted war with Islam.[102] These powers are the *a'daa' Allah* (enemies of God). He interprets Islamic history as a series of Western invasions, assaults and harassment, conveniently airbrushing from the record the Arab world's own history of violent colonialism, racism and outright oppression.

But it is not enough for the Islamists to identify the alleged unbelief of their enemies. The Islamists believe that the Dar-al-Harb (the house of non–Islam) will forever be opposed to Islam and will perpetually seek to destroy it from without and to undermine it from within. Key thinkers have weaved an elaborate historical narrative to explain how "the unbelievers" have been at war with Islam for over a millennium. The Crusades play a central part in their narrative, for these are interpreted not as a defensive war by Christendom to halt Islam's territorial expansion, but as part of a concerted effort by the West to destroy Islam and convert Muslims at the point of a sword. Every subsequent interaction between the West and Islam is viewed in the same light. Indeed the Islamists believe that the "crusading spirit" shown by the unbelievers has never disappeared. Qutb argued that attempts by the West to colonize and subjugate Muslims in the modern era were the result of "crusaderist imperialism."[103]

The apotheosis of the West's alleged assault on Islam was the ending of the Caliphate, decried as "the mother of all crimes" by most jihadists. Kemal Ataturk, the founder of secular Turkey, has been denounced as a tool of world Jewry and "an agent of England," while his actions are viewed as another example of the West's enmity towards Islam. Islamists believe that the ending of the Caliphate marked the disappearance of Islam "from the living of life," thus explaining why the reestablishment of the Caliphate is so central to jihadist motivation.[104]

Just as Islamists view Ataturk as a treacherous ally of colonial powers, so too do they denounce today's Arab rulers as apostates who follow the bidding of their Western backers. Thus the leaders of Egypt, Jordan, Pakistan and Saudi Arabia are seen as latter-day pharaohs whom a cabal of unbelievers control for their own nefarious purposes. It should not be forgotten that Bin Laden's motivation for forming al-Qaeda was the Saudi government's decision to allow American troops onto its soil before the First Gulf War. Israel is seen as a part of the Crusader war on Islam, a colonialist implant of the West designed to subjugate Muslims permanently.

However, Qutb argued that the Western powers in the modern age had cleverly masked their "crusading" spirit and deceived the world into thinking that their intentions were benign, when they actually sought to exploit Muslim peoples.[105] Qutb did not think of exploitation here in Marxist terms as a form of economic exploitation. Instead he believed that through the global reach of the media, a ubiquitous cultural and intellectual assault (via liberalism, secularism and globalization) was being made on the Islamic world. He argued that a number of progressive developments, including new developments in science and technology, had tested Muslim faith in the infallibility of the Koran, while the Western doctrines of nationalism and multiculturalism had falsely persuaded Muslims to integrate with non–Muslims.

But it was the American (and Western) cultural obsession with confining religion to the realm of private conscience (church/state separation) that exercised Qutb. As the ideologue himself explained, he feared "an effort to confine Islam to the emotional and ritual circles, and to bar it from participating in the activity of life, and to check its complete predominance over every human secular activity, a preeminence it earns by virtue of its nature and function."[106] The confrontation between Islam and America was "not over control of territory or economic resource, or for military domination." America was Qutb's foe because of an ideological, not political, disagreement.

At bottom the Islamist grievance of Western oppression is about how the West's cultural universe, its freedoms of expression and belief, its sexual liberalism, its religious tolerance and separation of church and state, impinges on highly traditional Muslim belief and practice. Islamism is less a cry of distress from the poor and oppressed and more an outraged cry from those whose sense of identity has been assailed by the experience of modernity.[107] In essence, as Walid Phares puts it, the global jihadist movement "is not a mere reaction to the foreign policies of industrialised powers, nor is it a collective response by a frustrated Muslim world to American, European, and allied 'aggression.'"[108] And as the Islamists rage against the modern world, there is one minority group above all others that they have in their sights.

Jihad Against the Jews

At this stage, objectors will say that while Islamists do genuinely desire a renewed Caliphate, they still have a fundamental problem with Israel. They often point to "Palestine" as a grievance upon which they base their terrorist activities. Thus in 2008, Bin Laden declared the following in an audio message: "The Palestinian cause has been the main factor that, since my early childhood, fueled my desire, and that of the 19 freemen [Sept. 11 bombers], to stand by the oppressed, and punish the oppressive Jews and their allies."[109] This suggests that the Israeli occupation is indeed a liability and is responsible, even in part, for the terrorist assault on the West.

Undoubtedly, the Islamists do hate Israel's control of the West Bank, the settlements, the checkpoints in the West Bank, the wall and various other Israeli policies. They loathe the fact that in her wars of self-defense, Israel has killed Palestinians and Arabs, some of whom are civilians. But more simply still, they hate Israel as a Jewish state, regardless of its behavior. Yet their hatred stems from something deeper still, namely their deep-seated and longstanding loathing of Jews with its roots in the theological anti–Semitism of the holy texts. It is this deep-seated Judaeophobia that explains why the Islamists, and many non–Islamist Muslims, so profoundly detest everything about the Jewish state, and why they can never come to terms with it. Thus the Islamists hate Israel, not primarily because of what it does but because of what it is—namely a bastion of Jewish, secular and liberal democracy in the heart of the tribal Arab and Muslim world. As we shall see, such hatred has deep roots.

Islamic Anti–Semitism

The early history of Islam is bound up with the battles between Muhammad and the Jewish tribes in the Hejaz. After Muhammad preached his new faith of Islam, he sought to win over local tribes in the Arabian Peninsula, including pagan Arab tribes and the region's Jewish population. But the Jews of Medina rebuffed his advances, in particular an attempt at enforced conversion, leading Muhammed to condemn their outright "disobedience." He would go on to expel the Nadir and Qaynuqa tribes from Medina.

But the most infamous act in Muhammad's dealings with the Jews was his attack on the Qurayza tribe in Medina. After he was informed that this tribe was forming a Meccan alliance against him, Muhammad's forces besieged the Qurayza for 25 days until they were forced into unconditional surrender. Muhammad then refused to show mercy and ordered the beheading of between 600 and 900 Jewish males, then burying their headless bodies in trenches. Women and children were sold into slavery. After the defeat of the Qurayza Jews in 628, Muhammad turned against the Jews of Khaibar, a fertile oasis that contained the largest of the Arabian Peninsula's Jewish communities. The Jews were forced to surrender and those that remained had to pay a humiliating tax or *jizya*. The Jews had been humiliated and were seen as objects of derision and ridicule. This necessitated living in a state of subjugation, or dhimmitude, to their Muslim masters.[110]

Turning to the Koran, one can find many indictments of Jews as a people. One central theme is how the Jews, through their purportedly treacherous and deceitful nature, have manipulated the truth about Islam and persecuted the prophets. According to the Koran, they have rejected Allah's revelations, unjustly killed Jesus (Isa) (Sura 4:155), and ridiculed Muhammad (2:104, 4:46). They are guilty of disobedience (4.46), of misleading others (3:69), of deliberately perverting scripture (2:75), of not acknowledging the faith (9:29), of confounding the truth (3:71), of sorcery (2:102) and of trying to "debar believers from the path of Allah" (3:99). They are said to be blind and deaf to the truth (5:71) and are denounced as "spreaders of war and corruption" (5:64). Elsewhere, they are condemned as senseless people of little faith (2:89) who are guilty of sinfulness and idolatry. In sum, they are said to be "the most hostile in intent towards the believers" (5:82).

Due to these various flaws, which seem to be permanently etched in the Jewish character, the Koran warns that a "grievous scourge" awaits them (58:14–19). They are said to be associated with Satan and consigned to hell (4:60) as fitting punishment for their sins. In a much-quoted verse, Allah has the Jews transformed into apes and swine (2:65). They are also warned that they should long for death if they truly believe they are chosen (62:6). Anti-Semitic references of this sort can also be found in the hadiths, which continually "portray the Jews' hatred and jealousy of Muhammad."[111] In one widely quoted hadith, Muhammad rails against the two monotheistic peoples who have rejected the Islamic revelation: "O Lord, perish the Jews and Christians. They made churches of the graves of their prophets. There shall be no two faiths in Arabia."[112] The negative interpretation of all these verses has been backed up by leading Muslim authorities around the world.

It is argued that the Bible too contains hostile verses against unbelievers and that it mandates violence for those who do not accept divine revelation. Indeed, Islam has no monopoly either on providing scriptural justifications for violence or on producing texts whose literal interpretation runs contrary to liberal values. But there is a big difference too. Today all the Koranic verses just cited, unlike Biblical ones, are taken to offer a divine mandate for anti-Semitic atrocities, in line with the literalism that dominates Islamic thinking. For jihadists, these verses have application in the here and now and cannot be overridden.

But the Koran offers more than a mere litany of abuse towards Jews. Together with Christians, Jews are regarded as "peoples of the book" (Ahl al-Kitab). The Judaeo-Christian prophets were (and are) also prophets in Islam, even being referred to by Arabic names. The Jews are said to have had wisdom and prophethood bestowed upon them, and they are granted scriptures (45:16). Allah resettles them in a sanctified land (10:93), and it is said that those Jews who understand the Koran's revelation will enjoy the blessings of Paradise (27:76–81).

Historically, these more positive elements in Koranic literature allowed Jews (and Christians), unlike polytheists and pagan worshippers, to receive special protection when living under Islamic rule. It is undeniably true that there were periods of Jewish cultural revival under Muslim rule, such as the Golden Age of Andalusia in Spain from the 9th to the 13th century, when great Jewish poets and philosophers thrived. Jews were also allowed to own land, practice their own religion, and engage in the commercial life of the towns in which they lived. Nor were they in this period confined to ghettos as was their experience in Christian Europe. There were also significant periods of prosperity for Palestine's Jews during the era of Ottoman rule.

But such points should not create too rosy a picture of Islamic-Jewish relations. Jews in Muslim lands were subject to dhimmitude, a form of "protection" that came in exchange for subordination to their Muslim masters. This entailed second-class citizenship and a host of humiliating restrictions. Anyone subject to dhimmitude faced many forms of discrimination in their social and economic life.

Dhimmis could not adopt Muslim names, could not prevent anyone converting to Islam and could not inherit anything from a Muslim. A male could not have sexual relations with or marry a Muslim woman even though a Muslim male could take a Jewish wife. They suffered legal discrimination for, as dhimmis, they could not give evidence in court against Muslims. They were subject to religious restrictions, including the law that prevented dhimmis from building a place of worship higher than a mosque and forbidding Muslims from converting to the dhimmi faith. A dhimmi's property would also revert to Muslim ownership on death until it could be proved under Sharia to belong to the dhimmi community. They had to give right of way in the street to Muslims, and their inferior status was reinforced by special payment of the *jiyza* (poll tax). In addition, they were forced to wear distinctive clothing such as a yellow badge in order to further separate themselves from their Muslim masters and in order to emphasize their inferior status. They were generally considered impure and were segregated from the majority Muslim community.

Jews were subject to periodic massacres across the Muslim world, from Morocco to Yemen and from Algeria to Iraq. Jewish life was also marked by ghettoization, occasional forced conversion, stone-throwing and the arbitrary confiscation of goods. Yet despite this, Bernard Lewis is right to say that in comparison to their experience in Christian Europe, Jews fared better under Muslim rule. Under this rule, he adds, "most of the characteristic and distinctive features of Christian antisemitism were absent."[113] There was no Islamic Holocaust or Inquisition, though it is equally true that there was no Islamic emancipation.

With such a long history of anti–Jewish prejudice in the Muslim world, and with many hostile messages in the Koran, it is hardly surprising that anti–Semitism has been such a powerful feature of Islamist writings. Thus Ibn Taymiyyah used verses from the Koran that stigmatized Christians and Jews to defame them further. He argued that the Jews' rejection of Muslim prophets, specifically their refusal to acknowledge Muhammad and their treatment of Jesus, invalidated their status as dhimmis. He insisted that the strictures on Jews regarding their clothing and religious practice be strictly enforced. He also issued a *fatwa* allowing Muslims to curse and insult Jewish holy books.[114]

In *Kitaab at-Tawheed*, Wahhab venomously denounced Jews for their alleged betrayal of Muhammad and their "idol worship." He regarded both Christians and Jews as "sorcerers" who believed in devil worship. He accused both groups of turning the graves of their prophets into places of worship and warned Muslims not to repeat such idolatry. He concluded: "The ways of the people of the book are condemned as those of polytheists." A key theme in Wahhab's writings is the danger of Jewish unbelief, which is the inevitable result of their untrustworthiness and "deceitful" nature.[115]

The idea of the Jew as treacherous and untrustworthy resonated with Islamists who were anxious to rationalize the humbling defeat of Muslim powers in the twentieth century. Using verses from the Koran, they became obsessed with an "archetypal Jew" whose allegedly perfidious, deceitful and corrupting nature threatened the very fabric of Islam. But mixed in with these traditional Islamic themes was a twentieth century European import: the fear of a Jewish conspiracy to take over the world. The combination of the two strains of anti–Semitism produced an intoxicating form of race hatred.

Mawdudi said that Jews (and Christians) had "corrupted their faith" since they had "distorted certain basic components of that [true] faith (i.e., Islam)."[116] He accused them of showing "hostility to Prophets" with events in the life of Jesus constituting "a shameful chapter in the record of the Jewish nation." In essence, he regurgitated the ancient charge of deicide against the Jews. As a result of that crime, Mawdudi said that God had "no alternative but to lay His curse and damnation on that nation."[117]

For Qutb, the sole aim of Jews (and other unbelievers) was "to destroy or cause harm to the Muslims." As such, they could only ever be described as the "enemy" of Muslims worldwide. This enmity was traced back to the original holy texts that purported to explain the "eternal" conflict between Muslims and (especially) Jews. For Qutb, the Jewish "original sin" was to reject the Muhammadan revelation, something that revealed their "wickedness," "deception," "mercilessness" and "moral shirking." "The Jews" he wrote, "perpetrated the worst sort of disobedience [against Allah], behaving in the most disgustingly aggressive manner and sinning in the ugliest way."[118] This essentialist interpretation locates the source of hatred in the perceived negative traits of the "Jewish character."

But it was not enough for Qutb to explain Jewish rejectionism in this way, for he had to show how their perfidy in the modern world was an ongoing threat to Muslim civilization. He blamed Jews for "the doctrine of atheistical materialism" embodied in Marxism, the Freudian doctrine of "animalistic sexuality" and Durkheim's rationalistic sociology. All these "subversive" and "heretical" influences not only contributed to the decline of religious belief but also undermined the Muslim attachment to authentic Islam.[119] Jewish and Christian societies are "jahili societies." They are in this state because "their forms of worship, their customs and manners are derived from their false and distorted beliefs ... because their institutions and their laws are not based on submission to God alone. They neither accept the rule of God nor do they consider God's commandments as the only valid basis of all laws; on the contrary, they have established assemblies of men which have absolute power to legislate laws, thus usurping the right which belongs to God alone."[120] Clearly, the strong Judaeo-Christian respect for democracy is a target for Qutb's invective here.

Qutb believed that Jews have continued to perpetrate unbelief, a rejection of Muhammad's revelation, which is a threat to Muslim life if it spreads. But again Qutb gives this phenomenon an essentialist twist. The Jewish insistence on "pagan" worship reflects "wickedness" and "deception," character traits that are seen as part of a perennial Jewish nature: "These features have accompanied the Jews in every generation and remain typical of their behaviour even today."[121]

For Qutb, the contemporary battle between Muslims and Jews is simply an updated account of Muhammad's struggle with Jews in the 7th century. Just as Muhammad had expelled or killed Jews in the Arabian Peninsula, so too Qutb advocates a draconian and violent response to the perceived threat from Jewry. Muslims, he wrote, must "let Allah bring down upon the Jews people who will mete out to them the worst kind of punishment." He adds: "Allah brought Hitler to rule over them."[122]

Qutb's virulent anti–Semitism reflected the deeper strains of prejudice animating the Muslim Brotherhood. In the 1930s the Brotherhood advocated *jihad* against the British and the Jews in defiance of the government in Egypt. Opposition to partition proposals in Palestine was manifested in a Nazi-style anti–Jewish boycott campaign and false rumors that the Jews were plotting to destroy holy places in Jerusalem.[123] In the Brotherhood's newspaper *al-Nadhir*, headlines appeared that blamed Egyptian Jews for the country's multitude of ills. The names and addresses of Jewish businesses were published in the paper's columns, and passages were quoted from the Koran that spoke of the inferiority of the Jews.[124] At the same time, from the 1930s, "Hassan al Banna and many of the first members of the Brotherhood offered their services to the Abwehr (German intelligence). Apart from their resistance to the British presence in Egypt, Hassan Al Banna's commitment was a result of a real admiration for Hitler and the Nazi regime." During the war, the Muslim Brotherhood distributed Arab translations of *Mein Kampf* as well as the *Protocols*.

One prominent member of the Brotherhood, Haj Amin al-Husseini, grand mufti of Jerusalem, was an even more enthusiastic Nazi supporter and sympathizer. In the 1930s he had formed a youth wing of the Brotherhood (the Nazi Scouts), whose outfit included "Hitler Youth style shorts and leather belts."[125] He embraced Nazi race theory fervently in the prewar years. Husseini then spent much of the war years in Berlin, from where he helped inspire a pro–Nazi coup in Iraq and gathered thousands of Bosnian Muslims to kill Jews in Yugoslavia. His speeches on Berlin Radio were essentially exhortations to kill as many Jews as possible. Husseini continued to be supported by many Palestinians even after his war crimes (see Chapter 6) were revealed to the world.

After the Second World War, the Brotherhood led an anti–Semitic campaign against the Jews of Cairo and denounced America for its anti–Zionist press and cinema, which were believed to be undermining Islam. It looks as if this campaign had some effect for in 1948, following the establishment of the state of Israel, there were riots in Cairo that killed dozens of Jews. In October 1956, at a time when some leading Nazi ideologies had been welcomed into Arab countries, the organ of the Muslim Brotherhood in Damascus declared: "It must not be forgotten that in contrast to Europe, Hitler occupies a respected place in the Arab world. His name arouses in the hearts of our movement sympathy and enthusiasm."[126]

The current spiritual leader of the Muslim Brotherhood, Sheikh Qaradawi, whose views are regularly aired on Al Jazeera, told an audience in 1989, "On the hour of judgment, Muslims will fight the Jews and kill them."[127] The man, described by some as the "mufti of television," has also said, "There is no dialogue between us and the Jews except for the sword and the rifle."[128]

Not surprisingly, the Brotherhood's hostility to Jews has strongly influenced its political activities. Sadat's peace with Israel was seen as a deliberate assault on Islam itself, and for one fundamentalist, Umar al-Tilmisani, it constituted "the most dangerous cancer eating away at all the life cells in our bodies." In graphic terms Tilmisani depicted how normalization of relations with Israel would destroy Islam from within, as the Jews would bring with them "all manner of moral evils such as cabarets, drinking of liquor and white slavery" and would "spread their poison among the youth." The Jews, he went on, "fight all varieties of Islamic tradition."[129] Another Egyptian scholar expressed the same paranoid fear of Jews undermining Muslim life. Abd al-Halim Mahmoud wrote in his book *Holy War and Victory*: "Among Satan's friends—indeed his best friends in our age—are the Jews. They have laid down a plan for undermining humanity, religiously and ethically. They have begun to work to implement this plan with their money and their propaganda."[130]

In the Middle East today, Hamas (the Palestinian branch of the Muslim Brotherhood) is often proclaimed as a force of resistance to Israeli occupation. Beneath the veneer of political dissidence, however, is the unmistakable echo of paranoid anti–Semitism, which is freely interspersed with a venomous hatred of Israel. Hamas regards Palestine as being part of the *dar as Islam* and, as such, a land that can never remain under permanent non–Muslim rule. They also believe that the creation of the state of Israel has violated a cardinal principle of Islamic law, namely that for the first time, the Jews no longer have dhimmi status and have instead attained sovereignty over other Muslims. For Hamas, like other Islamists, Israel also remains just another potent example of the erosion of Muslim power at the hands of the West, and further evidence of Jewish "deceit" and "treachery."

The opening words of Hamas' first leaflet from January 1988 gave a sign of how virulent their racism would be. It denounced Jews as "brothers of the apes, assassins of the prophets, bloodsuckers, warmongers," and continued: "Only Islam can break the Jews and destroy their dream."¹³¹ The Hamas Charter, the organization's foundational document, could have been written by the Nazis, such was (and is) its venomous tirade against international Jewry. It spoke of how the Jews "took control of the world media, news agencies, the press, publishing houses, broadcasting stations," used their money, and "stirred revolutions in various parts of the world with the purpose of achieving their interests and reaping the fruit therein." It went on: "There was no war that broke out anywhere without their [Jews'] fingerprints on it." It offered a diatribe against "limitless" Zionist "imperialism" and claimed that the Zionists aspired to "expand from the Nile to the Euphrates."

Hamas today rejects any notion of a long-term compromise settlement that might create a just, viable Palestinian state. Section 13 of the Hamas charter denounces "the so-called peaceful solutions ... to resolve the Palestinian problem" for "renouncing any part of Palestine means renouncing part of the religion." Put simply, Jewish sovereignty over even one square inch of Israel is unacceptable. Article 22 states that with their money, the Jews "took control of the world media, news agencies, the press, publishing houses, broadcasting stations, and others." With this financial clout "they stirred revolutions in various parts of the world with the purpose of achieving their interests and reaping the fruit therein."

Hamas accuses Jews of being "behind the French Revolution, the Communist revolution and most of the revolutions we heard and hear about, here and there." Indeed, they allege that there "was no war that broke out anywhere without their [Jews'] fingerprints on it." Where Zionism is condemned, the specter of the world Jewish conspiracy is raised. In article 32, the "Zionist plan" is described as "limitless." For once the Zionists have Palestine, they "aspire to expand from the Nile to the Euphrates. When they will have digested the region they overtook, they will aspire to further expansion, and so on."

The ideological basis for this belief is *The Protocols of the Elders of Zion*, the notorious anti–Semitic forgery that has proliferated throughout the Arab and Muslim world in the twentieth century. This is nothing but a vicious charter of hate that embodies the more familiar conspiracy theories involving world Jewry: that they control the media, foment war in their own interests and seek global power by manipulation.¹³²

The statements of Hamas representatives provide the firmest evidence that their rejection of Israel is ultimately rooted in a theological hatred of Jewry: "The Jewish faith does not wish for peace nor stability, since it is a faith that is based on murder: 'I kill, therefore I am' ... Israel is based only on blood and murder in order to exist, and it will disappear, with Allah's will, through blood and Shahids [martyrs]."¹³³ Elsewhere we find statements such as these: "The Jews killed the prophets ... slaughtered the innocent ... imprisoned our pious.... NO PEACE WITH THE MURDERERS."¹³⁴ In other statements Jews are described as a "cancerous lump ... in the heart of the Arab nation."¹³⁵

Like Egypt and its Islamist allies within Palestinian politics, Saudi Arabia has been at the forefront of a campaign to propagate the most virulent strains of Islamism and anti–Semitism. WAMY, a Saudi non-governmental organization that helps to spread Wahhabism around the world, has produced numerous publications with venomous anti–Semitic and anti–Christian messages.

In a book entitled *Tawjihat Islamiya (Islamic Views)* they make the following appeal: "Teach our children to love taking revenge on the Jews and the oppressors, and teach them that our youngsters will liberate Palestine and Al-Quds [Jerusalem] when they go back to

Islam and make jihad for the sake of Allah."[136] The Saudis have helped to finance thousands of schools whose curricula rigidly follow Wahhabi teachings. According to a recent study by Freedom House, the textbooks used in these Saudi schools actively promote a hatred of non–Muslims. They have commanded Muslims to hate "Christians, Jews, 'polytheists' and other unbelievers"; they have also taught notorious anti–Semitic forgeries such as *The Protocols of the Elders of Zion* as historical fact.

Throughout the 1980s and 1990s, Wahhabi clerics preached a message of violent hatred for other faiths. They condemned Judaism and Christianity as illegitimate, polytheistic religions that were incompatible with Islam. Jews were also described as "the brothers of pigs and monkeys." One prominent Wahhabi cleric, Sheikh al-Auda, called for a jihad to "bring about the certain fall of the West."[137] When Bin Laden launched his crusade against Jews and Crusaders in 1998, he had clearly been influenced by a generation of Saudi clerics. His writings over the years reveal a barely disguised contempt for Jews and Judaism. Take this statement, which smacks of the Qutbian essentialism we saw earlier: "What will explain to you who the Jews are? The Jews are those who slandered the Creator, so how do you think they deal with God's creation? They killed the Prophets and broke their promises.... These Jews are masters of usury and leaders in treachery. They will leave you nothing in this world or the next.... These Jews believe as part of their religion that people are their slaves, and whoever denies their religion deserves to be killed."[138] Elsewhere he has warned Muslims "to be very wary and careful about befriending Jews and Christians" and has said that uttering one word to them is equivalent to apostasy.[139]

Bin Laden shared the views of other Islamists that the Jews were engaged in a diabolical plot to undermine Islam and gain global power at the expense of Muslims. Thus Bin Laden alleged that Jews controlled the White House, the American economy and the American media generally, and that Israel was "behind all the attacks on states in the Islamic world."[140] This latter comment was made after a U.S.–British air attack on Iraq in 1998.

As early as 1994 Bin Laden described Israel as "the current Jewish enemy" that was "a corrupter of religion and the world."[141] In his 2002 "Letter to the American People," he issued a series of diatribes against the American way of life, the country's constitution and its economic system. But he also lambasts the Jews for being exploitative puppet masters of the country: "In all its different forms and guises, the Jews have taken control of your economy, through which they have taken control of your media and now control all aspects of your life, making you their servants and achieving their aims at your expense." In 1998 he had given vent to a similarly racist conspiracy theory when he claimed that the Jews had "the upper hand" in America's sensitive ministries, such as the CIA and the Ministry of Defense.[142] Such remarks do not express political disagreement but reflect instead a Manichean worldview, one where the role of devil incarnate has been taken by world Jewry.

Other leading figures in al-Qaeda share this fathomless and obsessive hatred of Jews. Ayman al-Zawahiri, who took command of al-Qaeda after Bin Laden's death, once denounced Jewish security experts in Russia who conducted the war against the Chechens while saying that in the United States, Jews were "in control of the media and propaganda tools."[143] When Zacarias Moussaoui, the man suspected of being 9/11's "twentieth hijacker," appeared in court, he openly vented his wrath on Jews. He described himself as "openly hostile to the Jews and the United States" and said that the Jews had "incurred the curse of Allah and his wrath at those he transformed into monkeys and swine."[144]

Shiite fundamentalism, for all its ideological differences with Sunni extremism, has not been immune to the most virulent strains of anti–Semitism. The idea that Jews posed a threat to the Islamic nation and faith is central to some of Ayatollah Khomeini's writings. In 1962 he warned that the independence of Iran and its economy was "about to be taken over by Zionists" who would drive the country "to complete bankruptcy."[145]

In his book *Islamic Government*, Khomeini wrote, "Since its inception Islam was afflicted with the Jews who distorted the reputation of Islam by assaulting and slandering it, and this has continued to our present day."[146] The Jews, he added, were "opposed to the very foundations of Islam" and wished "to establish Jewish domination throughout the world." Muslim apathy would, he warned, "allow a Jew to rule over us one day."[147] He added: "From the very beginning, the historical movement of Islam has had to contend with the Jews, for it was they who first established anti–Islamic propaganda and engaged in various stratagems, and as you can see, this activity continues down to the present."[148] Not surprisingly, the *Protocols* have influenced the thinking of the regime towards Zionism and world Jewry.[149] Since the 1979 Islamic Revolution, Jews have been treated as dhimmis, despite the Ayatollah's *fatwa* granting the community protection. The revolution "ushered in a steadily intensifying reign of terror. Jewish businesses became the targets of vandalism and boycotts; Jews were physically harassed and attacked on the streets."[150]

Today, Iran continues to be plagued by a virulent anti–Semitism. The country's Jews have been accused of past collusion with the Shah and of colluding today with Israel and the United States to harm Iranian interests. As in Egypt, copies of *The Protocols of the Elders of Zion* are widely available in Iran and purportedly lend credence to the more outrageous accusations of Jewish perfidy and cunning. The regime of Mahmoud Ahmadinejad has, in recent years, earned international opprobrium by denying the Holocaust and organizing a Holocaust denial conference. The language used towards Israel is unsurprisingly vitriolic. It has long been the official policy of the Iranian regime to call for Israel's destruction. Ali Khamenei has described Israel as a "cancerous tumour" that must be removed, and his refrain "Death to Israel" is repeated endlessly.[151] Former President Ahmadinejad has extended the microbiological analogy by calling Israel a "filthy germ."[152] In 2005, in a speech to a conference called "A World Without Zionism," he addressed Ayatollah Khomeini with these words: "O dear Imam. You said the Zionist Regime is a usurper, an illegitimate regime and a cancerous tumour that should be wiped off the map. I should say that your illuminating remark and cause are going to come true today."[153] One of Iran's alleged moderates, Akbar Rafsanjani, once extolled the advantages of an Islamic nuclear attack on Israel. "Application of an atomic bomb would not leave anything in Israel but the same thing would just produce damages in the Muslim world," he said.[154] Another reformer, President Khatami, has described Israel as a "parasite in the heart of the Muslim world."[155]

Today the Lebanese-based Hezbollah remains a potent Iranian client organization. It is committed to the core ideological principle underlying the Iranian revolution, namely that of *Vilayat-i Faqih* (rule of the jurisprudent) and explains why Nasrallah refers to himself as Khomeini's representative in the Levant.[156] Hezbollah has stated its anti–Zionist position most unequivocally. In its 1985 manifesto, it talks of how its struggle with the "Zionist entity" will end "only when this entity is obliterated," adding: "We recognize no treaty with it, no ceasefire and no peace agreements, whether separate or consolidated."[157]

But this stems from a prior hatred of Jews. The group has regularly disseminated its virulent anti–Semitism on their TV station, Al Manar, which is viewed by millions of people across the Muslim world. In 2003 Al Manar broadcast a vicious anti–Semitic series called *Ash-Shatat* ("*The Diaspora*") that depicted hook-nosed Jews purporting to plot the takeover of the world. There are constant references to *The Protocols of the Elders of Zion*, while Jews are shown as violent, treacherous, manipulative and evil, the very character traits in Qutb's writings. In one horrific scene, an actor, playing an archetypal Jew, kidnaps and then kills an innocent Christian child before using the child's blood to make matzah. This is an update of the infamous blood libel that played such a prominent role in medieval Christian anti–Semitism.

In any case, Hezbollah's aim is not just to "liberate" Palestine but also to annihilate world Jewry. Their leader, Hassan Nasrallah, stated this brazenly enough when he said: "If Jews all gather in Israel, it will save us the trouble of going after them worldwide."[158] He is on record as saying that Jews "invented the legend of the Holocaust" while also lauding some of the world's leading Holocaust deniers, including David Irving. Irving was praised for having "denied the existence of gas chambers."[159] Nasrallah has been quoted as saying: "If we searched the entire world for a person more cowardly, despicable, weak and feeble in psyche, mind, ideology and religion, we would not find anyone like the Jew. Notice, I do not say the Israeli."[160]

Some would argue that such levels of profound anti–Semitism, even if they long predate Israel's creation, must be seen within the context of the Arab-Israeli conflict. But that argument is belied by one important fact: a profound hatred of Jews persists even in those nation-states that have formal peace agreements with the Jewish state.

In 1979 Egypt and Israel concluded a peace treaty that saw the return later of the Sinai Peninsula. But in Egypt, the virus of Jew hatred persists with a force and intensity quite unlike anything else in the country. Cartoons that appear in the country's press, mirroring those produced in other Arab countries, engage in the wholesale demonization of Jews in a manner worthy only of Nazi Germany.

The Jew is depicted as a malevolent, Satanic figure whose inherent wickedness and immorality corrupts every society on earth. Jews are frequently depicted as animals, thus suggesting that they are subhuman creatures worthy of extermination. Such zoomorphism, where Jews are likened to spiders, vampires and octopuses, is one of the crudest and most powerful means to dehumanize Jewry. The medieval blood libel, the notion that Jews use the blood of Gentiles to bake matzah, is another regular feature of such cartoons. Many cartoonists also engage in outright Holocaust denial, charging the Zionists with fabricating stories of massacres in order to extort money from the postwar German government.

However, other columnists are less convinced by denial and prefer to laud Hitler for his crimes, only cursing him because his genocide did not succeed in killing all the Jews. One columnist in a leading Egyptian newspaper has described Jews as the "most vile criminals on the face of the earth," a sentiment that would resonate with a vast number of Egyptians.[161]

International Jewry is also charged with engaging in a secret plot to control and dominate the world and seize control of its media, the global banking system and its cultural life. The popularity of *The Protocols of the Elders of Zion*, seen as the key document for exposing a secret Jewish conspiracy for global domination, goes some way to explaining this. They are charged with using this domination, often by proxy, in order to defame the Muslim world and retard its socio-economic development. They are also accused of deceit, treachery, trickery and corruption, in line with what is perceived to be their perennial character, and of inventing past persecution to justify extortion and control.

As should by now be clear, this draws upon theological sources that depict the Jew in starkly negative terms. Jews are accused of controlling the world and using their evil inclination to spread harmful influences, such as prostitution, AIDS and drugs. The familiar motifs of Jews as hooked-nosed crooks, liars and manipulators are ubiquitous in the Egyptian press. Quite simply, the country has become a "world leader in disseminating hatred of Jews."[162] And this country was the first to have a peace treaty with Israel!

Outside of the Middle East and thousands of miles from the conflict, conspiratorial anti–Semitism finds ready acceptance in Muslim nations. In Pakistan, newspapers often explain the country's woes by some reference to Jewish control and influence. Thus in 2010 when Pakistan's cricketers were accused of involvement in a match-fixing scandal, a Pakistani newspaper alleged that "Indian and Jewish lobbies" in the UK had trapped the team in order to defame the country. A year earlier, another Urdu magazine alleged that a "dangerous Jewish conspiracy" was responsible for the global campaign to eradicate polio. Right-wing sections of the Pakistani intelligentsia blamed the Mumbai attacks on the work of fanatical Zionists. Indeed, even bird flu has been blamed on a Jewish conspiracy.[163]

There is a widespread belief in Pakistan that 9/11 was a carefully executed Mossad job that has been wrongly blamed on Muslims. Even Facebook has been described as part of a Jewish conspiracy that allows Israel to recruit spies from Muslim countries. As Gabriel Schoenfeld explains, Pakistan's ubiquitous anti–Semitism is the product of an educational system dominated by hardline Sunni clerics who have taken advantage of Saudi funding to construct a maze of madrassahs. The fundamentalist ideology taught in such schools combines anti-Western ideas with anti–Semitism and contempt for Shiite Muslims.[164]

Malaysia is one of a number of Muslim majority nations that does not permit Israelis to enter the country. Mahathir Muhammed, a former prime minister of Malaysia and a leading advocate of economic modernization, raised a few eyebrows in 1997 when he blamed Jews for the collapse of his country's currency. But he had spent decades making virulently racist statements about the alleged designs of international Jewry. In one speech to the Organization of Islamic Conference, he declared, "Jews rule this world by proxy" as "they get others to fight and die for them."[165]

What was even worse was that far from decrying the ugly anti–Semitism on display, Muhammed was given a standing ovation, a response that he might well have expected. On another occasion, he declared that he was "glad to be labelled antisemitic." He said: "How can I be otherwise, when the Jews who so often talk of the horrors they suffered during the Holocaust show the same Nazi cruelty and hard-heartedness towards not just their enemies but even towards their allies should any try to stop the senseless killing of their Palestinian enemies."[166]

In sum, the antipathy to Jews throughout the Arab and Islamic world has what Bernard Lewis calls "an obsessive character." No longer are the Jews merely a despised minority waiting to receive their comeuppance at the hands of Muslims. They are now a "major threat overshadowing the whole Islamic world," and the Jew is a "figure of cosmic evil."[167] This discourse assigns to the Jews a truly demonic quality whereby they plot, scheme and manipulate their way to world domination. Apologists for this pathological frenzy claim that the real antipathy is for Zionists and Israelis, not Jews. It is Israel's purported crimes that engender such hostility. But in the Arab and Islamic literature, it is the Jew, not the Israeli or Zionist, who comes under attack. And there is a dearth of countervailing literature to help set the record straight.

For the Islamists in particular, Israel is charged with violating a fundamental tenet of Islamic law, namely that the Jew deserves at most protected and submissive status as a *dhimmi* and cannot attain independent status or sovereignty. As Raphael Israeli observes: "Their [the Jews'] claim to a separate political existence amounts to an insult, as it were, to the holy tradition of Islam."[168] As Robert Wistrich puts it, the Jews are seen as an "insidious and permanent enemy," with the battle against them part of a wider battle to "throw back the diabolical conspiracy sapping the foundations of the true faith." In this fight, "no compromise is possible."[169]

That such a nation should come into existence and then survive repeated onslaught by the forces of Islam is a further grievous blow. It also points to the peculiar crisis that besets modern Islam, a religion once in the ascendant and now surpassed by Western forces, epitomized by the *dhimmi* Jew. As Gove puts it, there is one question that Arab subjects pose that Arab leaders do not like to hear: "How can the peoples of Allah have been allowed to fall so far behind those who were their second class subjects for so much of history?"[170]

Negotiated Peace Would Not Remove the Terror Threat

Finally, it could be argued that a resolution of the Israeli-Palestinian conflict might reduce al-Qaeda's ability to recruit Muslims to its cause. This was certainly the position advocated by Tony Blair in the aftermath of 9/11 as he invited Yasser Arafat to London and pledged British support for a Palestinian state. At first glance, this is an odd argument to make, because it assumes that Palestinians form a large percentage of al-Qaeda's recruits. But as the Jerusalem Centre for Public Affairs points out, the nationalities recruited for the cause come from other conflict areas, each with their own discernible, localized grievances: "Kashmir, western China, Uzbekistan, Saudi Arabia, Chechnya, Iraq, and Morocco."[171] Nor should it be forgotten that of the 19 hijackers, 15 were Saudi. If the continuation of the conflict were a real spur to al-Qaeda's recruitment and popularity among Muslims, surely the Palestinians would be much more prominent among its ranks. Of course, it could be argued that other Muslims, motivated by concern for the plight of Palestinians, are being recruited to the jihadist cause. It is these Muslims, so the argument goes, that we need to be concerned about. They have adopted a militant posture because their co-religionists are perceived to be suffering injustice; they are the ones that al-Qaeda exploits.

This argument is already flawed because it assumes that terrorism is the only option available to deal with grievances, and it also ignores the point made earlier about how jihadists are recruited by black and white, distorted pictures of Western (and Israeli) infamy. There are further flaws in this argument. If it were true that creating a Palestinian state would reduce the flow of recruits to the jihadist cause, would we not have seen a reduction in terror prior to 2001? After all, during the 1990s, Israel made a concerted effort to make peace with the PLO through the Oslo Accords, Oslo II, the Wye agreement and the talks at Camp David and Taba.

Yet throughout the 1990s, al-Qaeda instigated a series of devastating attacks against Western targets, including the first attack on the World Trade Center in 1993, the bombings of the U.S. embassies in 1998 in Kenya and Tanzania and the attack on the USS *Cole* in 2000.

Al-Qaeda was also busy planning the successful attack on the World Trade Center and other targets in 2001. Concessions did not diminish the global terror threat one iota. If anything, there was a correlation between Israeli peacemaking and increased global jihadism.

Of course, this is not an argument against Israel's many (and bold) efforts at making peace with her neighbors. Successfully resolving the conflict would be a tremendous boon for the region, for Israel and for those neighbors who felt able to reconcile themselves to a Jewish state. But it would not bring a change of heart to the al-Qaeda leadership or to any of the violent Islamist groups in the Middle East. As proof, one need only remind oneself about the fate of Anwar Sadat in 1981.

When the Islamists talk of Palestine, they are not thinking about a purely localized grievance that might be resolved by changing Israel's foreign policy. Such a view of Islamist ambitions would be hopelessly reductionist. Their grievance is the existence of Israel, seen as a barrier to a restored Caliphate, and an un-Islamic intrusion in the Muslim world. Thus were Israel to be forced to cede territory to the jihadists, as part of some grand bargain, this would not alter their overall aim, methods or strategy. They would remain fundamentally unappeasable.

To think otherwise is to commit the same egregious fallacy as the interwar appeasers when they assumed that Hitler was merely a disgruntled nationalist seeking redress for the Versailles treaty. Hitler was a revolutionary who sought to create a pan–German European empire purged of Jews, Bolsheviks and non–Nazi influences. He did not seek co-existence with his enemies and interpreted their peace overtures as evidence of weakness and lack of resolve. Today's Islamists are no different. They too are fundamentalist totalitarians fighting a relentless war against civilization. They too demand an empire, albeit an Islamic one that would be purified by the emasculation of Western influence. They too interpret Western actions as evidence of their enemies' irresolute and ineffectual nature.

That is why Israel's previous territorial retreats, some the result of Western pressure and some of Israel's own making, have been met with more, not less, terror. Hezbollah interpreted Israel's withdrawal from Lebanon as evidence of political exhaustion and within a decade had assumed a position of dominance in the country. Hamas viewed Israel's Gaza pullout in much the same manner, paving the way for a decade-long terror assault against the citizens of southern Israel. Such evidence of Israeli weakening has an intoxicating effect on Islamist radicals, empowering extremists and weakening moderates, both in the immediate region and beyond. As Michael Gove puts it so aptly, Israeli territorial concessions in the eyes of radicalized Muslims represent "a vindication of violence, a reward for those who issued threats, and a promise that future threats would yield yet greater rewards." In their worldview, such concessions from Israel represent "a retreat, won by force of arms, secured by the persistence of terror, proof of the ultimate weakness of the enemy and an incentive to press yet harder against a buckling opponent."[172] Worse, by making this false linkage between Israel and the war on terror, the West is signaling its preparedness to sink an ally while risking enflaming the jihadists even further. This "Czechoslovakia strategy" has distinctly immoral undertones.

Placing the emphasis for defeating Islamism on Israeli shoulders is blind and self-defeating. It shows at best profound ignorance, at worst willful denial, of the Islamists' true aspirations. It is political self-deception in its most glaring form. Western elites are effectively pretending that if, contrary to the available evidence, Islamist fanatics are liberal-minded people animated by identifiable grievances, then the West can perhaps come to terms with them after all.¹⁷³ Unfortunately, we must confront enemies as they are, not as we would wish them to be.

Ultimately, it is only by taking the battle to radical Islamic groups, denying them access to resources and funding, destroying their safe havens, capturing their leaders and tackling their ideology on multiple levels, that the West may eventually prevail. But equally, it is only by spearheading efforts at genuine democratization in the Arab world, and thereby tackling the endemic misery, corruption and tyranny on which an Islamist opposition thrives, that sound alternatives to jihadism can emerge. Moderate forces throughout the Islamic world need to be supported by the West, rather than "nonviolent" jihadists like the Muslim Brotherhood. But in this momentous battle, Israel, the region's only true democracy, remains a vital ally.

PART II: CHANGING THE NARRATIVE

5. The Jewish Historical, Legal and Moral Right to the State of Israel

The first half of this book has tried to show the main themes in the diplomatic assault on Israel. It is alleged that at the heart of the Middle East's many woes are a number of immoral Israeli policies and actions: the illegal occupation of Palestinian land; a grasping, thieving settlement policy; genocide, ethnic cleansing and apartheid towards Arabs; the manipulation of Western governments through the strong-arm tactics of the pro–Israel lobby and the encouragement of a global Islamist terror war. Together, these insidious charges form part of a relentless propaganda war which has been winning hearts and minds in the West. But it is not enough to demolish the specific lines of criticism leveled at Israel or to reveal the bankruptcy of the demonizers. It is also vital to offer a new narrative that offers an unapologetic assertion of Jewish historical, moral and legal rights to the state of Israel. Such an exercise is not designed to negate the Palestinian right to self-determination, a right that remains qualified by the Palestinians' willingness to live in peace alongside Israel. Instead it aims to undermine a key plank of the Palestinian propaganda war against Israel. Once this war is ended, the Palestinians will be better able to make historic compromises for peace, ones that may enable them to achieve self-determination and prosperity.

Before explaining the historical, moral and legal rights of the Jewish people to Israel, it is worth identifying how Israel's critics tend to explain this conflict historically. Their narrative might run something like this:

The Received Wisdom

Palestine existed for centuries as a peaceful independent state with an indigenous Arab population. Its ethnic people, the Palestinian people, possessing their own language, religion and culture, were the area's original inhabitants (at least for two millennia) with an unbroken connection to the land. At Palestine's heart was Jerusalem, a spiritual city with an Islamic character, which formed an integral part of this Arab nation. By contrast to the Palestinians, with their permanent attachment to this land, the Jews were a scattered or dispersed people who, since 2,000 years ago, had lost any physical or geographical connection with Palestine. Indeed it is not clear they were ever a collective nation, as opposed to people living in various countries who shared a common religion.

The Zionist movement was formed at the end of the nineteenth century, influenced by contemporary European nationalists. The Zionists sought a national refuge for Jews fleeing persecution and believed that Palestine was an empty land in need of a population. It was deemed to be a land without a people for a people without a land. In Palestine, as elsewhere in the Arab world, Jew and Arab had lived side by side in peace, but the aspirations of the Zionists would come to change all that. They cared little for the Arabs, who were held in contempt.

The Arab-Israeli conflict started after World War I. As a result of the imperialistic Balfour Declaration in 1917 and the subsequent political maneuvering of the colonial powers, the whole of Palestine was illegally taken away from its rightful Arab owners. This reflected the duplicitous bargaining of the Allied powers as they made successive and contradictory promises to the Arabs and the Zionists. The Arabs were denied self-determination as the British encouraged a Zionist "invasion" of Jews from Germany and other European countries. Gradually the Jews began to displace the peaceful native Arab inhabitants from the 1920s onwards. Zionist leaders, such as Ben-Gurion, formulated plans for the expulsion of the Arab population and for the creation of a Jewish-only enclave.

The Arabs naturally sought to revolt against British plans to set up Jewish overlordship of their country. Extreme statements by right-wing Zionists led to the Arab revolt of 1929 while Britain's provocative immigration policies led to a general strike in 1936 and the crushing of Palestinian power by the British authorities. The violence led to recommendations of partition so that Palestine could be divided between the Arabs and Jews. But as the Jews owned only 5 percent of the land, the Arabs naturally rejected any such proposal. Similarly, in 1947 the General Assembly recommended partition into a Jewish and Arab state. But the Jews were given the most fertile land on the coastal plain and the proposed Jewish state would be bigger than the Arab one, despite Jews' forming a mere one-third of the population and owning less than one-tenth of the land. The Arab leaders were simply rejecting what would have been an unjust division of their land.

In 1948 Israel was created. This came about because of two main factors. The first was Western guilt over inaction during the Holocaust, when 6 million Jews were murdered by the Nazis. The Palestinians effectively paid the price for this mass slaughter of Jews, something that their leaders had nothing to do with. In particular, the United States was the prime force in the West behind the creation and survival of the Jewish state. The second was the bloody campaign of terrorism carried out by Jewish groups like Irgun and Lehi, targeting both British soldiers as well as Arab civilians.

During the war of 1948, the Jewish state drove out the majority of Palestine's Arab inhabitants, turning them into stateless refugees. In one particularly brutal episode, Jewish fighters carried out a massacre of hundreds of Arab men, women and children at the village of Deir Yassin. Ever since 1948, Israel has defied international law by refusing to allow these refugees to return to their homes. These refugees now number some 5–6 million people who survive on food handouts from the UN. Instead of giving them the humanitarian option of return, Israel effectively forced them into Bantustan-style refugee camps in Lebanon, Syria and the West Bank. While she denied the right of return to Palestinian Arabs, she offered this unlimited right to Jews around the world. This meant in effect a two-tier, apartheid system of rights. Worse, it meant that Arab homes and villages would be turned over to the Jews, forever preventing any chance for an Arab return.

In 1967 Israel defeated several of her neighbors in the Six-Day War, which saw the country's borders expand fourfold. She occupied the Sinai desert, the West Bank, the Golan Heights and Gaza, a clear form of aggression against her weaker neighbors. The UN did not take long to decide that Israel had to return these territories to their rightful neighbors, via resolution 242. From 1967 to this day, Israel has simply ignored this resolution, and many others. During the 1970s, she has since engaged in colonization policies by planting hundreds of thousands of illegal settlers in those territories, a violation of the Third Geneva Convention. These settlers are supported by the Israeli government because they share the same messianic view of Israel as a land for God's chosen people. Subsequent wars of 1973 against Egypt and Syria, and Lebanon in 1982, showed up Israel's imperial character once again as its borders expanded to the west and the north.

During the 1990s the PLO took brave steps towards reconciliation, including their decision to recognize Israel and abandon the use of terrorism. They signed agreements such as Oslo and Oslo II. However, the subsequent peace agreements have broken down, largely because Israel has refused to offer a contiguous Palestinian state, its insistence on controlling all of Jerusalem and denying to the Palestinians their cherished right of return. In the meantime, Israel continues to create facts on the ground with settlement expansion, the prime cause of the Middle East conflict.

The Jewish Historical Right to the Holy Land

The essence of the Palestinian complaint can be summed up by the author Dawoud el-Alawi: "On what basis did the British believe that they were entitled to promise to the Zionists a land that belonged to others?"[1] If Palestine did indeed belong to another people, the Zionists could justly be accused of misappropriation, land theft and colonial conquest. But the charge has no merit. The reality is that the Jews had a longstanding historical attachment to the land stretching back more than three millennia. This was acknowledged in the British Mandate for Palestine in 1922, in which the Council of the League of Nations gave recognition to "the historical connexion of the Jewish people with Palestine and to the grounds for reconstituting their national home in that country."[2]

It was some three thousand years ago that King David established a strong and united Israelite kingdom with Jerusalem as his fortress capital. Jerusalem was to become established as a spiritual focal point of the Jewish faith. It is mentioned no fewer than 669 times in the Hebrew Bible. Jewish tradition has it that Solomon's Temple was built on Mt. Moriah, the spot chosen by the patriarch Abraham to bind his son Isaac.[3] In the Genesis account, it was the place where Jacob slept and dreamt of a ladder connecting heaven and earth. The Temple was viewed as the spot from where the Jews could come closest to the divine presence, and worshippers flocked there on the three pilgrim festivals. Under King David, Jerusalem became a national capital with considerable regional influence. Archeological evidence has corroborated the idea that the House of David was the head of a powerful royal kingdom, some of that evidence provided by the Israelites' enemies.[4]

This united kingdom split into the two kingdoms of Israel and Judah after the reign of Solomon, David's son. The northern kingdom set up its capital in Samaria and the southern one was established in Jerusalem. The southern kingdom called itself Judea, from which we derive the word Jew. Both kingdoms were overrun, the northern by the Assyrians in 722 BCE and the southern by the Babylonians in 586 BCE. Under Nebuchadnezzar, the Babylonians destroyed Solomon's Temple and sent the Jews into exile. Their lament for the loss of national independence is summed up by Psalm 137: "If I forget thee, O Jerusalem, let my right hand wither." The Persians under King Cyrus conquered Babylonia, allowing Jews to return to Jerusalem and rebuild the Temple. After Persian rule came the Greeks, against whom the Jews revolted in an attempt to prevent the imposition of Hellenistic culture.

After gaining a degree of autonomy under the Hasmoneans, the kingdom came under the control of the Romans and a series of increasingly oppressive and corrupt local governors or procurators, climaxing in the appointment of Gessius Florus in 64. In 66, the Jews launched a revolt against Roman rule, which was brutally put down over the next seven years. In 70, Titus captured Jerusalem and destroyed the Second Temple, before returning to Rome with booty from his triumph. In 73 AD, the defenders of the stronghold of Masada committed suicide rather than surrender to the Romans.

In 132–135, the Jewish warrior Simeon Bar Kokhba led a guerrilla insurgency against Roman rule, resulting in the capture of Jerusalem and the defeat of the Roman governor. But Bar Kochba's war of national liberation produced only a short-term victory. The Romans put down the rebellion in 135 CE, razing 985 villages so that, in the words of Dio Cassius, "nearly the whole of Judea was made desolate." More than 500,000 Jews died in the struggle. What followed was a determined Roman effort to crush the Jewish faith, with prohibitions on the celebration of Hanukkah, the eating of unleavened bread and the public study of Torah. The Romans banned the Jews from returning to Jerusalem with one exception: they could return one day a year to commemorate the destruction of the Temple by weeping by its only surviving remnant, the Western retaining wall (Wailing Wall).

Over the next centuries, the Jewish presence in the Holy Land remained undiminished despite the vicissitudes of foreign rule. By 300 CE, Jews still formed half the population of the Galilee and a quarter in the rest of the region.[5] Jews temporarily returned to Jerusalem during the rule of the Roman Emperor Julian, only to find themselves once again banned by his successor, Jovian. By the time of the Arab conquest of Palestine (as it was now known) in the seventh century, there were active Jewish communities in the northern Galilee, in Jerusalem and in the Jordan Valley. During the early period of Islamic rule after the second Caliph defeated the Byzantines, a Jewish quarter was built in the city and remained populated until the First Crusade.

During the Crusader conquest, thousands of Jews were massacred in Palestine and others were sold into slavery. Yet this appalling setback failed to diminish the Jewish yearning to return to their Promised Land. At the end of Crusader rule in 1210, more than 300 rabbis travelled to Palestine to help rebuild the communities affected by the Crusades. Among the great rabbis to make the pilgrimage to Jerusalem were Maimonides and Nachmanides. Jerusalem was not the only magnet for Jewish immigration. In the eleventh century, there were Jewish communities in Gaza, Rafah, Jaffa and Caesarea. From the thirteenth century, Jews also flocked to Safed, which later became the leading center for the study of Jewish mysticism. By 1530, as many as 10,000 Jews lived in and around the city, where they traded in a variety of foodstuffs and spices.[6] By the start of the following century, Safed boasted schools, a printing press (in 1577) and 21 synagogues. A number of Jewish villages in the neighboring countryside produced wheat, barley, vegetables and fruit.

In 1561, the Turkish Sultan, Suleiman I, gave the city of Tiberias to a Portuguese Jew,

Don Joseph Nasi. Don Nasi rebuilt the city and built up thriving wool and silk industries, attracting an influx of Jews.[7] The sixteenth century also saw the revival of the Jewish community in Hebron, where the Jewish quarter at Hebron was rebuilt around 1540. Together with Jerusalem, Tiberias and Safed, it was one of the 4 holy cities in Judaism. Life was by no means easy for, in Hebron alone, the Jews suffered arrests, threats of deportation, violence and even, in 1775, a blood libel.

By 1800, there were estimated to be 10,000 Jews in Palestine, though demographic data from this period cannot be known with certainty. During the nineteenth century, the community was given a boost by the philanthropic efforts of Sir Moses Montefiore. He bought land in Jaffa, Jerusalem and the Galilee region, just prior to the First Aliyah in the 1880s, when Jews from Eastern Europe and Russia travelled to Palestine. By 1860, Jerusalem had a clear Jewish majority, which it has maintained ever since.

Throughout the 1800 years of exile, there was a continuous Jewish presence in the Holy Land. Despite the terrible tribulations of foreign conquest, the harsh realities of foreign rule, the heavy taxation and the problem of dhimmitude, Jews were never deterred from immigrating to Palestine. Such a constant wave of movement and resettlement in the face of adversity speaks of one thing only: "The phenomenal affinity of the Jewish people to the land of Israel."[8]

The point of reciting this potted history is to disprove the notion that the Zionists had a phoney attachment to the land of Israel. It is simply not true, as the Palestinian academic Dawoud el-Alami says, that "the history of Jewish Palestine ended effectively in 137 CE."[9] The Jewish historical presence has been long, meaningful and continuous for well over three millennia, and that attachment did not disappear when the Romans conquered Jerusalem in 70 AD. As the 1937 Peel Commission so eloquently noted: "While the Jews had thus been dispersed over the world, they had never forgotten Palestine. If Christians have become familiar through the Bible with the physiognomy of the country and its place-names and events that happened more than two thousand years ago, the link which binds the Jews to Palestine and its past history is to them far closer and more intimate. Judaism and its ritual are rooted in those memories. Among countless illustrations it is enough to cite the fact that Jews, wherever they may be, still pray for rain at the season it is needed in Palestine. And the same devotion to the land of Israel, Eretz Israel, the same sense from it, permeates Jewish secular thought."[10]

But the decision to grant Jews self-determination was not based purely on past claims to the Holy Land; it had a pressing application based on *contemporary* demographics. Since the 1880s, Jews had been arriving in Palestine en masse quite legitimately, purchasing the land of absentee landlords at inflated prices. By the First World War, dozens of Jewish towns and agricultural settlements had been built with Jewish labor, creating a *de facto* Jewish national home. By the time of the San Remo conference in 1920, therefore, this sizeable Jewish community could quite legitimately claim a right of self-government, and it was this right that was subsequently recognized and enshrined in international law.

Was Palestine Ever an Arab State?

But some will still argue that even if there was a continuous (and present) Jewish presence, Palestine was a largely Arab state with a history of Muslim rule and an indigenous Arab population and character. This arguably overrides any prior Jewish claim to self-determination and gives added impetus to the Palestinian demand for a right of return to their historic homeland. To merely summon up the word Palestine is enough to convince many that the land is intrinsically Arab and Palestinian, and that the Zionists are usurpers.

But again, this flies in the face of the historical reality. The word *Palestine* bears no intrinsic relationship to an indigenous Arab population residing in the area. It comes from Syria-Palaestina or Palaestina, the name imposed on Judea by the Romans to stamp out any Jewish connection to the land. Many scholars argue that Palaestina was derived from Peleshet, or Philistia in Latin, the name given to the "region of the Philistines," who inhabited Canaan in the second millennium BCE.[11] The Philistines had no connection with Arabian culture, as they were widely considered to be an Aegean people. Similarly, the Romans called Jerusalem Aelia Capitolina to stamp out any Jewish association with the city. These are basic points of etymology that supporters of the Palestinian cause conveniently overlook.

Nor was Palestine ever a separate Arab nation-state ruled by an indigenous Palestinian Arab leadership. Instead it was a small administrative region ruled by a succession of imperial occupiers, whether Romans, Byzantines, Sassanids, Abbasids, Seljuks, Crusaders, Mamluks, Ottomans or British. As Bernard Lewis writes: "From the end of the Jewish state in antiquity to the beginning of British rule, the area now designated by the name Palestine was not a country and had no frontiers, only administrative boundaries; it was a group of provincial subdivisions, by no means always the same, within a larger entity."[12] Expressed another way, the word Palestine did not refer to "a defined political, demographic, cultural or territorial entity."[13]

As the area of Palestine was under Ottoman control from the sixteenth century onwards, officials or pashas in Sidon and Damascus were responsible for administering the area as well as areas of modern Lebanon and Syria. The area that encompassed Palestine (but which included neighboring areas) was split into two principal administrative districts in the nineteenth century. The northern sector was part of the vilayet of Beirut and was composed of the sanjaks of Acre and Nablus. The southern part of Palestine consisted of the Independent Sanjak of Jerusalem and was overseen from Istanbul.[14] There were other subdivisions, right down to the village level. In the central mountain region of Palestine, political authority lay in the hands of prominent local notables or chiefs, and in many villages, dominant families vied for influence, wealth and power.

The Muslim subjects of Palestine were loyal Ottomans at the turn of the twentieth century, though their more immediate loyalties were to their "clan, tribe, village, town or religious sect."[15] Clans and villages were frequently divided by longstanding feuds, and a "fault line divided the sedentary rural population from neighbouring Bedouin tribes," while "real fissures also separated townspeople from villagers."[16] Quite simply, such antagonisms stood in the way of a feeling of belonging to a separate "Palestinian" nation.

If there was no separate Palestinian Arab nation, this was partly a function of the territory's shifting population, one that was composed of peoples recently arrived from areas *outside of Palestine*. In a detailed survey of land ownership and settlement in Palestine, Arieh Avneri traced the significant number of immigrants who came to Palestine in past centuries. Following the Napoleonic conquest of 1799 and the later rule of Ibrahim Pasha, thousands of Egyptians fled the country, with many choosing to travel to Palestine. Many settled in and around Jaffa, while others went to the Jordan Valley and the south.[17] After 1856, Algerian refugees arrived in Palestine, founding some villages in the Lower Galilee and settling in Safed, Jaffa and Tiberias. There were other groups of North African immigrants in Ramle, collectively known as Mugrabis.[18] In 1878 the Sultan gave protection to Circassian refugees in Transjordan, though some settled west of the Jordan.

Among Arab refugees who found sanctuary in Palestine were those from Yemen, arriving in 1908, while thousands of others came from mountainous regions of Iraq (the Turkomans). Greek communities had been forming in Palestine since the mid seventeenth century, while some 3,000 Albanians settled in Acre in the late eighteenth century. Many of these ethnic groups had been imported by various conquerors over the centuries, while others had simply migrated. In other words, claims of an ethnically homogenous Arab community in Palestine living continuously in the land for two millennia are belied by the facts.

Further evidence for Palestine's ethnic heterogeneity comes from an article in the 1911 *Encyclopaedia Britannica*. The population, it discovered, contained "very large contingents from the Mediterranean countries, especially Armenia, Greece and Italy," as well as "a number of Persians and a fairly large Afghan colony... German 'templar' colonies... Circassian settlements ... a large Algerian element in the population," and inhabitants originating from Sudan, Persia and Bosnia. The article concluded that with such a "widely differing" group of inhabitants speaking "no less than fifty languages," it was "no easy task to write concisely ... on the ethnology of Palestine."[19]

This was no less true in 1931, when the census found at least 51 languages in use by Muslims and Christians as well as dozens of birthplaces listed for the non–Jewish community.[20] All this strongly disproves the idea that today's Palestinian Arabs have some longstanding "family" tie to the land, stretching back uninterruptedly over thousands of years. Put another way, their claim to self-determination is a thoroughly modern one.

While there was no Palestinian Arab national identity as such by 1900, many inhabitants did feel a sense of loyalty to the greater Arab nation of which they were an indissoluble part. Professor Michael Curtis of the Begin-Sadat Center for Strategic Studies has observed: "Both historically and in contemporary times, the Arabs living in the area now known as Palestine were regarded both by outsiders and by their own spokespeople as members of the greater Arab population, without a separate or distinct identity."[21] Arabist Historian Charles Smith makes a similar point. While acknowledging that by 1900, the Arab population of Palestine formed the overwhelming majority of the population, this fact "does not permit us to postulate the widespread existence of a Palestinian Arab national consciousness at this time."[22] After all, nationalism was a European construct based on the notion that a people united by common descent and with links to a given land deserved self-determination, free from foreign rule.

In addition, almost all Palestine's Arabs would have had a strong religious identity as members of the Islamic faith, coupled with an "exlusionist attitude to all religious 'others' and resistance to change."[23] So it is not surprising that the motive behind the Arab riots in 1929 was a rumor that the Jews intended to occupy the Temple Mount in Jerusalem. Nothing could stir the masses like an ominous warning that Muslim holy places were under threat, particularly if the alleged violators were Jews.

Indeed, if Palestine's Arabs identified with an entity other than the Arab nation or Islam, it was to imperial Syria or *Sham*, "the historical region of Syria which included the modern states of Syria, Lebanon, Israel and Jordan." This is evidenced by the views of Arab leaders themselves. Muhammad Amin Husseini, later the mufti of Jerusalem, presided over the Arab club, which called for Palestine to be incorporated into southern Syria. In 1919, the First Congress of the Muslim-Christian Association met in Jerusalem, prior to the Paris Peace Conference, and adopted a resolution that Palestine was "nothing but part of Arab Syria and it has never been separated from it at any stage." The ties of Palestine to Syria were "national, religious, linguistic, moral, economic, and geographic," and as a result, it had to be "undetached from the independent Arab Syrian Government." Similarly, in 1919 the General Syrian Congress requested on July 2, 1919, that "there should be no separation of the southern part of Syria known as Palestine, nor of the littoral Western Zone, which includes Lebanon, from the Syrian country."[24]

In 1919, American envoys, the so-called King-Crane commission, interviewed Jews and Arabs in Palestine, together with Arabs in Syria and Lebanon, to ascertain which power they would like to govern them. The commission concluded that an Arab state of Greater Syria be created, including Lebanon and Palestine, and recommended curtailing the Zionist program. What is interesting here is that an early survey of Arab opinion in Palestine did not reveal an overwhelming desire for a separate Arab state in Palestine.

During the Peel Commission, an Arab leader, Auni Bey Abdul-Hati, expressed similar sentiments. Decrying the concept of partition, he told the commission, "There is no such country [as Palestine]! 'Palestine' is a term the Zionists invented! There is no Palestine in the Bible. Our country was for centuries part of Syria."[25] Fares Khouri told the UN General Assembly in 1947, "Had it not been for the Balfour Declaration and the terms of the mandate, Palestine would now be a Syrian province as it used to be."[26] Such sentiments were shared by Syria's authoritarian ruler, Hafez al Assad.[27]

There is also evidence that such views found accord within the PLO. Ahmed Shuqeiri, chairman of the PLO, also said that it was "common knowledge that Palestine is nothing but southern Syria." In 1977, the head of the PLO Military Operations Department, Zuhair Muhsin, declared that there "are no differences between Jordanians, Palestinians, Syrians and Lebanese.... We are one people. Only for political reasons do we carefully underline our Palestinian identity.... The establishment of a Palestinian state is a new expedient to continue the fight against Zionism and for Arab unity."[28] Interestingly, under British Mandate rule, all inhabitants of the area, Jewish or non–Jewish, were called Palestinians.

All this gives the lie to the claim, so often made, that the Great Powers, in dividing up the land in 1919, imposed a settlement that violated the right to national self-determination of a Palestinian Arab people. There is no evidence in 1919 of a widespread "national consciousness" among Palestine's Arabs, no sense of a separate and distinctive Palestinian Arab national identity. Thus, in dividing up the Arab land mass, the claimants were not so much Palestine's Arabs and Jews as the Arab national movement and the Jews (Zionists). The fact that a distinctive Palestinian Arab national consciousness developed later (especially after 1967) hardly invalidates the prior Jewish claim that came to be recognized by the international community.

The Arab claim to sovereignty proceeded with enormous success. Within a short period, new Arab states had emerged from the old Ottoman Empire: Lebanon, Syria, Mesopotamia (Iraq) and the Arabian Peninsula. Eventually there would be more than 20 separate Arab states, in area more than 100 times the original area allocated for the Jewish national home; the Jews were allocated a "tiny notch," to quote Lord Balfour. There was no encroachment on existing Arab *national* claimants. As the renowned legal scholar Julius Stone correctly observes, "Jewish and Arab claims in the vast area of the former Ottoman Empire came to the forum of liberation together."[29] If one accepts that there was a need to grant Jews, like every other people, the right of self-determination, if that meant a state where those rights could flourish and where Jewish cultural identity could be preserved, then the Allied powers were right to propose a Jewish national home.

But even the tiny notch allocated for the Jewish national home was deemed to be too generous a disposition of land for the Zionists. In 1922, very nearly four-fifths of the original Palestine mandate was hived off to create yet another Arab state, that of Transjordan, which later became the Kingdom of Jordan. As well as settling disputes within the Hashemite clan, the new Transjordanian state provided a new territorial unit for Arabs within the geographical area of Palestine. This was the true example of the encroachment of one form of self-determination over another, except this was a case of Arab self-determination eroding the rights given to the Jews. It brought much resentment from Zionist leader Chaim Weizmann, who spoke of eastern and western Palestine as "a unit."[30]

Regardless of this fact, the new state east of the Jordan River became a *de facto* Palestinian Arab homeland. Today a majority of Jordan's inhabitants are Palestinian, even though they are second-class citizens and suffer political discrimination. As Crown Prince Hassan told the National Assembly in 1970: "Palestine is Jordan, and Jordan is Palestine."[31]

These historical observations are not being used to deny the Palestinians their claim to self-determination, provided that they pursue their claim peacefully and with respect to Israel's security and territorial integrity. But the Palestinian leadership has argued for these contentious points of history, and put them at the core of their people's victim-centered narrative. As a result, it is necessary to offer a historical rebuttal.

Was Zionism Pursued Illegitimately?

But even if all these points are accepted, some will still try to assert that Zionism is an illegitimate movement because of how the cause was pursued. The Jews, they scream, came into Palestine and stole Arab land, colonized Arab villages and acted illegally in pursuit of their redemptionist dream. But the strategy of the Zionists was anything but illegitimate. In the latter part of the nineteenth century and in the early part of the twentieth, the Zionist movement proceeded by a process of legal emigration and land purchase, as well as negotiations with world powers.

Theodore Herzl, the figure most often associated with secular Zionism, spent the last few years of his short life petitioning political figures and trying to persuade them of the merits of political Zionism. Thus in 1896 he met the grand vizier in Constantinople, though he had wanted to meet with Sultan Abdulhamid II. In 1898 Herzl met Kaiser Wilhelm in the same city and asked whether a chartered company for Jews in Palestine could be created. But the kaiser showed little interest, anxious not to lose for Germany the advantages of a burgeoning commercial relationship with the Ottomans. Undeterred, Herzl met the sultan in 1901, but no results from this meeting were forthcoming. Despite Herzl's promises of financial reward, the sultan was anxious not to cede any further parts of his tottering empire.

So Herzl now tried to influence the British government, and he gave evidence before the Royal Commission on immigration. He urged the government to facilitate Jewish emigration to Palestine as the only place of refuge for Jews suffering from anti–Semitic persecution. The British entertained the notion of establishing a Jewish state in East Africa, an idea rejected out of hand by the Russian Zionists. Among the other figures that Herzl met in the last years of his life were the Tsar's minister of the interior, Vyacheslav von Plehve, the king of Italy and the pope.

Herzl did far more than simply negotiate with foreign statesmen; he provided an intellectual blueprint for a Jewish state in his famous book *Judenstaat* (Jew state), in which he argued that Jews would never be accepted as a minority in the counties in which they resided. They would always be seen as outsiders until they organized themselves into a national collective with a state of their own. He was also the driving force behind the convening of the First Zionist Congress in Basle in 1897, and he remained its president until he died in 1904. Herzl's methods were therefore legal and non-violent. He did not advocate armed subversion nor did he seek the overthrow of Ottoman rule, relying instead on the power of persuasion and the force of the written word.

While Herzl was seeking to garner political support for Zionism, there was a parallel process of land purchase in Palestine itself. Here the charge of land expropriation is utterly false. Far from stealing land or swindling the local Arab landowners, the Zionists bought their land, often from absentee landlords and at vastly inflated prices. Time and again in the official records, there are Arab complaints about Zionists buying Arab land. The Peel Commission report noted the "Arab alarm at the continued Jewish purchase of land" while a report to the League of Nations on the administration of Palestine mentioned "the sale of lands to Jews," which had been "a permanent feature of political opinion in Palestine for the past ten years." Even Tom Segev, one of Israel's New Historians, has acknowledged, "The Zionist movement had always planned to buy Palestine with money."[32]

Moreover, the Jews were forced to pay inflated prices for often poor-quality land. The Ottomans banned Jewish permanent residence and land purchase from 1881, making the process of land acquisition much harder. Nonetheless, Jews purchased land from a variety of figures: absentee landlords, land agents, farmers, and senior figures in the Arab national movement, including many of those who publicly expressed vehement opposition to the Zionists. All knew that with such enormous demand, they could inflate the prices that they charged, often by a factor of ten.

Far from being exploited, the Arab land-sellers were the ones exploiting prospective Jewish landowners. A great deal of the land bought by the Jewish pioneers during two periods of intense emigration between 1880 and 1914 was wasteland and sand dunes, much of which had been neglected by its former owners. The pioneers had to contend with malarial swamps,[33] treeless land and attacks from local Bedouin. Today, Israel's commercial hub is Tel Aviv, with a population of over 400,000. But the city was founded in 1909 on nothing more than sand dunes.[34] Thus the idea that the Zionists staked their claim for self-determination in an illegitimate manner is baseless.

It is true that Zionist land purchases did have an impact on the rural Palestinian economy. These purchases inevitably meant dispossession for rural peasants, leaving them at the mercy of landlords and opening the possibility of eventual landlessness. Among the various sectors of Arab society in Palestine, the fellahin (native peasants) largely failed to benefit. A third were below the subsistence level, and many were burdened by enormous debt. They cannot be said to have prospered from land sales, unlike the landlords who sold on land at enormous profit.

But if these purchases had a detrimental effect on the livelihoods of Arab peasants, what do we say about the Arabs who were selling their land in the first place? There were, after all, two parties to the transaction. As Segev points out, "Arab landowners were not forced to sell."[35] In any case, the total number of Arabs dispossessed through Jewish land purchasers was but a tiny fraction of the Arab population. A memorandum submitted by the Mandatory Government to the Peel Commission declared that until 1 January 1936, 3,261 claims for dispossession had been filed and only 654 were considered to be valid.[36]

Many of those who protested most loudly about the sale of Palestinian Arab lands were themselves engaged in the sales. As Benny Morris points out in his volume on the 1948 war, "a giant question mark hangs over the 'nationalist' ethos of the Palestinian Arab elite: Husseinis as well as Nashashibis, Khalidis, Dajanis, and Tamimis just before and during the Mandate sold land to the Zionist institutions and/or served as Zionist agents and spies."[37]

In any case, Zionist organizations often sought to buy land that was free of landless tenants. In 1920, Ben-Gurion told a group of people from *Poale Zion*, "Under no circumstances must we touch land belonging to the fellas [native labourers] or worked by them. They must receive help from Jewish settlement institutions, to free themselves from the dead weight of their oppressors, and to keep their land. Only if a fellah leaves his place of settlement should we offer to buy his land, at an appropriate price." Ben-Gurion preferred Jewish settlement in desert and wasteland areas, rather than on land that was being cultivated by local Arabs, though much of the land eventually bought was on the coastal plain, purchased in an effort to create a contiguous territory.[38] It is important to remember that a majority of Zionist land purchases between 1878 and 1936 were from large landowners and not peasants.[39] Only 9.4 percent were from the fellahin.[40]

There is other evidence that the exercise of Jewish self-determination was not intrinsically harmful to the economic condition of Palestine's Arabs. As Martin Gilbert points out, "Between 1922 and 1939 more Arabs had entered Palestine than Jews. These were Muslim immigrants, including many illegals, from Morocco, Algeria, Tunisia, Libya, Egypt, Yemen, Iraq, Iran and Syria—as well as from Transjordan, Sudan and Saudi Arabia. These immigrants were drawn to Palestine by its opportunities for work and its growing prosperity—opportunities and prosperity often created by the Jews there."[41] The population was attracted to the region's burgeoning economic opportunities and industrialization.

In addition, the rate of Arab emigration from Palestine was slashed by two-thirds from its prewar level. According to the 1937 Peel Commission report, "the general beneficent effect of Jewish immigration on Arab welfare is illustrated by the fact that the increase in the Arab population is most marked in urban areas affected by Jewish development." The report noted a rise of 86 percent in Haifa and 62 percent in Jaffa, as opposed to a rise of 7 percent in the purely Arab towns of Nablus and Hebron.[42]

Both those of an Arabist and pro-Zionist disposition acknowledged these points. The former civil commissioner for Iraq, Sir Arnold Wilson, told the House of Commons on 20 July 1939 that the Arabs would never accept the Zionist enterprise despite "the material benefit which has accrued to the inhabitants of Palestine." Making the Zionist case before the Peel Commission, Winston Churchill made the following observation: "Why is there harsh injustice done if people come in and make a livelihood for more, and make the desert into palm groves and orange groves? Why is it injustice because there is more work and wealth for everybody? There is no injustice."[43] For Palestinian Arab leaders, the argument carried little weight. As Musa al-Alami, the assistant mandate attorney general, put it: "I would prefer that the country remain impoverished and barren for another hundred years, until we ourselves are able to develop it on our own."[44]

The Jewish influx had a positive impact on Arab welfare too. There was a substantial fall in deaths from malaria, owing to the Jewish efforts to eradicate the disease. There was also a decline in Arab child mortality and a substantial rise in life expectancy, "well ahead of the natural increase of other Arab/Muslim populations."[45] Many of the poorer Arabs received treatment at the tuberculosis hospital in Safed and the Radiology Institute in Jerusalem. Palestine's Arab population was thus direct benefiting from the increasing scientific and economic opportunities being created by the Jewish population.

Were Zionist Leaders Hostile to Palestine's Arabs?

It is often alleged that the Zionist leaders were willfully blind to the existence of an Arab community in Palestine. They are accused of concocting their plans for Jewish national revival rather myopically and with callous disregard for the native population. Allegedly the Zionists thought that Palestine was "a land without people for a people without land." The Zionists also stand accused by many of planning to transfer all Arabs from Palestine to make way for the Jews. Which population would not wish to drive out such newly arrived "interlopers"? For Alexei Sayle, the Arabs were "not considered fully human by the Zionists" and they could "be murdered without qualms."[46]

When one surveys what Zionist leaders actually said about the Arabs of Palestine, this accusation becomes grossly unfair. Here one should start with Theodore Herzl, the indefatigable founder of political Zionism. Often accused of having a patronizing attitude towards Palestine's Arabs in line with other "colonialist" rulers, Herzl in fact promoted the idea of civic equality for all the country's inhabitants, Jewish or otherwise. Thus in a letter from 1899 to Yussuf Ziah el-Khaldi, a former mayor of Jerusalem, Herzl promised in regard to Palestine's non–Jews that "their well-being and individual prosperity will increase as we bring in our own."[47] In 1902 he wrote *Altneuland* (*Old-New Land*), a utopian novel from 1902 that doubled as a plan of action for a future Jewish state. In the novel, two travellers come across a rabbi called Dr. Geyer (modeled on Vienna's anti–Semitic mayor Karl Lueger) who is busy promoting the belief that only Jews should be given rights of citizenship.

This racist and discriminatory policy runs counter to the liberal views of another character, Litvak, who tells the rabbi: "My colleagues and I make no distinction between one man and another. We do not ask to what race or religion a man belongs. If he is a human being, that is enough for us." In a rowdy election meeting, Litvak succeeds in turning voters away from Geyer's viewpoint and winning them over to a tolerant, liberal viewpoint.

This belief in civic equality was extended to religious affairs: "Every man will be as free and undisturbed in his faith or his disbelief as he is in his nationality." He added that if "men of other creeds and different nationalities come to live among us" they should be accorded "honorable protection and equality before the law."[48]

Altneuland features an encounter with Rashid Bey, an Arab engineer from Haifa who continually lauds his status as an equal citizen in the Jewish homeland. He offers fulsome tributes to the Jewish pioneers who have made the deserts bloom and improved the Arabs' economic standing. The notion that Palestine's Arabs would be won over by improved economic circumstances, a view that can be found in Ben-Gurion's writings, may seem somewhat naive today. Nonetheless, *Altneuland* reveals Herzl's awareness that Palestine, far from being an empty land waiting for Jews to arrive, was populated with, among others, a significant Arab population. It also reflects Herzl's "vision of a society devoid of discrimination and in which religious, racial and gender equality prevails" and in which non–Jews were "partners in citizenship."[49] He did not seek to make Palestine *Arabfrei*. Instead he wanted to create a liberal, peaceful society based on civic rights for all.

Nor was he alone. The Russian essayist Ahad Ha'Am (Asher Ginsberg), founder of cultural Zionism, wrote "Truth from Eretz Yisrael" in 1891. In it he expressed his disdain for those people outside Palestine who believed that the Arabs were "all desert savages, like donkeys, who neither see nor understand what goes on around them." On the contrary, he argued that the Arabs possessed "a sharp intellect" and were "very cunning." Aware of this, he advised Zionists to be "careful in our conduct toward a foreign people among whom we live once again, to walk together in love and respect, and needless to say in justice and righteousness." He castigated those in Palestine who had an "impulse to despotism" and who walked with Arabs "in hostility and cruelty, unjustly encroaching on them, shamefully beating them for no good reason."[50]

In 1905, Yitzhak Epstein, a Russian-born teacher and agriculturalist, proposed a charter between the Jews and Arabs in Palestine and said that the settlers should not enter the country as if they were colonial conquerors. In his book *Ha-Shiloah*, he wrote: "We must on no account cause harm to any people, and in particular to a great people whose hostility would be highly dangerous." The Jews and Arabs in Palestine were "two ancient and gifted Semitic peoples with great potentialities who complement each other."[51] One of his contemporaries, Yehoshua Radler-Feldmann, spoke of the need for Palestine's Jewish and Arab communities to unite "for a single objective and for mutual assistance."[52]

Nahum Sokolow, another prominent Zionist leader, told Egyptian paper *Al-Ahram* in 1914 that he desperately wanted Jews and Arabs to be partners in a collaborative exercise that would enable them "to build up together a great Palestinian civilisation."[53] Others such as Arthur Ruppin were proposing a binational state in order to do justice to the national aspirations of both Arab and Jew. He wrote, "Zionism can find its justification only in racial affiliation of the Jews to the peoples of the Near East." He added, "Zionism will end in a catastrophe if we do not succeed in finding a common platform."[54] Binationalism was proposed by members of Brith Shalom (Peace Covenant), a group formed in 1925. They wanted Jewish immigration to be carried out only with the consent of the Palestinian Arabs, an idea at odds with official Zionist policy (and the Revisionists), and advocated a bi-national state with equal civil, political and social rights for each community.

In Britain, Chaim Weizmann declared that he wanted Palestine to be "as Jewish as England was English" but later clarified that this did not imply the expulsion of Arabs. He wanted the Jews to help develop the Near East in a spirit of friendship with the Arab community. His associate, Harry Sacher, concurred with this position: "I don't want us in Palestine to deal with the Arabs as the Poles deal with the Jews…. That kind of chauvinism might poison the whole yishuv."[55] Another of Weizmann's associates, the psychoanalyst David Eder, was warning that the Zionists had to show respect for Arab aspirations if they wanted their own to be respected.[56]

The young Zionist leader, Chaim Arlosoroff, writing in 1921 in the aftermath of Arab riots that killed dozens of Jews, did not want the Zionist movement to abandon ties with Arab leaders. He argued that only a policy of peace, conciliation and mutual recognition would enable the Zionists to succeed. This view was officially adopted at the 12th Zionist Congress held at Karlsbad in 1921. The congress passed a resolution that declared that Zionism sought "to live in relations of harmony and mutual respect with the Arab people" and that called on the executive to achieve a "sincere understanding with the Arab people."

And what about Ben-Gurion, the closest figure that Israel has to a founding father other than Theodore Herzl? Throughout his career, Ben-Gurion was committed to the Zionist project of settling Jews in Palestine in order to facilitate a Jewish majority that would eventually attain statehood and national independence. But he was equally aware of Arab economic and political rights in Palestine and thus sought to bridge the divide between the two communities through dialogue and agreement. These twin aims, of strengthening the yishuv and reaching an accord with the Arabs, were never irreconcilable.

Ben-Gurion anchored the Jewish right to settle Palestine as much in historic right as on their ability to improve and cultivate the land. He argued for many years that only the Jews could make the desert bloom and that no one on that basis could deny them the right of unlimited entry to Palestine. The Arabs, he wrote, "have no right to close the country to us" or to uninhabited spaces such as the Negev. Palestine had to be open to the Jews because it was their tender care and nurture that would turn a malaria-infested, barren landscape into an outpost of civilization and prosperity.

But he equally acknowledged that Palestine's Arabs had undeniable rights on the land and stated, "On no account must we injure the rights of its inhabitants."[57] He declared, "The Arab community is an organic, inextricable part of Palestine," and added: "It is not to disinherit this community or to thrive on its destruction that Zionism came into being."[58] Ben-Gurion also looked favorably on the fellahs, who he saw as descendants of Jews who had lived in the land at the time of the Arab conquest. They were "the most important economic asset of the native population." Ben-Gurion stressed the cardinal importance of preserving their land rights in the country. "Under no circumstances must we touch land belonging to fellahs or worked by them." He added that they "must receive help from Jewish settlement institutions" and that the only time that Jews should offer to buy his land is when a fellah "leaves his place of settlement."[59]

In 1918 he admonished those who felt that Palestine could be taken over as if it had no existing population: "Eretz Israel is not an empty country…. West of Jordan alone houses three quarters of a million people. On no account must we injure the rights of the inhabitants. Only 'Ghetto Dreamers' like Zangwill can imagine that Eretz Israel will be given to the Jews with the added right of dispossessing the current inhabitants of the country. This is not the mission of Zionism. Had Zionism to aspire to inherit the place of these inhabitants—it would be nothing but a dangerous utopia and an empty, damaging and reactionary dream."[60]

In 1924 Ben-Gurion, while espousing his belief that the ultimate aim of the Zionists was the creation of a Jewish state, made it clear that he had no desire to rule harshly over the Arabs. "We have no intention, no desire, and no need to rule over others. When we say a state we mean two things: that others shall not rule over us, and that anarchy shall not rule over us." He went on: "We demand the same national autonomy for the Arabs as we demand for ourselves."[61] He added in a lecture in 1930: "It is imperative that the Arab knows that we have not come here to dispossess him, to subjugate him, or to worsen his condition."[62]

As he envisioned it, Palestine's Arabs had less a right of sovereignty (as this could be used to block Jewish immigration) than autonomy, more specifically "full internal autonomy in all cultural, economic and social affairs."[63] As he put it elsewhere: "The Arabs have full rights as citizens of the country, but they do not have the right of ownership over it."[64] This position was fully in accord with the legal rights under the league's mandate. A principle of separation meant that there would be cooperation between "neighbours," hence the title of one of his articles, "We and Our Neighbours." This principle of separation explains why he advocated the notion of "Avodah Ivrit" (Hebrew labor), contradicting the charge that he sought to exploit cheap Arab labor.

Later events showed Ben-Gurion just how implacable the Arab community was to the Jewish national home. In particular, he made grudging acknowledgment of an Arab national movement that sought to destroy Jewish hopes for national self-determination. Throughout the 1920s and 1930s, he came to believe that only a strong and heavily populated yishuv[65] would bring peace to Palestine and deter Arab aggression. He advocated bringing in massive numbers of Jewish immigrants in order to facilitate a Jewish majority and send an unequivocal message to the Arabs that the Jews of Palestine could not be conquered. Instead, they would have to reach a settlement.

This may sound similar to Jabotinsky's Iron Wall, but Ben-Gurion desisted from sounding an overly militant tone. He continued to advocate reconciliation with the Arabs of Palestine, even in these most trying of circumstances. Thus he could declare in 1925: "I am unwilling to forego even one percent of Zionism for 'peace'—yet I do not want Zionism to infringe upon even one percent of legitimate Arab rights."[66] Four years earlier he had written: "The establishment of comradely relations between Hebrew workers and the masses of Arab laborers, grounded in common economic, political and cultural action is an essential condition for our redemption as a working people, and the liberation of the working Arab people from servitude to propertied oppressors."[67] His vision of Jewish-Arab cooperation was heavily tinged with his belief in utopian socialism, but it was no less sincere for that.

In a letter to his son in 1937 he wrote: "We do not wish and do not need to expel Arabs and take their place. All our aspiration is built on the assumption—proven throughout all our activity in the Land—that there is enough room in the country for ourselves and the Arabs." The great Zionist enterprise, he told the Twentieth Zionist Congress in 1937, "will be a role model to the world in its treatment of minorities and members of other nations.... Just as an Arab policeman helping Arab rioters will be severely punished, so a Jewish policeman failing to protect an Arab from Jewish hooligans will be severely punished."[68] Sentiments such as these can be found in numerous letters, articles and speeches made by Ben-Gurion over the years.

His acceptance of an Arab national claim to the land led him to change tack. He came to propose a federal plan for Palestine in the 1930s that would satisfy an Arab demand for political as opposed to economic rights and convince them that the Jews had no desire to "dominate or dislodge them."[69] Jews and Arabs would share power initially prior to the establishment of a Jewish state as part of an Arab federation.

At all times, Ben-Gurion sought to keep open lines of communication to the country's Arab community. Thus in 1929 he asked the mandatory authorities for a publishing license for a newspaper, to be called *Al-Haqiqa* (the truth) which was designed to explain to them the justness of the Zionist cause and to stress the racial ties between Jews and Arabs. Later, as executive director of the political wing of the Jewish Agency, Ben-Gurion had a number of meetings with key figures in the Pan-Arab movement including the Palestinian nationalist, Musa Alami. No agreement was reached, but Ben-Gurion remained buoyed by the prospect of reaching a settlement. "Greater Zionism," he wrote, "will find a common language with the greater Arab movement."[70] There can be no doubt that while remaining committed to Zionism's ultimate goals, he sought every chance for compromise and reconciliation. When it was clear, by 1935, that no accommodation was possible, Ben-Gurion prioritized Jewish immigration from Europe. Peace, so he hoped, would be built by strength.

With his hopes for peace dashed in the final tumultuous years of the 1930s, Ben-Gurion lost any illusions about the possibility of a Jewish-Arab political accord. With perhaps a touch of melancholy, he would reflect on the Arab as "a political creature who is unable to withstand the pressures of his environment or the emotive and collective drives of his people."[71] As late as 1941, Ben-Gurion was writing the outlines of Zionist policy. In it, he insisted that any future Jewish state would be based on complete equality of all its citizens but that equality also meant "equalization," whereby Arab living and educational standards had to be raised to the Jewish level. He spoke of how the Biblical precept "Thou shalt love thy neighbor as thyself" had to be "the basis of the constitution of the Jewish state."[72]

An altogether more militant approach was taken by Vladimir (Ze'ev) Jabotinsky, the leader of a revisionist strand of Zionism that was the forbear of today's Likud party. He argued, sometimes in patronizing terms, that it was pointless trying to reach an agreement with the Palestinian Arabs so long as they still believed that the Jewish national home could be wrecked. They would not consent to becoming a minority in the country if they were in a position of strength and the Zionists were weak. The Jews had to build an unassailable military and diplomatic power base in Palestine, an "iron wall," to demonstrate to the Arabs that Jewish aspirations for statehood were serious and impossible to challenge. Only then would talks yield fruitful results and enable both peoples to "live together in peace, like good neighbours." His Revisionist supporters also talked of incorporating Transjordan into the Jewish national home.[73]

But even the more hard-line Jabotinsky was not the extreme anti–Arab figure of popular thinking. He distanced himself from any suggestion that he wanted to expel Arabs from Palestine: "I consider driving the Arabs out of Palestine, in whatever form, absolutely impossible; there will always be two peoples in Palestine.... I am ready to swear, on behalf of ourselves and our descendants, that we ... will never attempt driving out or oppressing [the Arabs]."[74] In 1934, he helped to draft a constitution for Jewish Palestine in which Hebrew and Arabic had equivalent legal standing and in which the burdens of statehood were to be shared by the two communities.[75]

Occasionally, some individual Zionists would flirt with the idea of Arab "transfer" and population exchange, particularly when it was clear that the demographics of Palestine were not yet favoring a Jewish majority. Benny Morris argues that this idea had "a basis in mainstream Jewish thinking, if not actual planning, from the late 1930s and 1940s."[76]

One of those most associated with this idea was the novelist and playwright Israel Zangwill, who wrote in the *New Liberal Review* in 1901: "Palestine is a country without a people; the Jews are a people without a country."[77] A year later he spoke of how Palestine "remains at this moment an almost uninhabited, forsaken and ruined Turkish territory." But he soon spoke of the "Arab peril" in Palestine and how the Zionists would either have to reconcile themselves to an "alien population" or drive the Arabs out in order to create a viable political entity. Palestine, he would later say, could not be the country of two peoples. As a result, he founded the Jewish Territorialist Organization, which sought to create a Jewish homeland in any other part of the world, including Uganda. But by this time, he could reasonably be judged as outside the mainstream Zionist camp.

The discussion of transfer in mainstream Zionist circles became more prominent in the period 1937–8, and this came at the instigation of the British Peel Commission, not the Zionists. The commission recommended the partition of Mandatory Palestine into a Jewish and an Arab state. In order to create stability between the two states, it proposed a land and population exchange, as there were some 225,000 Arabs in the Jewish state but 1,250 Jews in the Arab one. In the aftermath of World War I, exchanges of population between different nations, such as between Turkey and Greece, were seen as relatively uncontroversial, even by the League of Nations.

The attitude of Ben-Gurion and others was that this was viable only if it was approved by the League of Nations, carried out by Britain and did not involve compulsion. In Ben-Gurion's eyes, it represented compensation for reducing the Jewish patrimony to a rump. This much is proved by a letter he wrote to his son in 1937: "We have never wanted to dispossess the Arabs. But because Britain is giving them part of the country which had been promised to us, it is only fair that the Arabs in our state be transferred to the Arab portion."[78] By ignoring this situational context, Shlaim therefore completely distorts the record when he accuses Ben-Gurion of being "one of the earliest converts to the idea of transfer as the best way of dealing with the problem of an Arab minority."[79] In addition, transfer was never an official policy adopted by the main Zionist parties or leaders.[80]

Indeed if it had been, it would surely have been a key component of the UN Partition Plan of 1947. But even though that plan envisioned a Jewish state with a substantial non–Jewish population, Ben-Gurion did not call for transfer. In a speech given on 13 December 1947, the soon-to-be prime minister did acknowledge that the proposed population ratio did not "constitute a solid basis for a Jewish state." But his solution was not the mass evacuation of non–Jews but the bringing to Israel of "one and a half million Jews" from around the world. In other words, he called for the emigration of Jews to Israel as a solution to the demographic problem. He added that for Arab inhabitants of a future Jewish state, "the state will be their state as well."[81]

Shlaim writes that the history of Zionism is "full of manifestations of deep hostility and contempt towards the indigenous population." There were a few, to be sure, but the voices just mentioned give an altogether different picture.[82] Taken together, this evidence suggests that far from seeking an active confrontation with the Arab population, the Zionist leaders preferred accommodation and compromise.

Admittedly, language differences did constitute a barrier between the two populations, and certain cultural norms common to the Jews (equality between the sexes, communal living) were alien to the country's Arabs. But it was always assumed by most Zionists that efforts were necessary to cross the divide. Many also came to believe, somewhat naively, that Palestinian Arabs would be won over by the promise of social betterment and enhanced economic opportunities resulting from the Zionist enterprise. Such illusions would be shattered by the late 1930s. For all these reasons, it is reasonable to conclude that the Jewish claim to self-determination was historically valid, that it was pursued legitimately and that it created no fundamental economic injustice to Palestine's non–Jewish population.

Israel Has a Legal Right to Statehood

It is sometimes asserted that Israel's legal legitimacy rests on the UN Partition Resolution 181 of 1947, which called for the division of Palestine into a Jewish and an Arab state. According to Resolution 181, which the Zionists accepted and the Arabs rejected, the Jews were to receive some 55 percent of Palestine (mostly the Negev Desert) and the Arabs the remainder, much of it in fertile areas. Some scholars cite this fact in order to invalidate Israel's (minimal) claim to all land west of the "green line" (78 percent of the current state), claiming that a viable partition of the land would have to proceed on the basis of this earlier and more generous resolution. They argue that any attempt to base a negotiated treaty on the idea that the Palestinians would receive a mere 22 percent of the land is seen as grotesquely unjust.

But Israel's legal legitimacy does not rest on Resolution 181 or ultimately on any decision or acknowledgement of the UN. Resolution 181 has no legal validity today because it was a resolution of the General Assembly rather than the Security Council. As such it had a non-binding character and was a mere recommendation instead. As Sir Hersch Lauterpacht, a former member judge of the International Court of Justice, put it: "The General Assembly has no legal power to legislate or bind its members by way of recommendation."[83]

In any case, the Arab leadership rejected the resolution out of hand and then went on to wage war against the Jewish community. It cannot now be brought back to life for the benefit of one party. Nor does Israel's foundational legitimacy rest on the Balfour Declaration, the letter written by British Foreign Secretary Arthur Balfour to Baron Rothschild in 1917, in which the British government made a public declaration of sympathy with the Zionist movement, or any earlier treaties such as the Sykes-Picot agreement. In particular, Resolution 181 abrogated a set of prior legal obligations that had been established by the League of Nations nearly three decades earlier.

The true legal basis for a Jewish state rests on the international settlement that was put in place in the aftermath of the First World War. The League of Nations, birth child of U.S. president Woodrow Wilson, was established in 1919 as part of the Versailles Treaty imposed on Germany. One of its guiding principles was the idea of self-determination—that nations had the right to rule themselves and determine their destiny rather than being ruled by a foreign power. The Great Powers accepted that the land of a defeated enemy would not automatically be annexed as in the past.

Article 22 of the Covenant of the League of Nations called for the national independence of those people living in territories that were previously under Turkish and German control. In somewhat patronizing fashion, the league declared that the "tutelage of such peoples should be entrusted to advanced nations who by reason of their resources, their experience or their geographical position can best undertake this responsibility, and who are willing to accept it." Thus was born the mandates system, according to which the governing power would help the indigenous communities in the mandated territory to develop political, economic and social institutions in order to facilitate self-government and independence. The "well-being and development" of such peoples formed "a sacred trust of civilisation."

After 1918, Palestine was part of the territory formerly belonging to the defeated Ottoman Empire. Under Article 22, it was considered to be one of those communities from the former Ottoman Empire that had "reached a stage of development where their existence as independent nations [could] be provisionally recognized subject to the rendering of administrative advice and assistance by a Mandatory until such time as they are able to stand alone." It became a Class A mandate with Britain as the mandatory power.

The key document that laid the legal foundation for Jewish national statehood was the San Remo resolution of 1920. At the San Remo Conference in Villa Devachan in San Remo, Italy, in April 1920, the principal Allied powers from World War I—Britain, France, Italy, and Japan—represented by Lloyd George, Millerand, Nitti and Matsui (the Japanese ambassador), with the United States as an observer, dealt with some unresolved territorial issues from the previous Versailles treaty. In accordance with Woodrow Wilson's 14 points, which stressed the centrality of self-determination, the aim of the conference was to divide up the territories of the defeated Ottoman Empire and examine the territorial claims made on their behalf, including those of the Zionists. The Zionists claimed territories on both the west and east banks of the Jordan River and for Britain to be the mandatory power, in accordance with the 1917 Balfour Declaration. At San Remo, three mandates were assigned, with the French becoming the mandatory power in Syria and Lebanon and Britain receiving control of Iraq and Palestine.

As regards Palestine, the high contracting parties agreed to the following: "Mandatory will be responsible for putting into effect the declaration originally made on November 8, 1917, by the British Government, and adopted by the other Allied Powers, in favour of the establishment in Palestine of a national home for the Jewish people, it being clearly understood that nothing shall be done which may prejudice the civil and religious rights of existing non–Jewish communities in Palestine, or the rights and political status enjoyed by Jews in any other country." This latter stipulation did not confer a right of national self-determination on Palestine's Arab community, no right of sovereignty as such, but did insist on respect for their civil rights. Such rights would receive recognition in Israel's 1948 Declaration of Independence.

The San Remo Resolution of 1920 was reportedly described by Lord Curzon as "the Magna Carta for the Zionists," and with good reason. Political authority had now been vested in the Jewish people worldwide and the ultimate objective of the resolution was the reconstitution of a Jewish national home. It is important to stress this point, for it helps to rebut the charge that in making a case for Jewish self-determination, the wishes of the majority were unfairly or illegally excluded. The principle of self-determination had a wider application than merely to the existing population of Palestine. This is because in 1919 the Arabs outnumbered the Jews by a factor of six to one and would have vetoed any plan for Jewish self-determination had a plebiscite been held. Such a plebiscite would have been unjustified in any case, for the claims for Arab self-determination had already resulted in a plethora of nation-states carved out of the former Ottoman Empire.

Self-determination, as Howard Grief has pointed out, was vested in the Jewish people as a whole, not just the small remnant of world Jewry then present in Palestine. It was they who became the "national beneficiary of the Mandate or Trust" and effective "sovereign owner of Palestine."[84] Indeed it could hardly have been otherwise, for the creation of a Jewish national home, the whole point of the mandate, would have been impossible in the absence of substantial emigration by the globally scattered Jewish nation.

The San Remo Resolution was subsequently incorporated into the 1920 Treaty of Sevres and, more crucially, inserted into the preamble to the League of Nations Mandate for Palestine. The mandate, approved by the Council of the League of Nations on 24 July 1922, was subsequently binding on fifty-one League of Nations states, and they also received the endorsement of the U.S. Congress that same year. The Anglo-American treaty of 1924 incorporated the text of the mandate, showing that the United States officially recognized the mandatory power's legal obligations.

The mandate for Palestine[85] explicitly recognizes both "the historical connection of the Jewish people with Palestine" and "the grounds for reconstituting their national home in that country." Under Article 2, Britain was "responsible for placing the country under such political, administrative and economic conditions" as would secure "the establishment of the Jewish national home." Under Article 5, Britain was obliged to see that "no Palestine territory" would be "ceded or leased to, or in any way placed under the control of the Government of any foreign Power." As legal expert Dr. Cynthia Wallace points out, Article 5 meant that the members of the Supreme Council "produced binding resolutions relating to the recognition of claims to the Ottoman territories." The agreement "had the force of a legally binding decision of the Powers."[86]

Under Article 6, it was the task of the Palestine Administration to "facilitate Jewish immigration under suitable conditions" and "encourage close settlement by Jews, on the land, including State lands." There were provisions "to facilitate the acquisition of Palestinian citizenship by Jews who take up their permanent residence in Palestine" under Article 7. This latter provision could be seen as the pre–1948 legal basis for Israel's law of the right of return. Finally, Britain was answerable to the league for its actions, as it had to give the council "an annual report in reference to the territory committed to its charge" under Article 24.

The land that was earmarked for the Jewish state covered all of what is today Israel (including the West Bank and Gaza) and the state of Jordan, though in earlier Franco-British negotiations, it was clear that the Jews would receive an even greater portion of land to cover Biblical Palestine. But Article 25 of the mandate allowed Britain "to postpone or withhold application of such provisions of this mandate as he may consider inapplicable to the existing local conditions." Subsequently, in the 1922 Churchill white paper, Britain did indeed hive off three-quarters of the land that had been earmarked in Palestine for the Jewish national home, installing Sharif Abdullah bin al-Hussein as ruler. This action, undertaken for political convenience, could be seen as a direct violation of Article 5 of the mandate, which required the mandatory power to ensure that no Palestine territory was ceded to, leased to or placed under the control of the government of any foreign power.

Israel is often accused of offering the Palestinians a mere 22 percent of historic Palestine, covering the entire West Bank. In reality, it is Israel that had to settle for just over a quarter of the historic homeland with which they had been legally entrusted. The San Remo Resolution and the subsequent mandate created a set of binding obligations under international law. This was not an optional exercise for Britain but a solemn undertaking. As mandatory power, Britain had a fiduciary duty to facilitate the creation of a Jewish homeland in historic Palestine, together with the social, economic and administrative structures necessary to support such a state.

Yet over the next 20 years, Britain would continue to betray the legal provisions of the mandate. Its most egregious breach came in 1939 with the MacDonald white paper, which limited Jewish immigration to 15,000 Jews for each of the next five years, followed by any further immigration being dependent on Arab agreement. In effect, this was tantamount to denying any form of Jewish statehood in Palestine. This decision specifically violated Article

27 of the mandate, which stipulated: "The consent of the Council of the League of Nations is required for any modifications of the terms of this mandate."

The rights laid down in 1920, subsequently ratified in 1922, did not cease with the change of sovereign and were not overruled by the end of the mandate in 1948. Further, the UN Charter included Article 80, which specifically allowed for the continuation of existing mandates (including the British Mandate). Article 80 stated, "Nothing ... shall be construed in or of itself to alter in any manner the rights whatsoever of any peoples or the terms of existing international instruments to which Members of the United Nations may respectively be parties." In other words, all the rights the Jewish people had to the land of Israel, as guaranteed by the League of Nations under the British mandate, remained unaffected by the newly created UN.

Israel's existence as a Jewish homeland rests therefore not only on a justified claim to self-determination but also on solid legal foundations. Arguably, its existence rests on a surer legal footing than more established states, ones whose existence predates any international legal body.

Today, the Palestinian Arab leadership claims a state in the disputed territories, adding to the small state in Gaza and the *de facto* state in Jordan. This claim is based on a right of self-determination that they have built up after living for a number of generations in that area. There is no need to elaborate on the right of self-determination, as it has been covered already. However, the important qualification is that in the exercise of that right, only a peaceful state is allowed. The leaders of "Palestine" must create a climate of coexistence and peace, rejecting terrorism and the demonization of Israel in their education system and media. Any future Palestinian state must be demilitarized, with the exception of police forces and a token security force, and cede control of its airspace and borders. That such a proto-state is far from being created owes much to the poor leadership decisions of the Palestinian Authority and the failure of the West to hold it to account.

Moral Justification

It sounds odd to argue that there is a moral reason why a state should exist. In a world where claims to national sovereignty have so often rested on the outcome of war, subjugation and conquest, as well as secret treaties with other states, the idea that there is an ethical basis for statehood seems contrived and far-fetched. Countries just exist, their presence taken for granted in international forums, regardless of any wrongs they may have been committed in their past. But Israel is different in that there was always a profound moral basis to establishing Jewish nationhood in the world.

Today, Israel represents the world's only guaranteed safe haven for Jews fleeing persecution, discrimination and oppression. It is a sanctuary that will always open its doors to Jews regardless of the prevailing socio-economic or political circumstances. Historically this has been a vital part of Israel's very raison d'être. During its 68 years, Israel has opened its borders to Holocaust survivors from Europe as well as Jewish communities threatened with pogroms in the Arab world. While Western countries have enacted laws to protect the civil and religious rights of their Jewish populations, they do not have the safe-haven function that Israel alone can offer. This protective capacity invests the Jewish state with a unique mission and moral purpose in the life of world Jewry and within the international community.

There have been occasions when this principle has been tested. In the raid on Entebbe in 1976, Israeli paratroopers rescued a large group of Israelis who were being held hostage in Uganda by Idi Amin's government. Without a Jewish state, those hostages would almost certainly have remained the captives of that African tyrant. Eventually, they might all have been murdered, abused or traded for some of the world's most notorious terrorists. Similarly, in Operation Solomon in 1984, Israel rescued thousands of Ethiopian Jews who were threatened with death during the civil wars enveloping that country. No other country would have carried out such an operation, certainly not with the consummate preparation and skill of the Israeli forces. "Israel, alone," declared the *Sunday Times*, "was capable of plucking a whole people from the nightmare of the Ethiopian famine with such brilliant élan and brushing aside all its own material problems in order to welcome its African brothers."[87]

Those who believe that no such "safe haven" is necessary would appear to have forgotten the long and tragic history of persecution that has beset the Jewish people for more than two millennia, culminating in the demonic genocide of the Second World War. Indeed the late nineteenth century Zionist movement was forged in a European atmosphere replete with the virulent stench of anti–Semitism. Much of this prejudice was racial, not religious, in nature. Jewish communities were increasingly portrayed as alien and inferior forces that were undermining their host nations; their liberal values, ethnic particularism and economic success increasingly regarded as a destabilizing and insidious threat to civilization. For sure, the more poisonous brand of anti–Semitism built upon a centuries-old tradition of Christian demonization, transmitted through sermons, ballads and pamphlets, in which the Jew was charged with deicide, usury and ritual murder. But this insidious Jew-hate persisted despite the progressive ideals of the French Revolution and the emancipation of European Jews that it spawned.

But it was in late nineteenth century Russia that Judaeophobia spawned the most violent convulsions. Following the assassination of Tsar Alexander II in 1881, Jews were branded as subversives and reactionaries and were punished by the state's increasingly draconian laws. A series of pogroms took their toll on the community and destroyed any lingering sense of complacency. These pogroms and the wider issue of European anti–Semitism, including the Dreyfus Affair, persuaded the Zionists to search for a territorialist solution. Assimilation and exile would only bring renewed persecution. For Moses Hess, writing in *Rome and Jerusalem*, Jews would inevitably be viewed as strangers in the nations they lived in. Leon Pinsker, in *Auto Emancipation*, claimed that Jews would never escape anti–Semitism as long as they were in a minority and in this, he would have agreed with the secularly minded Herzl. It was the terrible experience of suffering, persecution and prejudice that gave the Zionists added moral zeal for their cause. No longer could Jews simply exist at the whim of their cruel rulers. They had to be masters of their own fate.

During the 1930s, anti–Semitic movements, which were stoked by the fires and hatreds of ethnic nationalism, spread like wildfire across Europe. The catalyst came from Nazi Germany where a once-thriving and highly assimilated Jewish community of some 500,000 was increasingly subjected to legal restrictions, racial discrimination and poisonous, state-sponsored hatred. When Germany forcibly added Austria and Czechoslovakia to the Reich in 1938-9, hundreds of thousands of Jews suddenly became trapped within the confines of the most Judaeophobic nation on earth.

Italy promulgated the Manifesto of Race in 1938, which stripped Jews of citizenship and banned them from holding any government position. In Hungary, Prime Minister Teleki introduced the second anti–Jewish law in 1939, banning Jews from holding government positions and imposing severe quotas on Jews in all major professions and in commerce. In Romania, the government of Octavian Goga passed laws in 1938 that stripped many thousands of Jews of their citizenship.[88] Conditions were awful too in Poland, the location of Europe's biggest Jewish population. Jews were barred from many professions with prejudice manifesting itself in many forms.[89] It was, as Walter Laqueur has written, "the declared policy of successive Polish governments to make the position of Polish Jewry intolerable and compel them to emigrate."[90]

But as the gates of hell were descending upon the Jews of Europe, the gates to the free world were slamming shut. France had restricted entry to Jewish immigrants in the post–World War I years, with trade unions voicing opposition to an influx of "cheap labour."[91] Canada had a highly restrictive policy on Jewish immigration, allowing in a mere 5,000 refugees from Nazism in the 1930s. Under the Mackenzie government, vigorous efforts were made to keep out Jewish emigrants. The architect of this policy was the anti–Semitic Frederick Charles Blair, director of Canada's immigration branch from 1936 to 1943. Blair's most infamous act was to turn away more than 900 German Jews who were aboard the M.S. *St. Louis* in June 1939. The ship was forced to turn back to Europe, where 254 of those on board later perished.[92]

From 1880 to 1924, the United States had become a safe haven for over 2 million East European and Russian Jews. For the Jewish immigrants, America came to represent a beacon of hope in a world dominated by tyranny, oppression and the secret police. But the anti-communist Red Scare of 1919 and the growth of nativist sentiment, symbolized by growth in support for the Ku Klux Klan, led to a series of restrictive quotas on further immigration. The Emergency Immigration Act of 1921 and the Johnson-Reed Immigration Reform Act of 1924 severely limited the number of immigrants (largely Eastern European Jews) who could enter the country by the imposition of ethnic quotas. The annual number of Jewish immigrants fell sharply from between 100,000 and 150,000 to 49,000 and later to 11,000. In the 1930s, these quotas blocked the escape route for vast numbers of European Jews who were desperate to flee the worst excesses of their governments' extremism and discrimination. A bill in 1939 to bring 20,000 German Jewish children into America was blocked by a wall of congressional opposition, much of it spurred by testimony from extreme nationalistic groups who disavowed the rescue of Jews.

No doubt, the opposition of Congress to a pro–Jewish immigration policy reflected public opinion. Indeed in one poll conducted in April 1939, only 8.7 percent of respondents favored the admission of refugees.[93] In a wider sense, there was widespread hostility towards America's Jewish minority in the 1920s and 1930s. During the Depression, many sought to blame their nation's unprecedented economic catastrophe on a convenient Jewish scapegoat. Opinion polls from the late 1930s onwards show widespread hostility towards Jews in America, with over half the population believing that they were greedy, dishonest and possessed of too much power, particularly in business and politics.

According to polls taken from 1938 to 1945, roughly 15 percent of those surveyed would have supported "a widespread campaign against the Jews in this country," another 20–25 percent would have sympathized with it and 30 percent would have opposed it. Jews were not allowed into some social clubs, while there were quotas for entrance to colleges. There were certainly many anti–Semitic agitators, chief among them Henry Ford, arch proponent of *The*

Protocols of the Elders of Zion, and Father Charles E. Coughlin, whose Sunday radio broadcasts reached 3.5 million listeners.[94] Admittedly, these American demagogues lacked the reach of their European counterparts, but they still had some influence within American society.

The most telling and tragic symbol of global indifference to the plight of the Jews was the ill-fated Evian Conference. In July 1938, following the call of President Roosevelt some three months earlier, representatives of 32 countries and several dozen organizations arrived at Evian-les-Bains in France in order to discuss a coordinated rescue plan for German Jewish refugees. Chaim Weizmann asked to address the conference, but his request was flatly refused by the American who presided over the conference. Golda Meir was able to attend the conference but not allowed to address it.

In a telling display of hypocrisy, one national representative after another made public declarations of sympathy for the refugees before explaining why their country would offer little or no help to resettle them. The Belgian delegate said that his country deemed it "a point of honour not to assume fresh international obligations whose consequences she [couldn't] estimate."[95] Ireland could "make no real contribution," while Switzerland considered it "essential to exercise very stringent control over the admission of any further foreigners."[96] Canada's immigration department, headed by Frederick Blair, was determined to block Jewish immigrants from entering the country. One of Australia's delegates, Thomas White, offered these infamous words to explain why Australia would not help take in more than the existing quota of refugees: "It will no doubt be appreciated also that as we have no real racial problem, we are not desirous of importing one by encouraging any scheme of large-scale foreign migration."

Incredibly, the Dominican Republic offered to take in 100,000 Jews, though the imposition of an entrance tax of $500 for all immigrants somewhat dulled its viability. Though Britain and the United States did allow Jewish refugees to enter their countries, the former through the *Kindertransport* program, each acted rather more cynically. The British demanded that the issue of Palestine not be raised while the United States barred any interference with their existing quota system. As one German newspaper commented on Evian: "We can see that one likes to pity the Jews … but no state is prepared to … accept a few thousand Jews."

In words that were more poignant than he could possibly have realized, Weizmann spoke of Europe's Jews on the eve of war: "There are in this part of the world six million people pent up in places where they are not wanted, and for whom the world is divided into places where they cannot live and places where they may not enter."[97] With so many of the nations failing in their moral duty, the homeland cherished by the Zionist dream offered the only viable alternative. Indeed how could those who were sympathetic to Jewish concerns argue otherwise?

The moral imperative of creating a safe haven was cemented by the Holocaust and the destruction of two-thirds of European Jewry. But it was not just the appalling slaughter of six million Jews that necessitated the creation of a Jewish safe haven. It was the fact that during the Second World War, no foreign Allied government *prioritized* the plight of Jewry. No nation offered a guarantee to open its gates to those fleeing the Nazi genocide. As the mandatory power, Britain must bear a burden of responsibility for its wartime record.

The British War Cabinet consistently "resisted any suggestion that those Jews who could escape from Nazi-controlled Europe should be allowed into Palestine."[98] Those Jews who were caught trying to reach Palestine had been deported to a number of colonies, including the island of Mauritius. Others, such as the estimated 781 Jewish refugees on board the *Struma* who reached Istanbul *en route* to Palestine, were stopped from entering the country because of the white paper then in force. When their ship was ordered out of Turkish waters by the then-neutral Turkish government, it was sunk, killing all but one of the passengers.

On 5 March 1942 the War Cabinet went so far as to decide that "all practicable steps should be taken to discourage illegal immigration to Palestine," this at a time when Jews were desperately seeking to escape the brutal and relentless Nazi extermination machine. When, on 23 March 1943, the archbishop of Canterbury, Cosmo Lang, moved a resolution that called for the granting of temporary asylum to beleaguered Jews in Europe, the government declined his suggestion. Immigration restrictions would remain in place, said Viscount Cranbourne, because opening the door to fleeing refugees would lead to shortages of food and housing.[99] Thus during the bleakest chapter of Jewish history, when the Jews of Europe were collectively subjected to the most appalling and inhumane treatment ever witnessed in history, Britain's government remained passive, indifferent and hostile.[100]

In the USA, the fate of potential Jewish emigrants was sealed by the fact that the man in charge of refugee policy, assistant Secretary of State Breckinridge Long, was anti-immigrant and anti–Semitic.[101] In 1940 and 1941, Long tightened visa restrictions and imposed increasingly draconian quotas, leading to a number of protests. As the war went on, Treasury officials discovered that Long and the State Department not only had secretly cut immigration even further but had also blocked the transmission of information about the Holocaust coming from Switzerland.

A report was produced with the title "Acquiescence of This Government in the Murder of the Jews." It revealed that State Department officials had used government machinery designed to rescue Jews to actually prevent their rescue, had attempted to block information about ongoing massacres and had tried to cover up their guilt by concealment, misrepresentation and the issuing of false information. Realizing that the release of this document would be political dynamite (1944 was an election year), and under intense pressure from prominent individuals and organizations, Roosevelt created the War Refugee Board, designed to facilitate the rescue of European Jews, and other persecuted minorities, in Axis territory. But it received scant support from the administration, and only a tiny percentage of its funding came from government.[102] Jews in the 1930s and 1940s could no more rely on the USA, home to the world's most powerful Jewish community, than they could on any of Europe's nations. It is little wonder that Abba Eban declared: "The Holocaust and the world's response to it mark the lowest point in the moral history of mankind."[103]

To make matters worse, the postwar British government of Clement Attlee was resolutely opposed to allowing Jewish refugees to enter Palestine. To prevent "illegal" immigrants entering Palestine from Europe, the British returned captured immigrants to displaced camps in Germany or held Jews in former prisoner of war camps. Forcing these refugees to return to parts of Europe in which they had experienced such unprecedented suffering, torture and maltreatment was just another act of inhumanity unworthy of such a great nation.

Those who question Israel's moral legitimacy or deride its law of return should therefore revisit their own countries' prewar and wartime records in regard to the Jews. If those countries were so indifferent to the rescue of Jewish refugees at a time of unprecedented peril, it was only right to create a state that actually would rescue Jews.

This does not mean that the Holocaust has become the primary or sole justification for a Jewish state—far from it. If it were, then some might sympathize with Ted Honderich's suggestions that after the war, "a homeland for the Jewish people ought to have been created out of Germany." Completely ignoring events before 1945, he sought to justify this position by saying, "It was not the Palestinians who voted for Hitler in a German democracy and then ran the death camps."[104] But of course, no one would seriously suggest that the Palestinians were primarily responsible for the Holocaust, a classic straw man strategy. The demand for a national home to be sited in Palestine had little to do with the Holocaust. Instead it was primarily about the historical and spiritual connections that Jews had with the area for three millennia. The Holocaust simply added a further layer of moral justification.

6. The Actual Cause of the 90-Year Conflict: Arab and Palestinian Rejection and Western Appeasement

It is often said that Jewish national aspirations in Palestine were inevitably going to set up a clash between Jew and Arab. There is certainly some evidence of local Arab opposition to Zionism in the early years of the movement. An example is the petition sent in 1891 from a group of Jerusalemites to Constantinople demanding an end to land sales to Jews and an end to Jewish immigration. Six years later, an Arab commission was formed in Jerusalem to examine the sale of land to Jews, the subsequent protests from which led to a temporary halt to such sales. In 1905, Naguib Azoury wrote *Le Reveil de la Nation Arabe* (*The Awakening of the Arab Nation*), in which he predicted that Palestine's Arabs and Jews would clash violently for control of the country. Later, in 1917, Sharif Husayn expressed his concerns with the Balfour Declaration, arguing that while he could accept an influx of Jews to Arab countries, he could not accept an independent Jewish state.[1]

Nonetheless, harmony could have prevailed in Palestine from the moment when Zionist ideals were being firmly imprinted on the map. A sign of what might have happened can be seen from the exchange between Amir Faysal ibn Hussein of Mecca and Chaim Weizmann, a prominent Russian Zionist living in Britain. The Amir, "mindful of the racial kinship and ancient bonds existing between the Arabs and the Jewish people," struck an agreement with the Zionist leader on 3 January 1919. He promised "all necessary measures to encourage and stimulate immigration of Jews into Palestine on a large scale" and those measures that would "settle Jewish immigrants upon the land through closer settlement and intensive cultivation of the soil."[2]

Nor was Hussein the only Arab notable to adopt such sympathetic sentiments. Ahmad Ziwar Pasha, Egypt's prime minister from 1924 to 1926, "took part in the celebrations of the Balfour Declaration in 1917." His pro–Zionist position was shared by former Egyptian cabinet minister Ahmad Zaki, who in 1922 celebrated the "victory of the Zionist idea."[3] There were also village sheiks in parts of Palestine who signed petitions that supported Jewish immigration to the country.[4] Their motives included the promise of economic gain, the self-interest of their claim, and their rejection of militant Arab violence.

It is possible that moderate leaders might have emerged from within the ranks of Palestine's Arab community. These would have been leaders of a pragmatic mindset, unencumbered by fanaticism or personal ambition and aware of Zionism's economic benefits to the indigenous Arab population. But such an outcome is usually confined to democratic societies in which the will of the majority is genuinely respected. Sadly, there was no tradition of liberal or participatory government in the Ottoman Empire or in the wider Muslim and Arab world. Instead the leadership of Palestinian Arabs during the mandate years fell to an extremist called Hajj Amin al Husseini. Husseini's visceral anti–Semitism, religious extremism and personal corruption would set Palestine's communities on a disastrous collision course for decades to come.

Like the other Palestinian and Arab leaders who would come after him, Husseini rejected as illegitimate the Jewish claim to self-determination. He seethed with hatred for international Jewry, launching endless diatribes in which he accused Jews of undermining the Muslim prophet, of being deceitful and treacherous, of corrupting the morals of Palestinian Arab society and of seeking to undermine Muslim holy sites in Jerusalem. Much like today's Palestinian Authority, the mufti used his extensive influence (newspapers, pamphlets, school system) to fulminate against alleged Jewish wrongdoing in the most venomous tones. In one diary entry he wrote: "How can the Jews be respected for their wealth at a time when they spread wickedness and misery throughout the world?"[5] The mufti made particular use of the charge that the Jews were a threat to the Temple in Jerusalem and were planning to destroy the al Aqsa mosque built upon it, charges that were used to incite violence against Palestinian Jewry. He also distributed *The Protocols of the Elders of Zion*, the notorious forgery purporting to reveal an insidious Jewish conspiracy to dominate the globe.

But Palestinian rejectionism alone is only half the reason this conflict has persisted for so long. What accompanied this intransigence was a mindset of appeasement from other powers, whether this was the British mandatory authority, the United Nations, European powers or Israeli leaders themselves. Together, irreconcilable hostility to Zionism and indulgent appeasement created a potent cocktail that ignited the bonfire of murderous violence well into the twenty-first century. Rejectionism met by appeasement only made Palestinian leaders think that their tactics of violence, terrorism and intimidation were succeeding, and that the forces arrayed against them were unwilling to uphold their interests and legal obligations. As a result, they were never satisfied with the concessions made to them, ultimately because their aims were non-negotiable.

We can see this fateful combination at work as early as 1920, the year that the mufti incited an Arab mob to attack the Jewish community in Jerusalem and kill five people. Husseini fled the country and was sentenced to a ten-year prison term *in absentia* but was then pardoned months later by Sir Herbert Samuel, the British governor in Palestine. Husseini's reward for the 1920 riot was to be appointed the next mufti of Jerusalem in 1921, the most important religious post in Palestine as the occupant was a "supreme legal adviser in questions of religious canon law."[6]

That Husseini was even included on the list of nominees was down to British influence; the groups entitled to vote for the next mufti did not include Husseini owing to his lack of educational qualifications. Even then, he received a lower share of the votes than the top three candidates and thus should have been dropped altogether after the vote had been counted. As it was, Samuel wished to balance the power of the two leading Arab families in Jerusalem (the Husseinis and the Nashashibis) and thus persuaded one of the leading candidates to exclude himself, allowing Husseini to be accepted.

Prior to Samuel's agreeing to the appointment he had dined with Husseini, and the Palestinian had assured him that there would be full cooperation with the mandate. Thus British administrators supported and later subsidized the mufti (half his salary was paid by the government in Palestine) because they assumed that their patronage would generate goodwill. Instead their largesse would fund religious intolerance and lethal violence. What is also clear, however, is that Samuel was trying to accommodate Arab opinion, only for the tactic to lead to bitter recrimination.

Later in January 1922, Husseini became the president of the Supreme Muslim Council, giving him a commanding platform in Palestinian political, financial and religious life. He used this office to disseminate his zealous anti–Semitism and to agitate against the Balfour Declaration. His control of *Waqf* funds allowed him to create "an army of paid propagandists, agitators, thugs and gunmen" and neglect expenditure on education and welfare.[7]

After further anti–Zionist riots in May 1921 in Jaffa, in which 47 Jews and 48 Arabs were killed, the British authorities set up the Haycraft Commission of Inquiry. Though the commission established that the Arab mobs were responsible for the bloodshed, it also concluded that the violence resulted from fears about Jewish immigration and was critical of Zionist methods and ambitions.

The British authorities proceeded to undermine the Zionist movement by removing more than three-quarters of the area that had been allotted at San Remo for the Jewish National Home and giving it to Emir Abdullah. This area would henceforth be closed to Jewish development. In response to the outbreak of Arab violence in Jaffa in May 1921, Samuel ordered an immediate temporary suspension of Jewish immigration to Palestine. Though the prohibition on immigration was soon lifted, the notion of imposing some limit was discussed and later accepted by both Samuel and the Colonial Office. Jewish immigration would now be based on the "economic absorptive capacity of Palestine," an idea that would later be wholly at odds with the requirements of Article 6 of the 1922 mandate, which called for "close settlement" of the land. Major Young, a leading advisor at the Colonial Office, told Colonial Secretary Winston Churchill that Samuel's policy was telling the Arabs in Palestine that the British commitment to its mandate obligations had "wavered" and that they "must be prepared to take a stronger line."[8] Not for the last time, the Palestinian Arabs were learning that violence brought its share of rewards.

Nonetheless the British concession would do little to satisfy Arab critics of Zionism. In August 1921, Churchill received an Arab deputation in London that demanded a total ban on Jewish immigration and the nullification of the principle of a National Home for the Jews. The deputies refused to meet Chaim Weizmann. Churchill made a revealing remark to the deputation, namely, "Many of the British officials in Palestine are very, very friendly to the Arabs, more so than to the Jews."[9] Churchill's view would be echoed by Sir John Shuckburgh, the head of the Middle East Department at the Foreign Office, when he wrote to Churchill on 1 December 1921, "It is unfortunately the case that the army in Palestine is largely anti Zionist."[10] However, hostility to Britain's Palestine policy was not confined to these quarters alone. In 1921, the House of Lords voted by 60 to 29 against the Balfour Declaration.

Samuel attempted to win over Arab objectors by establishing a legislative body that incorporated all sections of Palestinian society. In the British constitution for Palestine, there was a plan to establish a consultative body to advise the high commissioner, some members of which would be elected from the population. It would consist of eight Muslims, two Christians and two Jews. Both Muslims and Christians decided to boycott the elections, in part because they would have been unable to discuss Britain's Zionist obligations. Attempts to create an Arab agency, rivaling the Zionist Executive, similarly failed. Any such institutions, no matter how imperfect, would have implied some form of Arab acquiescence in the Balfour Declaration and Zionist policy. Again, the Nashashibis favored such participation.

In 1929, there was a bloody wave of attacks against Jewish communities across Palestine. The old Jewish quarter in Jerusalem came under attack, while a ferocious assault was launched against Jews in Hebron and Safed. A total of 133 Jews were slaughtered by the rampaging mobs before the British authorities helped to restore order. One hundred and sixteen Arabs also died, though most were killed by British forces.[11] In the words of Sir John Chancellor, high commissioner of Palestine from 1928, there were "acts of unspeakable savagery upon Jewish people."[12]

That the mufti had played a role in instigating the violence is undeniable. For the previous year, he had spread rumors that the Jews were plotting to take possession of the al-Aqsa mosque and encouraged Arab disturbances at the Wailing Wall. He had seized upon an incident on 24 September 1928 when Jews had put up a portable screen in front of the Western Wall, claiming that this was a desecration of Islamic property. (This claim was dismissed by British officials.)[13]

Yet the Shaw Commission, which was set up by the British government to investigate the causes of the carnage, exonerated the mufti. It concluded that he had largely cooperated to quell the violence and to restore peace and order. A senior official from the League of Nations Permanent Mandates Commission expressed his surprise that the report concluded there was "no premeditation or organization of disturbances on the part of the Arab leaders," in particular Husseini.[14] However, one member of the Shaw Commission was alert to the mufti's sinister machinations, and said he had to "bear the blame for his failure to make any effort to control the character of [the] agitation."[15]

This was accurate, for the mufti had helped to instigate an orgy of insurrection and violence and shown himself irreconcilably hostile to British policy. The mandatory authorities were within their rights to imprison him or send him into permanent exile. Instead he was rewarded with yet another British concession, the Passfield White Paper of 1930, which recommended restrictions on land purchase by Jewish immigrants, as well as severe restrictions on Jewish immigration itself. The report concluded that the cause of the outbreak was "the Arab feeling of animosity and hostility towards the Jews consequent on the disappointment of their political and national aspirations and fear for their economic future." There was criticism of Zionist land policy, which was blamed for worsening Arab unemployment. The report caused alarm in London, where the MacDonald government was only too aware that a loss of Jewish immigrants would reduce tax revenues, thus forcing up government expenditure in Palestine.[16]

MacDonald issued a letter to Weizmann explicitly repudiating the Passfield White Paper, but Jewish immigration was still cut. Not that this mollified the mufti. With the logic of appeasing the unappeasable kicking in, this concession simply radicalized him further. He refused to recognize any Jewish right of worship at the Wailing Wall, or for that matter in Palestine. Further, he told Lord Passfield that he wanted Britain to abandon the Balfour Declaration and bar all future land sales to Jews.

At this stage, the mufti and his supporters picked up a valuable lesson about violence. The British would try to prevent Jewish self-defense while making delayed and inadequate attempts to prevent sporadic Arab attacks. After each major confrontation, the British would hastily convene an inquiry to investigate the causes of the riot, only to conclude that the Arabs had legitimate fears of displacement as a result of Zionist policy. The logical response was to address those fears by curbing Zionist immigration or land sales, thus dealing a blow to the Jews of Palestine. The policy virtually guaranteed incessant Arab violence and rejectionism.

Thus in 1936, the mufti led yet another campaign of terror and intimidation, except this time the targets were Palestine's Jewish communities, the British authorities and Arab dissidents. The Arabs launched a general strike in April 1936, and Jewish shops, farms and houses were attacked and destroyed. Within six months, some 80 Jews had been killed and much property pillaged. The mufti's forces, who were well armed and well trained, carried out acts of violence "in a planned and co-ordinated attempt ... to force various demands on Britain."[17] They sabotaged the oil pipeline in North Palestine, mined the roads, set forests on fire, raided villages and terrorized neighborhoods. Despite this tumult, the Jewish Agency continued to urge a policy of restraint (*havlagah*) in the face of the rising violence, something accepted by both official Zionists and revisionists alike.

There was also a wave of assassinations of the mufti's rivals, including leading mayors, sheiks and other notables. The pillaging of Arab villages by the rebels was a constant feature of the terror, and it has been estimated that far more Arabs than Jews died in the three-year revolt. The mufti's thugs would descend on isolated villages, demanding men, clothing and food. Given that the alternative was certain death for the villagers, no refusal was possible.

Now that the British authority was itself a direct target of Arab violence, stern measures were taken against the radicals. British reinforcements were sent into Palestine and repressive measures were used, including house demolitions and the destruction of rebel villages, to quell the violence. But even though prominent Arab leaders were arrested, the mufti was undisturbed, having convinced the authorities that he was working in the government's interests. Thus all of the Arab agitators arrested and deported to Sinai were members of rival parties; the mufti's followers were not deported. He also persuaded the mandatory government to appoint him as president of the new Arab Higher Committee, another sign of how easily his duplicitous sentiments and sponsorship of violence brought political dividends. As Schechtman puts it, this meant that Husseini "became the sole actual chief of the Arab rebellion."[18]

Only later would the AHC be disbanded and declared illegal, with the mufti escaping to Lebanon from where his campaign of murderous violence could be continued. But his enforced departure only came about because instead of merely attacking Jews and Arab critics, the mufti's gangs had killed a Briton, the district commissioner for the Galilee, L. Y. Andrews. Had he refrained from attacking British officials, there is every reason to think that the mufti could have remained in Palestine. Moreover, his evil machinations were being hatched from Lebanon while he remained undisturbed by either the British or the French. In 1938, his bands killed 297 Jews and a number of his political opponents.

In purely political terms, the Arab revolt could be seen as a considerable triumph for the Palestinian radicals. It forced the British government to rethink the terms of the mandate. In 1937, the Peel Commission, which had been set up a year earlier to investigate the causes of the revolt, recommended the partition of Palestine, a position wholly at odds with the terms and spirit of the mandate. The proposal was to divide Palestine into a Jewish and Arab state with the Jews receiving a mere 15 percent of the territory, the Arabs the other 85 percent and Jerusalem being under international control. It hardly needs to be pointed out that this was a blatant repudiation of Britain's legal commitment under the mandate.

The Zionists, sensing their own weakness and the need to bring more Jews into Palestine from fascist-dominated dictatorships in Germany and Poland, had mixed feelings. The Twentieth Zionist Congress in Zurich voted against the borders set out by the commission but allowed the executive to negotiate for better terms. In effect, this was a vote to back the *principle* of partition. As Chaim Weizmann put it: "The choice lies between a Jewish minority in the whole of Palestine or a compact Jewish State in a part."[19] For Ben-Gurion, a mini-state was a stepping stone to eventual statehood in the whole country, though he left it unclear how the rest of the land could be reclaimed. It is wrongly assumed that this would involve war instead of negotiation and land purchase.[20]

With such a generous proposal in their favor, the Arab leadership could have voted to adopt the Peel proposals. Instead the Arabs rejected this two-state solution (the first of four in the last 75 years). The Arab Higher Committee declared the proposals "incompatible with the justice promised by the British government" and called on Arab states to show unity in the face of such "injustice."[21] When the mufti had appeared before the Peel Commission to give evidence, he made it clear that Palestine had to be handed over to a sovereign Arab body, that such a body would not digest the country's Jewish population and that Arab-Jewish cooperation was impossible. At best, he would allow only those Jews who were resident in Palestine before 1917 to stay in the country while the rest would be forced to leave.

This rejectionist stance was echoed by the other Arab leaders who appeared before the commissioners. Both the Saudi king and the Iraqi prime minister denounced the partition proposals, with the latter declaring that any Arab who led a post-partition Palestine would "stab the Arab race in the heart" and "be regarded as an outcast throughout the Arab world."[22] According to one British official: "All Arabs including Christians are quite definitely ... utterly opposed to partition in any form.... There is no moderate political opinion on this political issue."[23] The Nashashibis, though no less critical of Zionist dominance (as they saw it), advocated cooperation with the British and supported partition, no doubt fearing that they would lose influence under the rival Husseini clan.[24] Sadly, their pragmatic voice did not prevail.

Not surprisingly, the Peel Commission concluded rather despairingly: "Not once since 1919 has any Arab leader said that co-operation with the Jews was even possible."[25] Perhaps some of these leaders shared the mufti's aims, or perhaps they were merely terrorized into acquiescence. Either way, the British simply had no moderate interlocutor on the Arab side. All sought to end the Yishuv in one way or another.

There were some militants on the Zionist side too. In 1931, a Zionist revisionist group called Irgun Zvai Leumi (or Etzel) was formed. Believing that the policy of appeasement had brought no dividends, the group carried out a series of murderous attacks in 1938 that included the planting of five bombs in Arab markets that killed 100 civilians. Within the mainstream Zionist leadership there was widespread condemnation of these acts of terror, causing a halt to the attacks. Another militant nationalist group, Brit Habiryonim, was founded in 1930 by the Russian journalist Abba Ahimeir. However, the group had a limited following and its reputation was severely tarnished after Ahimeir was charged with plotting the assassination of Haim Arlosoroff, the head of the Political Department of the Jewish Agency. Lehi, an even more militant revisionist organization, came to be founded in 1940, with the aim of evicting British forces from Palestine.

With the Arab violence continuing into 1938, much of it directed by the mufti from his exile in Lebanon, the British policy of appeasement reached its apotheosis. A commission headed by Sir John Woodhead recommended dropping the partition proposals and in May 1939, the colonial secretary, Malcolm MacDonald, issued Britain's infamous white paper. Britain declared that it was "not part of their policy that Palestine should become a Jewish state." Instead the plan was to establish an "independent Palestine" within 10 years in which Arab and Jewish Palestinians would "share authority in government" and eventually be put in charge of all departments of government. While this sounded like a policy of evenhandedness, it effectively catered to the Arab majority. For over the next five years, a maximum of 75,000 Jews would be admitted to Palestine and any further immigration would be subject to Arab approval. A quota of 10,000 Jewish immigrants was imposed with additional space for 25,000 refugees, though even this was subject to qualifications. After that five-year period, no further immigration would be allowed "unless the Arabs of Palestine are prepared to acquiesce in it." There would also be powers to prohibit and regulate transfers of land, in violation of Article 6.[26]

Chaim Weizmann denounced the white paper as a final break with the legal obligations that Britain had undertaken in 1922. Not surprisingly, the policy was strongly criticized in a report by the league's Permanent Mandates Commission. It was also condemned by President Roosevelt, though in private and unofficially. But more tellingly, in the words of one high official in the Palestine administration, the British authorities had "let the Jews down rather badly," a sentiment that would reverberate throughout the Yishuv in 1939.[27] What was equally telling in this tale of egregious perfidy was the Arab rejection. Anti–Zionist Arab states ought to have queued up to embrace a policy that meant that Palestine would never have a Jewish majority. Instead, no Arab government publicly endorsed the white paper.

In general, the policy of appeasement in the 1930s was motivated by geopolitical concerns. Throughout the decade, the British chiefs of staff warned the government that Britain, with all her globally scattered imperial commitments, was in an especially vulnerable position. She faced the strategic possibility of a war on three fronts: one in continental Europe against a formidable German foe, one against Italy and one in the Far East against Japan. From the moment that Japan invaded Manchuria in 1931, Britain's Far Eastern colonies were extremely vulnerable, especially Hong Kong and Singapore. Mussolini's desire to recreate the Roman Empire in what he called "Mare Nostrum" posed a clear threat to Britain's Mediterranean possessions, as well as to the Suez Canal. German militarism posed an immediate threat to France and the Low Countries, countries whose independence was essential for the maintenance of the balance of power in Europe. There were fears that a simultaneous war with a combination of all three fascist powers would overwhelm Britain, with its miniscule army and inadequate defense spending. Britain's chiefs of staff thus looked to foreign policy in order to prevent this happening, and that meant appeasement.

Many British diplomats and administrators believed that a pro–Zionist policy would lose Britain valuable Arab friends, jeopardize her interests in the Suez Canal and inflame Muslim sentiment in overseas colonies, especially India. The colonial secretary, Malcolm MacDonald, told Chaim Weizmann that if Britain accepted a Jewish state, even one of minuscule proportions, she would "lose much of the friendship of the authorities and peoples of a number of important surrounding countries like Egypt, Saudi Arabia, Iraq and Syria."[28] The Foreign Office had a number of missions in the Arab world and reported back Arab views of Palestine to London on a regular basis. A typical report came from Charles Bateman, British minister in Egypt, advising in August 1938 that "placating the Arabs" was essential, for the alternative was that Arab hostility might force the closure of the Mediterranean and the Red Sea. Britain, he added, would be left in "queer street."[29] His view was that curtailing Jewish immigration was advisable and in this, much of the Foreign Office's Middle East department would have concurred.

There were also fears that in the event of a global conflict, much of the Arab world would side with the totalitarian powers and threaten Britain's imperial interests. Egypt was of crucial importance for it "gave Britain control of sea and air communications with India and the Far East," Iraq and Persia had vital oil assets while the port of Aden, again an important Royal Naval base on the route to India, could be threatened by a recalcitrant Yemen or Saudi Arabia. Thus the chiefs of staff argued that to protect Britain's imperial strategy, it was vital to maintain "the goodwill of Egypt and the Arab countries in the Near East."[30] They knew well enough that they could rely on the pro–British instincts of the vast majority of Palestine's Jews. But they equally had sound reasons for fearing that Arab countries would gravitate towards the Axis powers. After all, they had similar enemies in the guise of the colonial powers (Britain and France) and the Jews. Nazi anti–Semitism in particular had a strong appeal to Arab sensibilities at a time when the Jewish National Home aroused such strong antipathy in many Arab countries. When the Nuremberg laws were formulated in 1935, Hitler received numerous telegrams from across the Arab and Islamic world. A number of Nazi and fascist-style political parties were formed in Syria and Egypt.[31]

Overall the direction of British Palestine policy in the late 1930s was well summed up by an edition of the *Palestine Post* in December 1938: "The present British cabinet is committed to a policy of appeasement, in Europe and elsewhere. It is anxious for peace and is not prepared to examine too closely the price."[32]

But if the British government had hoped to convert the Arab world to the Allied cause, they were to be disappointed. It is true that some Middle Eastern countries declared war on Nazi Germany (Egypt, Syria, Saudi Arabia, Iraq and Lebanon), but this was early in 1945 (Iraq in 1943) with an Allied victory all but certain. In addition, some key figures sought German help and ammunition during the war, including Saudi Arabia's Ibn Saud and Hikmat Suleiman, the former prime minister of Iraq. Ibn Saud declared: "All Arabs and Mohammedans throughout the world have great respect for Germany, and this respect is increased by the battle that Germany is waging against the Jews, the archenemy of the Arabs."

Egypt's King Farouk was a known admirer of Hitler and sent him a message in 1941 expressing his "great admiration for the Fuhrer" and his hope for a German "victory over England."[33] As a non–Arab but Islamic country, Persia did not escape Nazi influence. According to Arthur C. Millspaugh, who was administrator general of Persian finances during the war, "Reza Shah handed Persia over to Hitler." During the war, the country was crawling with German agents who disseminated a vast amount of Hitlerite propaganda.[34] In Iraq, a short-lived pro–Nazi coup in 1941 led to the massacre of nearly 200 Jews in the *Farhud*.

By contrast, the Jews of Palestine fought on the Allied side from the start. By the end of September 1939, 100,000 men and 30,000 women from among Palestinian Jewry had volunteered for military service. Ben-Gurion, not disguising his contempt for the prewar policy, famously declared: "We shall fight the war as if there were no White Paper and the White Paper as if there were no war." Yet their reward was scarcely forthcoming, at least in terms of the government's Palestine policy. Despite being a vehement critic of the 1939 white paper,

Churchill maintained the policy during the war.³⁵ He was no doubt aware that he would have had to overrule a vast army of bureaucrats, diplomats and military advisors at a time when he was under the most severe strain to win the war. He also battled for four years to authorize the creation of a Jewish fighting force or Jewish division, eventually overcoming the objections of the War Office. And while the Nazi regime was engaged in the systematic slaughter of Europe's Jews, British officialdom, in what must surely count as one of the darkest chapters in its history, largely closed Palestine's doors to Jewish immigration (see Chapter 5).

Above all, the mufti, the Palestinian darling of the Arab world, was a passionate devotee of the Nazi cause and would spend the entire war years praying and working for an Axis victory. After fleeing Lebanon, Husseini arrived in Baghdad in October 1939. Despite Husseini's record of deception and betrayal, and his willingness to incite violence, the British offered him an amnesty in return for agreeing to the white paper. Not surprisingly, their largesse was to go unrecorded. The mufti tried unsuccessfully to reignite the revolt in Palestine while forbidding ordinary Palestinians to volunteer for military service. He also sought to foment unrest in Iraq in order to force the government to adopt a more pro–Axis policy. Later he would be an instigator of the pro–Nazi coup that saw Rashid Ali seize power in Baghdad. In 1941 the mufti lobbied Mussolini for a public endorsement of his ambitions to create a pan–Arab regional empire.

But it was the Nazis for whom the mufti reserved his greatest admiration. Even before the war, the mufti had organized the "Nazi scouts" on the model of the Hitler youth and welcomed the advent of National Socialism in Germany. Such was the depth of his anti–Semitism that his sermons and speeches could have appeared quite easily in *Der Stuermer* or *Volkischer Beobachter*. Already in Iraq (from 1939 to 1941), the mufti, who received a generous financial stipend from the government, was building up a loyal political base in the country. Convinced that an Axis victory was inevitable, and that it would eventually lead to the creation of a pro–German Arab Empire stretched across the Middle East (with the mufti at the head), he started to conduct negotiations with the Germans.

In one letter to Hitler himself, the mufti praised Germany's "Great Leader" and the "courageous German people" and expressed his interest in initiating "negotiations necessary for a sincere and loyal collaboration in all spheres."³⁶ Following the pro–Axis coup in 1941, the mufti broadcast a *fatwa* against Britain and called for a jihad against this "strongest enemy of Islam."³⁷ When the coup failed, the mufti was forced to flee for the sanctuary of Berlin, though not before his anti–Jewish incitement, together with that of the Nazis, bore fruit: the Farhud or pogrom that killed up to 180 Jews.

Then on 28 November 1941, Husseini and Hitler met in Berlin. During the meeting, Husseini promised the Nazi dictator that the Arabs "were prepared to co-operate with Germany with all their hearts and stood ready to participate in the war" provided that the Nazis endorsed his plans for Arab independence. They were, he declared, "engaged in the same struggle." Hitler lauded Husseini's political ambitions and welcomed their shared loathing for international Jewry, informing the Palestinian leader of his plans for a "final solution" to the Jewish question. In Husseini's own words: "Our fundamental condition for cooperating with Germany was a free hand to eradicate every last Jew in Palestine and the Arab world. I asked Hitler for an explicit undertaking to allow us to solve the Jewish problem in a manner befitting our national and racial aspirations and according to the scientific methods innovated by Germany in the handling of its Jews. The answer I got was: 'the Jews are yours.'"³⁸

In other words, the mufti, like Hitler, sought nothing less than the industrial genocide of the Jews. Husseini became an honored guest in Nazi Germany, where he remained until the end of the war. He was put in charge of pro–Nazi propaganda for the Arab and Muslim world and gave speeches on Berlin radio that gave vent to his loathing for Jews. His broadcasts called on Muslims in the Far East to support the fascist regime in Japan and to overthrow British rule in India. He was also active in establishing pro–Axis military units from among the millions of Muslims in the Soviet Union. For his services he was paid over 90,000 marks a month.[39]

Husseini played a significant role in organizing and recruiting thousands of Muslims for a unit of the Waffen SS (the Handschar division). They would go on to murder 90 percent of Bosnia's Jewish community. In addition, the mufti actively opposed Jewish emigration from Axis countries. Thus in June 1943, he wrote letters to the governments of Hungary, Romania, Bulgaria and Italy insisting that they "withdraw their authorization for Jewish emigration" and demanding that Jews be sent instead to Poland.[40]

There is also evidence of his role in the systematic destruction of European Jewry. In January 1944, Dieter Wisliceny told Dr. Rudolf Kastner that he thought the mufti had "played a decisive role in the decision to exterminate European Jews." He later declared that the mufti had been "one of the initiators of the systematic extermination of European Jewry" and that he had been a "collaborator and advisor of Eichmann and Himmler in the execution of this plan."[41] That he knew of the Final Solution is made clear by a reference, in a broadcast from 1944, to the Arab world to "repulse the Jews who number not more than eleven million."[42] Given that it was common knowledge that there were approximately 17 million Jews alive in 1939, it is entirely likely that, being a close confidante of those who were at the forefront of perpetrating the Holocaust, he knew exactly how many Jews had been killed during the war to date. However, some historians strongly question the claims made by Wisliceny.

The mufti also directly intervened with Heinrich Himmler, the architect of the Holocaust, to prevent the release of over 4,000 Jewish children and 500 adults in exchange for 20,000 German prisoners of war. The Jews were sent to Auschwitz instead. He also sought to block the entry of Jews from Hungary into Palestine. On 25 July 1944, he wrote to Hungary's foreign minister saying it was preferable to send 900 Jewish children to a country like Poland where they would be held "under active control" rather than to Palestine. In 1943, he blocked a negotiated attempt to rescue 500 Jews from the Arbe concentration camp.

The mufti should have been tried at Nuremberg, as he had the blood of thousands of Jewish and non–Jewish victims on his hands.[43] However, the Labour government expressed no interest in bringing the mufti to justice, even claiming that he was not a war criminal. Britain's continuing indulgence of the mufti was based on simple calculations of national self-interest. Mark Curtis is probably right when he states that the government's refusal to indict the mufti as a war criminal was based on the "fear that moves against the still popular al-Husseini would increase unrest against the British presence in Egypt."[44] In short, upsetting him would destabilize British imperial interests in the region, or so it was feared. Once again, appeasement was the order of the day.

The mufti then cheated justice in 1946 by fleeing intentionally lax French custody to the security of Egypt. While in Paris, he was given privileged treatment, as he was allowed to stroll around Paris, open his own office and have unrestricted visits by Arab nationalist leaders. Surveillance was nominal and described as "for his protection only." There is speculation that his "escape" was part of a shady deal concocted between the French authorities and the mufti; in return for his not acting against French interests in North Africa, the mufti would be released. Britain and the United States, which had both said that the mufti had to face punishment, made light of his escape, the former withdrawing an extradition request.[45] (Many other Nazi war criminals would escape justice and came to Egypt after the war, finding that the pro–Axis sympathies within the country made for a conducive climate.) With good reason, Simon Wiesenthal would later describe the mufti as an "unexploded bomb" that "people avoid because they haven't yet found the expert able to defuse and render it harmless for those around it."[46] It would not be the first time that European powers would place national interests ahead of moral considerations.

From Egypt, the mufti strengthened his position in the reconstituted Arab Higher Committee and began a campaign of intimidation against his opponents. It is worthy of note that Husseini's record as a Nazi war criminal did not stop Arafat from lauding him. As one of Arafat's biographers points out, "He [the mufti] was a man whom Arafat came to adore and emulate, and whose name he later used as his own."[47]

In April 1946, an Anglo-American committee recommended the admission of 100,000 Holocaust survivors into Palestine. A pan–Arab summit in Cairo denounced the idea of a Jewish national home and warned it would use arms to resist Zionism. The committee wrote that in neighboring Arab countries, "hostility to Zionism was as strong and widespread there as in Palestine itself." They also reported that these Arab governments saw a Zionist state as a means to "impede their efforts towards a closer Arab union."[48] The AHC's vice president, Jamal Husseini, summed up the committee's anti–Zionist rejectionism when he told the Egyptian newspaper *al-Musawwar* in 1946: "There is not a single Palestinian Arab in the world who believes in political means. They all know that bloodletting is the only way to resolve the problem, and every one of them is prepared to shed his blood for the holy cause."[49]

But the Arab states did take comfort from the decision of Britain's Labour government, in September 1945, not to lift the white paper nor admit the 100,000 Jewish refugees, again in contravention of the mandate. Attlee's government was happy to see Holocaust survivors resettled in Germany and other European countries, the very ones that had just instigated the mass murder of 6 million of their co-religionists and merely feigned concern for their welfare. Alternatively, America was seen as a suitable destination, though certainly not Britain.

What was crucial for Britain was not upsetting the Arab states by allowing mass emigration to Palestine. As the notoriously anti–Semitic foreign secretary Bevin later put it to Lord Halifax (British ambassador to the USA) in 1948: "I think that to fly in the face of the Arabs after all the undertakings that have been given would cause a breakdown at the beginning." Britain, after all, had treaties of alliance with Transjordan, Iraq and Egypt and wanted in particular to strengthen Transjordanian claims to the Negev (in violation of the later 1947 Partition Plan) in order to ensure that a line of contiguous territory stretching from Suez to the Jordan River was in the hands of an ally. Worse, in the eyes of British officialdom, the Zionist movement was indelibly tinged with communist influence and would become a base for Soviet influence in the Middle East. Above all, the fact that in the wider Arab region, there were states with huge energy reserves that could be of commercial benefit to the UK was not lost on British policymakers either. Taken together, the overriding concern was to protect Arab interests.[50]

From August 1946, "illegals" travelling on ships towards Palestine from Europe were sent to Cyprus to be detained in camps. Earlier, on 29 June 1946, the British had implemented a fierce crackdown on the *Yishuv*, arresting Jewish leaders, interning some 2,700 suspects, imposing curfews and occupying the Jewish Agency's building in Jerusalem. What became known in Zionist history as "Black Sabbath" was a response to military actions carried out by the Palmach, including the blowing up of road and rail bridges linking Palestine to neighboring countries. There are numerous accounts of venomous anti–Semitic abuse being directed by soldiers towards Palestine's Jews, and of such bigoted attitudes prevailing among British officials.[51]

In 1947, the British government, headed by Labour's Clement Attlee, handed over the Palestine question to the UN. A special committee was formed, UNSCOP, which spent several weeks travelling throughout Palestine and interviewing different communities. At the end of August 1947, UNSCOP proposed the termination of the British mandate and the partitioning of Palestine into an Arab and a Jewish state. By a vote of 51 to 16, the General Zionist Council passed a resolution that described UNSCOP's proposals as "an earnest effort to bring the problem to a just conclusion."[52] Rather predictably, the Arabs decided not to cooperate with UNSCOP.

On 29 November 1947, the UN General Assembly voted by 33 votes to 13, with 10 abstentions, in favor of partitioning Palestine, with the Jews receiving approximately 55 percent of the land (though most of this was the Negev Desert), the Arabs some 42 percent and the Jerusalem area being governed by a body called the UN Trusteeship Council. The Zionists, through the Jewish Agency, reacted with jubilation. They fully endorsed the UN vote, despite reservations about the borders imposed on the state. Just as in 1937, they were prepared to forego their legal right to the entire land because of their urgent need to create a state and accommodate immigrants who were desperate to arrive. Or as Ben-Gurion had put it in a letter to Weizmann: "I would accept a Jewish state in a sufficient section of the country instead of a British mandate and paper rights in the whole country."[53]

However, the Palestinian Arab reaction was a predictably negative one. Arab spokesmen, both at the General Assembly and elsewhere, lined up to denounce the partition vote as invalid, often using the most virulent anti–Semitism to buttress their case. Some even had the temerity to compare Zionism with Nazism, despite the clear evidence that the leader of the Palestinian Arab movement was himself a Nazi war criminal.[54] Fawzi al-Qawuqji, one of the commanders of the 1936 Arab revolt, promised that a vote for partition would have dire consequences: "We will have to initiate total war. We will murder, wreck and ruin everything standing in our way."[55] This would indeed be the outcome of the vote, though only because it was rejected unequivocally by the Arab side.

Some Arab leaders did say that partition alone would create a viable solution to the conflict. Thus Abdullah, emir of Jordan, declared that a two-state formula was "the only realistic solution to the conflict." The emir's main enemy was the mufti, not the Zionists. The prime minister of Iraq, Muzahim al-Pashashi, said, "There would have to be an acceptance of the Jewish state's existence" but "to acknowledge this publicly … would cause a revolt in Iraq." Even the head of the Arab League, Abd al-Rahman, said in 1947, "There is only one solution: the partition of Palestine."[56] As Hillel Cohen also observes in his scholarly study of Palestinian collaboration with Zionism, there were also many Arabs in Palestine who continued to see the economic benefits of a Jewish presence, and thus tried to prevent locals from carrying out military actions.[57] However, these voices did not prevail during the ensuing bloody maelstrom.

From 30 November 1947 until 14 May 1948, the Arabs directed a systematic campaign of mob violence and terror against the Jewish community in Palestine. Shootings and stabbings occurred on a regular basis, Jewish shops and businesses were ransacked and buildings were torched. There were also attacks on Jewish convoys and on the transportation network. Some 180 Jews had been murdered by the end of 1947, more than in the 1929 riots. There was also evidence that the British authorities, including the police, were bystanders to some of these events. Gradually the Arab effort to strangle the proposed Jewish state drew in elements from outside Palestine: a force of the Muslim Brothers crossed from Egypt into Palestine, thousands of men under the Arab leader Abdel Quader al-Husseini operated in Jerusalem and Ramallah, with the help of European volunteers, while another Arab group, operating under Hassan Salameh, who had been trained in Germany, operated around Jaffa.

It is true that there was also violence directed towards Arabs by Jewish extremist groups, often in the form of reprisals for previous violence, as well as targeted attacks against British authorities. The main groups responsible were Lehi and Irgun Zvai Leumi. Lehi, initially led by Avraham Stern (and dubbed the Stern Gang by the British), sought an alliance with Nazi Germany in 1940, believing that Britain rather than Germany was Zionism's main enemy. One operative was sent to Beirut for a meeting with a German official at the Foreign Ministry, but the Germans expressed no interest (not surprisingly) and the operative was jailed on his return to Palestine. It had no more than 500 members. A further attempt to forge a Lehi-Germany alliance failed the following year. The Lehi was a tiny and insignificant group, thwarted by tip-offs from Haganah and Irgun.[58] As Benny Morris points out, their operations "were limited almost completely to thefts of weaponry and bank robberies."[59] They did, however, succeed in assassinating Lord Moyne, minister resident in Egypt, in November 1944 and UN mediator Count Folke Bernadotte in 1948. Their idea of an alliance with fascist powers proved unpopular with mainstream Zionists who craved the defeat of Nazi Germany as much as they wanted independence in Palestine.

The operations of Irgun were more successful and represented a greater challenge to the British authorities. Between 1944 and 1947, Irgun squads attacked police stations, government offices and a variety of other military targets. They also blew up a wing of the King David Hotel in Jerusalem, a British military and administrative headquarters, killing 91 people. They did provide coded warnings beforehand, however, that were ignored. In addition, they kidnapped and killed a number of British soldiers in Palestine, causing outrage back in Britain.

However, neither Irgun nor its tactics represented mainstream Zionist policy. Weizmann, who spent most of his life putting faith in cooperation with the British, was consistent in his condemnation of the extremists. So too was Ben-Gurion, who condemned those he called "Jewish Nazis" and "a bubonic plague."[60] He also described the King David Hotel bombing as "the dastardly act of dissident terrorists" that had been "condemned by ... all the official institutions of the community."[61] Ben-Gurion disavowed the use of "indiscriminate reprisal action" against the Arab community. "Fight the attackers—yes. But leave the innocents alone."[62] In other quarters, Irgun militants were condemned as "misguided terrorists" and "young fanatics" and towards the end of the war, the *Haganah* declared an open hunting season (the *saison*) on the group.[63] The head of military intelligence in Palestine, Colonel C.R.W. Norman, admitted that the Haganah had tried "with some easure of success to suppress the Irgun and Stern Gang ... some of their actions have prevented serious loss of life amongst the security forces."[64] The activities of Jewish extremists and militants were largely disowned by the mainstream Zionists, whereas the Arab terror against the country's Jews was far more an authentic expression of their leaders' genocidal intentions.

As the campaign of violence intensified, the Haganah responded and gradually took the offensive, preventing the attempted Arab takeover of Jewish villages and settlements and protecting vulnerable and isolated communities. Far from embarking on an imperialist war to take over Arab land, the Jews had, in the words of the ALA commander, "constantly endeavoured to narrow the theatre of operations." He put this self-restraint down to a desire for Arab acquiescence in a Jewish state, something that could come about only if most Arab villages and communities were left untouched by the violence. As Ahron Bregman, a historian not afraid of challenging mainstream Israeli historiography, has put it: "The principal aim of the Jews in Palestine in the period immediately after the UN resolution to partition Palestine, was to gain effective control over the territory allotted to them by the UN and to secure communication with thirty three Jewish settlements which, according to the UN plan, fell outside the proposed Jewish state." These Jewish settlements in Arab areas "relied heavily on outside supplies, which made the keeping open of routes a necessity for them."[65]

This was also the rationale behind the much-debated Plan D (Plan Dalet), which was a Haganah plan for rebuffing an expected Arab invasion. Its rationale was to "secure the territorial integrity of the Jewish state and to defend its borders, as well as the blocs of Jewish settlements and such Jewish population as were outside those boundaries, against regular, semi regular, and guerilla forces operating from bases outside or inside the Hebrew state."[66]

The plan also called for operations to be mounted "against enemy population centers located inside or near our defensive system in order to prevent them from being used as bases by an active armed force." This would involve "Destruction of villages ... especially those population centers which are difficult to control continuously" and "in the event of resistance ... the armed force must be destroyed and the population must be expelled outside the borders of the state." In other words, if Arab populations were to be expelled, if was only those that were considered hostile or potentially hostile to the Jewish state rather than the entire Arab population. The essence of the plan was to establish territorial contiguity within, and the future borders of, the prospective Jewish state. It did not involve a premeditated plan for the systematic expulsion of the Arab population.[67]

The creation of the Palestine refugee problem during 1947 and 1948 remains one of the most potent weapons hurled by Israel's critics to delegitimize the state. It is used by them to justify their own rejectionism and to demand a "right of return" for Palestinian Arabs into Israel. Yet the basic facts tell a different story. It is undeniable that between November 1947 and November 1948, at least 580,000 to 600,000 Palestinian Arabs became refugees and lost their homes within the borders of the Israeli state. Some were indeed expelled at certain stages of the war, largely due to reasons of military necessity. Many fled to neighboring states (Jordan, Egypt, Lebanon) while others ended up in Gaza or the districts of the West Bank that were later annexed by Transjordan.

Several points are in order, however. A vital one that should never be forgotten is that if the Arabs had accepted the 1947 partition plan, there would have been no war from 1947 to 1949, no Palestinian refugees, and a Palestinian Arab state would have been created on some 45 percent of the land. That the Arabs chose to launch a war of extermination against their Jewish neighbors is the single most important reason for the creation of the Palestinian refugee problem.

The second point is that the majority of the Palestinian Arab refugees fled Palestine as the area descended into civil war. Like most people caught up in a war zone, the Arabs in big cities such as Haifa and Jaffa, as well as those in the countryside, panicked and took flight to safer zones. Many had heard lurid rumors of alleged Jewish atrocities, with one event in particular standing out: the capture of the village of Deir Yassin on 9 April 1948. Today, Deir Yassin is held up as a prime example of Zionist cruelty and bloodletting, part of a deliberate plot to kill or expel Arabs from the country.

An objective reading of the evidence does reveal that a horrific battle took place that day that caused terrible loss of life for some of the village's noncombatants. Deir Yassin was an Arab village that overlooked the highway between Tel Aviv and Jerusalem. Jews in the Old City had been under siege for five months, and the highway was the only supply route that could be used to bring in food and vital supplies. On 17 April 1948 the *Economist* noted, "A desperate fight is being waged by the Arabs to cut off the community of some 100,000 Jews who live in the Holy City and by the Jews to enable convoys of supplies to reach their beleaguered fellow countrymen." The capture of the village therefore made strategic sense.

According to Benny Morris' account, some "100–120 villagers (including combatants) died," "the IZL [Irgun] and LHI troops systematically pillaged the village" and remaining villagers either fled or were trucked outside the Old City walls.[68] The IZL and LHI lobbed grenades in houses, blew up houses and shot those fleeing into alleyways. Morris talks of "atrocities" being committed by Zionist forces against civilians, including accounts of rape.

However, to paint Deir Yassin as a war crime comparable to, say, the massacre at My Lai would be mistaken. For starters, the Zionist troops used a loudspeaker to urge all citizens of the village to leave, although it is unlikely this was heard. Secondly, there was strong resistance from those inside the village, who opened fire on the Jewish fighters repeatedly. Irgun suffered 41 casualties, including 4 fatalities. To paint all the villagers as innocents caught up in war would therefore be highly inaccurate. None of this excuses the deliberate killing of civilians at Deir Yassin or pillaging, which explains why there was vigorous condemnation of the attack from the Jewish Agency. Yet another question remains: Why would both Irgun and Lehi have allowed hundreds of Arabs to leave if their sole intention was to carry out a massacre?[69] Surely no Arabs would have survived a deliberate massacre, nor would Irgun have allowed into the village a representative of the Red Cross if such a calculated crime had been committed. Moreover, why do Israel's critics single out this terrible event when others, such as the Hadassah Medical Convoy massacre, were as bad, if not far worse?

Deir Yassin did matter for one fundamental reason, namely in its political consequences. According to the *Economist*, "The news of what happened at Deir Yassin had been widely circulated among the Arabs all over Palestine."[70] The Arab media, in the aftermath of the battle on April 9, "broadcast reports about the atrocities—usually with blood curdling exaggerations." The result was as intended—to spark outrage among foreign Arab governments who pledged, as did King Abdullah, to restore honor for the dead, but also to cause "further panic flight from Palestine's villages and towns."[71]

Others were exhorted to leave, with the promise that they would soon return in the aftermath of an Arab victory. Still other Arabs, particularly villagers in various regions in Palestine, were coerced into leaving.[72] Dr. Adel Husein Yahya, director of the Palestinian Association for Cultural Exchange, concluded: "When refugees were asked why they left, the overwhelming majority of them, more than 92 per cent, responded that they left out of fear

... [or] to allow the Arab armies to fight ... or out of plain ignorance on their part of the stakes involved."⁷³ Contemporary evidence for Palestinian *flight* comes not so much from Jewish as from contemporary Arab and British sources.

According to the *Economist* in October 1948, "the most potent of the factors" behind the flight of more than 50,000 of Haifa's Arabs was "the announcements made over the air by the Higher Arab Executive, urging the Arabs to quit."⁷⁴ This was confirmed by the Cyprus-based Near East Arabic Broadcasting Station, which stated on 3 April 1949: "It must not be forgotten that the Arab Higher Committee encouraged the refugees' flight from their homes in Jaffa, Haifa and Jerusalem." In September 1948, Emil Ghoury, secretary of the Arab Committee, had the chance to officially blame the Jews for expelling the Arab refugees from Palestine. Instead he declared that the refugee problem was "the direct consequence of the action of the Arab states in opposing partition."

On a similar note, the Jordanian paper *Filastin* on 19 February 1949 lambasted the "Arab states" which "encouraged the Palestine Arabs to leave their homes temporarily in order to be out of the way of the Arab invasion armies."⁷⁵ Articles from the *London Times*, a paper unfriendly towards the Zionist cause, published nearly a dozen articles on the Palestine conflict in the spring of 1948. None mentioned a policy of expulsion. So it would not be surprising that, according to Sir John Troutbeck, "while the [refugees] express no bitterness against the Jews ... they speak with the utmost bitterness of the Egyptians and other Arab states."⁷⁶

When Sir John Troutbeck, head of the British Middle East office in Cairo, met Palestinian refugees in Gaza in 1949, he found out that they expressed "no bitterness against the Jews" but did "speak with the utmost bitterness of the Egyptians and other Arab states." Referring to their Arab brothers, the prevailing sentiment was that they had been betrayed after they were "persuaded unnecessarily to leave their homes."⁷⁷ They had another reason to feel bitter towards the Arab states in particular. Had Palestine been conquered by Egypt or Jordan, there would have been no Palestinian state. Palestine was a mere vehicle for the imperial ambitions of both countries. As it was, the West Bank was annexed by Jordan following the war and all its residents became Jordanian citizens. For their part, the Egyptians ruled Gaza as an occupied military zone and did nothing to create a sense of Palestinian identity in the area.

That said, there were some expulsions of Palestinian Arabs from the towns of Lydda and Ramle in July 1948 in order to prevent these strategically located cities from forming a hostile armed base in the event of an armed attack. But these exceptions show that expulsion was an *ad hoc* affair carried out for military necessity rather than the result of premeditation. By the end of 1948, some 160,000 Arabs remained in the new borders of Israel and became Israeli citizens. They became subject to the foundational document of the state, its declaration of independence, which gave a constitutional guarantee of "political equality of rights" and which urged Arab citizens to "take part in the building of the state on the basis of full and equal citizenship and on the basis of appropriate representation in all its institutions."

If there was a full-scale program of ethnic cleansing as some claim, if the nascent Israeli state wanted to establish "an exclusive Jewish community" in the words of one left-leaning historian,⁷⁸ why were these Arabs allowed to remain instead of being expelled? Why were they allowed to multiply to their present numbers, instead of being uprooted and displaced? It's a question that apologists for the Palestinian cause would do well to ask themselves.

In addition, there is considerable evidence to suggest that in mixed towns, such as Haifa, Tiberias and Jaffa, the Palestinian Arabs left despite the exhortations of Jewish leaders for them to stay. In Haifa, the Arab population was rapidly being depleted despite the tearful entreaties of Mayor Levy for the refugee flood to stop. The Arab committee in the town rejected a truce that would have allowed the remaining Arabs to stay. According to a report from the Haifa District HQ on 26 April 1948: "Every effort is being made by the Jews to persuade the Arab populace to stay and carry on with their normal lives."[79] Following the mass Arab flight from Jaffa, a Haganah communiqué noted: "This is not the time to rejoice. The city of Jaffa is almost empty. We promised the [remaining] residents a peaceful and dignified life and it is incumbent on each and every one of us to uphold this commitment; this is a matter of honour and the hard moral core of our army."[80]

Sir Henry Gurney, in no way a friend of the Zionists, knew exactly who to blame for the flight of Arab residents in Jaffa: "It is pathetic to see how the Arabs have been deserted by their leaders, and how the firebrands all seek refuge in Damascus, Amman and elsewhere when the real trouble starts."[81] "Speaking of the Arabs who had fled Palestine," the *Economist* commented, "this does not suit the Jews who are trying to persuade the Arabs to return to Haifa, where they count on using cheap Arab labour."[82]

The third point which must never be forgotten is that as a result of this conflict, there were two refugee crises, not one. From 1947 onwards, Jewish communities across the Middle East and North Africa, communities that dated back more than two millennia, were forced to flee their homes either because of the threat of Arab violence and intimidation, or because they were physically expelled. Most found sanctuary in the Jewish state, though they were forced to leave their assets behind.

The Jews who fled the Arab world were largely not voluntary emigrants. The Jewish communities in Egypt, Morocco, Algeria, Tunisia, Iraq, Aden, Libya, Iran and Syria were many centuries old, in some cases millennia old, and had long played a vital role in the commercial, political, cultural and social life of those countries. Over centuries, they had experienced bouts of tolerance and goodwill together with the ever-present reality of pogroms, persecution and discrimination. They usually lived at the whim of whichever caliph or ruler was imposed on them. The Jewish exodus from the Arab world was an enforced one, brought about by the scarring effects of anti–Semitic incitement and murderous violence.

A wave of riots in Tripoli and other Libyan cities in 1945 led to the murder of 129 Jews. A Muslim mob in British-controlled Aden carried out a three-day rampage in the Jewish quarter, killing 82 Jews. Anti–Jewish violence in Aleppo led to the exodus of most of its 7,000 Jews, while the Muslim Brotherhood whipped up a frenzied hatred of Jews and Zionists in Cairo. Articles in the Lebanese press accused Jews of poisoning wells. As the War of Independence intensified, so too did the mob violence. Dozens of Jews were killed in attacks on Cairo's Jewish quarter and in Tripoli in June 1948, as well as in a number of Moroccan cities.

This orgy of violence had already been predicted. Jamal al-Hussayni, who represented the Arab Higher Committee of Palestine at the UN, told assembled delegates: "It must be remembered that there are as many Jews in the Arab world as there are in Palestine whose positions ... will become very precarious. Governments in general have always been unable to prevent mob excitement and violence."[83] Egypt's Heykal Pasha, shortly before the UN vote on partition, told the UN to "not lose sight of the fact that the proposed solution might endanger a million Jews living in the Moslem countries." He added that a UN vote on partition would make that body "responsible for the massacre of a large number of Jews." More ominous still was a warning from senior Arab diplomats who met in Beirut in March 1949: "If Israel should oppose the return of the Arab refugees to their homes, the Arab governments will expel the Jews living in their countries."[84] Some Muslim rulers, such as the Moroccan sultan Muhammad V, condemned this orgy of violence and called for his Jewish subjects to be protected, while simultaneously denouncing Zionism.

After the failure to destroy Israel in 1948, the repercussions for Jewish populations in the Arab world were severe. In Iraq, Jews were systematically removed from public life, so that within a year, "ninety five per cent of all Jews in official positions ... had been dismissed."[85] In November 1948, the promulgation of Zionism was made a criminal offence with a punishment of 7 years' imprisonment or a heavy fine. Secret police arrested and tortured suspected Zionists, with many Jews fearing for their lives. Eventually the vast bulk of the community was allowed to emigrate in 1950–1, though at the cost of permanently revoking their Iraqi citizenship. In Egypt, a mass exodus of Jews came about following the Egyptian government's response to the Suez War. Some 24,000 received deportation notices and were forced to leave Egypt within days.[86] Thus the former Canadian minister of justice, Irwin Cotler, is right when he says: "the displacement of 850,000 Jews from Arab countries is not just a 'Forgotten Exodus' but a "Forced Exodus."[87]

The 850,000 Jewish refugees who came from Arab countries "came with nothing, and were taken in, sheltered, fed, housed and found places in the workforce, despite the heavy financial costs to the Israeli government."[88] Today, half of Israel's Jews are descendants of these refugees. Clearly, in any future settlement, both Palestinian Arab and Jewish refugees deserve compensation for lost property, though in monetary terms, the Jewish claims would be greater.

The Arab war against a Jewish homeland intensified shortly after David Ben-Gurion announced the creation of a Jewish state on 14 May 1948. A day later Israel came under attack from the armies of Syria, Iraq, Egypt, Transjordan and Lebanon. It is true that the Jewish state faced a number of advantages, particularly in terms of manpower, preparation, superior lines of communication and sheer determination. Arguably, this detracts from the notion that this was a David vs. Goliath struggle that Israel won miraculously.[89] Nonetheless, for a people already scarred by the Holocaust and listening to the blood-curdling rhetoric coming out of Arab mouths, this appeared to be a precarious, life-or-death struggle. There is no doubt that for the invading Arab forces, this was a war of conquest and extermination. Arab victory would be counted in Jewish blood.

The first secretary general of the Arab League, Azzam Pasha, declared: "It does not matter how many [Jews] there are. We will sweep them into the sea." Elsewhere he added: "I personally wish that the Jews do not drive us to this war, as this will be a war of extermination and momentous massacre which will be spoken of like the Tartar massacre or the Crusader wars."[90] For al-Quwwatli, this would be a war to "eradicate Zionism." Ahmed Shkeiry promised "the elimination of the Jewish state," while the Syrian president invoked the language of the Crusades.[91]

The war would end with Israel in control of nearly 80 percent of British-mandate-controlled Palestine (excluding Transjordan) and with Emir Abdullah illegally annexing the West Bank. For the Arab leaders, the crux of the battle was eradicating any vestige of Jewish independence and statehood in any part of Palestine. As the Arab League put it, "The establishment of [a] Jewish state in [the] country lies at [the] root of [the] present dispute."[92] Thus the decision to launch an Arab invasion was, as the author Yaacov Lozowick points out, "a reflection of a deeply felt conviction, stated openly, whereby in this part of the world only Arabs, preferably Muslims, can rule."[93]

After the war, Ben-Gurion would not countenance the return of the refugee population, seeing the majority as a potential fifth column that could be exploited by the Arab states in a future conflict. At the 1949 Lausanne Conference, under U.S. pressure, he relented and stated that some 100,000 refugees could be repatriated provided that there was an Arab agreement to make a comprehensive peace on the basis of the current borders. No such agreement was forthcoming.

During the 1950s, many of these refugees made attempts to return to their former homes, travelling from refugee camps in Lebanon, Syria, Jordan and Egypt. Sometimes they were armed and committed acts of murder, theft and robbery; some 200 Israelis died as a result and many more were wounded or suffered property damage.[94] The IDF went after these infiltrators, killing and capturing some and occasionally launching reprisal raids against neighboring countries, including Jordan and Egypt. Sometimes, Israel's response to Palestinian attacks was unjust and heavy handed, such as the October 1953 Qibya raid, led by a young Ariel Sharon, which killed over 60 inhabitants of that West Bank town. But the logic was deterrence and a desire to make the Arab world realize that Israeli blood could not be spilled with impunity.

During this same period, attempts were made to secure peace with Arab states, but they all foundered on what these states demanded in return. Thus Syria's Hosni Zaim demanded half of the Sea of Galilee, depriving Israel of much of its water supply. Jordan's King Abdullah I wanted a corridor from the West Bank to the Mediterranean, effectively cutting Israel in half. Egypt's Nasser reportedly wanted the port of Eilat in return for peace, together with the return of Palestinian refugees.[95] All such plans were unrealistic, the more so considering that all these countries were bases for terrorism against Israel. In particular, Nasser's peace feelers had a purely tactical feel. He wanted U.S. economic aid to shore up his country's ailing economy and to pressure Britain to withdraw from Suez, both of which required some form of Israeli acquiescence. At the same time, he could hardly abandon the war against Israel, given its cardinal importance in the eyes of Arab nationalists and Islamists alike.

In the late 1950s, a group of Egyptian students in Kuwait, angry at how Arab governments had manipulated the Palestinian cause for their own selfish ends, decided to launch a new movement. They came together to form the Palestinian Liberation Movement, and their initials, when read backward, spelled Al-Fatah, the Arabic word for conquest. They were led by Yasser Arafat, a supporter of the Muslim Brotherhood in his youth, who was also known by his *nom de guerre* Abu Ammar.[96] Interestingly, much of Arafat's personal identity was entirely fabricated. The charismatic "face" of modern Palestine was not himself Palestinian but Egyptian. He had no personal experience of dispossession or exile, as he was born and brought up in Cairo. Yet he was at pains to deny these facts for obvious reasons.[97] In 1962, Arafat and other Fatah leaders had visited Algeria, at the time embroiled in a guerrilla war against its French colonial overlords. Fatah was told that the "Palestinian struggle" had to be prevented as "a struggle for liberation." Arafat visited China in 1964, a country that would later provide aid to Fatah.

In 1964, Egypt helped to create the Palestine National Council, which consisted of representatives of the Palestinian communities inside and outside "Palestine." They established an executive wing called the Palestine Liberation Organization (PLO), with Ahmad Shukeiri as its first chairman. It was founded as "the sole representative of the Palestinian people." Its goals could be discerned by reading its foundational document, the Palestinian National Charter or Covenant (amended version, July 1968).

In the charter, Palestine is described as an "indivisible part of the Arab homeland" and the Palestinians as "an integral part of the Arab nation" (Article 1). Under Article 15, the "liberation of Palestine" is regarded as a "national duty." For the sake of clarification, to liberate Palestine means "to repel the Zionist and imperialist aggression against the Arab homeland" and "the elimination of Zionism in Palestine." Indeed, Zionist claims to the land are regarded as morally and historically illegitimate. Thus Jewish claims of historical or religious ties to Palestine are deemed "incompatible with the facts of history" and Jewish claims to self-determination are invalid, as Jews do not "constitute a single nation with an identity of its own" (Article 20). Zionism is seen as "racist and fanatic in its nature, aggressive, expansionist and colonial in its aims, and fascist in its method," with Israel described as "a geographical base for world imperialism placed strategically in the midst of the Arab homeland to combat the hopes of the Arab nation" (Article 22). Article 21 stated, "The Arab Palestinian people ... reject all solutions which are substitutes for the total liberation of Palestine and reject all proposals aiming at ... the internationalization."[98]

This charter was originally produced several years before the occupation of the West Bank or Gaza, the alleged grievances underlying Palestinian terrorism. And that is because the charter called for the outright destruction of Israel, though the euphemism "Zionist presence" was designed to be more palatable for Western observers. From 1968 Fatah would come to dominate the PNC and in 1969, Arafat became PLO chairman, and public face of the Palestinian movement.

Yet there is no doubting that Fatah's aims and ideology mirrored those of other Palestinian factions, and the PNC as a whole. Fatah's aim, as expressed in 1967, was the military defeat of Israel and "the blotting out of the Zionist character of the occupied land, be it human or social."[99] The PLO pinned their hopes for Israel's destruction on the combined force of the Arab states. It was indeed a combination of Arab states, led by Nasser's Egypt, that threatened to destroy the Jewish state in the 1967 Six-Day War. The war was effectively started by the Egyptian closure of the Straits of Tiran, a waterway vital to the Israeli economy and through which freedom of navigation had been guaranteed since 1957. At the time, an Egyptian commander readily acknowledged that this action would constitute "a declaration of war."[100] Nasser also ordered a United Nations Emergency Force, stationed in the Sinai Peninsula, to withdraw from the territory in order that he could mount his own forces there.

Again, the intentions of the belligerent powers could not have been made any clearer. "Our basic objective," Nasser declared on 26 May 1967, "will be to destroy Israel." Ahmad Shukeiri, chairman of the PLO, said of the Israelis: "Those who survive will remain in Palestine, but I estimate that none of them will survive."[101] Blood-curdling announcements made on Arab radio suggested that the streets of Israel would soon be running with Jewish blood. As Golda Meir recalled in her memoirs, every Israeli "knew that the enemy we faced was committed to our annihilation."[102]

Once again, however, the appeasement and weakness of outside powers acted as a spur and a tonic for Arab rejectionists. If Nasser's confidence was up, it was because he had been aided by the weak-willed response of the UN. When Nasser sought UNEF's withdrawal from Sinai, General Secretary U Thant simply capitulated rather than refer the matter back to the

General Assembly. This contradicted an earlier undertaking given by Thant's predecessor whereby no such action would be undertaken without the assembly's approval. Over the blockade, Thant showed a similarly lily-livered approach. He proposed to Nasser that in return for lifting the blockade for a fortnight, the Israelis would be asked not to use the waterway for the same period. Instead of confronting Nasser's belligerent behavior, he was "comparing Egypt's right to engage in an act of war with Israel's right to use international waters for peaceful commerce."[103] There can be little serious doubt that such inept diplomacy only encouraged Nasser's warlike behavior and that of his allies, Jordan and Syria.

In the end, the Arab states suffered a shattering defeat at the hands of Israel. Within a fortnight, the Israeli Cabinet voted by 11–10 to return Sinai to Egypt and the Golan Heights to Syria in exchange for peace, with the future of the West Bank remaining subject to future negotiation. The response of the Arab League was the famous Khartoum resolution of 1 September 1967: "No peace with Israel, no recognition of Israel, no negotiations with it." There seems little doubt that this was a defiant and unequivocal statement of rejectionism by the defeated powers. Abba Eban put it so well: "I think it would be the first war in history that on the morrow the victors sued for peace and the vanquished called for unconditional surrender."

But it was also clear to them that Israel could not be defeated militarily, and in the next war, of 1973 (the Yom Kippur War), the war aims of Egypt and Syria were less ambitious than six years earlier. They wanted, at the very least, the return of captured territories from 1967 and the restoration of national pride.

This much was clear from the reaction of Jordan's King Hussein to the "Allon Plan." Shortly after the conclusion of the Six-Day War, General Allon produced a plan that allowed Israel to maintain control of parts of the West Bank while withdrawing from the majority. Israel would leave the hilly spine of the territory, including its major population centers (Hebron, Ramallah, Bethlehem, Nablus and Jenin) and retain the Jordan Valley and East Jerusalem. Jordan would have to agree to permanently demilitarize those areas handed back and allow Israel to enter them in the pursuit of terrorists.

In a series of secret meetings between senior Israeli figures and King Hussein, the former offered the Jordanian monarch at least 90 percent and possibly up to 98 percent of the territory he had lost. Admittedly, right-wing parties within the Labor-led coalition had no appetite for disengagement, and so the Allon plan was shelved. But what is telling is Hussein's rejection of the offer. According to his own account, he rejected these Israeli concessions and demanded 100 percent of the West Bank, adding: "I could not compromise."[104] The king personally told Moshe Dayan (defense minister): "You must get it into your head that no Arab King can propose that a single village be taken away and become Israeli ... without being accused of treason."[105] The maximalist position prevailed.

With the Arab states unwilling to accept the principle of land for peace, Israel's control of the West Bank, Gaza, Sinai and Golan deepened in the years after 1967. To assess the overall effect of Israeli control on the lives of Arab inhabitants, one must balance some of the negatives in these early years—occasional curfews and closures, the difficulties associated with border crossings and checkpoints, an extensive permits system regulating Palestinian behavior, censorship and administrative detention, and the sometimes harsh military response to Palestinian violence—with the advantages accruing to the local population: increased rates of employment and higher wages, rising GDP, enhanced educational opportunities, the advantageous introduction of drip irrigation, longer life expectancy and improved access to hospitals, telephones and electricity. Settlement expansion was another feature of Israeli policy, though this only became noticeable after the triumph of Likud in 1977. Of course there are legitimate criticisms of Israeli policy within the context of human rights, but these require sensitivity to context, a factor sorely missing in many analyses.

From 1968 onwards, the Palestinian leadership under Yasser Arafat made international terrorism a primary tactic in the war against Israel. A variety of terrorist groups carried out airline hijackings, attacks on civilians at airports, fatal assaults on Jewish and Israeli civilians and assassinations of public figures. They also took schoolchildren hostage in northern Israel, eventually killing dozens. These tactics had at least two purposes. They would give prominence to the Palestinian cause, which represented the destruction of Israel. They would also increase Israel's international isolation by frightening her allies and trading partners into putting pressure on the Jewish state. In turn, this would supposedly force Israel to make concessions that would weaken her and boost the Palestinian terror organizations.

It wasn't just the Israelis that were plagued by Arafat's murderous violence. When the PLO set up camp in Jordan, they effectively created a lawless state within a state. Violence and thuggery abounded as Palestinian guerrillas set up their own police and court system, and there were many violent clashes with Jordanian forces. Diplomats and journalists were regularly kidnapped. Eventually King Hussein expelled Arafat in 1970 when it was clear that he could become the PLO leader's next target.

Once again, Palestinian violence would be met with appeasement. The general pattern was that Palestinian terror attacks, whether in the form of airline hijackings or attacks on civilians, were followed by a lenient European response, often with political concessions made in an attempt to avoid future attacks. Alan Dershowitz, in his book *Why Terrorism Works*, has catalogued the numerous instances in which Palestinian terror groups planned and carried out attacks, only for the captured terrorists to be released weeks or months into their sentences. Sometimes, a hijacking would be followed by another hijacking, the second of which would be used to free those convicted of the first. On innumerable occasions, European and Arab governments capitulated to pressure, desperate to protect their own interests. As a result, of 204 terrorists convicted of terror-related felonies in countries outside the Middle East between 1968 and 1975, only three remained behind bars in 1975.[106]

This pattern of behavior was on display most infamously in the aftermath of the abduction and killing of 11 Israeli athletes in the Munich Olympics. According to recent evidence, West German chancellor Willy Brandt made a deal with Palestinian terrorists whereby they would hijack a Lufthansa plane with civilians on board, allowing him to feign horror at this "hijacking" and giving him a pretext to release those guilty of the Munich massacre.[107] Italy too allowed the PLO to use their country as a base of operation on condition that non–Jewish Italians were not harmed, a deal that the PLO would later violate. Britain, which had already capitulated to Palestinian terror for decades, was not immune. In 1970, Ted Heath's government released Leila Khaled and a number of other Palestinian terrorists in return for the release of hostages that had been taken on board five airliners on 6 September 1970. According to declassified documents, the British governments saw Khaled as an "embarrassment to the British government" and they genuinely feared reprisals by Palestinian terrorists.[108]

But it was not just European nations that were appeasing terrorism. On 2 March 1973, a group of PLO terrorists, acting on Arafat's orders, stormed the Saudi embassy in Khartoum and took hostage the American ambassador to Sudan, Cleo A. Noel, his charge d'affaires, George Curtis Moore, and other diplomats. After Western governments refused to release terrorists in exchange for the men, the two Americans were brutally murdered. Instead of indicting Arafat as a bloodthirsty murderer who had just committed a heinous crime against U.S. interests, American officials proceeded to hide the proof that Arafat's hand was directly behind the murders. The CIA in particular came to believe that Arafat could become a useful intelligence asset and provide valuable information on other terrorist groups. It is far from clear what grand intelligence he was expected to provide nor why he should have been considered reliable.[109]

In appeasing terrorism, the UN played a highly significant role too. In 1970, the General Assembly passed Resolution 2708, which reaffirmed "its recognition of the legitimacy of the struggle of the colonial peoples and peoples under alien domination to exercise their right to self determination by all the necessary means at their disposal." Contrary to Article 51 of the UN Charter, force was now legitimate not just in self-defense but also against a "colonial" state. There can be little doubt that such a description suited the PLO, for whom Israel was a colonial state, and that "all necessary means" included terrorism. The UN had given a stamp of legitimacy to the most illegitimate form of warfare.

Later in 1982, the UN would associate the Palestinian "struggle" against Israel with that of the black struggle with white South Africa. A resolution affirmed "the legitimacy of the struggle of peoples against foreign occupation by all available means, including armed struggle." Given that the targets of choice were civilian, the UN was undeniably giving its stamp of approval to international terrorism.

In 1974, the UN legitimized Arafat himself by inviting him to speak at the UN General Assembly, the first time that the head of a terrorist group had been so honored. Dressed in military garb with a holster by his side, he was treated like a visiting head of state and, despite his connections with other violent terror groups (the IRA, Baader-Meinhof and the Japanese Red Army), was applauded warmly by the world's premier diplomatic body. He then gave a speech in which he justified "armed struggle" and compared his campaign of terror to the liberation struggles taking place around the world against racism and colonialism. Though promising to use the diplomatic track as a complement to armed struggle, it was clear that nothing short of Israel's elimination would satisfy him.

Arafat's reward was Resolution 3237, which gave the PLO observer status at the UN, followed in 1975 by the infamous vote equating Zionism with racism and the establishment of a "Committee in the Exercise of the Inalienable Rights of the Palestinian People." In 1979, the UN gave a further boost to Arafat's terror campaign by observing the first international day of solidarity with the Palestinian people, an event repeated annually on 29 November. There were special messages of solidarity for the Palestinians, with a host of films, special exhibits, cultural events and publications being produced around the world. No other stateless or refugee population was being treated to such an outpouring of global largesse, and at a time when its leaders were murdering civilians and demanding the destruction of another UN member state.[110]

The UN was showering the PLO with legitimacy; indeed, by the end of the 1970s, more countries recognized the PLO (86) than Israel (72).[111] This was aided by the formation of a solid voting bloc at the UN, with Soviet-controlled countries and the Non-Aligned Movement automatically providing the PLO with a majority in the General Assembly.

Yet far from pacifying Palestinian terrorism, it merely exacerbated it. During these same years, the PFLP hijacked an Air France airliner and forced it to land in Uganda, necessitating a successful Israeli rescue mission, while the same group carried out attacks on airports in Paris, Istanbul and Brussels. Arafat's Fatah organization also carried out a seaborne raid in 1978 that killed 26 civilians. Such violence was mirrored in his increasingly intemperate and bellicose language, revealing him to be as much a foe of compromise and moderation as his predecessor, the mufti, had been. Thus in 1970 he declared: "We don't want peace, we want victory. Peace for us means Israel's destruction and nothing else."[112] To *Reuters* in 1976 he added: "We will not concede even an inch of Palestine." A year later he revealed that he was not "a man who makes deals or compromises. I shall struggle until the very last inch of Palestine be regained."

Nonetheless, one Arab state decided that pragmatism warranted an end to hostility with Israel. Egypt's Anwar Sadat flew to Israel in 1977 and addressed the Knesset, something regarded as almost unthinkable up until that point. Peace negotiations were pursued between the sides and culminated in the 1979 Camp David Accords signed by Egypt and Israel. This led to a staged withdrawal from the Sinai Peninsula and the removal of settlements from Yamit.

Sadly, it would not lead to the normalization of relations between the countries, a key component of the treaty. Vicious anti–Israeli tirades appeared regularly in the Egyptian media, encouraging an almost unprecedented level of anti–Semitism across all strata of Egyptian society. Sadat, reviled for his "stab in the back," was assassinated in 1981 for his "crime" of recognizing Israel, causing him to suffer the same fate as King Hussein's grandfather in 1951. Israel would go on to establish the Begin-Sadat Center for Strategic Studies, but no similar institution was set up in Egypt. Under Sadat's successor, Hosni Mubarak, relations with Israel were cool. He only once set foot in Israel, for the funeral of Yitzhak Rabin in 1995, while Israeli leaders were usually received at Sharm el-Sheik and not Cairo. Mubarak was more than happy to encourage and inflame anti–Semitic passions among the populace to serve his own domestic purposes.

Sadat's interlocutor at Camp David, the Likud leader Menachem Begin, had come from the revisionist camp of Vladimir Jabotinsky. Likud's more militant philosophy, which had been manifested in violent attacks against British targets before Israel's founding, represented a sea change in Israeli politics. Up until 1948, the country's political system had been dominated by the socialist philosophy of Labour Zionism. From 1977, following Likud's stunning electoral upset, Begin took an uncompromising stance on the disputed territories. His promise not to give up one square inch of "Biblical Israel" resonated with a galvanized, religious-nationalist right, including the messianic group Gush Emunim. His program for expanding Jewish settlements throughout the West Bank, and his rejection of a Palestinian state in principle, could be seen as examples of Israeli political rejectionism.

Nonetheless, Begin agreed to freeze settlements for three months in the hope that it would galvanize other states to forge a more comprehensive, regional peace agreement. Begin also agreed to a five-year plan for Palestinian autonomy in the territories. As part of a two-stage process, Israel would agree to grant the Palestinians self-governing authority, prior to negotiating an agreement on the final status of the territories. Instead, the Saudis led the revolt against Sadat, cutting off aid to Egypt and moving the Arab League headquarters from Cairo. But the PLO also rejected these overtures and did not participate in any talks, maintaining their violent irredentism and maximalist position.[113]

In 1982, Israel invaded Lebanon in order to remove the PLO army that had set up camp in the country since its expulsion from Jordan in 1970. The pretext for the invasion was the attempted assassination of Israel's ambassador to the UK, Shlomo Argov, outside the Dorchester hotel. At first, some questioned the Israeli justification for invading Lebanon, given that the would-be assassin was from the Abu Nidal group, which had split years earlier from the PLO and was based in Syria, not Lebanon.

However, there was justification for military action, given that in the previous decade, the PLO had built up a terrorist army consisting of some 15,000–18,000 men, armed with enough rockets, mortars and missiles to equip five brigades. Lebanon had become a training ground for numerous terrorist groups, including the IRA, the Sandanistas and the Red Army faction.[114] Palestinian rule in Lebanon was marked by brutality and persecution, particularly towards the Christian population. Preceding this event there had been a series of terrorist attacks directed from Lebanon that killed 29 Israelis and wounded more than 300. Incessant terrorism and shelling spelled havoc for thousands of Israelis in the Galilee, forcing them into bomb shelters and disrupting the pattern of normal life. As Henry Kissinger had put it in the *Washington Post*: "No sovereign state can tolerate indefinitely the buildup along its borders of a military force dedicated to its destruction and implementing its objectives by periodic shellings and raids."[115]

Thus on 6 June 1982, the IDF launched "Operation Peace for Galilee" to protect the country's northern inhabitants from incessant PLO attacks. Such was the organization's tyrannical rule in Lebanon, including a decade of rape, mutilation and massacres, that many Lebanese cheered the IDF in June 1982. The objectives of the operation were initially to create a 25-mile safe zone in the south that would push the PLO away from Israel's northern border. Defence Minister Ariel Sharon envisioned a deeper operation that would destroy the PLO's economic and political strength in Lebanon, remove Syrian forces from the country and establish a Christian-dominated government in the country. Such plans appear not to have been communicated to Begin, who nonetheless came to endorse them.

This was a war in which Israel was censured doubly, both for initiating a war of choice and for the unacceptably high number of civilians and IDF soldiers killed in the war. Above all, the decision to allow Phalangist fighters into the refugee camps of Sabra and Shatila, following the murder of Lebanese prime minister (and Israeli ally) Bachir Gemayel, was mistaken. In revenge for the slaying of their leader, the Phalangists overran the camps and proceeded to kill hundreds of Palestinians, a savage episode that caused deep angst for many Israelis. The Kahan Commission found Israel "indirectly responsible" for the deaths, and Sharon personally responsible. The war would also prove to be socially divisive within Israel itself, attracting the biggest demonstrations to date in the country's history. It did, however, represent a short-term blow for the PLO.

The terror organization was a spent force by the war's end, having lost an important base and thousands of fighters. No Arab country agreed to host the organization until Tunisia offered a safe haven following pressure from the Reagan administration. The hope was that with U.S. assistance, the Palestinians would look more favorably upon Washington and improve America's standing among developing nations. But such largesse (or appeasement) did not pay dividends in terms of moderating the PLO's insatiable appetite for terror. Arafat understood that his tactics of terror and rejection had brought him rewards, thus disincentivizing him from a path of goodwill and moderation.

Throughout the 1980s, Palestinian terrorists, many linked to the radical Abu Nidal group, carried out a series of bomb, grenade and gun attacks on synagogues in Vienna, Paris, Rome and Istanbul. Among the dozens of victims were young children, including a two-year-old toddler. In 1985, they hijacked the Italian cruise ship *Achille Lauro* and murdered a wheelchair-bound American Jew, Leon Klinghoffer. There were further attacks on airlines and passenger terminals as well as the kidnapping and murder of an American official, William Buckley.

Despite these atrocities, Arafat continued to be feted around the world, treated like a head of state rather than a terrorist leader with blood on his hands. As well as addressing the United Nations General Assembly, he spoke before a session of the European Parliament, had meetings with Pope John Paul II and visited a number of European leaders to discuss the Middle East situation. The more he perpetrated indiscriminate outrages, the more his diplomatic standing was boosted and the more he was encouraged to persist with violent rejectionism.

He gained sympathy during the Palestinian intifada (uprising) in the territories, which started in 1987. In the West Bank and Gaza, there was an explosion of rage on the Palestinian street at Israel's continuing control of these territories, though the initial spark was a road accident. Over 1,000 Palestinians were killed during continued clashes with Israeli troops (160 Israelis died too), though at least as many and possibly more Palestinians died at the hands of other Palestinians, a repeat of the fratricidal violence of the 1936–39 Arab revolt. In 1988, the Jordanian government renounced any claim to the West Bank.

Arafat now seized on a new initiative, announcing the creation of a Palestinian state and calling for a peace settlement based on UN resolutions, including 242. On 15 November 1988, the Palestinian Declaration of Independence was produced. Referring to UN Resolution 181, it called for "the right of the Palestinian Arab people to sovereignty" and rejected violence "against the territorial integrity of other states," also demanding an end to "the occupation." In Geneva in December 1988, Arafat publicly recognized the right of all nations, "including the State of Palestine and Israel," to live in peace while condemning all forms of terrorism including "state terrorism," but not "resistance." Now even the United States under the hawkish Ronald Reagan was to open negotiations with Arafat.

Walid Khalidi suggests that the 1988 PNC resolutions were a "triumph of compassion for one's people over hatred of one's enemy." The decision "opened wide the gate towards a historic reconciliation while spelling out its irreducible minimum condition of statehood."[116]

But Arafat's tactics were a cruel form of deception typical of Islamic *Taqiyya*. Far from seeking a genuine accommodation with Israel, he was merely seeking to implement the "phased plan," devised in 1974. The phased plan, adopted at the 12th Session of the Palestinian National Council in Cairo, adopted a three-stage process for continuing the Palestinian struggle. In the first stage, the PLO would "employ all means, and first and foremost armed struggle, to liberate Palestinian territory and to establish the independent combatant national authority for the people over every part of Palestinian territory that is liberated." The second stage would involve using the territory to continue the PLO's warfare against Israel, principally using terrorism. In the final stage, they would provoke a war in which Israel's Arab neighbors would destroy it completely.

As Abu Iyad, Arafat's second in command, explained in 1988, "The establishment of a Palestinian state on any part of Palestine is but a step towards the [liberation of the] whole of Palestine."[117] As historian Yezid Sayigh has clarified, the PLO members "were keenly aware of the regional and international impediments to the destruction of Israel," including the limited resources of the Arab states. As such, their strategy was to adopt a staged approach to the elimination of Israel.[118]

By the early 1990s, however, the PLO was at a low ebb in military terms. They had been driven from their base in Lebanon after the war of 1982, a war in which they lost thousands of fighters and a huge amount of military infrastructure. Arafat had also incurred the wrath of Arab leaders after making an ill-advised decision to support Saddam Hussein in the 1990–91 Gulf crisis. In a twist of irony, it would be the Israelis, with substantial Western backing, who would give Arafat and the PLO an invaluable opportunity for rehabilitation.

The Oslo "peace process," initiated with a choreographed handshake on the White House lawn between Israeli PM Yitzhak Rabin and Arafat in September 1993, allowed the PLO to set up base on Israel's doorstep in the West Bank and Gaza Strip. Arafat was also a joint recipient of the Nobel Peace Prize. Over the next few years, substantial areas of the territories were put under Palestinian civil and administrative control, including Gaza, Hebron, Ramallah and hundreds of smaller Arab villages and towns. Israel transferred education and health, social welfare, culture, tourism and direct taxation to the Palestinians. Within two years, the two sides commenced final status talks on the most sensitive issues concerning borders, refugees and Jerusalem. There were also Palestinian security forces to patrol these areas, trained and armed by Western powers. The Israeli cabinet approved Oslo with only two abstentions and the Declaration of Principles was also approved, though by the slimmer majority (61–50). Despite opposition from the right and from religious quarters, a majority of Israelis also endorsed the Oslo process throughout the next decade.[119]

The arrangement (peace by stages) was to prove a major strategic blunder with dire repercussions for both Israelis and Palestinians. In the words of one PLO official, Israel was facilitating the establishment of a "trojan horse" into its vicinity.[120] The central reason was that Arafat was a monumental liar and a serial hoaxer, a man prepared to preach peace to a Western audience and war to an Arab one. For those who listened impartially to his Arab rhetoric, it was clear that the PLO leader had no intention of making peace with Israel or recognizing a Jewish state. On the contrary, his apparent peace overtures were nothing more than a tactical ploy to buy time, his concessions akin to the Treaty of Hudaibiya signed by Muhammad in 628.

To Western ears, Arafat talked of "the peace of the brave" and creating a just and lasting settlement in the region. He claimed to have turned his back on terror and violence and said that in a new age he would fight for the rights of the Palestinian people. But shortly after Arafat appended his signature to the Oslo Accords, he went to a mosque in Johannesburg and explained that the Palestinians would "continue their jihad until they had liberated Jerusalem." Though he tried to downplay the real meaning of his words, many Israelis were unconvinced. Two years later, Arafat told a group of Arab notables that he planned to "eliminate the state of Israel and establish a purely Palestinian state."[121] He would do this by using "psychological warfare and population explosion" to force Jews to leave Israel, creating a civil war that could be then exploited by millions of Arabs living in the West Bank and Jerusalem. More often than not, he explained to Arab audiences that the Oslo process was merely part of the phased plan from 1974 in which the PLO would seize any part of "liberated" Palestinian territory and use it as a base for liberating the rest.

His words were echoed by other Palestinian "moderates." Faisal Husseini made it clear in 1992 that Palestinians would never surrender "any of the obligations" to which they had been "committed for more than seventy years." He went on to say: "Sooner or later, we will force Israeli society to be incorporated into … our Arab society, and eventually to dissolve the Zionist entity." A decade later, he remained unwavering in his rejection of Israel's existence, for he said in 2001 that the boundaries of a future Palestine were "from the Jordan river to the Mediterranean Sea."[122]

Yasser Abd Rabbo, another key minister within the PA, said in 1996 that the goal of the talks was for Palestine to be liberated "from the sea to the river." Abu Ala in the same year claimed that in signing the Oslo Accords, "We did not and will not relinquish one inch of this territory or the right of any Palestinian to live on it with dignity."[123] For the Palestinian intellectual Hannah Ashrawi, the occupation that she so decried came about not in 1967 but in 1948 when Israel was created.

Ashrawi was committed to the notion that for peace to occur, millions of Palestinian refugees (though the vast majority were anything but refugees) had to be given the right of return to Israel. But this was simply a formula for the demographic destruction of Israel, a fact not lost on Palestinian leaders. Indeed throughout the 1990s, this became a virtual touchstone of Palestinian authenticity. Thus in 1999, shortly before the Camp David talks, Rafiq al-Natsheh, Palestinian minister of labor, said: "We will not agree to conclude the fulfillment of our national goals before the Refugee Problem is solved. We will not conclude the fulfillment of our national goals before Jerusalem becomes the sole and eternal capital of the Palestinian state.… The land is ours, the authority is ours, and Jerusalem is ours."[124]

Abd al-Rahman, the chairman of the PLO's refugee department, gave a press conference in February 1999 in which he discussed the future of the refugee problem in the context of an Israeli-Palestinian agreement. He made it clear that the only solution for the refugees was to implement Resolution 194, effectively a right of return, rather than allow for their return to a future Palestinian state. In his view, some 80 percent wished to return, and all needed compensation for "50 years of suffering and loss of revenue from their property."[125] No mention was made of the vastly greater property losses suffered by the Jews who had been forced to leave Arab countries from 1948 to 1967. These statements all indicate that the peace on offer was one in which Israel ceased to have a Jewish majority, ceased to exist. It was tantamount to no peace at all.

Worse still, despite a pledge to "abstain from incitement, including hostile propaganda" in the Gaza-Jericho agreement of 1994, subsequently reinforced by commitments made in Oslo II and the 1998 Wye River Memorandum, Arafat (like his successor Mahmoud Abbas) used every opportunity to turn Palestinians against Israel. Palestinian newspapers, including *al-Hayat al-Jadida*, constantly invoked the language of *The Protocols of the Elders of Zion* by referring to stories about Jewish control and dominance. Jews were accused of corruption, decadence and deception, invoking some of the worst tropes of Quaranic anti–Semitism. Israel was depicted as the center of a malevolent plot to divide the Arab world. Israeli forces were accused of injecting Palestinian children with the HIV virus, of dumping liquid waste in Palestinian areas, of harvesting the organs of dead Palestinian children and using patients for experimental medicines.[126]

Palestinian media referred to Israel behind the green line as "occupied Palestine," encouraging children to believe that the Jewish state was an illegitimate entity to be fought against in the future. Palestinian imams continued the process of demonization by likening Jews to the "sons of pigs and apes" and calling for their murder. Among the other themes in the demonization discourse was Holocaust denial, the ultimate rejection of the Jewish narrative of past suffering. More pertinent still was the denial of any Jewish historical attachment to the Holy Land. Thus in 1997, the Palestinian historian Jarir Qudwa declared that the events in the Old Testament had taken place not in Palestine but in the Arabian Peninsula. Denying that Solomon's Temple had ever existed in Jerusalem was another favorite of Palestinian leaders. Military camps were set up by the PA where teenagers could receive arms training, fighting skills and anti–Israeli indoctrination.

Worse still was the protracted wrangling over the Palestinian Charter that called for Israel's destruction. As a condition of signing the Oslo Accords, Yitzhak Rabin had demanded the abrogation of the clauses of the charter that called for Israel to be destroyed, among other things. Arafat wrote to Rabin before the signing ceremony and said that the "clauses in the Charter which are contrary to what I have stated in this letter are either no longer operative or will be nullified." He went on to promise that his letter would be sent to the Palestinian National Council "for their formal approval," as required by clause 33 of the charter.

When the PNC convened in April 1996 (nearly three years from the signing of the accords), they adopted a resolution that said that they had decided to amend the charter and agreed to "cancelling the Charter's articles opposing the exchanged letters between the PLO and the Israeli government on September 9th and 10th 1993." The next part of the resolution promised that a legal committee would be formed in order to draft a new charter. In January 1998, Arafat assured President Clinton in a letter that, in accordance with Article 33 of the charter, all of the provisions of the charter that were inconsistent with the commitment to recognize and live in peace with Israel were now no longer in effect. He specifically declared that the various clauses had been annulled in the earlier resolution of 1996. But this was nonsense. That resolution had appointed a legal committee to draft changes to the charter, and there is no evidence that such a committee had been formed or had convened.

In December 1998, the PLO's Executive Committee and Central Committee reaffirmed Arafat's letter to Clinton. Then on December 14, a vote of members of the PNC, the PLO Central Committee and PNA ministers voted to endorse the 1996 resolution. The only problem, once again, was that the resolution from 1996 was at the very least ambiguous—it did not revoke the charter but called instead for a legal committee to be formed. Moreover, the PLO and the PA did not move to create a new and amended charter, to the consternation of Israeli officials.[127] Hence, not surprisingly, leading Palestinians to this day deny that any amendment to the charter took place. In 2009, Azzam Al-Ahmad, a central committee member, declared "It (the charter) will remains as is. It won't be subject to discussion."[128]

But Israel had to contend with a yet graver problem during this alleged decade of peace: terrorism. In the Gaza-Jericho agreement, the new Palestinian Authority was tasked with taking all measures necessary "to prevent acts of terrorism, crime and hostilities" and to ensure that there were no armed forces operating in the territories other than the official police force. Arafat urged the Israelis to allow for the creation of a Palestinian security force, the better to allow him to curb the activities of Hamas terrorists.

Yet terrorism, far from being curbed, was intensified. From May 1994 to the fall of the Labour government in May 1996, 123 Israeli civilians were murdered and hundreds more injured in acts of terror. There were also numerous failed attempts at suicide bombing that, had they been successful, would have amplified those casualty figures considerably. These suicide bombings were carried out by Hamas, an extremist Islamist organization founded in 1988, and Islamic Jihad. Hamas was the Palestinian branch of the Muslim Brotherhood, a fanatical Islamist movement striving for world domination through jihad and, as such, was a natural enemy of the West. It stood for *Harakat al Muqawama al Islamiya*, or Islamic resistance movement, and embodied a belief in attritional war: if they could inflict severe casualties on Israelis, then eventually, over a very long period of time, the Jewish state would wither as its population became increasingly demoralized.

Hamas had developed a reputation for honesty and propriety with its network of charitable and educational work, and thus stood in contrast to Fatah with its stark record of endemic corruption. Hamas too, as Jonathan Spyer points out, was "untainted by the perceived failure of the peace process and by the inherently humiliating involvement in it."[129]

Apologists for Arafat claim that he did authorize the arrest of terrorists from groups other then Fatah. Under pressure, Arafat would occasionally cooperate with Israel. Attempts were made to block attacks and sometimes criminals were handed over to Israel. Palestinians who were arrested could be brought to court, where they were often sentenced rapidly and without due process. Sentences could be harsh and without proper legal redress for those convicted, reflecting the corruption within the PA.

However, there were times when PA "ineptitude and laxity" failed to stop the Hamas terror campaign, while Hamas members were even recruited to join Fatah, after falsely pledging to abstain from violence. Some terror attacks were also carried out by Palestinian police.[130] There was also a "revolving door policy" in which suspects were arrested and later released, allowing them to pursue their violent activities unhindered.

All the while, Arafat was complicit in the creation of a vast terrorist infrastructure in Gaza. Thousands of weapons were now being smuggled there via Egypt, including sophisticated TNT explosives, all contrary to the commitments made in Oslo. There was talk of Palestinian areas becoming "Lebanonized," with the terrible echoes of Arafat's tyrannical rule in the past. In tacitly approving the terrorism against Israelis, Arafat was simply repeating the lesson he had learned in the 1960s and 1970s, namely that mayhem and terror were bound to bring political dividends. Specifically, he hoped to pressure the governments of Rabin, Peres, Netanyahu and Barak to cave in to his demands.

By constant incitement, terrorism and outright mendacity, the Palestinian leadership was signaling that it had no interest in pursuing the path of coexistence and normalization with its neighbor. Rabin was outraged and exasperated both by the escalating acts of terror and by Arafat's refusal to condemn or stop them. Several times he called on the Palestinian leader to take action, even threatening to suspend the Oslo process, but to no avail. On several occasions, Israel closed off the territories with predictably negative consequences for the Palestinian economy.

In the end, Rabin refused to punish Arafat for his deceitful behavior, insisting that he remain a "partner" in peace. He continued to make concessions under fire and against the advice of some in the security establishment, including an agreement in 1994 to transfer various forms of civilian authority in the West Bank and Gaza and the interim agreement of 1995. That same year, he went further, excusing Arafat's failure to curtail terrorism by declaring, "Even in areas under our control we cannot claim to have completely eradicated terrorism."[131]

For a man so possessed of the need to maintain the peace process, Rabin had less time for his critics. He once said of them: "They can spin around like propellers for all I care." On another occasion, he referred to a group of American Jewish leaders as "pariah Jews" for daring to criticize the PA. Rabin dubbed those who were cut down in suicide bombings as "the sacrifices for peace."[132] Quite how an escalation in murderous violence was compatible with peace is hard to fathom, but having staked his career on signing the Declaration of Principles, Rabin would have had to admit to a strategic blunder if he had lost faith in Arafat's promises. Little was he prepared to acknowledge that the man he called a "partner for peace" was responsible for some of those murders (partly by paying the salaries of terrorists and giving payments to their families) and was merely feigning concern for Israeli victims of terror.[133]

Yet Rabin would never live to see the outcome of the Oslo process. In 1995, he was shot dead by a right-wing Jewish fanatic, Yigal Amir, in Tel Aviv. Amir's slaying of Rabin was a low point for the country. Prior to Rabin's assassination, the language used to attack his government was incendiary and inexcusable. Some compared him to an SS officer, and he was accused of treason, insanity and wickedness. Ultra-nationalists and religious extremists produced a toxic cocktail of abuse and invective that poisoned the political atmosphere in the country. They were offering a potent challenge to Israel's secular majority, both in their fanatical attitudes towards the Arabs and on a range of domestic issues. That challenge was highlighted by the brutal murder of 29 Arab citizens in Hebron by a fanatical settler and Kach supporter, Baruch Goldstein. Both Amir and Goldstein represented an extreme section of the hawkish electorate, one that rejected peace overtures to the Arabs and believed in the legitimacy of murderous violence. Yet neither of these men was any more a part of the Israeli mainstream than Lehi or Irgun had been in the 1940s. Their actions were roundly condemned.

Rabin's argument for continuing negotiations was given an emotional boost after his assassination. In 1996, Benjamin Netanyahu, a Likud leader who condemned the Oslo Accords while in opposition, was elected prime minister. Netanyahu believed that the peace process thus far represented a capitulation to terror and was strategically dangerous for Israel. Nonetheless he continued the Oslo process, respecting the international commitments that his predecessors had made while trying to ensure that future concessions were made on a *reciprocal* basis.

He was to be disappointed. While agreeing to the Hebron Protocol in 1997, which led to a major Israeli redeployment in that town, Arafat was busy preparing for a new round of violence and confrontation with Israel. In March 1997, Arafat gave Hamas a green light to continue their terrorist war against the Jews and promptly allowed dozens of senior Hamas figures to be released from jail. Suicide bombings swiftly followed, including one in a Jerusalem market that killed 16 Israelis and injured 178. Later, Hamas figures were found being transported in vehicles belonging to members of Jibril Rajoub's Palestinian security service. At the same time, Arafat was rejuvenating Tanzim, Fatah's military arm, even though he was required to dismantle it in the 1995 Interim Agreement.[134]

In 1999, Labour's Ehud Barak powered to victory in the country's national elections. It was a sure sign of how the electorate was becoming increasingly disenchanted with the slow pace of the peace process. The Labour leader had been a critic of the gradualist approach of Oslo and now sought to offer an all or nothing peace deal that could not be derailed by rejectionists. After failing to reach a settlement with Syria's Hafez Assad over the Golan Heights, he made the PLO its most generous offer yet. After a series of negotiations at Camp David in summer 2000, Barak agreed to the following: an independent, demilitarized and contiguous Palestinian state in the West Bank (with a road for access to Gaza) covering (eventually) some 91 percent of the West Bank and all of Gaza, with compensating territory from pre-1967 Israel; sovereignty over Arab districts in Jerusalem, and control over parts of the Old City; a package of compensation for Palestinian refugees; and, though not a right of return, some refugees returning to Israel within a fixed time frame.

Yet Arafat turned down the offer and refused to put forward any counter-proposals. That Arafat was mostly to blame for walking away from this offer of statehood is attested to by numerous observers apart from Barak himself. In their revisionist account of the talks, R. Malley and H. Agha, who are determined to blame Barak more than Arafat for the failure at Camp David, admit that the Palestinians' principal failing at the talks was that "from the beginning of the Camp David summit onward they were unable either to say yes to the American ideas or to present a cogent and specific counterproposal of their own." The authors also report that at one point, the president reacted furiously to Arafat's behavior, telling him: "If the Israelis can make compromises and you can't, I should go home. You have been here fourteen days and said no to everything. These things have consequences."[135] Dennis Ross, the U.S. Middle East envoy, noted that there was a discrepancy between the Palestinian leader and the more junior members of his delegation. It was pointed out to him that only Arafat could symbolically deliver an agreement to his people, that only he had true legitimacy to negotiate on behalf of his people.

Further evidence of Arafat's uncompromising manner is evidenced by a comment made by Abbas, who was part of the Palestinian negotiating team in 2000. He admitted in 2001, "We made clear to the Americans that the Palestinian side is unable to make concessions on anything."[136] This was particularly noticeable on the thorny issue of Jerusalem. The Israelis were prepared for the city to be divided in practice but in a manner that would allow them to save face. By contrast, the Palestinians were not prepared to shift their position with Arafat, even denying that there was ever a Jewish temple in the city.[137] Viewing himself as a latter-day Saladin, he sought nothing more than the total retaking of the Holy City. As he put it: "It is not in my capacity, or the capacity of any Palestinian leadership, to leave al-Aqsa and Jerusalem under Israeli sovereignty."[138]

Furthermore, Abbas admitted the crucial role of the right of return in Palestinian thinking, claiming in November 2000, "The issue of the refugees was at least as important as the Jerusalem issue." He added that he had clarified to the Israelis that "the Right of Return means a return to Israel and not to the Palestinian state."[139] As Ephraim Karsh puts it, "No Israeli government could yield to the Palestinian demand on this issue without signing away its country's national existence."[140]

Dennis Ross, a senior member of Clinton's negotiating team, would later comment: "When you question the core of the other side's faith, that is not exactly an indication that you are getting ready to try and end the conflict."[141] Both President Clinton and Dennis Ross would later blame Arafat for the talks' failure and in a revealing article, so too would Saudi prince Bandar, who advised the Palestinian leader to accept the Barak proposals. Indeed, he believed it would be a "crime" to turn down the peace overtures, such was the long Palestinian history of rejection.

There is no mystery about why Arafat chose to take such intransigent positions on the emotive issues of refugees and Jerusalem, ultimately scuppering the talks. One of the biggest misconceptions about Arafat was that he was a secular leader. In fact, he had a deeply religious character, which may have owed much to his strict Islamic upbringing. In addressing Palestinian crowds, he would frequently regale them with Islamic teachings and phraseology, injecting his speeches with fiery rhetoric about the necessity for a holy jihad and martyrdom to liberate Palestine. He spoke of the sanctity of Jerusalem and of the martyrs that would liberate the city from oppressive rule. In justifying his signature on the Declaration of Principles, he invoked the treaty of Hudaibiyya in his speech in a South African mosque. This was a temporary truce signed by Muhammed, a *hudna*, which could be broken later when more propitious circumstances arose.

These quasi-religious sermons had a political rationale in part. They would enable him to win over those Palestinians who might otherwise prefer the Islamist rule of Hamas. But they also reflected his most cherished beliefs, explaining why he found it impossible to compromise on any of the core issues. For Arafat, the liberation of Jerusalem and the right of return were invested with a sacred aura; he was entrusted not to renege on them because of their inestimable value to the Muslim world.

Arafat responded to the Camp David breakdown by launching a new terrorist offensive, the second intifada. He ordered Tanzim to orchestrate a wave of violence against civilian and military targets across the territories, hoping to induce a strong Israeli response that would spur on other Palestinian martyrs. A wave of terror attacks was encouraged by a Palestinian media that, even by its own standards, exhibited no restraint. Broadcasts encouraged Palestinians to martyr themselves, while Israel was presented as a demonic force to be resisted. The vilest anti–Semitic libels were commonplace.

Contrary to the myth that would later be propagated, the intifada was not directly caused by then opposition leader Ariel Sharon's visit to the Temple Mount on 28 September 2000. Jibril Rajoub, a top Palestinian security official, had been consulted in advance, and the visit was to prove largely uneventful in any case, with only sporadic and limited clashes between Palestinians and Israeli police. Further proof that Sharon did not cause the intifada comes from the words of the Palestinians themselves. Imad Faluji, the PA's minster of post and communications, revealed that the PA "began preparing the present intifada and bracing for it since the return from Camp David at the request of President Yasser Arafat." The PLO leader, he went on, "envisaged the intifada as a complementary measure to the Palestinian steadfastness in the negotiations, and not as a protest over Sharon's visit to al-Haram al-Sharif."[142]

For his part, Marwan Barghouti, one of the key figures in the Palestinian terrorist war, revealed four months before the Camp David talks that the negotiations over key issues such as Jerusalem and refugees had to be "accompanied by a campaign on the ground, that is, a confrontation."[143] Perhaps the smoking gun came from no less a person than Suha Arafat. She told an interviewer on Dubai television: "Immediately after the failure of the Camp David [negotiations], I met him in Paris upon his return.... Camp David had failed, and he said to me, 'You should remain in Paris.' I asked him why, and he said, 'Because I am going to start an intifada.'"[144]

Indeed, a day before Sharon's visit, Hamas had circulated an incendiary statement to its supporters warning that plans to "demolish the Aqsa mosque and build the so called Jewish temple in its place" were "no longer the aspirations of limited or extremist groups in the Zionist society." This was followed by a sermon the next day at the Temple Mount in which an imam accused "the Jews" of plotting to replace the mosque with a synagogue. He added ominously: "Should we respond to [Sharon's visit] only by throwing stones or by condemnation?"[145]

Nonetheless, Sharon's visit was condemned as being highly provocative, particularly in light of the lethal force used by Israeli police to disperse protestors the following day, which resulted in the deaths of twelve Israeli Arabs as well as one Jewish and one Palestinian citizen. Nonetheless, to blame Sharon for provocation, especially when the riots took place the day after the visit, was to absolve those who carried out premeditated acts of violence.[146] Barak too came under fire, in part because he had been warned that there was a grave risk of Palestinian violence and that Arafat had no intention of reaching a deal. Few can doubt that his all-or-nothing approach was a high-risk gamble.[147] But Clinton too was part of the problem at Camp David. For the president had previously assured Arafat that he would not blame him if the talks failed to produce a meaningful outcome.[148]

Still, Arafat's decision was rooted in the logic of his past terrorism. He would resort to violence, both to divert attention from his underachievement at Camp David but also to elicit international sympathy for the predictable scenes of Palestinian youths dying at the hands of a "tyrannical" Israel. He hoped that such sympathy could then be translated into political pressure on Israel to make even further concessions to the PLO. Violence, he hoped, would continue to pay rich dividends. At the same time, he could "bag" the concessions made to him at Camp David as if nothing had happened.

What also spurred him on was Ehud Barak's policy of appeasement in Lebanon. Barak had been desperate to disentangle Israeli troops from their northern neighbors and, in a precipitate move, ordered the IDF to vacate their outposts in the south of the country on 24 May 2000. The withdrawal from Lebanon was carried out without any reciprocal concessions from Syria or the terrorist group Hezbollah. For the Palestinians, this was proof that the Zionist Goliath had suffered a defeat at the hands of well-armed guerrillas. They saw it as the ultimate vindication of the armed struggle and henceforth, the "Lebanese model" would be used to force Israel out of the territories.

Yet despite the ongoing violence, the Palestinians were rewarded yet again, confirming the rationality of Arafat's strategy. For starters, much of the international community fell for the deceitful line that the current violence engulfing Israelis and Palestinians alike was due to Sharon's visit to the Temple Mount. Typical was UN Resolution 1322, which condemned the visit as a provocation and called for a return to negotiations. The United States did not veto the resolution. George Mitchell arrived on a fact-finding mission and he would eventually absolve Sharon of direct blame for starting the intifada. But then no finger was pointed at the party that did start the violence.

Moreover, the political dividends would soon follow. President Clinton now offered a new peace plan, incorporating some ideas from Israeli doves, which again envisioned an end to the conflict. These were the famous Clinton "parameters." Now the Palestinians were being offered the following: 94–96 percent of the West Bank and 100 percent of Gaza, with compensating territory from pre–1967 Israel; a phased Israeli withdrawal to take place over three years overseen by international monitors; a limited IDF presence in the Jordan Valley for three years; a division of the old city of Jerusalem in which Israel would only control the Jewish quarter, the Mount of Olives and the City of David, and the surface of Temple Mount would be under Palestinian control; some resettlement of refugees in Israel but otherwise a right of return to "Palestine," and fund of $30 billion for compensation and resettlement; the Palestinian state would be demilitarized but with a strong security force. Thus contrary to Honderich, the Palestinians were not offered a "dog's breakfast of bantustans" at the negotiations.[149]

On 27–28 December 2000, Israel's Cabinet voted to accept Clinton's proposals, with a follow-up letter being sent shortly afterwards that asked for various clarifications. In effect, as Clinton later acknowledged, Israel had agreed to the offer. Some Palestinian commentators claim that Arafat too assented to these proposals. But instead of finally agreeing to the most generous concessions he would ever be offered, he effectively turned them down by offering reservations that were a flat denial of what Clinton was proposing.

The Palestinian negotiating team rejected the putative state in the West Bank (described as "three separate cantons connected and divided by Jewish-only and Arab-only roads") and disputed the quality of the land in pre–1967 Israel that was being offered. They also rejected the ideas for shared Jewish/Islamic sovereignty over the Temple Mount, taking instead an all-or-nothing approach. They disliked the idea of an Israeli military presence in the Jordan Valley and, above all, said they could not "surrender the right of return of Palestinian refugees."[150] As a result, they could not agree to the additional clause that stipulated an end to the conflict. In the words of Dennis Ross, a senior member of the negotiating team: "He [Arafat] said yes, and then he added reservations that basically meant he rejected every single one of the things he was supposed to give."[151] Not surprisingly, the two sides also failed to reach any agreement at the January 2001 talks at Taba.

Arafat's rejection of the Clinton offer was also confirmed by an adviser, Mamduh Nawfal, who said that Palestinian negotiators had told their Israeli and American counterparts that the proposals were "far from the international legitimacy resolutions on the Palestinian-Israeli conflict."[152] For Abed Rabbo, the parameters represented "one of the biggest frauds in history."[153] Saib Erekat claimed that Clinton had asked Arafat to acknowledge that the Temple of Solomon was "located underneath the Haram-Al-Sharif." According to Erekat, Arafat responded by saying, "I will not be a traitor. Someone will come to liberate it after 10, 50 or 100 years. Jerusalem will be nothing but the capital of the Palestinian state."[154]

The sabotaging of the peace talks by January 2001 coincided with a dramatic upsurge of violence, again characterized by the return of suicide bombings and other violent attacks. Between 2001–5, there would be dozens of suicide bombings, and other attacks, killing over 1,000 Israelis (mostly civilians) and wounding thousands more. A number of these attacks were carried out by the Fatah-based al-Aqsa Martyrs Brigade in coordination with operatives from Hamas and Islamic Jihad. Israel responded with a major defensive operation designed to smash the terrorist infrastructure that Arafat had built up in the West Bank. Israeli forces launched major incursions in Ramallah, Bethlehem, Jenin, Nablus, Qalqilya and Tulkarm, arresting and detaining thousands of suspects, seizing weapons and destroying bomb laboratories. Inevitably these operations incurred the loss of innocent Palestinian lives though, as in the battle for Jenin, this was largely due to the use of human shields and the Palestinians' booby-trapping of their own buildings.[155] Indeed in Jenin, the IDF ruled out aerial power and instead conducted hand-to-hand combat to minimize casualties.

But now no one could doubt Arafat's own role in the terror war against Israel. In 2002, Israel seized the *Karine A*, laden with 50 tons of weapons, including Katyusha rockets and anti-tank missiles, that were destined for Gaza. They also seized a vast cache of documents from Arafat's headquarters showing the price he was to prepared to pay for suicide bombers and the links between Arafat's al-Aqsa Martyrs Brigade and other Islamist groups.

Despite his distaste for the Palestinian leader, President Bush in a speech on 24 June 2002 went out of his way to endorse a Palestinian state, albeit one that was not compromised by terror and corruption. He slammed a Palestinian leadership for "encouraging, not opposing terrorism" and demanded "new leaders" and "new institutions" for the Palestinians. He slated Israeli settlement policies, saying that they "must stop," and in 2003 endorsed the "Performance Based Roadmap to a Permanent Two State Solution to the Israeli-Palestinian conflict." He also insisted that Israel withdraw to the positions it had occupied prior to 28 September 2000.[156] Washington's calls for political reform fell on deaf ears; in effect, they were forlorn expressions of hope that were predictably ignored by Palestinian leaders.

In the same year, the Saudis produced an initiative at an Arab League summit that was designed to end the conflict. It called on Israel to withdraw to the pre–1967 lines, giving up all of the West Bank, Gaza and Golan Heights; to recognize a just solution to the refugee problem based on Resolution 194; and to agree to a Palestinian state with East Jerusalem as its capital. In return, the Arab states would consider the conflict over and establish normal relations with Israel.[157] Though on paper this appeared to offer a viable basis for resolving the conflict, it was a non-starter. For one thing, it required a set of Israeli concessions without making demands of the Palestinians, including the need to stop terrorism. It required Israel to absorb a potentially huge number of refugees and withdraw from holy Jewish sites in Jerusalem. Crucially, Israel would have to take grave risks with her security through a pullback to the pre–1967 lines before she received Arab recognition, a reversal of Camp David. The "peace plan" was a clever form of impression management by the Saudis. They were anxious to be seen as peacemakers following the revelations of Saudi involvement in the 9/11 attacks.

Arafat died in 2004, though there is no proof that it was from polonium poisoning as some claim.[158] But if the Americans and Israelis had hoped for more from his successor, they were to be much mistaken. On the plus side, Mahmoud Abbas has largely rejected the use of terror for tactical reasons, primarily because he does not believe it will bring political dividends to the Palestinians. He has stated his commitment to reaching an accommodation with Israel based on two states for two peoples and has spoken out against the BDS movement. Yet in other respects, Abbas has been a clone of Arafat, both in his uncompromising attitude towards negotiations and in the media frenzy directed towards Israel.

Abbas' Palestinian Authority from 2004 has been guilty of inciting hatred and glorifying terrorists. Palestine Media Watch has documented dozens of examples where the PA has named sporting events, summer camps, schools, streets and public squares after murderers. Two examples are Dalal Mughrabi (who led the 1978 bus hijacking that killed 37 civilians) and the PLO's Abu Jihad. Another honored "martyr" was Abd al-Baset Odeh, a suicide bomber who killed 30 Israelis in 2003 but who had a football tournament named after him.[159] Such actions have given a sense of honor to killers as well as providing a lethal incitement to murder. Not surprisingly, the PEW organization found that 68 percent of Palestinians polled justified suicide attacks, either often or sometimes, a figure far higher than in other Arab countries.[160]

Worse, the PA has paid the salaries of Palestinian prisoners held in Israeli jails for terror offenses, as well as "monthly stipends to the families of suicide bombers." The total spent amounts to a minimum of 6 percent of the PA's annual budget. Much of this was overseen by

Salam Fayyad, a man regarded by Western politicians as a true Palestinian moderate. In 2011, Fayyad made an amendment to this law by massively increasing these salaries.[161]

The PA media regularly launch hate-filled diatribes against Jews and Israel. Programs on Palestinian television demonize the Jews, likening them to poisonous animals and willingly reproducing the most vicious anti–Semitic images. Palestinian textbooks still contain maps that describe Israel as "occupied Palestine" and thereby blot out the existence of the Jewish state. PA-appointed imams, including the mufti of Jerusalem, describe the conflict as an ongoing "religious war" (*ribat*) and demonize Jews as "the enemies of God." Then there are the libels, such as that Israel has spread AIDS, cancer, drugs and prostitution to undermine Palestinian society, that Israel steals the organs of Palestinians and treats prisoners as guinea pigs for medical experiments, that Israel seeks to destroy the al-Aqsa mosque and is planning to build a new temple on Muslim sites, that it foments crises in the Arab world and that it poisoned Arafat.[162] It is hardly surprising to hear that an Arabic translation of *Mein Kampf* is a bestseller in the disputed territories.

Mahmoud Abbas has also engaged in Holocaust denial. He gave a powerful boost to the denial movement with his 1983 book, *The Other Side: The Secret Relationship Between Nazism and Zionism*. In the book, Abbas described the murder of 6 million Jews as a "myth" and a "fantastic lie." He argued that the number of Jews killed was probably less than one million and, to support his thesis, quoted Robert Faurisson, the French academic who denied that the gas chambers ever existed. Like many others on the hard left, Abbas also blamed the Zionist movement for the massacres. He wrote that the Zionists "gave permission to every racist in the world, led by Hitler and the Nazis, to treat Jews as they wish, so long as it guarantees immigration to Palestine."

In 2003, Abbas declared that his views had changed, describing the Holocaust as a "terrible, unforgivable crime against the Jewish nation." In April 2014, the *New York Times* reported that Abbas had shown further contrition, describing the Holocaust as "the most heinous crime to have occurred against humanity in the modern era." But the issue was not whether Abbas believed the Holocaust to have occurred, though he has doubted the numbers. The issue is who was responsible. Abbas clearly continues to believe that the Zionists, with their "Nazi links," helped to engineer it, and has claimed that he has a further 70 books on this subject that he has yet to publish.[163]

In any case, Holocaust denial remains rampant in Palestinian society, particularly in the education system and in the media. After a visit to the territories in 2012, Ed Husain, a former Islamist and now senior fellow for Middle Eastern studies at the Council of Foreign Relations, observed, "Holocaust denial continues to be part of the normative mindset among so many" in the territories.[164] Holocaust denial is not surprising, either in the territories or in the wider Arab world. Acceptance of the genocide perpetrated against the Jews would make normalization with the Jewish state much easier. It would provide moral justification for a Jewish state and strip away the pretense that Palestinians are the greatest victims of the modern age.

Attempts to deny Jewish historical links with the Holy Land have been among the most salient characteristics of Palestinian discourse under Abbas' rule. At a speech in Doha in 2012, Abbas accused Israel of trying to obliterate the "Arab-Islamic and Christian" character of east Jerusalem by "Judaizing" the city. He questioned whether a Jewish Temple ever existed in Jerusalem and claimed that Israel was seeking to destroy the al-Aqsa mosque. Abbas stated that the holy city would "forever be Arabic, Islamic and Christian" with no mention of the Jews having a three-thousand-year connection to the place.[165]

The Palestinians also managed to persuade UNESCO that two of the holiest Jewish sites, Rachel's tomb in Bethlehem and the Patriarchs' Tomb in Hebron, were actually mosques and that the Cave of the Patriarchs in Hebron ought to be removed from Israel's list of national heritage sites. Palestinians have claimed that Jesus was a Muslim and that the Jebusites and Canaanites were Arabs. They have gone further and stated, "The nation of Palestine upon the land of Canaan had a 7,000 year history BCE"; they added, "We are the people of history."[166] This led to Saeb Erekat declaring that he was the "proud son of the Canaanites who were there 5,500 years before Joshua bin Nun burned down the town of Jericho."[167] In actual fact, Erekat's family hailed from Saudi Arabia and not Palestine. This falsification of history is designed to present the Jews as colonial usurpers who have conducted a ruthless land grab of the Palestine patrimony. But then the PLO's charter enshrines the following: "Claims of historical or religious ties of Jews with Palestine are incompatible with the facts of history."

In line with previous policy, Western powers have systematically ignored or downplayed this appalling legacy of hate and rejectionism, preferring the well-trodden path of unconditional reward and appeasement. But before dealing with the "Quartet," it is worth reflecting on Israel's own concessions to the PA. In 2005, Ariel Sharon's government evacuated remaining settlers from Gaza (some 9,000) plus two settlements in the northern West Bank. Israel would control the area's airspace and borders. Gaza was to be handed fully to Palestinian control and used as a litmus test of Palestinian intentions, allowing the Israelis to assess the viability of withdrawing from large parts of the West Bank at a later date.

At the same time, Israel signed an agreement on movement and access. It was designed to "promote peaceful economic development and improve the humanitarian situation on the ground."[168] Under the agreement, Israel would allow the passage of convoys to facilitate the movements of goods and persons, and movement within the West Bank would be eased, consistent with Israel's security needs. There were plans in the agreement for a seaport and an airport. Thriving greenhouses were also left to Gaza's residents. Israel was offering the Palestinians a chance to build a state in Gaza en route to further disengagement elsewhere.

However, in 2006, the jihadist group Hamas won parliamentary elections in the Strip and proceeded to exacerbate the firing of rockets from Gaza into towns in Israel. The following year, Hamas seized control of the Strip in a violent coup, killing dozens of Fatah members by throwing them from the rooftops of buildings. Hamas' victory only worsened the security problem for Israelis, as rockets continued to be launched at Israeli communities in the south. The evacuation, though no doubt necessary for demographic reasons, offered false hope that simply handing back land to the Palestinians was a recipe for peace and stability.

In November 2007, Washington launched the Annapolis peace conference with Secretary of State Condoleeza Rice declaring, "There could be no greater legacy for America" than the creation of a Palestinian state. Not that the PA was paying much attention. When there was a possibility of renewing negotiations from 2008 onwards, Mahmoud Abbas "missed the bus" completely. In 2008, Abbas had a series of meetings, as many as 35, with Ehud Olmert in a repeat of the secret diplomacy that had characterized the pre–Oslo years.

In September 2008, Abbas was offered a map by Israeli PM Ehud Olmert, showing the proposed contours of a future Palestinian state. Olmert proposed to annex some 6.3 percent of the West Bank, areas containing three-quarters of the settlers, and offered land swaps to make up the difference. There would have been a road on sovereign Israeli soil offering safe passage from the West Bank and Gaza. In addition, the old city of Jerusalem would be administered by a five-nation trust with the Palestinians and Israelis each claiming Jewish and Arab neighborhoods for their own capitals. No more than 5,000 Palestinian refugees would be able to return.[169] Olmert gave a subsequent account of the meeting in the *New York Times*, the main details of which have since been confirmed by Saeb Erekat and Mahmoud Abbas:

> I saw that he was agonizing. In the end, he said to me, "Give me a few days. I don't know my way around maps. I propose that tomorrow we meet with two map experts, one from your side and one from our side. If they tell me that everything is all right, we can sign." The next day they called and said that Abu Mazen had forgotten that they needed to be in Amman that day, and they asked to postpone the meeting by a week. I haven't met with Abu Mazen since then. The map stayed with me.[170]

Olmert was replaced by the more hawkish Benjamin Netanyahu. Netanyahu had long been highly lukewarm on making the kind of concessions offered under his predecessors, Barak and Olmert. Before his first period in office, he was extremely critical of the Oslo process. But once again, the evidence shows that while Netanyahu was prepared to make some concessions to the PA, Abbas spurned the opportunity to end this conflict.

In a speech at Bar Ilan University in 2009, Netanyahu pledged himself to the creation of a demilitarized Palestinian state in the West Bank, but a state not compromised by terror. This commitment to two states for two peoples was reaffirmed in a speech given to the Conference of Presidents of Major American Jewish Organizations on 11 February 2013.[171] After Benjamin Netanyahu made his Bar Ilan speech, Fatah could have shown a willingness for compromise and negotiation. The opposite occurred. The Fatah Conference resolved to "totally reject recognizing Israel as a Jewish state" and "to be creative in finding new forms of struggle and resistance."[172]

The speech coincided with the election of President Obama, who now decided that freezing Jewish settlements was an essential precondition for the resumption of peace talks between the two sides. Netanyahu agreed to a 10-month settlement freeze in the West Bank (not including east Jerusalem). However, for almost the entire period, Abbas refused to sit down and talk to his Israeli counterpart. He cited the need for a range of preconditions to be met before the resumption of talks.

In 2011, Netanyahu reversed course on a policy he had long criticized by agreeing to a prisoner swap with Hamas. The militant jihadist outfit had been holding soldier Gilad Schalit hostage since 2006 without access to the Red Cross, in contravention of international law. Years of negotiation had broken down, with Netanyahu coming under intense media pressure to bring Schalit home. The case for a deal was strengthened by the campaign from Schalit's parents, who used a sympathetic media to drive home their case. Eventually a deal was brokered whereby over 1,000 Palestinians, some serving multiple sentences for mass murder, were released in return for Schalit. It was a classic case of capitulation to terrorism and, in the short term, arguably strengthened Hamas at the expense of Fatah. It was not the first time that such generous terms had been agreed in a prisoner swap.[173]

In 2012, Abbas made a bid for unilateral Palestinian statehood at the Security Council and, when this failed, for non-member observer status in the General Assembly, which he obtained. This was designed as a means to an end. As an observer state, he would have the opportunity to launch a range of criminal prosecutions against Israel in the International

Criminal Court and to argue for the illegality of Israel's presence in the disputed territories. In effect, without offering the Israelis anything, he would be trying to create a hostile Palestinian state "in a de facto state of war with Israel."[174]

At different stages in his presidency, Barack Obama promised that he would work for a Palestinian state and would do everything possible to "get beyond the current impasse." That led to a renewed incarnation of the peace talks, overseen by Secretary of State John Kerry in 2013, which lasted nearly a year. An incredibly detailed account of these talks appeared in the *New Republic*, based on interviews with many of the key negotiators. In July 2013, Abbas managed to sell the idea of renewed negotiations via the United States to the Palestinian leadership. The price was Israel's agreement to release 104 pre–Oslo prisoners currently languishing in Israeli jails. For his part, Abbas would agree not to apply for membership in any new UN bodies, and Israel was granted the right to build 2,000 new settlement units. The choice of releasing prisoners rather than freezing settlements appears, in retrospect, a mistaken judgment.

Nonetheless, the talks dragged on between representatives of each side for several months. And with continuous disagreements over various issues, ranging from settlements and tit-for-tat murders to Palestinian threats to sign UN treaties, no clear agreement was going to be signed by the 29 April 2014 deadline. However, what is significant is that Netanyahu, in spite of his previous skepticism about the peace process and the right-wing coalition he was leading, suddenly softened to American proposals. He was prepared to allow some Palestinian refugees to enter Israel on a humanitarian basis, though he refused to accept any division of Jerusalem. Most importantly: "After decades of railing against any mention of the 1967 lines, Netanyahu accepted that '[t]he new secure and recognized border between Israel and Palestine will be negotiated based on the 1967 lines with mutual agreed swaps.'"[175]

Despite Abbas refusing to believe that Israel would make concessions, President Obama was upbeat. In March 2014, in a meeting at the White House, the president tried to assure the PA leader: "The occupation will end. You will get a Palestinian state. You will never have an administration as committed to that as this one." However, neither Abbas nor Erekat were impressed with this, leading to a stinging rebuke from Susan Price, who accused the Palestinians of not being able to see "the big picture."[176]

Over the next month, there were frantic disagreements over the issue of prisoner releases, with Israel withholding the final batch until it was certain that Abbas would agree to continue the talks. The Palestinians were threatening to sign UN treaties and conventions. Eventually, Abbas made good on his threat. But what really brought the talks to a shuddering end was the decision late in April 2014 to create a Hamas/Fatah unity government. The day after this announcement was made, the Israeli Cabinet voted to suspend the talks.

But it is not clear if the talks would have produced a substantive agreement in any case. Trust between the sides was incredibly low to begin with and only worsened as the talks progressed. Both sides entered negotiations without believing that they would produce anything substantive. However, it is clear that, despite the massive domestic pressures from his coalition, Netanyahu was moving steadily closer to the American peace formula. By contrast, Israeli demands were simply ignored by Palestinian leaders. Netanyahu demanded recognition of Israel as a Jewish state, the right of return for refugees to Palestine and not Israel, Jewish rights of sovereignty to the Old City and the need for an Israeli presence in the Jordan Valley. All these were rejected by Abbas and his negotiating team, with the support of the Arab League.[177]

The issue of accepting Israel as a Jewish state was a particularly big sticking point. Nabil Shaath, a leading "moderate," justified the refusal to accept Israel as a Jewish state: "Do you think that any Palestinian leader in his right mind can ever accept this?"[178] He has not been alone in this position. In 2007 Saeb Erekat said: "We will not agree to recognize Israel as a Jewish state" as "there is no country in the world where religious and national identities are intertwined." He later warned Netanyahu that he "will have to wait 1,000 years before he finds one Palestinian who will go along with him."[179]

In 2013 Abbas said: "If we will be asked to recognize Israel as a Jewish state, we'll refuse, because we already recognized the State of Israel, but if Israel wants to go to the UN and change its name to whatever it wants, that's its own business."[180] For Yasser Abed-Rabbo, "the issue of recognition is for internal [Israeli] consumption only" as "only a Zionist party" is concerned with defining Israel as a Jewish state. In other words, the very thing that the Palestinians demand from Israel and the outside world—recognition of their national rights—is denied by them to Israel. Some claim that this is purely a matter of Israeli self-definition, and is therefore an issue that the Palestinians scarcely care about. If so, then why did Yasser Abdel Rabbo face calls to resign when he said that the PLO might after all recognize Israel as a Jewish state in exchange for a sovereign Palestinian state within the 1967 borders?[181]

Shortly after the talks collapsed, another Israel-Gaza war erupted to match the intensity of Operation Cast Lead. This one had a great deal to do with the financial and diplomatic weakness of Hamas and the state of intra–Palestinian politics. Hamas faced grave financial difficulties, owing to the fact that its civil servants needed to be paid and Fatah refused to do, despite their unity deal. The jihadists were also badly isolated, principally because they had lost their Muslim Brotherhood patron in Cairo and been ostracized throughout much of the region.

The war was precipitated by the kidnapping and murder of three Israeli teenagers, an event that caused anguish throughout Israel. Israel rounded up hundreds of Hamas supporters in the West Bank and, in a brutal revenge attack, a sixteen-year-old Palestinian boy was murdered by Jewish extremists. Hamas then launched hundreds of rockets deep into Israel, many reaching as far as Tel Aviv and Jerusalem. After rejecting several ceasefire requests (which Israel accepted and initiated), Israel launched Operation Protective Edge, a series of air strikes and military incursions designed to curb the threat from rockets and tunnels in Gaza. Over 2,000 Palestinians and 70 Israelis would be killed, though the number of Palestinian civilian casualties remains disputed. Despite many Western nations supporting Israel and its right to self-defense, there were many calling for an unconditional ceasefire, even though Israel was being attacked by terrorists. Halfway through the war, John Kerry produced a ceasefire proposal that was much to the liking of Hamas and its Arab backers but that was rejected by Egypt, the PA and Israel. If this was not a reward for terror, it is hard to see what was.

True to form, after Operation Protective Edge, Palestinian extremism received a most needed shot in the arm. The UN Human Rights Council announced that it would hold an international commission of inquiry into alleged war crimes committed during Operation Protective Edge. The UNHRC resolution behind this inquiry was to investigate "the widespread, systematic and gross violations of international human rights and fundamental freedoms arising from the Israeli military operations in the occupied Palestinian territory." It made no reference to the Hamas rockets or their vicious charter and was thus one-sided from the outset. It would be headed by law expert William Schabas. In the past, Schabas had declared that Benjamin Netanyahu should have been "in the dock of an international court" and called for President Shimon Peres to appear before the ICC. He was therefore tainted with bias from the outset, making him highly unsuitable to lead such an inquiry. The enquiry was therefore judicial nonsense from start to finish.[182]

As of 2016, the pessimists are in the ascendancy. Even though most Israelis still support a two-state solution, most believe that this will not end the conflict. It may be harder to extract concessions from Netanyahu's right-of-center Likud coalition, but the problem lies more squarely on the other side. Characterizing Abbas' behavior over the last decade, one is led to conclude that he (like Arafat) is excellent at extracting Israeli concessions, only to then renege on any written commitment, walk away and later demand those exact concessions as a starting point for further talks. No meaningful Palestinian concessions are ever offered.

Some argue that Israeli leaders are just as liable to the charge of rejectionism. After all, during the 1970s and 1980s, Israeli prime ministers Golda Meir, Menachem Begin and Yitzhak Shamir refused to countenance any notion of Palestinian statehood. They outlawed contacts with the PLO and decried as fanciful the idea that territorial changes would bring peace to Israelis and Palestinians. The most that Begin was prepared to consider at Camp David was a formula for Palestinian autonomy, a formula that might have led, after a 5-year period, to citizenship for Arabs either within Israel or in Jordan. There is much in the accusation, frequently made by Israel's New Historians, that these leaders sought at all costs to prevent the creation of a Palestinian state.

Of course, it is equally true that not all Arab leaders in the last century have been diehard opponents of Israel, as the examples of Anwar Sadat, Jordan's King Hussein and Morocco's King Hassan II amply demonstrate. There have also been some genuine Palestinian moderates who were prepared to negotiate with other Israelis *in good faith* on the basis of a two-state compromise. One such was the journalist and diplomat Said Hammami. After joining the PLO and becoming a member of the Palestinian National Council, he took up a position as representative in London. He met a number of left-leaning Israelis and, in numerous interviews, openly advocated a two-state solution. Yet he came to suffer the same fate as other Palestinian moderates when he was fatally gunned down in 1978. This was merely a continuation of the mufti's policy of eliminating rivals in ruthless fashion.

But in some ways, the accusation of Israeli rejectionism misses the point. Had Begin, Meir or Shamir sat down with Palestinian representatives, either during the Egypt/Israel peace talks or later, would their experience have been more profitable than that of Barak or Peres in the 1990s? It is hard to see how Arafat would have been any less intransigent in the decades during which his terrorism was in the ascendant. A Palestine under his control would have been a corrupt center of global terror in a state of permanent war with Israel. The Israeli "rejectionists" believed, and were not afraid to say, that Arafat was never committed to peace and coexistence with Israel, or the future well-being of his own people. The tragedy of the Palestinian people is that this description so easily fits all those who have championed their cause since 1920.

7. Israel Is an Invaluable Asset to the West

The Common Argument

It is often argued that the West's alliance with Israel does incalculable harm to its interests, particularly in the Middle East. Israel's existence, so it is argued, is a running sore for much of the Arab world, especially the Arab "street." There is a profound loathing of the sinister machinations of this "Zionist entity" and the harm it inflicts across the region. It is regarded as an affront to Islamic unity. Western countries, by virtue of their extensive trade, military and diplomatic links with Israel, are seen as complicit in her behavior and "illegal" policies. Thus the alliance with the Jewish state backfires against the West because it can only incur a popular backlash.

This is particularly irrational because the West's real interests in the Middle East are purportedly to support Arab national interests. They are vastly more numerous in terms of their geographical extent, demographic strength and overall economic resources, particularly in terms of cheap energy. All those interests are allegedly under threat when the West backs Israel. You hear such views from a range of critics, including American academics Mearsheimer and Walt and a former French ambassador to the UK, Daniel Bernard, who was overheard describing Israel as a "shitty little country" that was in danger of leading the West to World War III.

Inevitable Assumption

The assumption is that when Western nations support Israel, it reflects either the seeming omnipotence of the pro–Israel lobby or some form of post–Holocaust Western guilt. This argument has a seductive appeal even to some pro–Israel supporters who assume that because "the Arabs have the oil," there must be something brave and romantic about supporting tiny Israel. It cannot be a matter of calculated self-interest.

Supporting Israel is indeed brave for world leaders because they often run the gauntlet of irrational anti–Israeli hostility. Supporting Israel may well exacerbate (rather than create) anti–Americanism and anti–Western feeling on the Arab street. But here is the crucial and never-to-be-forgotten point: Western nations support Israel primarily because of self-interest, namely because their political and strategic needs, to say nothing of their guiding values, align with those of the Jewish state. Hard-headed pragmatism, rather than romanticism, is the true driver of a strong relationship, despite the misty-eyed rhetoric from some quarters.

Indeed, the evidence shows that the Jewish state is one of the West's greatest assets in the region. To show why, it is necessary to identify the principal Western interests in the Middle East. Essentially, these boil down to four (in no order of importance): first, the containment of radical, potentially hegemonic anti–Western nations, including those with a desire to proliferate weapons of mass destruction; second, preventing violent extremism in the region, particularly Islamist terror; third, preserving the free flow of cheap oil in the region; and fourth, the promotion of genuinely liberal, democratic forces in the region, which includes the protection of Israel itself.

Containment of Radical, Potentially Hegemonic Nation-States in the Region and Preventing Their Acquisition of Weapons of Mass Destruction

For most of the second half of the twentieth century, the central threat to Western interests in the Middle East was represented by the Soviet Union and its sponsorship of radical Arab states, including Egypt (until 1973), Syria, Iraq and Libya. Among non–Arab states, the principal threat has come from the Islamic Republic of Iran.

These regimes have had much in common: they are violently illiberal, ideologically hostile to America and Israel, and manifest a relentless loathing of Western values. Historically, states such as Syria, Iraq and Iran engaged in a form of covert warfare with the West, hiding behind a variety of anti–Western proxies to destabilize neighboring states, cower and intimidate their enemies through state-sponsored terror and engage in violence to bolster their regimes. These radical states have also long sought and obtained weapons of mass destruction.[1]

Israel has consistently shown that it can help the United States, and her allies, to hold back or deter the most radical regimes within the region. In May 1958, a civil war broke out in Lebanon between the pro–Western president, Chamoun, and the Muslim Socialist National Front, which wanted to join Nasser's United Arab Republic. The Iraqi king was overthrown in July 1958 in a military coup, and there was a deep concern that the Hashemite regime in Jordan would be next. Western intervention swiftly followed, with Israel agreeing to allow overflights by Anglo-American forces as it had a joint interest in the survival of King Hussein's regime. The crisis highlighted Israel's crucial significance to the great powers.[2] Later, Israeli intelligence would play "an important role in ensuring the survival of Jordan's King Hussein," who faced assassination threats, together with "Egypt's President Sadat, and Saudi Arabia's King Faisal."[3]

Next one can consider the result of the 1967 war. Egypt and Syria, Soviet client states, were heavily defeated by U.S.–backed Israel, demonstrating so clearly both the superiority of American arms and allies and the inferiority of Soviet support. By 1973, Sadat had become painfully aware that Soviet support would not deliver the territories that were lost in the 1967 war. Thus in the mid–1970s, he was weaned away from the USSR and into the U.S. camp, itself a major diplomatic success for the Nixon administration. But again, it was only Israeli military prowess that made this possible, for a decisive Egyptian victory might have produced a different set of consequences.[4] It was Israel's ability to fight and defeat the Soviet-backed states that proved it had the mettle to resist Soviet expansion, thus making it a reliable bulwark during the Cold War.

As former vice president Walter Mondale once put it: "No Soviet strategist can consider an offensive operation in the eastern Mediterranean without weighing the strength of Israel's defense forces. No Soviet proxy can undertake aggression without risking a crushing rebuff."[5] But it was equally the sense of Israeli invincibility that frustrated the Soviet-backed client states and that persuaded at least one (the key one as it turned out) to become a U.S. ally, naturally in the hope that American leverage with Israel would deliver territorial gains that were impossible with Soviet help.

It was thanks to Israeli ingenuity that the United States was able to analyze captured state-of-the-art Soviet weaponry. *Operation Diamond* (1965) was perhaps the greatest achievement of Meir Amit, Mossad's director during the 1960s. It involved persuading an Iraqi Christian pilot, Munir Redfa, to defect from Iraq to Israel, bringing with him a Soviet MiG-21. The capture of this military hardware was a boon to the Israeli airforce but also caused ripples of astonishment throughout the West.[6] Israel also seized a Russian ground-to-air missile system in the 1967 war and downed Soviet missiles in the 1982 Lebanon war. In the latter war, Israeli air force pilots flying American jets downed 86 Soviet MiGs without the loss of a single plane, an impressive achievement at the height of Cold War tensions.

In all these examples, Israel gave successive American administrations a valuable chance to assess the military capability of their foremost military adversary, and remind them of their qualitative military edge. It is little wonder that in 1979, Ronald Reagan wrote: "Only by full appreciation of the critical role the State of Israel plays in our strategic calculus can we build the foundation for thwarting Moscow's designs on territories and resources vital to our security and our national well being."[7]

ISRAEL'S VALUE TO THE WEST IS EVIDENCED BY HOW IT HAS HELPED PREVENT ANTI–WESTERN MIDDLE EAST STATES FROM ACQUIRING WEAPONS OF MASS DESTRUCTION

In 1981 the Israelis bombed the Osiraq nuclear plant in Iraq, thus curtailing Saddam Hussein's pursuit of atomic weapons. Though condemned at the time, Israel's action reaped a dividend for coalition forces in the first Gulf War. By preventing Saddam from having a credible nuclear deterrent, Israel smoothed the path for the removal of Iraqi forces from Kuwait. With a nuclear shield, the Iraqi dictator might have felt emboldened to invade other oil-rich Gulf states with catastrophic and potentially irreversible consequences. In 1990, Israel's intelligence agency Mossad allegedly killed Dr. Gerald Bull, the rogue scientist who was helping to construct a supergun for Saddam Hussein. This too was a blow to the Iraqi dictator's regime before the First Gulf War. Israeli intelligence also reportedly alerted the United States to Iraq's attempts to *reconstitute* its nuclear program while it played a critical role in helping UNSCOM to "penetrate Iraq's concealment mechanism and to dismantle Iraq's residual WMD programs in the mid to late 1990s."[8]

In 2007, the Israeli Air Force destroyed a Syrian nuclear reactor at Dir al-Zur that had been constructed with North Korean and Iranian assistance. This operation, the result of meticulous planning and incredible intelligence work, prevented another regional sponsor of terror from acquiring the world's worst weapons. One should not forget that the administration of George W. Bush refused to carry out this course of action. A year later, Israeli naval sharpshooters reportedly killed General Muhammad Suleiman at his residence near the Syrian city of Tartus. Not only was Suleiman a close confidante of President Assad but he had also played a key role in Syria's clandestine nuclear program. At the time of his death, he was said to be planning another reactor.

In recent years, the prime focus of Israel's attention has been the Iranian nuclear threat, and many operations credited to Mossad are said to have slowed down their programs. In 2006, there was a mysterious explosion in the Natanz underground facility caused by malfunctioning equipment planted by foreign saboteurs. Further delays at Natanz were the result of faulty products purchased abroad, with the Iranians discovering later that this rogue material came from front companies set up by Mossad and Western intelligence agencies. Mysterious explosions rocked Iranian nuclear facilities at Arak and Isfahan and brought down several planes that were carrying scores of Revolutionary Guards. Several of Iran's leading nuclear scientists have also died in targeted assassinations, with the deaths attributed by British intelligence to Mossad double agents.

Then in 2010, much of Iran's nuclear infrastructure was hit by the powerful Stuxnet computer virus, an extremely sophisticated cyberweapon likely to have been built by Israel and the United States. In 2011, at least half of the Iranian centrifuges were immobilized by the attacks.[9] Not for nothing do the authors of a recent book on the Mossad describe the organization as "the best defence against the Iranian nuclear threat" and "against terrorism."[10]

The decade-long covert war against the Iranian regime and its nuclear arms apparatus will always be associated with one of Mossad's most esteemed directors, Meir Dagan. Dagan's feats in tackling Israel's enemies would become the stuff of legend, so much so that they would lead the Egyptian paper *Al-Ahram* to describe him as "the Superman of the State of Israel."[11] Yet in reality, much of Mossad's work to counter the Iranian nuclear threat has been carried out with the help of the CIA and MI6, a powerful security triumvirate collaborating to contain Tehran's ambitions.[12] They work together to deal with the critical threats posed to their countries, with Israel's counter-terror techniques now used increasingly by other intelligence agencies.

In all these cases, Israeli action has exercised a "chilling effect" on rogue regimes that might otherwise have become more advanced in their pursuit of WMD. One retired U.S. Air Force intelligence chief, Major General George F. Keegan, once said, "The ability of the U.S. Air Force in particular, and the Army in general, to defend whatever position it has in NATO owes more to the Israeli intelligence input than it does to any other single source of intelligence, be it satellite reconnaissance, be it technology intercept, or what have you." He also claimed "Five CIAs"[13] could not have yielded Israel's intelligence on the Soviet air force.

All this without a vast contingent of American troops permanently stationed on Israeli soil, making the Jewish state historically very unlike South Vietnam, West Germany or South Korea. As Alexander Haig once put it: "Israel is the largest American aircraft carrier in the world that cannot be sunk, does not carry even one American soldier, and is located in a critical region for American national security."[14]

Preventing Violent Extremism in the Region, Particularly Islamist Terror

Today, the Middle East is convulsed by the multiple threats posed by terror groups, both Sunni and Shia. Sunni groups include Hamas, al-Qaeda, the Muslim Brotherhood, the

Nusra Front and Islamic State, while the Shiite groups are primarily represented by Hezbollah. These terrorist organizations are deeply anti–Western in orientation and have attacked Israeli and other targets over many decades. Some, such as al-Qaeda, Hezbollah and Islamic State, are in open warfare against the West.

Israel has multiple roles to play in the war on terror and against jihadist extremism. She has long battled against violent Islamist terrorists with years of experience in tracking the movements of Hamas terror operatives, removing key figures in the chain of command and neutralizing terrorist plots before they can be actuated. She has a specialty in HUMINT, that is, human intelligence based on information gathered by sources on the ground. Israel's renowned secret service, Mossad, is famed for planting agents in foreign countries where they blend naturally in to their surroundings. Israel has the advantage of an ethnically diverse citizenry who hail from dozens of countries around the globe and who speak a vast array of languages.

Naturally, this intelligence expertise benefits the West too. Thus when in 2008 a Mossad team reportedly hunted down and killed Imad Mugniyeh, the military commander of Iran-backed Hezbullah, they were removing one of the world's most wanted terrorists, not just an enemy of Israel. Mughniyeh had been responsible for hundreds of American and Western deaths in the 1980s and 1990s.

Israel also plays a more indirect role in the war on terror through the use of sophisticated military technology. Israel invented the modern unmanned aerial drone that is now being used in Afghanistan for intelligence gathering and combat warfare. The UAV is a remarkably cost-effective instrument of national security that allows for precision targeting of the enemy at no cost to Allied troops. According to Dyke Weatherington, "It is difficult to find any other technology in the Department of Defense that in a single decade has made such a tremendous impact."[15]

The American navy has benefited from a defensive gun system developed in Israel that provides defense against terrorist dinghies and other hostile small vessels. From 2016, a sophisticated Israeli helmet-mounted display system will be "part and parcel of all American stealth aircraft produced."[16] Israel is also America's most sophisticated partner in the field of rocket and missile defense.[17] Israel is the only country on earth with a national missile defense system protecting all its population centers. It has been argued that the United States and other Western countries are being influenced by the success of Iron Dome and David's Sling into acquiring similar systems to protect troops deployed in areas that are subject to rocket attack. Joint U.S.–Israeli drills have been carried out to protect against the threat of ballistic missiles.[18]

America has also learned lessons in urban warfare from Israel, a country that has had to fight two intifadas against terrorists embedded in civilian areas. Prior to the 2003 war, delegations from the U.S. Army, Marine Corps, and Joint Staff travelled to Israel to learn the lessons Israel had drawn from their operations in the West Bank. Two lessons learned included the use of "add on armor to enhance the survivability of armored vehicle crews in the lethal urban environment" as well as "the use of D9 armored bulldozers." After the invasion, thousands of U.S. troops trained at Baladia City, Israel's urban warfare training center.[19]

The American military used a number of Israeli innovations (checkpoints, roadblocks, security barriers) in Iraq during the extensive insurgency. To counter the lethal threat of improvised explosive devices, they used "IED-detection dogs, and special search dogs" acquired from Israel. The dogs are "credited with having saved many American lives."[20]

Israel has also developed expertise in airline hostage rescue, with its most famous feat being the Entebbe rescue in 1976. It has since "pioneered a number of the tactics, techniques, and procedures eventually adopted by counterterrorism units around the world, including America's Delta Force and SEAL Team 6."[21] In terms of extrajudicial killings, the United States has "incorporated Israeli tactics, techniques, and procedures for targeted killings in operations in Iraq, Afghanistan, Pakistan, and Yemen."[22]

The American military has also used the emergency bandage invented by Israeli Bernard Bar Natan, which stops potentially fatal bleeding from traumatic injuries.[23] American soldiers benefit from the recuperation method known as Prolonged Exposure. Developed by an Israeli professor of clinical psychology, Edna Foa, the treatment helps to alleviate the symptoms of battle-induced post-traumatic stress disorder. It has been widely used by American veterans groups.[24]

There are also extensive working relationships between U.S. law enforcement and Homeland Security agencies. Tens of thousands of officials in these areas have received extensive training on counterterrorism techniques, including bomb disposal. Israel has enhanced the U.S. capacity to defend itself from sophisticated cyber-warfare, while Israeli software has helped create a computerized database for the FBI, improving the agency's ability to evaluate potential terrorists before they strike. Nor can it be forgotten that Israel has led the way in airline defense for several decades: the use of armed sky marshals on El Al planes, together with thick metal doors to protect the cockpits and the extensive use of profiling passengers, are all crucial counterterrorist measures that have prevented hijackings.[25] Such airline security measures have become standard on U.S. airlines following 9/11.

In addition, American public health and emergency services officials have travelled to Israel to deal with "emergency planning and mass casualty incident response." Israeli homeland security firms "have an extensive global presence" with Nice systems, which provides integrated digital recording and management solutions, serving 25,000 customers in 150 countries, including "over eighty Fortune 100 companies."[26]

It isn't just the United States that has benefited from the fruits of Israeli military technology. Colonel Richard Kemp, former commander of British forces in Afghanistan, revealed that when he took command in 2003, he relied on Israeli advice for tackling the threat of Afghan suicide bombers. After contacting a friend at the Israeli embassy, he received a detailed, four-hour briefing from an Israeli brigadier-general that was used as the basis for the British army's manual for tackling suicide bombers. Kemp also revealed that after the 7/7 attacks, he received a call from contacts that he had in the Israeli security services "who offered every assistance they could provide." He said that he received "few other such calls from our allies around the world."[27]

Intelligence sharing and cooperation extends to Iran too, so much so that, according to Con Coughlin, defense editor of the *Daily Telegraph*, Britain "cannot afford a diplomatic rift with Israel."[28] But Israeli military technology has other applications of profound importance to the UK. The Hermes 450, an aircraft designed by Israel's Elbit Systems, has been used extensively in Afghanistan and is credited with being vital in protecting British lives.[29] London's metropolitan elite firearms unit SO19 has also used techniques derived from Israel's counter-terror agencies. Also, according to one report produced by the Henry Jackson Society, Israeli technology has been used to safeguard Buckingham Palace and Heathrow Airport, to name just two iconic structures.[30]

The EU has benefited profoundly from its strong military ties with Israel. In the field of counter-terrorism, Israeli expertise has proved invaluable after a decade in which Islamist terrorists have struck on the European continent, most notably the 2004 Madrid bombings that killed 191 people. The HJS report noted that EU governments, mindful of the terror threat, "have dramatically upgraded security collaboration with Israel." In particular, the report cited above reveals how Israeli intelligence has been invaluable in tracking the movements and activities of Hezbollah, whose track record includes the 1983 bombing of French barracks in Beirut and a 2013 suicide bomb attack in Bulgaria.

The EU also benefits from Israeli military technology. Israel exported $1.6 billion in arms to the EU in 2012. Among its exported military hardware is the Spike anti-tank portable missile system, designed by Rafael, which has been bought by the UK, Spain, Netherlands, Belgium and Italy. Like the United States, the EU has also benefited from the unmanned aerial drone, "accounting for 40% of all sales globally."[31] This device is crediting with helping to save the lives of European troops in conflict zones such as Afghanistan, Mali and Libya. Such is Israel's reputation for security management that an Israeli company was tasked with protecting athletes during the 2004 Athens Olympics.[32]

Israel has also conducted joint training exercises and missile defense drills with the armed forces of European nations. It hosted the air forces of Germany, Italy, Poland and the United States in December 2013 (Blue Flag) and, in 2011, conducted long-range airforce bombing runs with Greece, Germany, Holland and Italy.[33]

In recent years, Israel has been developing closer ties with NATO. Shortly after Jaap de Hoop Scheffer became the first NATO chief to visit the country in 2005, they signed a plan to cooperate in 27 areas. In 2009, the chairman of NATO's military committee visited Israel to study IDF tactics in dealing with terrorism in built-up areas, and how they might be applied to the war in Afghanistan. Israel has also agreed to the installation of a U.S.–NATO missile defense system in the Negev Desert that is designed to protect Europe from Iranian ballistic missiles. Israel and Germany have also been reported to be working on a secret project for differentiating nuclear-tipped from decoy missiles in the event of a nuclear war.

Overall, the military cooperation is of profound benefit to Western countries. It is true that, on occasions, Israeli military relationships, particularly that with the People's Republic of China, have created disagreements between Israel and the West. The case of Jonathan Pollard[34] has also caused considerable consternation. But the overall picture is surely a positive one as far as the West is concerned.

Preservation of Cheap Energy Supplies

According to Pulitzer Prize–winning oil expert Daniel Yergin, "Petroleum remains the motivating force of industrial society and the lifeblood of the civilization it helped to create. It is an essential element of national power, and a major factor in world economies."[35]

A key Western regional interest is to secure the free flow of oil from the Persian Gulf, in particular from energy-rich Saudi Arabia. Arabists in the State Department, the oil industry and among the diplomatic corps have long believed that the insatiable need for cheap energy necessitates the forging of closer links between the United States and the Saudis, keeping their Israeli ally at arm's length. There is a plenitude of evidence that former diplomats as well as those in the energy sector have lobbied U.S. presidents to take a more pro–Arab line (particularly a pro–Saudi line) and adopt a cooler approach towards Israel. They argue that the West will suffer deleterious consequences from supporting Israel over the Arab states.

As evidence, they cite the oil embargo initiated by OPEC as punishment for supporting Israel in the 1973 Yom Kippur War. They also cite repeated Saudi threats to lower oil production unless the U.S. pressures the Jewish state on the Palestinian issue. Without doubt, the last 60 years of the U.S.–Saudi alliance have shown a consistent willingness by Washington to kowtow to Riyadh's demands on everything from arms sales to covering up the Saudi link to jihadism.

However, this does not show that Israel is a liability, and it is a misconception that America must choose between supporting Israel and securing cheap energy. For all the posturing about Palestinian suffering by members of the Saudi royal family and members of other Gulf sheikhdoms, there is little chance that oil supplies from the Gulf will be suspended. The Saudis are dependent on the sale of oil to Western (and now increasingly Eastern) customers and would only be threatening their own economic interests if they caused a dramatic surge in commodity prices. To lower production and raise oil prices would be to risk the very thing the Saudis most fear, namely the investment by her customers in alternative sources of energy. Many of these fears are being realized in any case. U.S. oil imports have been declining too in recent years, with domino effects for her dependence on Middle East oil.[36] Imports have declined because of higher domestic production on private and state lands, the use of hydraulic fracturing and horizontal drilling technology for shale products, and the increased production of corn-based ethanol.[37]

Fundamentally, the prime interest of the House of Saud, apart from generating stupendous revenues from producing and exporting petroleum products, is not to protect the human rights of Palestinians (even just those living under Israeli occupation) but to guarantee their own survival. In the 1950s, the Saudis were concerned that their newly founded state might be taken over by its former Hashemite controllers. Later they became concerned about Nasser's imperialist ambitions as a leader of the Arab world, particularly following the takeover of Yemen. After 1990, there was grave concern about the threat posed by Saddam Hussein's invasion of Kuwait and the possible capture by Iraqi forces of Saudi oil fields.

Today, the Saudis, like the Bahrainis, fear the threat posed by Shiite Iran, and its leaders' dire warnings to close the Straits of Hormuz in time of war. The Saudis know that with a nuclear shield, Iran could use its status as a nuclear power to bully smaller oil-rich powers into lowering oil production or forcing them to change their foreign policy. Hence the "moderate" arc of Sunni powers, including Saudi Arabia, Bahrain, Jordan and Egypt, are united in their suspicion of Iranian intentions. National self-interest dictates the policies of these states, Saudi Arabia in particular, not any abstract concern for the rights of fellow Arabs. Jimmy Carter would have agreed with all this. In 1979 he stated that he had "never met an Arab leader that in private professed the desire for an independent Palestinian state."[38]

Democracy Promotion

The fourth Western regional interest, particularly in recent years, has been to promote and support liberal democratic movements in the Middle East, seeing them as a vital bulwark to radical anti–Western regimes and international terrorism. Democracy promotion became an article of faith with American neoconservatives, such as Paul Wolfowitz and Douglas Feith, in the George W. Bush administration. They saw in the fall of Saddam Hussein (and other autocracies) the chance for a democratic revolution in the region that would usher in the spread of liberty, pluralism and intellectual freedom. They exulted in American exceptionalism, the notion that the country has a unique mission to spread the core enlightenment values of freedom, equality and democracy to the downtrodden peoples of the Middle East.

Seen in this light, the alliance makes sense. Israel is a stable oasis of democracy in a region beset by tyranny. Since its founding, it has operated a multi-party system of participatory democracy in which free and fair elections are the norm. It boasts a genuinely free press that is openly critical of the government, and which contains all shades of opinion. Its Supreme Court has time and again delivered judicial rebukes to Israeli governments and provided an essential check and balance to executive power. Following every major conflict since 1973, the supreme court has carried out a major judicial investigation into the military and civilian handling of the war, the result of which has led to the resignation of several serving PMs. This shows Israel's commitment to the rule of law and respect for human rights.

Unlike every one of its neighbors, Israel's record on women's rights is exceptional. As early as 1951, these rights were enshrined in the country's Basic Laws. Golda Meir became the world's third female prime minister in 1969. Women have the legal right to be artificially inseminated at taxpayers' expense, while Israel boasts stringent anti–sexual harassment laws. Israel also protects its religious minorities. This explains why the Baha'is, a religious minority persecuted for their beliefs in Iran, have found safe haven in Israel, where they have established their global headquarters. Similarly, while members of the moderate Ahmadiyya sect of Islam flourish in Israel, they face hatred and persecution in Gaza, the West Bank, Pakistan and other Muslim countries where they are branded *kuffar* (infidels). In Israel, Christians flourish openly in a country that contains many of their most venerated holy places. Other minorities such as the Druze have played important roles in the military and diplomatic spheres.

Israel allows space for mass protest, particularly during unpopular wars (1982 Lebanon war), and through the operation of independent trade unions. A variety of NGOs openly scrutinize the country's record on human rights and publish searching critiques of government policy. It is also a haven for sexual tolerance, providing a space for gay and lesbian people that cannot be found anywhere else in the region. Israel thus shares the West's political values and its abiding belief in liberty, democracy and social progress. What better reason is there for the special relationship between the two countries? Indeed, the ideological bonds uniting Americans and Israelis stretch further. Both countries were shaped by immigrants who sought to create a just society built around individual freedom. At the outset, both were (and remain) imbued by the pioneering ethos of their founders, which celebrated drive, enterprise and initiative. Today, both see themselves as models of democracy and Western governance in a deeply unstable world.

Some caution is needed here, however. For all America's talk of promoting democratic governance, the United States continues to support bulwarks of Middle East autocracy in the interests of stability and energy security. In the 1970s, key American allies included Egypt's Sadat and Iran's repressive Shah, neither man being noted for his commitment to liberal democracy or human rights. American governments have long supported Bahrain's autocratic Khalifa monarchy, which, in turn, has hosted the U.S. Fifth Fleet. And successive American governments have made a devil's bargain with the oppressive Saudi monarchy in the interest of preserving cheap energy.

Some cite these alliances as evidence that democracies are not always reliable allies. Recent history is replete with examples of democratically elected governments making geopolitical commitments that are subsequently reneged upon by successor governments, partly due to unpredictable shifts in public opinion. Spain's military commitment to the Iraq war, followed by its withdrawal of forces in 2004, is one example. This is also a reason why democracies are not always deterred from *allying* with non-democratic regimes. They know that commitments entered into are unlikely to change because of varying popular sentiment. An autocrat can, after all, remain unmoved by shifts in popular mood.[39] But the flip side of this argument is that when there is overwhelming popular support for a political alliance within a representative democracy, that relationship is thereby solidified. It has the backing of the public, regardless of which party is in power. As Bernard Lewis pointed out in 1986 in his discussion of the USSR's Cold War strategy: "The Soviets know very well that strategic alliances are more effective and more secure when they are underpinned by real affinities, and not merely political choices of current leaders."[40]

America in particular enjoys a consistently high level of public support in Israel. Israelis value the United States, the American way of life, American consumer culture and America's role in the world. A Pew Survey from 2011 found that 72 percent of Israelis had a favorable view of the country, rising to 83 percent in 2013. In another poll from 2009, 68 percent of Israelis thought that the United States was a loyal ally, with some 10 percent disagreeing. Some 91 percent believed that close relations between the two countries were vital to Israel's national security. Such strong and friendly links are reinforced in trade and investment figures. As of 2013, Israel was the United States' 23rd-largest export market for goods in the world with Israel being the United States' 21st-largest supplier of goods imports.[41] America's very first free-trade agreement was signed a quarter of a century ago—with Israel. Israel has streets named after iconic American presidents Lincoln and Washington, honors the memory of Kennedy and has two replicas of the Liberty Bell. Israel has also signed formal agreements with the United States in a host of areas, including economic cooperation, agricultural production, education, security and defense, and social policy.[42]

At the UN, Israel votes over 90 percent of the time with the United States, making it America's ally-in-chief in terms of diplomatic support. (By contrast, America has only vetoed just over one-third of the hostile anti–Israel resolutions at the Security Council, and did not do so until 1972.) What this suggests is that, regardless of which party is in power in either the United States or Israel, there will be healthy support for the strategic alliance between the two countries.

Israel's status as a liberal democracy matters in three other fundamental respects. It is little contested today that full-fledged democracies rarely if ever go to war with one another. Instead, their disputes and confrontations are usually settled by processes of negotiation, diplomacy and compromise. In his book *Never at War*, Spencer Weart cites a considerable body of historical evidence to demonstrate this very point. He shows that over the course of a millennium, and particularly in more recent history, well-established democracies "are inhibited by their fundamental nature from warring on one another."[43] In part, this is explained by the nature of leadership prevailing in established democracies, where custom dictates tolerance of dissent, openness to opposition and the settlement of internal disputes by nonviolent debate. If these are the means for solving domestic issues, it is hardly surprising that they create a paradigm for resolving inter-state disputes. When democracies do go to war, as they often do, it is almost always with tyrannical or otherwise non-democratic regimes, or on occasion, barely established democracies.

To appreciate the importance of democracy, one need only look at how alliances with undemocratic regimes have often failed. The clearest example for the United States was its relationship with Iran before and after 1979. Whereas under the Shah, Iran–U.S. ties were close given the proximity of their economic interests, they were irreparably damaged after his overthrow. The ayatollah regime that emerged in the wake of the Shah's overthrow was violently hostile to both America and Britain and, despite cosmetic domestic changes, remains so to this day. For three decades, the United States viewed President Mubarak as a key regional ally, despite the hostility of much of the Egyptian people and commentariat. Swept along by the current of the Arab Spring, the undemocratic Mubarak was overthrown and replaced by a Muslim Brotherhood government that was antagonistic to the West. The danger is that because autocratic governments are not immune to a populist overthrow, any agreements reached with them that lack the imprimatur of public opinion cannot be trusted. Deals made with tyrannies are frequently dependent on the will of a strongman and when such a figure is removed, political alignments shift accordingly.

Secondly, Israel's democratic status gives a vital moral dimension to the alliance with the West. Western nations that promote the rule of law, judicial independence, minority rights, freedom of religion, sexual tolerance—in short, democratic ideals—suffer less reputational damage from allying with fellow democracies as opposed to thuggish, oppressive and tyrannical regimes. The war on terror involves, at least in part, a battle to "win hearts and minds." If so, this is more easily achieved by rewarding other bulwarks of liberty than by supporting regimes that are on a moral par with the terrorists they fight. Making alliances with autocratic dynasties in the Gulf may make economic sense, but it exposes the United States to the charge of hypocrisy: of espousing disdain for the values of terrorists while backing states that are equally repressive.

But democratic Israel's contribution to Western interests does not end there. It is a great pillar of innovation, technological progress and astounding scientific achievement. Since its founding, the tiny Jewish state has produced an enormous array of scientific and medical advances that have impacted directly on the lives of millions. Today Israel is a world leader in fields as diverse as electric car technology, fish farming, desalination, airline security, missile defense, crop protection, stem cell research, clean energy, cardiovascular medicine, cyber-protection and earthquake relief. These technologies are exported around the world every year, particularly to countries in the developing world, where they save lives.

Israel's medical sector is particularly renowned. Her doctors have been engaged in pioneering research for treating an array of diseases including leukemia, Parkinson's, multiple sclerosis, diabetes, Ebola, cancer and asthma. Israeli medical research has produced innovative systems for detecting breast cancer, amniocentesis (a standard procedure for detecting genetic abnormalities in pregnant women), blood detoxification techniques, tumor imaging, and the discovery of the protein ubiquitin.[44]

Among the dazzling array of medical devices invented by Israel are the optical heartbeat monitor, BabySense (a product that helps to prevent crib death), a spine assist, a robotic tool for performing spinal surgery, and ReWalk, which has given mobility to those who would otherwise be paralyzed.[45] At the Jerusalem-based Hebrew University's Interdisciplinary Center for Neural Computation, a micro-computer is being designed that will revolutionize treatment for paralysis. Haifa-based company InSightec has developed the use of sound waves to treat tumors and lesions, with impressive results to date.[46] "The Diverter," an implant that can reduce the occurrence of strokes, is the brainchild of Israeli doctor Ofer Yodfat.

Professor Yoel Margalith, known as "Mister Mosquito," developed an environmentally friendly means of eliminating mosquitos. He won the 2003 Tyler Prize for environmental achievement and, according to the Tyler executive committee, his work on mosquito eradication had a profoundly important impact: "The sight of millions has been saved and repopulation of deserted river valleys has been initiated. Additionally, malarial infections from pesticide resistant mosquitoes have dropped by 90% along the Yangtze River, China, which has a population of over 20 million people."[47] Innovative methods of drip irrigation, pioneered by Israeli company Netafim, have helped to "increase crop yields, preserve scarce water resources and protect the surrounding environment." They are being used to boost food production in dozens of countries to the benefit of millions.[48]

Israeli high tech is renowned the world over. Any time that people use an Internet connection, they rely on the miniature modem pioneered by Israel-based RAD systems. When they pick up a mobile phone, the technology behind voice mail, text messaging and the transmission of pictures and movie clips has come from Israeli engineers. The ICQ chat facility was the brainchild of three young Israelis who sold their multi-million-dollar invention to AOL.[49] The antivirus software used on so many computers was first developed in Israel too, as was the USB flash drive. It has just produced a smartphone designed for disabled customers, allowing them to make calls, send text messages and use the Internet.[50] Israel is also a world leader in security encryption technology. Perhaps the most exciting area for Israeli scientific innovation is in the field of nanotechnology. This seemingly esoteric branch of science involves manipulating particles that are the size of molecules and promises applications in health care and space exploration.[51]

The result of all this is that dozens of American companies, among them Intel, Google and IBM, have set up major research and development centers in Israel, where they rely on the expertise of Israeli engineers. The architecture for so many of Intel's successful computer chips "was invented in Israel, accounting for an estimated 40 percent of the firm's revenues."[52]

In the words of the high priest of technology, Bill Gates, the "innovation going on in Israel is critical to the future of the technology business."[53] Indeed, Israel's high-tech community is surpassed only by Silicon Valley. These prodigious accomplishments are undoubtedly beneficial for Israelis and reflect the open, liberal, democratic and entrepreneurial environment in which they live. What is equally important is that they also offer untold benefits for millions worldwide.

The United States and the Arab World

The conflict between Israel and her neighbors has clearly not sapped America's interests with the Arab world. Eisenstadt and Pollock point out that, today, "U.S.–Arab trade is booming," with U.S. exports to the Middle East up by 15 percent in 2011, reaching $56 billion while, in recent years, oil exports to the United States from most Arab producers "rose or remained steady, regardless of political tensions." Furthermore, "defense cooperation remains as close as ever, with massive arms deals to Saudi Arabia and the UAE."[54] They sum up clearly:

"Since the Arab oil embargo of 1973, one can search in vain for even a single instance in which any Arab government penalized the United States for its support of Israel."[55]

But while Washington continues to uphold its interests in the Arab world, it is not so clear that those interests represent a grand strategic bargain for the United States. There are some severe costs associated with America's partnership with various countries in the Middle East, in particular Pakistan, Egypt, Saudi Arabia and Qatar.

The Pakistani intelligence service ISI stands accused of providing support to the Taliban, particularly before 9/11. Indeed, it was largely created through the vast financial and military support provided by Pakistan. In 2009, Robert Gates, the U.S. defense secretary, accused it of maintaining links with the Afghan terrorists to help Islamabad gain influence in the country. In 2010, considerable evidence emerged from the "Wikileaks" cables about the close links between the ISI and various militant groups fighting coalition forces in Afghanistan. These troubling links came under further scrutiny when, a year later, Osama Bin Laden was found hiding in the Pakistani city of Abbottabad. Pakistan has also long stood accused of institutionalizing clerical support for violent and sectarian jihadism through its vast network of more than 10,000 madrassahs.

In 2011, Admiral Mike Mullen, chairman of the Joint Chiefs of Staff, told the Senate Armed Services Committee that the Pakistani government was allowing the Quetta Shura, the Taliban's supreme military and political command, and the Haqqani Network to "operate from Pakistan with impunity." These were proxies of the government, attacking both Afghan troops and civilians as well as U.S. troops. After citing a number of terror attacks that had been carried out by the Haqqani network, he went on to declare: "The actions by the Pakistani government to support them—actively and passively—represent a growing problem that is undermining US interests and may violate international norms, potentially warranting sanction."[56]

Yet none of this has stopped an incessant aid flow from the United States and UK. The United States alone has provided nearly $20 billion since 2002 in aid to Pakistan. Despite Pakistan's deep geo-political significance, Washington pays a price for that country's jihadist sympathies and dual loyalties in the war on terror.[57]

For several decades Egypt has been viewed as a key American ally, responsible for helping secure vital U.S. interests in the region. As such, it has received over $40 billion of American aid, amounting today to nearly $2 billion a year over the period. On the plus side, President Mubarak abided by the Camp David accords signed by his predecessor and cooperated with Israel and the United States on security issues. He opposed leading terror organizations, such as Gamaa al-Islamiya, and staged military exercises with the United States. Yet despite this, he never sought to upgrade Egyptian-Israeli relations to the level of "normalization" as required by the Camp David accords. To this end, he permitted the most atrocious anti–Western and anti–Semitic incitement in state press and television channels. He also failed to completely crack down on the smuggling of weapons from Egypt into Gaza, especially when it did not have domestic implications.

Despite cracking down on the Islamists at home, largely for domestic reasons, Mubarak permitted the Muslim Brotherhood to become the main opposition group in the country. This was used to increase Western support for his regime; in effect, he was blackmailing the West by arguing for his own indispensability in the face of an inevitably growing Islamist opposition. But giving such a wide berth to the Brotherhood simply upped the radical threat and today, the virulently anti–American Islamism that the Brotherhood embodied remains a potent force in the country, despite General Sisi's military coup in 2013. Mubarak ruled with an iron fist through his police state, the very apparatus of terror that encouraged many people to support a more radical alternative.[58]

Qatar is another key American and Western ally. It hosts the headquarters of U.S. Central Command and the al-Udeid military airbase, which serves "as the hub for all American air operations in the region."[59] With its immense reserves of oil and gas and its huge sovereign wealth, Qatar offers attractive commercial prospects to Western investors. Its financial muscle has allowed Qatar to purchase Harrods, Al Jazeera, football clubs and other investments. But Qatar is also one of the world's leading sponsors of global jihadist terror.

It has given guns and money to Islamist rebels in Syria, including Ahrar al-Sham, a group that has cooperated with IS, and Jabhat al-Nusra. It has provided support to the Muslim Brotherhood and has long hosted the organization's spiritual leader, Shiekh Yusuf al-Qaradawi. For years, donors in Qatar have also provided lavish amounts of material support to ISIL while the state, through its promotion of an intolerant brand of militant Wahhabism, has given it ideological succor. Qatar has also hosted the Hamas political leader Khaled Mashaal and directly funded the terror group's activities. Terrorist financiers operate in the country, including those who serve as interlocutors between Qatari donors and ISIL. One family member, according to a report in the *New York Times*, operated a safe house for Abu Musab al-Zarqawi, who later led al-Qaeda in Iraq.[60] It is stating the obvious to point out that these activities directly militate against all Western interests in the region.

But these three examples pale into insignificance when one considers the price that America has had to pay for its "special relationship" with Saudi Arabia. Today the desert kingdom is the world's leading incubator of Sunni jihadi terrorism. For years, the Saudi religious establishment has been given free rein to export its interpretation of Salafi Islam around the globe. The annual $4 billion budget for "Islamic activities" has been used to fund the creation of schools, madrassahs, youth organizations and mosques, many of which are to be found in Western countries, including the United States. Indeed one terrorism expert has estimated that as many as 80 percent of American mosques are run by Wahhabi imams.[61] These institutions have propagated a virulent strain of intolerant Wahhabism, the main themes of which are to sow discord between Muslims and non–Muslims, to spread hatred of the unbeliever, to demean Christians and Jews, to condemn homosexuality and to promote Sharia law. In other words, they are at the forefront of disseminating the intellectual underpinning of the modern jihadist movement.

Saudi clerics in the 1980s and 1990s were the intellectual progenitors of Bin Laden's jihad, and it is hardly surprising that more than three-quarters of the 9/11 hijackers turned out to be Saudi. According to the 9/11 Commission report, Khalid Sheikh Muhammad revealed "that Saudis comprised the largest portion (some 70%) of the pools of recruits in the al-Qaeda training camps."[62]

Since the start of the war on terror, many thousands of Saudis have been recruited for terrorist activities and suicide bombings in Afghanistan, Pakistan, Somalia, Yemen and Iraq. Some 135 Saudis have been held at Guantanamo Bay since 2002, the second highest number of nationals after Afghanistan.[63] Little of this should be surprising, given the overwhelming support in the population for Bin Laden's organization. Moreover, Saudi terrorists have played a major role in undermining the U.S. presence in Iraq. One study has shown that of the 1,200 foreign fighters captured in Syria from mid–2003 to mid–2005, some 85 percent were Saudis. As Middle East expert Vali Nasr points out, they were undoubtedly encouraged to join the jihad by Wahhabi and Salafi clerics in the desert kingdom.[64]

With Washington knowing full well about the Saudi link to terror, one might have assumed that there would be some caution about issuing visas to Saudi nationals entering the United States. Quite to the contrary, in the months before 9/11, the U.S. embassy in Riyadh agreed to grant a visa to any Saudi without requiring a personal appearance. Such largesse may partly explain why the Saudi hijackers did not face sterner tests before arriving in the United States. The Bush administration's initial response to the terror attacks was to allow a planeload of Saudis to leave the country, despite a nationwide restriction on flights. And even worse, the FBI has admitted that there were "always constraints on investigating the Saudis. Officials were told to 'back off' from investigations involving other members of the Bin Laden family, the Saudi royals, and possible Saudi links to the acquisition of nuclear weapons by Pakistan."[65]

A year after the 9/11 attacks, a report from the highly respected Council on Foreign Relations about the financing of international terrorism included this statement: "For years, individuals and charities based in Saudi Arabia have been the most important source of funds for Al Qaeda." It continues, saying that Saudi officials "have turned a blind eye to this problem."[66] In June 2003, David Aufhauser, general counsel of the Treasury Department, described Saudi Arabia as the epicenter of terrorist financing.[67]

Again, in 2007 and 2008, Stuart Levey, the undersecretary of the treasury for terrorism and financial intelligence, named Saudi Arabia as the world's "leading source of money for al-Qaeda and other extremist networks."[68] These networks included the Taliban and the LET, which carried out the Mumbai terror attacks in 2008. To avoid embarrassing their Saudi friends, the Bush administration took the line that the country was an ally in the war on terror. In all the years since 9/11, there remains zero chance that the country will be placed on the list of countries sponsoring terror. This shameful appeasement of terror is the price that the United States has been willing to pay for its "special relationship" with the House of Saud.

Not surprisingly, the Saudis have barely supported their U.S. ally's proposals for resolving the Arab-Israeli conflict. Indeed, far from helping to promote dialogue between Israel and her neighbors, or advancing realistic proposals for ending the conflict, Saudi interventions have mostly served to fuel the conflict. Riyadh denounced the Camp David accords and in their aftermath, opposed reintegrating Egypt with the Arab world or allowing it a seat at the Security Council. They threatened sanctions against King Hussein if Jordan negotiated with Israel and openly supported the terrorist regime of Muammar Qaddafi.[69] Their 2002 peace plan was a complete non-starter for reasons already mentioned, and it was likely designed as a PR exercise.

The Saudis have also regularly voted against the United States at the UN General Assembly, especially on motions relating to the Arab-Israeli conflict. Saudi Arabia has also provided funding for the PLO and distributed tens of millions of dollars to the families of suicide bombers.[70] Vast sums have poured into the coffers of the virulently anti–Zionist, anti–Semitic Muslim Brotherhood as well as Hamas. This exposes the hollowness of Saudi claims to champion the rights of Palestinian people. If that were truly the case, we would have seen billions of dollars poured into Palestinian schools, hospitals, homes and infrastructure, in short, rebuilding their economy and developing their infrastructure. Instead, the money that has flowed from this oil-rich nation has financed decades of murderous, and futile, terrorism.

And while there has been *some* Saudi cooperation against terrorism since 9/11, this intelligence relationship can be highly volatile. In August 2001 Crown Prince Abdullah wrote to President Bush, warning that their two governments were "at a crossroads." He went on: "It is time for the United States and Saudi Arabia to look at their separate interests. Those governments that don't feel the pulse of the people and respond to it will suffer the fate of the Shah of Iran." Such an aggressive and potentially threatening statement was repeated the following year when a senior Saudi figure declared that his country might "contemplate joining with America's worst enemies." He said: "If reason of state requires that we move to the right of bin Laden, so be it; to the left of Qaddafi, so be it; or fly to Baghdad and embrace Saddam like a brother, so be it."[71] Such statements were made with impunity, because there was no response.

Perhaps such threats influenced the Bush administration to excise 28 pages of the Joint Congressional Inquiry into the 9/11 attacks. According to those who have read these redacted pages, the material looked at the Bush administration and its relations with the Saudis, offering evidence of complicity in the attacks by Saudi individuals and charities. President Bush's claim that the publication of the material would damage American intelligence operations has been dismissed. For one Republican congressman, Walter Jones, "there's nothing in it about national security." It's about the Bush administration and its relationship with the Saudis.[72]

It is not just America that displayed such an incredible level of appeasement. In December 2006, the UK–based Serious Fraud Office, reportedly under pressure from Tony Blair and the attorney general, curtailed an investigation it had been carrying out into an alleged slush fund used in the multi-billion-pound al-Yamamah arms deal. Payments had allegedly been made by BAE Systems to Prince Bandar bin Sultan, Saudi Arabia's ambassador to the United States. Lord Goldsmith tried to defend the decision in the House of Lords by citing the national interest: "It has been necessary to balance the need to maintain the rule of law against the wider public interest."[73]

He no doubt had in mind an earlier statement that had been made by Robert Wardle, head of the Serious Fraud Office, who stated that the Saudi ambassador to the UK had threatened to cease all counterterrorist cooperation with the UK. In the ambassador's words, "British lives on British streets were at risk."[74] The High Court would subsequently rule that the decision to drop the investigation into BAE Systems was unlawful and an outrage, adding that the government had buckled to blatant Saudi threats. What this sorry affair reveals is the extortionate price that has to be paid for obtaining the Saudis' limited cooperation against terror. If British lives were truly at risk because of the fickleness of the Saudi government, it surely says very little about such a choice of ally.

What compounds the problem of these unsavory alliances is that attitudes towards the United States in the Arab world are frequently negative. The respected Pew Research Global Attitudes Project asked respondents whether they had a favorable or unfavorable view of the United States. As of spring 2014, 85 percent of Egyptians surveyed had a very or somewhat unfavorable attitude towards the United States. Exactly the same figures pertained for Jordanian citizens. In Turkey the figure is 73 percent and in Pakistan 59 percent. Nor are these figures a one-off. Surveying the data from the Attitudes Project from 2002 to 2012, the percentage of Egyptians with an unfavorable view of the United States ranged from 69 percent in 2006 to 82 percent in 2010. Figures for Jordan were worse (from a low of 75 percent in 2002 to a staggering 99 percent in 2003 and averaging in the 80s) while Pakistan averaged a disapproval rating of 68 percent for the 11 years from 2002 to 2012, and Turkey 73 percent.[75]

Of course, opinion polling is not an exact discipline and must be treated with a degree of caution and skepticism. But this consistent polling data gives a telling indication of how the United States is perceived in much of the Islamic world. What ought to be worrying for the White House is that these countries are not the purported enemies of Washington, like Syria or Iran. They are its allies.

Some argue that these negative perceptions owe much to America's policies towards Arabs and Muslims in the region and, in particular, to its unstinting support for Israel. The hostility it arouses is allegedly entirely of the United States' own making, a result of the calculated, one-sided policy it adopts towards its Zionist friends and its neglect of Arabs. To correct the negative feelings that America arouses, so the argument goes, America must stop acting against Arab interests through its support for Israel.

The problem with this argument is that it fails to appreciate all those times that America has come to the aid of Arabs and Muslims. In recent decades, the United States helped to save Afghanistan from Soviet occupation by funneling support to the mujahideen. It rescued Kuwait from the tyrannical clutches of Saddam Hussein in 1991, and neighboring Saudi Arabia too, for that matter. It also became a major patron of Egypt from the late 1970s onwards, providing arms and financial support after the Camp David accords. After the second Gulf War, in which the United States removed a genocidal Arab dictator, the Bush administration pressured Syria to end its decades-long occupation of another Arab state, Lebanon. The United States intervened to prevent a massacre of the people of Benghazi by Libyan dictator Muammar Gaddafi in 2011 and provided massive development aid for the Afghan people following the ousting of the Taliban in 2001. Frantic Soviet–U.S. diplomacy in 2013 sought to prevent any further use of chemical weapons by President Assad against his own people. Outside of the region, the United States also intervened to stop the ethnic cleansing of the people of Kosovo and launched a humanitarian operation in Somalia. There were no major economic incentives for many of these interventions.

In respect of the Arab-Israeli conflict, the United States prevented the PLO from suffering total defeat in 1982 by arranging safe passage for Arafat's men out of Beirut, and later recognized the PLO as the legitimate representative of the Palestinian people. Throughout the 1990s, the United States poured billions of dollars of aid into the PA and trained Palestinian security forces in the West Bank. Then from 1993 onwards, American administrations tried to bridge the gaps between Israelis and Palestinians in successive rounds of peacemaking, putting considerable pressure on Israel to make concessions. This included a virtual guarantee of a Palestinian state with part of Jerusalem as its capital.

Of course, not all American interventions have been successful, and some have had harmful effects on Muslim populations. One thinks of the consequences of the Second Gulf War in particular. But in assessing these actions, one must also examine their beneficial consequences, including the removal of dictators who killed an untold number of Muslims and the promotion of more progressive and democratic regimes. In any objective analysis therefore, the United States has often acted positively towards Muslims and Arabs within the region. The negative perceptions of the U.S. role owe less to its actual catalogue of misdeeds than to the grossly distorted lens through which the country is seen.

In conclusion, Mearsheimer and Walt could not be more wrong. The Western relationship with Israel offers untold benefits for both sides. By contrast, the alliances with a number of Arab states in the region are rather less of a bargain.

8. Changing the Narrative: Turning on the Accusers

There are obvious drawbacks in confronting false but well-established narratives. For starters, by amplifying the voices of the bigoted, ignorant and ill informed, one potentially circulates opinions that might otherwise have a much smaller audience. This is particularly true when it comes to fringe figures who thrive on the oxygen of publicity because they are denied a mainstream platform. Publicizing incendiary statements from minor celebrities will obviously increase the audience for their comments and potentially give them a false sense of respectability.

Worse, in challenging the narratives of others, one is constantly forced onto the defensive. Having to relentlessly analyze, dissect and challenge viewpoints is a time-consuming affair that distracts from promoting one's own preferred viewpoint. Moreover, by engaging with the flawed narrative, there is the risk of lending it a level of legitimacy that is not warranted. As the old adage goes, it is better never to argue with a fool because, if you do, the world will never tell the two of you apart.

Unfortunately, it is necessary to challenge those who promote the anti–Israel narrative. This is partly because ignoring what people say is tantamount, for many, to refusing to debate the issues. Such evasion can be a highly risky strategy. In addition, the narrative has seeped into the political mainstream and counts among its adherents some of the Western intelligentsia's key opinion-formers. To allow such influential voices to go unchallenged is misguided.

But at the same time, there is a strong case for turning on Israel's accusers when they are motivated by hypocrisy, ill will or double standards. Many of Israel's fiercest critics have tarnished their credibility and integrity, whether they are academics who have feigned concern for truth, "progessive" politicians who have alienated minority groups, international organizations that have failed in their duties, or regimes that abuse their populations while projecting their faults onto Israel. By turning on the accusers, one can undermine their hallowed status in the eyes of adoring fans. Reputations take years to build up but minutes to lose. As they seek to ruin Israel's reputation, so they should be "hoist on their own petard."

This chapter examines the double standards and hypocrisy of hard left critics from around the world, demolishes the credibility of both the UN and the boycott movement and critically examines the real apartheid within the Arab world.

Exposing the Malevolent Agendas of Five Key Critics

George Galloway is one of the most popular political mavericks of our age. He is an articulate critic of Western foreign policy and of the abuses of power in British society. His demeanor and outlook make him a thorn in the side of the Westminster elite. In recent years, he has become an unofficial cheerleader for some of the most fashionable left wing causes: the closure of Guantanamo Bay, opposition to anti-terrorist legislation, the nationalization of our banking system, the crusade against President Bush and, of course, vehement opposition to Israel.

He would have his followers believe that he stands for noble values—support for human rights; freedom of religious conscience and individual liberties; the rule of law; and opposition to torture and dictatorship. Indeed Galloway's career would not be possible without those values. He is, after all, an elected politician who relies on free and fair elections to achieve power. He speaks freely at political meetings without being censored by a secret police. He demands that his (often largely Muslim) constituents attend places of worship without harassment. He would be the first to complain if he were arbitrarily removed from Westminster without recourse to appeal, subject to illegal interrogation and arbitrarily deprived of justice. But there is nothing noble about the kind of governments Galloway admires.

In 2002 he admitted to a journalist: "I think the disappearance of the Soviet Union is the biggest catastrophe of my life."[1] This was the same Soviet Union that had killed tens of millions of its citizens in gulags, prison cells and state-induced famines, that had operated an oppressive police state that imprisoned a vast number of political dissidents, that had denied the Soviet people their democratic rights for decades and that had imposed draconian censorship on its entire population. The disappearance of such a murderous and repressive regime was deemed a "catastrophe."

By contrast, one of the greatest days of his life was seeing the American ambassador fleeing Saigon and the United States being given a "bloody good hiding."[2] He chose to ignore the even bigger "hiding" that Ho Chi Minh's communists had inflicted on the Vietnamese people in the preceding two decades. According to a report from 1968, the Vietcong, by the end of 1967, "had committed at least 100,000 acts of terror against the South Vietnamese people." These included the destruction of hamlets that were thought to have any connection with the South Vietnamese government, the torture, rape and beheading of young children and the mass kidnappings of civilians.

During the land reform program launched in the 1950s, the Vietminh are thought to have executed between 150,000 and 200,000 people accused of being landowners. It has been estimated that one million people were imprisoned without charge as part of the notorious "re-education" program instituted by the communists after the fall of Saigon. Some 165,000 were killed and thousands more tortured and abused, with some prisoners being incarcerated for up to 17 years.[3] Still, perhaps this was a small price to pay for giving the United States a "bloody good hiding."

In the 1990s, Galloway developed sycophantic ties with Saddam Hussein's regime in Iraq. He had been a vocal critic of Saddam's excesses in the 1980s but switched to fawning admiration a decade later. Of course, there was an obvious reason: Saddam was, in part, supported by the West in the 1980s but became its enemy in the 1990s. Galloway met the Iraqi dictator in 1994 and told him: "Sir, I salute your courage, your strength, your indefatigability...."

I can honestly tell you that there was not a single person to whom I told I was coming to Iraq and hoping to meet with yourself who did not wish me to convey their heartfelt fraternal greetings and support." He later maintained that his words referred to the Iraqi people, not to Saddam himself. One wonders then why he bothered to tell the dictator in the same address these words: "I thought the President would appreciate to know that even today, three years after the war, I still meet families who are calling their newborn sons Saddam."[4] In 1999 he greeted Saddam's son, Uday Hussein, with tremendous warmth: "Your excellency.... I would like you to know that we are with you to the end."[5] Uday is believed to have tortured thousands of Iraqis over the years, and raped countless women in shocking displays of cruelty.[6]

While Galloway acknowledges now that Saddam "committed real and serious crimes against the people of Iraq," he thinks that these "do not compare with those committed against Iraq by us."[7] But even his condemnation of those crimes is marked by equivocation and anti-Western sentiment. In discussing the crime of Halabja, he concentrates primarily on Western perfidy in arming Saddam and providing him with financial support, suggesting that there is something obscene about our squeamishness. He also quotes Churchill's advice for dealing with Iraq's recalcitrant tribes (using poison gas), though Churchill, then colonial secretary, advocated a weapon to disarm people, not murder them. Amazingly, Galloway describes the massacres of Shiites that followed the war in 1991 as "a revolutionary struggle for power" that "involved massive violence on both sides."[8]

His vehement opposition to toppling Saddam led him to advocate Arab armed opposition to coalition troops. In 2002 he said: "Will they [the Arab states] send forces to defend Iraq this time in 2002 or will they allow the use of their forces, air space and land by the Crusaders and foreigners to attack Iraq and start a fire in an Arab, Muslim country that is part of their big entity?" He declared that he was "in favour of everything than can be done to stop it [the imminent invasion of Iraq]."[9]

Two years later he was accused of legitimizing murderous attacks against American and coalition forces by the Iraqi "resistance": "The Iraqi resistance have a right to defend their country against the occupying invader."[10] "Those poor Iraqis," he said later, "are writing the names of their cities and towns in the stars, with 145 military operations every day, which has made the country ungovernable."[11] The fact that so many innocent, working class Iraqis were being liquidated in these "operations" mattered less than the liquidation of American power and the destruction of its perceived imperial hubris.

Galloway is on record for praising President Assad's regime. He met with him in 2005 and later said: "We covered the whole world in 60 minutes. I was very impressed by his knowledge, by his sharpness, by his flexible mind. I was very, very impressed.... Syria is lucky to have Bashar al-Assad as her President."[12] One wonders how many of the hundreds of thousands of Syrians killed by Assad's forces, or the millions forced to flee the country, would have agreed with Galloway's assessment.

He has also praised the Iranian regime in his capacity as presenter for Press TV, a propaganda arm for the Islamic Republic. He has defended the Holocaust-denying former president, Mahmoud Ahmadinejad, and denied that the regime executes people because they are gay.[13] He has also defended the outcome of the 2009 elections, declaring: "Those who hate Iran, those who hate the Islamic revolution in Iran, those who wish the Shah of Persia, the tyrant, had never been overthrown in the first place, are lining up to give Iran a good kicking. Well, not me."[14] Not surprisingly, he has also lionized Hezbollah. In a 2006 op-ed for *Socialist*

Worker, Galloway declared: "I have no hesitation in saying that Hizbollah is not and has never been a terrorist organization." He added: "I glorify the Hizbollah national resistance movement, and I glorify the leader of Hizbollah, Sheikh Sayyed Hassan Nasrallah."[15]

Perhaps he has reserved his greatest admiration for Cuba's Fidel Castro. He has described himself as a "friend of and partisan for Fidel Castro" and "a partisan, for Cuba, for its revolution, for its leadership for its role in the world." He also believes Fidel Castro is "one of the greatest men of the twentieth century and that he will be remembered and revered."[16]

Perhaps he ought to have read a Human Rights Watch report from 1999 that declared, "Over the past forty years, Cuba has developed a highly effective machinery of repression. The denial of basic civil and political rights is written into Cuban law. In the name of legality, armed security forces, aided by state-controlled mass organizations, silence dissent with heavy prison terms, threats of prosecution, harassment, or exile. Cuba uses these tools to restrict severely the exercise of fundamental human rights of expression, association, and assembly. The conditions in Cuba's prisons are inhuman, and political prisoners suffer additional degrading treatment and torture."[17] There is also ample evidence of discrimination against black Cubans, who form the majority of the population.

Part and parcel of praising communist regimes is the implausible denial of their crimes. Thus Galloway has dismissed the notion that there was ever a massacre in Tiananmen Square in 1989. "It is a remarkable thing, that something we've been told for 20 years was a massacre, that not a single photograph of a single dead person has been adduced."[18] Clearly, the extensive firsthand footage and documentary accounts of the very real massacre that took place were no good for Galloway. Instead he preferred the communist regime's own implausible and self-serving denials. Then again, in his book *I Am Not the Only One*, he dismissed the mass murder of the Kurds and the Shia after 1991 as "a civil war with massive violence on both sides."

Were it not for the widespread contempt for George W. Bush among much of the Western intelligentsia, Galloway would long ago have been dismissed as a rather cranky demagogue from the left. As it, the roots of such skepticism run deep. The war on terror and the widespread protests against the Iraq war gave Galloway a new lease of life. He pictured himself as a charismatic crusader against Blairite excesses, appearing on the BBC's *Question Time* and penning columns for the *Guardian*. A columnist with identical views but hailing from the English Defense League would not have been so fortunate.

Galloway's gushing praise for dictatorship and tyranny, together with his disdain for Western power, is echoed by many on the left. This is certainly true of the former mayor of London, Ken Livingstone. In the 1980s, Livingstone distinguished himself by supporting a "rainbow coalition" of disadvantaged groups, including women, homosexuals and ethnic minorities. He publicly condemned prejudice, sexism and homophobia as the lingering evils of right-wing prejudice. Then in 2004, he invited Sheikh Yusuf Qaradawi, spiritual head of the Muslim Brotherhood, to City Hall, where he offered the leader a very public embrace. Livingstone defended Qaradawi in the face of "Zionist smears" and described him as a man who "preaches moderation and tolerance to all faiths throughout the world."[19]

Yet Qaradawi's version of Islamic moderation sits rather uneasily with any Western notion of liberalism or equality. Qaradawi, who has an enormous following across the Arab and Islamic world, defends the use of genital mutilation on girls. He also sanctions the practice of wife beating: "Islam doesn't call for beating but it is necessitated by certain circumstances for a certain type of woman and within limits."[20] On homosexuality, he is far more forthright, condemning the practice as a form of sexual perversion and demanding the death penalty for this form of "sodomy." He has advocated the execution of converts from Islam, saying, "If they left apostasy alone, there wouldn't have been any Islam."[21]

Though condemning the 7/7 attacks, Qaradawi has supported the use of suicide bombings against Israel. One should not be in any doubt that this is symptomatic of a visceral anti-Semitism. He has defended the Holocaust as a form of divine punishment, declaring: "Allah imposed Hitler upon the Jews to punish them—and Allah willing, the next time will be at the hands of the believers."[22] In another sermon on 9 January 2009, Qaradawi called on God to "kill them [the Jews], down to the very last one."[23] In 2013, he boycotted an interfaith dialogue conference in Qatar by saying: "I decided not to attend in order not to sit with Jews on one stage."[24] Livingstone argued that attacks against Qaradawi were part of a Zionist smear campaign that was Islamophobic, and he was joined in this view by supporters from the Muslim Association of Britain and the Stop the War campaign. But these Qaradawi quotes do not come from "discredited" Zionist sites. Instead, as Peter Tatchell points out, they are "a matter of public record on BBC Monitoring, Al Jazeera and Qatar TV, the Al-Sharq Al-Awsat newspaper—and in his own books, such as *Modern Fatwas*."[25]

Livingstone shares many of Galloway's blind spots about dictators. While trivializing the Tiananmen Square massacre, he has staunchly defended the Chinese government's occupation of Tibet because, he says, without such an occupation "they know that within a year there would be a huge American military base there, they would be surrounded on that side."[26] The mass persecution of the Tibetan people is therefore necessary to prevent the spread of American imperialism.

Livingstone, like George Galloway, was an admirer of Venezuela's Hugo Chavez. In the *Guardian* he wrote: "For many years people have demanded that social progress and democracy go hand in hand, and that is exactly what is now taking place in Venezuela."[27] In 2010, a report on Venezuela produced by the Inter American commission on human rights noted that the "punitive power of the State" was being used to "intimidate or punish people on account of their political opinions." It also noted "a pattern of impunity in cases of violence, which particularly affects media workers, human rights defenders, trade unionists, participants in public demonstrations, people held in custody, campesinos [small-scale and subsistence farmers], indigenous people, and women."[28] But just as Livingstone has dismissed criticism of Qaradawi as Zionist scaremongering, he would no doubt regard criticism of Chavez as the poisonous outpourings of neo-con propaganda.

Like Galloway, Livingstone has legitimized internationally proscribed Palestinian terror groups. Nor has he blamed fanatical Muslim terrorists for the 9/11 or 7/7 attacks. The latter atrocity was the result of the West's "meddling in Muslim nations," among which he includes Western support for Israel. He talked of how Islam was being demonized in the British press and even compared the experience of Muslims in Britain with that of Jews in Nazi Germany.[29]

One may well ask why advocates of the left, whose reputations have been based on defending the rights of workers, women, gays and minorities, so willingly side with regimes that openly repress these groups. It is only part of the answer to point out (quite correctly) that many on the hard left have a history of supporting, or turning a blind eye to, the depravities perpetrated by communist regimes, such as Stalin's Russia or Mao's China. The other part of the answer is that what animates radical leftists, above all else, is visceral anti-Westernism, most particularly anti–Americanism. Their overarching ideological goal is the defeat of capitalism and the humbling of Western powers. They see those powers as the cause of most of the world's economic and political problems and interpret their foreign interventions as malevolent and self serving.

Ken Livingstone once described President Bush as "the greatest threat to human life on this planet that we've most probably ever seen"[30] and claimed, "Capitalism had killed more people than Hitler."[31] He was joined in his view by Galloway who described capitalism and imperialism as "the greatest mass murderer in all history, quite dwarfing Hitler's genocide."[32] In 2004, he described Bush, Blair and Howard as "crusaders" and "empire builders," adding that they were "the world's worst leaders, deploying the world's most dangerous weapons."[33] For Noam Chomsky, "Washington has become the torture and political murder capitol of the world."[34]

As a result of this burning hatred, these radicals support every form of anti–American opposition and genuflect in admiration before any regime that does battle with the "American empire." Here they find common cause with the radical Islamists who despise American secular values within the *Dar al-Harb* (the House of War). They cannot tolerate a U.S. presence, direct or indirect, in the land that will soon become the restored caliphate. Both the hard left and the Islamists believe that a new moral order is possible without America's "malign" influence in the world and, for both, the humbling of the American empire must happen for their own utopian dreams to be realized. It is within the context of rabid anti–Westernism that the radical left's hostility to Israel must be viewed. Using the classic tropes of conspiratorial thinking now so widespread in the Middle East, Israel is seen as a pro–U.S. implant designed to disrupt the Arab world and serve Western purposes. In Galloway's words, "Israel was planted in the Middle East as an imperialist vanguard." Its Jewish population largely consists of "settlers" and the "advance guard of an empire."[35] Removing Israel from the map is part of a wider concern with Western power.

The combination of morally blind support for tyranny and unyielding hatred for America finds its loudest echo in the work of Noam Chomsky. Chomsky has spent half a century trying to eviscerate America's reputation. Books, lectures and pamphlets picture the country as a fount of evil, and as the principal progenitor of poverty, inequality, tyranny and corruption. He views America as a Great Satan that has plundered the Third World and launched "terrorist wars" right across the globe. He views the 9/11 attacks as justifiable retribution for America's past misdeeds. "For the first time in history," he wrote, "the victims are returning the blow to the motherland."[36] On many occasions he likens American foreign policy to that of Nazi Germany. Thus as early as 1969 in his book *American Power and the New Mandarins*, where he offered a robust critique of America's war in Vietnam, he declared that what America needed was "a kind of denazification."[37]

Chomsky has also repeatedly denounced American democracy as a fraud that enables the country to hide its "tyrannical" behavior behind a smokescreen. Ordinary people, he believes, are being "duped by the propaganda of the corporate media" into agreeing with the actions of their governments.[38] The apparent consent of the governed is merely "manufactured," an elaborate form of thought control akin to totalitarianism. As a result, he pictures American capitalist society as a sham that needs to be overthrown. Today, many still view Chomsky as a bold polemicist standing up to abuses of Western power.

For all his fame, however, Chomsky may be the most intellectually dishonorable thinker of the modern age. His writings are laced with false statistics, factual inaccuracies and mangled quotes. He avoids key facts and distorts the existing historical evidence, allowing him to reach hyperbolic conclusions that bear little relation to reality. He also relies on highly tendentious, one-sided sources, and sometimes the official, self-serving accounts given by disreputable regimes. Paul Bogdanor has compiled a most valuable list of Chomsky's more egregious factual and statistical errors, some 200 in all, which is required reading.[39]

Like many of his comrades on the hard left, Chomsky whitewashed the appalling crimes of the anti–Western tyrants. He did this by minimizing their actions, creating arguments based on specious moral equivalence and, more often, ignoring critical facts or contextual background.

Thus he ignored the many credible accounts that testified to the mass murders committed by the North Vietnamese Communists from the 1950s onwards. During the Land Reform Campaign conducted from 1953 to 1956, tens of thousands of Vietnamese peasants were brutally murdered by the regime. For Chomsky, these "laid the basis for a new society" that had "overcome starvation and rural misery and [offered] hope for the future."[40] Worse still he ignored the far more heinous crimes of the Vietnamese communists after 1975. Following the war, they engaged in a nationwide purge of former military officers, civil servants and intellectuals. Hundreds of thousands were imprisoned without charge, many succumbing to disease and malnutrition due to their confinement. The regime also deported up to two million Vietnamese to New Economic Zones, akin to the Soviet gulags, and then expelled a vast number of ethnic Chinese citizens. There were numerous credible eyewitnesses to these crimes, all of whom lived in Vietnam for years and had no prior pro–American leanings.[41] Yet in *The Political Economy of Human Rights* Chomsky whitewashed the regime's record, citing the evidence of political activists who were favorable to the regime and who had been vetted by Hanoi. Ignoring the persecution of the Vietnamese boat people, he denied that there was genocide in postwar Vietnam, stating that there was "no credible evidence of mass executions."[42]

It was hardly surprising that Chomsky would turn a blind eye to tyranny. He had already adopted such a position in endorsing the authoritarian leaders of Communist China in December 1967: "China is an important example of a new society in which very interesting and positive things happened at the local level, in which a good deal of the collectivization and communization was really based on mass participation and took place after a level of understanding had been reached in the peasantry that led to this next step."[43] Rather conveniently he glossed over the tens of millions who perished from state collectivization as well as the vast numbers executed by the regime in its early years.

On Cambodia, Chomsky argued that only 25,000 were killed by the vicious Pol Pot regime and that casualty lists had been exaggerated by a "factor of 100."[44] However, the truer figure was some 1.7 million victims, a figure based on extensive research by the Cambodian Genocide Program at Yale University's MacMillan Center for International and Area Studies.[45] Indeed, he compared the Pol Pot genocide to post-liberation France, "where tens of thousands of collaborators were massacred with far less motive for revenge." For Chomsky, these "allegations of genocide" served an insidious purpose: they were designed "to whitewash Western imperialism."[46] At one point he even described the Khmer Rouge ethnic cleansing as a "direct and understandable response to the violence of the imperial system." Pol Pot could hardly have stated it any better. This is genocide denial, pure and simple.

Chomsky was later forced to acknowledge that there had indeed been repression under the Khmer Rouge but he put this down to the undisciplined behavior of military units, revenge and a mixture of starvation and disease resulting from the U.S. war. He also blamed the U.S. bombing campaign for radicalizing the Khmer Rouge, whereas the truth is that the Stalinist tyrants had long sought to impose their fanatical vision on Cambodia and carried through their decimation of the country regardless of America's behavior. In 1988 in his book *Manufacturing Consent* Chomsky remained unrepentant about being an apologist for the Khmer Rouge and claimed he had been right to deny evidence of the genocide in the 1970s.

While denying the genocides of communist regimes, Chomsky has used the flimsiest pretext to accuse America of the same thing. Of the war in Afghanistan, he accused America of being engaged in "a silent genocide" and of carrying out plans that "may lead to the death of several million people in the next few months."[47] As evidence he quoted a *New York Times* report from the previous month, in which the United States "demanded from Pakistan the elimination of truck convoys that provide much of the food and other supplies to Afghanistan's civilian population." The reality is completely different. The American military carried out a massive aid operation to provide relief to millions of Afghan citizens. This consisted of food, clothing and medical supplies, lessening the kind of mass starvation that might constitute "slow genocide." In fact, more food was being delivered since the start of the bombing than before.[48] And all this was being carried out despite attempts by the Taliban to steal food from convoys and levy taxes on essential imports. Thus the charge of implementing slow genocide was just another egregious falsehood designed to tarnish America.

Chomsky's reputation took a further battering after the Faurisson affair. Robert Faurisson, a French academic and leading Holocaust denier, believed that the Holocaust was a Jewish hoax and a financial swindle, designed to empower the State of Israel and harm the interests of both the German and Palestinian people. He dismissed Jewish witnesses of the Holocaust as liars, simply because they were Jews, and misused and ignored evidence to suit his purposes. Not surprisingly, Faurisson faced legal challenges and suspension from his post at the University of Lyon because of his defamation of Holocaust witnesses and anti-intellectual behavior. He also received a suspended prison sentence for incitement to racial hatred.

Yet Chomsky signed a petition that stated that the Frenchman had been subjected to "a vicious campaign of harassment, intimidation, slander and physical violence in a crude attempt to silence him." Faurisson was described as a "respected professor of twentieth century French literature and document criticism" and a man whose "findings" were part of "extensive historical research into the Holocaust question." The petition went on to decry a "shameful campaign to silence him."

Chomsky went on to pen an essay in which he claimed to find no "credible evidence" that Faurisson was an anti–Semite and described the Frenchman as "a relatively apolitical liberal of some sort."[49] The essay was later used as the preface to one of Faurisson's books, without Chomsky's knowledge. Chomsky claimed that he was merely defending a "beleaguered" scholar's right to freedom of expression, quoting Voltaire to this effect. He also stated that he did not endorse Faurisson's view on the Holocaust.

But his actions went beyond a mere libertarian endorsement of freedom of speech. He ignored the fact that, in virtue of his Holocaust denial and falsification of history, the Frenchman had shamefully tainted his reputation as a serious scholar and objective searcher of the truth, destroying any claim to academic credibility. Defending Faurisson as an "apolitical sort of liberal" appeared to cross the line from defending his freedom of expression to giving his remarks a seal of approval. Chomsky was effectively defending the "political legitimacy" of Faurisson's writings by sugar-coating them and denying the author's obvious racism. This much was proven by remarks made by Chomsky in 1981 in the Australian magazine *Quadrant*. Chomsky stated: "I see no antisemitic implications in denial of the existence of gas chambers, or even denial of the holocaust.... I see no hint of antisemitic implications in Faurisson's work."[50] So for Chomsky, denying the mass murder of Jews on the grounds that all Jews are hoaxers is not racist.

As for anti–Semitism in his home country, Chomsky argued that it was a manufactured problem and that real racism occurred to others. The reason is that U.S. Jews were "the most privileged and influential part of the population" and only raised the issue of racism because "privileged people want to make sure they have total control, not just 98% control."[51] Like others on the hard left and hard right, Chomsky accuses Jews of controlling America's media.

What is tragic is that Chomsky could have been a credible commentator on the abuses of power in the modern world. Instead Chomsky destroyed his credibility by an all-consuming hatred of America and its values, a hatred that has caused him to embrace his country's enemies and indulge in wild and irresponsible conspiracy theories.

Another darling of the anti–Israeli left is Norman Finkelstein, a former academic who left De Paul University in 2007 after being denied tenure. The son of Holocaust survivors, he has chosen to view the Holocaust as a vehicle for financial exploitation and a political opportunity for Israel to justify its "expansionist" policies. He recounts a childhood in which the subject of the Holocaust was rarely raised and where he was never asked questions about his parents' experience. "In this light," he says, "one cannot but be sceptical of the outpourings of anguish in later decades, after the Holocaust industry was firmly established."[52] What exists now is a "current crass exploitation of Jewish martyrdom" characterized by "shelves upon shelves of shlock that now line libraries and bookstores."[53]

Finkelstein dismisses the modern world's angst at the Nazi genocide and derides the Holocaust literature in the most pejorative terms. Firstly, he is at pains to deny the uniqueness of the Holocaust, and second, he dismisses the notion that it resulted from an irrational hatred of Jews. But such a false narrative is useful, in his view, for supporting "extortionate" claims for compensation, which he derides as part of a "Holocaust industry." This is a campaign to "extort money from Europe in the name of needy Holocaust victims," something that has "shrunk the moral stature of their martyrdom to that of a Monte Carlo casino." He likens those who claim compensation to Nazis: "I really think that not even Julius Streicher were he editing Der Sturmer today, could have conjured up the image of Jews huckstering their dead, but that's exactly what this gang of wretched crooks have done."[54]

He believes that Jewish elites have knowingly exaggerated the number of survivors in order to milk compensation from European governments in Germany and Switzerland.[55] Elsewhere he trivializes the claims of Holocaust survivors: "I'm not exaggerating when I say that one out of three Jews you stop in the street in New York will claim to be a survivor."[56] Overall, the Holocaust narrative has become "an indispensable ideological weapon" for insulating from criticism "one of the world's most formidable military powers, with a horrendous human rights record."[57]

Like others in the anti–Israel movement, Finkelstein has no problem making comparisons between Israel and Nazi Germany, as when he said that during operation Cast Lead, the Jewish state was "committing a holocaust in Gaza." He has described Israel as a "satanic" and "lunatic" state and Israelis as "satanic narcissistic people." Israel, he goes on, is "Genghis Khan with a computer."[58]

Finkelstein's rather unhinged analysis is laced with poisonous language. He condemns the Simon Wiesenthal Center as "a gang of heartless and immoral crooks." Israel Singer, an executive V.P. of the World Jewish Congress, is "a complete and total hoodlum—something that crawled out of the sewer." Nobel Laureate Elie Wiesel is the "resident clown" for the Holocaust "circus."[59] He is a "ridiculous character" about whom the "expression 'there's no business like Shoah-business' is literally coined for him." He added: "Thanks to Elie Wiesel we have a distorted and disfigured and frankly meaningless version of the Nazi Holocaust and we only know about those genocides that serve the interest of the U.S. and Israel, and we forget the ones that don't."[60]

He says that prominent American Jews such as Abraham Foxman, Edgar Bronfman and Rabbi Israel Singer "resemble stereotypes straight out of Der Sturmer."[61] Nonetheless he praises Holocaust denier David Irving for making an "indispensable contribution to our knowledge of World War II."[62] Elsewhere he has said, "If David Irving is saying, 'Well, an Auschwitz survivor is born every day,' he can say that, because if you look at the numbers of the Holocaust industry, it's true."[63] It is surely no coincidence that Finkelstein was invited to Mahmoud Ahmadinejad's Holocaust denial conference and that he is cited approvingly by radical Islamists.

The Holocaust Industry was pilloried by leading historians. For David Cesarani, the "short, vitriolic polemic" offered a "misinterpretation of history and questionable use of sources" and was "distorted by a venomous dislike of the 'American Jewish elites.'"[64] Omer Bartov, a highly distinguished professor of history at Brown University, described the book as "juvenile, self-righteous, arrogant and stupid" with a thesis that "verges on paranoia."[65] For American historian Peter Novick, it was little better than a "twenty-first century updating of the 'Protocols of the Elders of Zion.'" He added that an examination of Finkelstein's footnotes "reveals that many of those assertions [about reparations] are pure invention.... No facts alleged by Finkelstein should be assumed to be really facts, no quotation in his book should be assumed to be accurate, without taking the time to carefully compare his claims with the sources he cites."[66]

In 2007, Finkelstein was denied tenure by De Paul University and fired. This followed a long campaign by Alan Dershowitz to highlight Finkelstein's distortion of evidence and his willingness to manipulate quotes. What is astonishing is how Finkelstein ever sustained a job as an academic or why anyone, bar a small group of extremists, should ever have taken him seriously. For as Finkelstein himself admitted, as of 2000, "Not one article by me has ever been published in a scholarly journal.... I also rarely give a class by day, mostly in the evenings."[67]

One final academic is worthy of brief discussion, if only because he is the most regularly quoted Israeli historian for the hard left: Ilan Pappe. As one of Israel's New Historians, Pappe distinguished himself by calling for a global boycott of Israeli academics while being one himself (at the University of Haifa). Pappe has often called for a one-state solution, meaning that Israel should be converted into a binational state of Israelis and Palestinians, even though this would eventually lead to an Arab majority and the destruction of Israel as a Jewish state.

Pappe's best-known book is *The Ethnic Cleansing of Palestine*. In it, he spells out his claim that the Middle East conflict was entirely the fault of Israel's leaders and of Zionist ideology. He claims that some 800,000 Palestinians were forcibly removed from Palestine in 1947–1948 and that this was not an *ad hoc* measure but the by-product of a deliberate Zionist policy of ethnic cleansing. In his own words: "From its early inception and up to the 1930s, Zionist thinkers propagated the need to ethnically cleanse the indigenous population of Palestine if the dream of a Jewish state were to come true." He dismisses the Partition resolution as "unjust" and "impractical."[68] He is even prepared to describe 1948 as "the worst chapter in Jewish history."[69]

In other words, Pappe fully endorses the "Naqba" narrative of the Palestinians. To back up his thesis, he quotes from the diaries of Ben-Gurion and from the writings of leading Zionists. He believes the premeditated plan for ethnic cleansing was spelt out in Plan D (Plan Dalet) and that in its implementation, it involved expulsion, massacres, demolitions and a variety of other war crimes. Indeed, he claims that what the Jews did in Palestine in 1948 was "what Jews had not done anywhere else in the previous two thousand years."[70] He also accuses the Israeli state of "memoricide," of deliberately erasing this crime from the collective national consciousness, something that was accomplished by Hebraizing Palestine's geography by the substitution of Jewish names for Arab villages. He also says that thanks to Israeli policy, "millions of Palestinian refugees around the world have no way to return home" and that those in the West Bank and Gaza face "the most brutal occupation the world has seen since World War II."[71] He argues that Hamas is engaged in "resistance" to Israel's occupation and supports their stance, even though he decries their "political ideology."[72] This is, in essence, the synopsis of Pappe's work, and he has never retracted his claims.

Pappe completely ignores the context for Israel's actions in 1947 and 1948, which was that Palestinian leaders and the Arab states, after rejecting partition, launched a war of genocide against the Jewish state. Israel's military actions make no sense when not seen in that light, yet for Pappe, all that matters is that he proves his thesis of Zionist premeditated ethnic cleansing. He makes light of the Zionist acceptance of the 1937 partition proposal that gave the Zionists less than one-fifth of post–1922 Palestine. He also exaggerates the number of Palestinian refugees in mendacious fashion, accepting the UN's own figures, which bear no relation to reality (see Chapter 1). He ignores the many statements made by Hamas spokesmen that reveal that what they are resisting is a Jewish state in any form, indeed the very existence of Jews *per se*.

Pappe has used his extreme anti–Zionist perspective to allege misdeeds and massacres that probably never took place. The most famous example is the so-called Tantura affair. In 1998 a student at the University of Haifa, Teddy Katz, submitted a master's dissertation alleging that in 1948, a battalion within the Israeli army had carried out a previously unknown massacre of 200 people in the Arab village of Tantura. He based his findings on a series of interviews that he conducted with residents from the village. When the allegations were publicly aired in an Israeli newspaper, veterans of the 33rd battalion of the Alexandroni brigade filed a suit for libel.

During the subsequent trial, Katz's evidence was taken apart. Tapes from his interviews were closely examined and found to directly contradict his conclusions; there were discrepancies between quotes in his thesis and his interviews. Faced with evidence of methodological sloppiness, Katz retracted his allegation under court order. He wrote:

> After checking and re-checking the evidence, I am now certain beyond any doubt that there is no basis at all for the allegation that after Tantura surrendered, there was any killing of residents by the Alexandroni Brigade, or any other fighting unit of the IDF. I would like to clarify that what I wrote was misunderstood, and that I did not mean to suggest that there had been a massacre in Tantura, nor do I believe that there ever was a massacre at Tantura.

He then retracted this confession, but this change of heart was dismissed, together with his appeal to a higher court. A committee in the University of Haifa also failed his thesis after finding similar fabrications of primary evidence.[73] Nonetheless, Pappe took a different view. In an article for the *Journal of Palestine Studies*, he described Katz's ideas as "a solid and convincing piece of work whose essential validity is in no way marred by its shortcomings." His work revealed "one of the worst massacres in the war."[74] The dubious testimony should have alarmed a serious historian, but it was meat and drink for Pappe. He followed up his support for Katz by calling for an international boycott of the University of Haifa, a call taken up (temporarily) by the AUT (Association of University Teachers).

But it is barely surprising that he has made such egregious mistakes. For as Pappe himself admitted in 1999, "ideology influences my historical writings.... I am not as interested in what happened as in how people see what's happened." The struggle, for Pappe, "is about ideology, not about facts. Who knows what facts are? We try to convince as many people as we can that our interpretation of the facts is the correct one, and we do it because of ideological reasons, not because we are truthseekers."[75] He willingly makes this glaring admission: "I use Palestinian sources for the Intifada: they seem to me to be more reliable, I admit."[76] In other words, the need to discover what truly happened in the past, the noble quest of any historian, seems to matter little for Pappe. If Pappe cannot be objective about his subject matter and if he is little interested in being a "truthseeker," then it is hardly a surprise that he is so cavalier in his observations and in his treatment of historical sources. As Neil Caplan observes, Pappe has "gone beyond merely criticising the Zionist narrative to openly adopting the rival, Palestinian narrative which he promotes in his work."[77]

The five figures just mentioned represent only a fraction of Israel's most hardened critics. Without doubt, it would take an entire volume to fully document the intellectual failings of the hard left over the last 100 years. But from this small sample, we gain an invaluable insight into the irrational and anti-intellectual thought processes of the Israel-haters, their distortion of reality and their sordid love affair with tyranny.

Against the Boycotters

The anti-Semitic hate fest also known as the 2001 Durban Conference initiated a campaign for boycotts, divestment and sanctions against the state of Israel. It was designed to isolate and delegitimize Israel and turn it into an international pariah, much like apartheid South Africa. In recent years, this campaign has taken on a number of targets: boycotts of Israeli academics by student unions and other universities, boycotts of Israeli journalists by unions, boycotts of sporting and artistic events featuring Israeli performers, boycotts of companies (such as Veolia) that do business with Israel, and boycotts of Israeli businesses. There have been repeated calls to divest from a number of Israeli universities, while a sizeable number of entertainers have refused to perform shows in Israel on "political" grounds.

Recent events provide a flavor of the anti–Israeli boycott movement just in the UK. In September 2011, a group of anti–Israeli protestors disrupted a performance of the Israel Philharmonic Orchestra at the BBC Proms. Though these trespassers were ejected and their interruptions dismissed by the paying audience, no charges were brought against them.[78] In May 2012, the Israeli theater Habima produced a Hebrew version of *The Merchant of Venice* to a packed audience at the Globe. A number of protestors unfurled banners condemning "Israeli apartheid" while disrupting the show; they too were removed.[79]

In September 2012, the Israeli contemporary dance group Batsheva performed at the Edinburgh International Festival. Their performances were interrupted on a number of occasions while protestors outside screamed intimidating slogans at theater-goers.[80] Their stance was backed by Scottish national poet Liz Lochhead, who called for the group to be banned. In 2014, the Jewish film festival was forced to change venues (a boycott, in effect) after the London-based Tricycle Theatre imposed a condition that the festival disown funding from the Israeli embassy. No similar condition was imposed on other national cultural events.[81] In the same year, the Edinburgh Festival axed *The City*, a play staged by Jerusalem's Incubator Theater, amid calls for a boycott of all Israeli products.[82]

In 2013, renowned scientist Stephen Hawking declared that he would not attend the Presidential Conference in Jerusalem in order to respect the boycott of Israeli academia.[83] But such principles did not extend to respecting the rights of Chinese or Tibetan academics. For in 2006, he accepted an invitation to attend an international physics conference in Beijing, his presence lending the event enormous legitimacy. Nor did he have any qualms in visiting the Islamic Republic of Iran for a similar purpose.

In February 2015, 700 British artists announced that they would not accept professional invitations to Israel, nor funding, "from any institutions linked to its government" until the "colonial oppression of Palestinians ends."[84] More recently, the TUC passed an anti–Israel resolution that called on its member unions to affiliate to the pro–Hamas Palestine Solidarity Campaign.[85]

Without doubt, the anti–Israel boycott movement represents gestural politics at its worst. It will do nothing to alter Israeli policy, help the Palestinians (especially those studying in Israeli universities) or create conditions for reconciliation. In fact, it is arguable that many of those advocating boycotts are not advancing a set of policies at all. They are not seeking to end the occupation but rather to defame the Jewish state and turn it into an international outlier deserving global condemnation. They intend to cause reputational damage rather than change on the ground. Thus Kenneth Stern is right when he says that boycotts "reinforce the narrative that is Israel is a deformed, illegitimate society that has no right to be treated by the same standards as other nation states."[86]

An academic boycott is particularly counterproductive, quite simply because many in the Israeli intelligentsia are among their country's most vocal critics. The boycotters are targeting the one group with which, in theory at least, they ought to have some ideological affinity. But in any case, boycotting academics because of their national origins violates the cardinal importance of academic freedom. Civilized societies thrive on the work of academics whose research opens up new ways of engaging with and understanding the world around us. By denying academics an international platform, one diminishes the possibility of expanding knowledge and research, sharing ideas and changing the world for the better. Such boycotts indicate that academic freedom is perceived to be "conditional on the identity or political views of the individual scholar" and that "knowledge cannot be judged objectively" but is instead "based on the identity of the originator."[87]

A boycott of Israeli journalists is an equally egregious example of such irrationality. The Israeli media is one of the freest in the world, certainly the freest in the Middle East, and guarantees that Israeli policies undergo an unprecedented level of critical scrutiny. Indeed, left wing journalists from *Ha'Aretz*, most noticeably Gideon Levy, frequently give oxygen to the BDS movement with their scathing indictment of Israeli policies. A boycott of Israeli journalists would provide the West with even less information about matters inside Israel, ones that may be the focus of legitimate concern. Boycotters from the NUJ should be concerned about the plight of journalists in the Arab world who are persecuted relentlessly for reporting their governments' crimes. But these regimes, being anti–American and anti–Israeli, are on the boycotters' side and thus the victims of their repression are of no concern to them.

The boycott groups claim to have a concern for the rights of Palestinians living under occupation. Of course, for all their condemnation of Israeli policy, the boycotters fail to mention the existential threat to Israelis from Palestinian terror and incitement, the factors that makes a continuing presence in the territories necessary. No context is ever given for Israeli house demolitions, the security barrier, the checkpoints or road closures, measures that have everything to do with the country's entirely legitimate security concerns. Instead these measures are viewed through a prism of colonial aggression and racial oppression. The boycotters' analysis is thus woefully one-sided.

Above all, their concern for human rights is never universalized. There are a number of countries in the world whose human rights record is on a par with the state of Israel and many whose record is far, far worse. Yet one only country is ever selected as the target of a boycott: Israel. The boycotters have little to say about tackling the perpetrators of genocide in North Korea and Darfur, the occupation of Tibet, the ongoing slaughter of Syria, the execution of gays in Iran or a host of other crimes. The boycotters would rather target an open, liberal democracy with an independent judiciary and mechanisms for addressing human rights abuses than a despotic regime where such abuses proliferate with immunity.

Some will argue that, as a democracy, Israel must be held to higher standards of behavior than a dictatorship. Indeed so, but in this context it is a specious argument. Quite naturally, we expect higher standards of behavior in democracies, but this gives no license to ignore the victims of despotic regimes. The selective boycott expresses no generalized concern for human rights or racist policies and is thus a politicized tool for demonizing the Jewish state. Moreover, Israel's record of human rights, while hardly perfect, compares favorably to other democracies fighting similar wars against terror. There has been no Israeli Abu Ghraib or Guantanamo Bay and no experience similar to the Russians in Chechnya.[88] Israel has achieved a lower ratio of noncombatant to combatant deaths in asymmetric warfare than other democracies. Yet there are few calls to boycott artists, academics and journalists from Russia, the United States or the UK.

The hypocrisy is manifested in other ways, too. The boycotters, claiming to be motivated by Palestinian suffering, are noticeably silent when Palestinians are the victims of Arab discrimination and unjust treatment. In 1991, Kuwait expelled hundreds of thousands of Palestinians who were resident in the country, as punishment for the PLO's support for Saddam Hussein. A small number remained, fearful for their lives. The protest in the West was conspicuous by its absence, nor do the boycotters mention it.[89]

In Lebanon, Palestinians "have faced institutionalized and non-institutionalized discrimination" and have until very recently been denied working rights within Lebanon. For six decades they could barely obtain work in the country, and there are at least 50 professions that are barred to them.[90] According to Amnesty, Palestinians in Lebanon suffer "discrimination and marginalization," which contributes to "high levels of unemployment, low wages and poor working conditions."[91] In Jordan, Palestinians suffer political discrimination, being vastly underrepresented in the Chamber of Deputies, and they experience discrimination in private and state sector employment. According to Amnesty, the country's security forces are more likely to torture a detainee if that person is a Palestinian. In 2015, ISIL took control of the Yarmouk refugee camp and was reported to be carrying out atrocities on its inhabitants.[92] Again, the silence from the rest of the world was palpable.

If pro–Palestinian boycotters were consistent, they would condemn any Middle East regime that made Palestinians second-class citizens. They would, at a minimum, be demanding a full cultural and academic boycott of Lebanon, Syria, Jordan and Kuwait. The fact that the boycotters target Israel alone in such a self-righteous manner reveals that it is not Palestinian suffering *per se* that motivates them. Their ultimate goal is to demonize, denigrate and ultimately dismantle Israel as a Jewish state.

In short, the boycotters achieve nothing through their one-sided, bigoted calls to isolate Israel and treat it as an international pariah. They do not advance the prospects for an Israeli-Palestinian peace one iota and merely fan the flames of hatred and distrust.

Against United Nations Hypocrisy

The UN was founded in 1945 after the most devastating global conflict in history. Its guiding aims were to uphold international peace and security, to prevent the triumph of tyranny and to stand up to the genocidal ambitions of dictatorships and discredited regimes. In the words of President Bush, the UN's founding members "resolved that the peace of the world must never again be destroyed by the will and wickedness of any man."[93] The UN certainly promised to perform better than its predecessor, the discredited League of Nations, which had presided over a collapse in international security and the rise of totalitarianism throughout the 1930s. Today, in many parts of the world, the UN is regarded as an embodiment of international virtue. As a transnational actor that eschews militarism and all the perceived ills that afflict nation-states, its word appears to have a hallowed status.

Yet this status is in so many ways unmerited. The UN has failed to confront threats to international security, turned a blind eye to genocide and encouraged international terrorism. In the specific context of the Middle East, it has developed an unhealthy obsession with Israel, in turn giving a free pass to genuinely rogue regimes.

On many occasions the Security Council, whose five permanent members alone have veto powers, has blocked the means by which to intervene against tyranny. In 1998, when the West wanted to stop Serbia's rampant genocide, a Russian veto at the council blocked the chance for a multilateral response. Instead President Clinton and his allies were forced into taking unilateral steps to halt the slaughter. Similarly, the chances of preventing bloodshed in Assad's Syria have long disappeared, in part because determined Sino-Russian pressure in the Security Council would block it. On other occasions the UN has recognized a clear and present danger but stifled any meaningful action. After 1990 a total of 17 Security Council resolutions under chapter 7 were passed against Saddam's Iraq, many of which were designed to deal with the threat from weapons of mass destruction. Saddam, by common consent, had violated his obligations under international law and flouted human rights routinely, yet the UN failed to deal adequately with his issue.

Many of the UN's problems stem from an inflexible belief in moral relativism and impartiality. In essence, when confronted by genocidal dictators or terrorists, the UN has chosen not to take sides but has given equal credence to both parties. Thus in the 1970s, Pol Pot's deputies were part of the UN-brokered peace process in Cambodia, despite the appalling genocide that had just taken place. Similarly, Hezbollah was regarded as an equal interlocutor in Lebanon despite being internationally proscribed as a terrorist organization. On 12 May 2006, the UN high commissioner for human rights, Louise Arbour, issued a press release concerning the "deteriorating situation in occupied Palestinian territory," stressing her concern at "the rising number of lives lost, whether as a result of targeted killings or suicide attacks, home-made missiles or artillery fire." By talking of a "cycle of violence," the UN has drawn no distinction between terrorists strapping bombs to their bodies and a nation defending itself from terror, between weapons targeting civilians and weapons designed to protect them.[94]

This lack of willingness to take sides, to take a stand against the aggressor, has resulted in the United Nations' becoming a bystander to genocide. As early as 1971 the UN was accused of being wholly ineffective at stopping genocidal violence in Bangladesh, violence that was only stopped by the Indian army. Twice in the 1990s, the UN was witness to some of the most wanton cruelty in modern history. In 1994 the commander of the UN peacekeeping mission in Rwanda, General Dallaire, received highly credible information from a Hutu informant of an impending plan to exterminate the minority Tutsis, as well as the location of Hutu arms caches.

Despite the fact that the peacekeepers had full UN cover to ensure that the capital was free of weapons, and even as reports reached the UN warning of impending genocide, Dallaire was told by Kofi Annan not to seize the weapons. Instead Annan informed him that the crucial issue was not to compromise his team's impartiality, as if one could be morally neutral between those about to commit mass murder and their hapless victims. The UN also refused to beef up the peacekeeping force or offer it more forceful powers and began instead to evacuate the country en masse, leaving nearly a million Tutsis to be slaughtered by their bloodthirsty neighbors. At the Security Council, nations, particularly France, rushed to protect their interests rather than intervene. The UN had literally become a bystander to genocide.

The same failure was observed in Bosnia and Herzegovina where the UN Protection Force (UNPROFOR) was tasked with the protection of "safe areas" from "armed attack or any other hostile act." When deployed in Goradze to protect Muslims from the Serb military, they failed to intervene when the Serbs shelled the city with their artillery. In Srebrenica, a contingent of Dutch peacekeepers abandoned thousands of Muslims to the Serbs even though the inhabitants had been given a guarantee of protection under resolutions 819 and 836. Subsequently, 7,000 Muslim men and boys were slaughtered by the Serb forces. And despite the pledges made by successive UN secretaries general to stop the genocide in Darfur, the violence continued unabated throughout the first decade of the twenty-first century.[95]

Worse, the UN General Assembly has created a climate in which legitimate, democratic regimes can be undermined and tyrannical, oppressive regimes can thrive. By 2014 some 55 percent of 195 nations were classed as not free or only partly free by Freedom House. As there are 193 UN member states, this means that the organization is dominated by illiberal regimes, many of which are highly autocratic. As resolutions are passed by simple majority vote, these regimes can condemn the cheerleaders of democracy (the United States and Israel) while covering up their own hideous crimes. It was hardly a surprise that in 2011, the General Assembly held a one-minute silence for Kim Jong-il following the dictator's death.[96]

Rogue states have received elevated positions within the organization. To take just one example, it was announced in May 2013 that Iran would chair the UN's most important disarmament negotiating forum during that month's session. Iran was being asked to preside over a disarmament commission, despite supplying an arsenal of weapons to Syria, Hezbollah and Hamas and defying the IAEA and the West over her own illicit nuclear plans. With good reason, Hillel Neuer (executive director of UN Watch) said: "This is like putting Jack the Ripper in charge of a women's shelter."[97]

By far the most obvious manifestation of such a hostile climate is the UN's longstanding obsession with attacking Israel. In the mid–1970s, an Arab/Soviet/Third World bloc was created in the UN that allowed countless anti–Israeli and pro–Palestinian resolutions to pass. These included the notorious 1975 resolution equating Zionism with racism, which was not rescinded until 1991. Every year since 1975, the assembly, dominated by the 57-nation Organization of the Islamic Conference and its associated allies, has passed an unending stream of anti–Israeli resolutions, over 800 to date since 1947. All these resolutions are deeply critical of Israel, with none balanced by a word of criticism of the Palestinians. Half of all its emergency sessions called since 1945 have focused on Israel.[98] It is rare for individual countries to receive censure from the General Assembly, yet of all those resolutions passed, three-quarters refer to Israel. With good reason, one historian speaks of how the UN has undergone "PLO-ization."[99]

The UN's massively disproportionate focus on Israel can be seen in other ways too. There is a separate committee, the Committee on the Exercise of the Inalienable Rights of the Palestinian People, established in 1975. The UN's Department of Political Affairs has a single division dedicated to the Palestinian cause.[100] It sponsors an annual day of solidarity with the Palestinian people that is observed at UN offices around the globe on the anniversary of the 1947 resolution. In May, it joins the Palestinians in an annual Naqba Day, commemorating the "tragedy" of Israel's creation. Quarterly conferences bring together hundreds of activists and NGOs who are encouraged to express their bitter hostility to Israel and to endorse boycott calls. Solidarity with Palestinian suffering is one thing; a near obsessive focus on it is another.

Nowhere is this anti–Israel bias better exemplified than in the UN Human Rights Council, which (as of 2013) has been presided over by such human rights luminaries as Libya, Mauritania, China, Angola, Cuba and Saudi Arabia. Since its inception in 2006, the council has launched a virulent and relentless campaign against Israel. Of the 103 resolutions passed by the UNHRC from June 2006 to July 2014, more than half (56) have criticized Israel, and of the 21 special sessions convened, one-third have focused on Israel.[101] The council also voted to make a review of Israel's alleged human rights abuses a permanent feature of every council session. It also has a special rapporteur for investigating "Israel's violations ... in the Palestinian Territories." Such resolutions receive sometimes near-unanimous majority in the council chambers, reflecting the inbuilt bias of this institution. Even Kofi Annan was forced into criticism: "There are surely other situations, besides the one in the Middle East, which would merit scrutiny at a special session. I would suggest that Darfur is a glaring case in point."[102]

Seeing this voting record, a Martian visiting earth would be forced to assume that Israel was a uniquely demonic force among the nations, a serial abuser of human rights without parallel in modern history. Yet what is truly demonic is how the council has systematically ignored human rights violations in the world's worst regimes in order to pursue a partisan campaign against a bastion of democracy. Again, UN Watch makes a telling observation: "The world body's obsession with censuring Israel at every turn directly affects all citizens of the world, for it constitutes (a) a severe violation of the equality principles guaranteed by the UN Charter and underlying the Universal Declaration of Human Rights, and (b) a significant obstacle to the UN's ability to carry out its proper mandate."

The collective presence of so many dictatorships in the UNHRC makes a mockery of human rights. Former UN ambassador Jeanne Kirkpatrick has written: "The UN has the image of a world organization based on universal principles of justice and equality. In reality, when the chips are down, it is nothing other than the executive committee of the Third World dictatorships."[103]

But this obsessive focus on one country also means that there is correspondingly less time available to investigate the far greater breaches of human rights, including the repressive occupation of Tibet by China, the genocide in Darfur, the massive violations of human rights in North Korea, the torture in Zimbabwe, and the civil war in the Congo, to say nothing of the denial of the rights of minorities, women and homosexuals across the Arab world. As UN Watch puts it: "Because every proposed UN resolution is subjected to intensive review by various levels and branches of government, a direct result of the anti–Israel texts is a crippling of the UN's ability to tackle the world's ills."[104]

In fact, the UN has consistently made the prospects for a negotiated peace in the Middle East much harder to achieve. We have already seen how the UN appeased the PLO throughout the 1970s and 1980s while the group was reveling in an orgy of terrorist violence. More recently, they have had a dubious track record in supporting terrorists in Lebanon. In 2000, Hezbollah launched an attack on the Israeli-Lebanese border, capturing and then killing three Israeli soldiers. This act of terror was carried out using faked UN vehicles and represented a clear breach of earlier agreements. Despite the act of aggression, the UN delayed handing over vital information to the Israelis, something made easier by the fact that among the countries contributing to UNIFIL were several that had no diplomatic relations with Israel.

Not surprisingly, some "peacekeepers" are believed to be sympathetic to Nasrallah's terrorists. In response to Hezbollah's aggression, the UN upgraded the group's diplomatic status to regional "player." Indeed even calling Hezbollah a terror organization was unacceptable. Instead the UN referred to the ongoing confrontation between Israel and Hezbollah in nonjudgmental terms as a "cycle of violence," implying that there was a moral equivalence between the two. Worse, the UN elevated Syria, Hezbollah's ally, to the Security Council in 2002. This high honor was given despite the country's hosting numerous regional terror groups and continuing to illegally occupy Lebanon, another UN member state. It was a brutal rebuke to all those Syrian and Lebanese dissidents who yearn for freedom in the Middle East.

The UN has also allowed the Palestinian refugee problem to persist. As mentioned in Chapter 1, it has a separate agency specially set up to deal with Palestinian refugees, the

United Nations Relief and Works Agency (UNRWA). More than three times as many staff work for this organization as compared to the high commissioner for refugees (UNHCR), and despite the latter serving a far larger refugee population.

Whereas the purpose of the UNHCR was to assimilate the refugees into their host populations, the UNRWA was designed to facilitate a spurious "right of return" despite the resolution on which this was supposedly based (194) being rejected by the Arab states. Moreover, the definition of a refugee, as stated in the 1951 Convention Relating to the Status of Refugees, was deliberately misapplied to the Palestinian refugees, meaning that the descendants of the original refugees from 1948 suddenly counted as refugees too. The sole reason for doing so was to avoid resolving the conflict peacefully, nurturing a dream of return that would overwhelm Israel and lead to its eventual demise. By falling in line with the machinations of Arab states, UNRWA has made itself part of the problem, not the solution.

Anti–Semitism, too, lingers among UN officials. In 1980, Hazem Nuseibeh, Jordan's permanent representative at the UN, declared, "The Zionists are the richest people in the world and control much of its destiny." In 1983 the Libyan representative told the UN, "It is high time for the United Nations and the United States, in particular, to realize that the Jewish Zionists here in the United States attempt to destroy Americans.... If we succeed in eliminating that entity, we shall by the same token save the American and European peoples."[105] Some comments merely reflect the blood libel against Jews, such as those made in 1984 by a Saudi delegate to the UN Human Rights Commission conference on religious tolerance: "The Talmud says that if a Jew does not drink every year the blood of a non–Jewish man, he will be damned for eternity."[106] In 1997, Israel was accused of injecting 300 Palestinian children with the HIV virus.[107]

More blatant anti–Semitism was on display at the 2001 United Nations World Conference Against Racism, Racial Discrimination, Xenophobia and Related Intolerance in Durban, South Africa. It turned out to be nothing of the kind, at least as far as its Jewish representatives were concerned. Jewish delegates at the conference were subjected to a primitive orgy of race hatred: copies of the notorious tract *The Protocols of the Elders of Zion* were openly on sale, Zionists were compared to Nazis, and there were reports of death threats made against Jews. The Arab lawyers' union produced cartoons that portrayed Jews with "hooked noses, blood dripping from fangs, with pots of money surrounding the victims."[108] One flyer that was distributed stated that if Hitler had won the war, Israel would not have come into existence. A motion to describe Holocaust denial as a form of anti–Semitism was roundly defeated. In a Palestinian-led march with thousands of participants, a placard was held aloft that read "Hitler Should Have Finished the Job."[109] At the parallel NGO conference, a resolution was adopted that called Israel "a racist apartheid state" that was guilty of the "systematic perpetration of racist crimes including war crimes, acts of genocide and ethnic cleansing ... and state terror against the Palestinian people."

In short, a conference with the entirely noble aim of confronting and combating racism descended into a medieval hate-fest worthy of Goebbels and Streicher. Yet in a twist of irony worthy of Kafka, these latter-day Jew-haters were lionized by the very body that was designed to oppose them.

Nor is such prejudice confined to the UN's lower echelons. In July 2011, Richard Falk, the United Nations special reporter on Palestinian human rights, posted a cartoon on his blog in response to the issuing of an arrest warrant for Colonel Gaddafi by the International Criminal Court. The cartoon showed a dog wearing a kippa with the word "USA" around his body. While feasting on the bones of a skeleton, it was urinating on a symbol of justice. It was designed to reveal the alleged double standards of "Jewish controlled" America, which, by ignoring Israeli actions to focus on Libya, purportedly denigrated the norms of international justice.[110]

After dismissing charges of anti–Semitism as "a complete lie," Falk issued a belated apology and removed the cartoon, though not before taking a swipe at the alleged motives of his critics. Yet despite denouncing the cartoon as "antisemitic" and "objectionable," Navi Pillay, the UN high commissioner on human rights, did not call for Falk's resignation. What makes this particularly galling is that Falk, who is Jewish himself, has a dreadful track record of hatred towards Israel, including excusing suicide bombings against Israelis on the grounds "that Palestinian resistance gradually ran out of military options and suicide bombers appeared as the only means still available to inflict sufficient harm on Israel."[111] Perhaps we should expect little better from a man who has sympathized with the 9/11 "truth" movement, which claims that the U.S. government was complicit in the attacks.[112]

In conclusion, the UN is barely worthy of its founders' ideals. It is a club dominated by dictatorships, failed states and pseudo-democracies. It has turned a blind eye to genocide on numerous occasions, including the tragedy in Rwanda. It gives special status to rogue states by inviting them to chair its commissions and draws unhealthy equivalence between democracies and terrorist groups. It has demonized Israel and fuelled hatred towards Jews through its infamous Durban "anti racism" conference. For all its occasionally good deeds in other areas, it has become a league of tyranny. Those who revere the UN as a true arbiter of international justice have their heads buried firmly in the sand.

Real Middle Eastern Apartheid

Apart from the Western left (and occasionally the hard right), the most persistent critics of Israel come from within the Arab and Islamic states of the Middle East. In Egypt, Jordan, Syria, Saudi Arabia, Lebanon, Iran, Libya and the Palestinian territories, a burning hatred of Israel, Zionism and world Jewry festers deeply. It is so institutionalized that it has come to form part of the region's social fabric, one of the "truths" that bind people together. One only needs to pick up a newspaper, watch a television show or attend a mosque in these countries to realize the startling depth of hatred that is directed towards the Jewish state and its Western backers. To the majority of inhabitants, it is natural to think that Israel's existence is an aberration and that Jewish "intrigue" and "perfidy" lie at the root of all their grievances.

Yet the charge that Israel is a constitutionally racist, sexist and inherently discriminatory state, firmly rebutted in Chapter 2, is an especially galling one to make. This is simply because those charges apply to the Arab and Muslim states themselves, particularly in terms of their treatment of religious minorities, their persecution of gays and their oppression of women. In other words, gender, religious and sexual apartheid is a ubiquitous feature of life in the Islamic world, particularly across the Middle East.

THE DENIAL OF WOMEN'S RIGHTS

It is undeniable that women's rights are affected across the Arab and Islamic world. Sexual inequality is underwritten by Islamic law, which stipulates that a Muslim man can have up to four wives whereas the female can marry only one man. As Nonie Darwish explains, this legally sanctioned polygamy "damages any expectation of loyalty or commitment from the husband to the wife" and "destroys the idea that a man and a woman are one in marriage."[113] Under Sharia, if a Muslim woman commits adultery, she can die by stoning.

Divorce too favors men, for in order to divorce his wife, a Muslim man need only say "I divorce you" three times; no reason is required. Such instant termination of marriage is in the gift of the male alone. By contrast, Muslim women cannot unilaterally divorce their husbands and have to petition courts for this purpose. In many countries, it will be harder for Muslim women to initiate divorce and if their requests are not granted by men, they can be prevented from remarrying. Some women are forced to pay back their dowry for the privilege of being unchained.[114] Under Sharia, a woman's testimony in court is worth only half that of a man, and women get half the inheritance of a man. A host of other misogynist laws turn Muslim women into second-class citizens.

Sharia laws relating to child custody, financial maintenance and wife support are frequently stacked against women. Under Sharia, a Muslim man is also allowed to beat his wife for "rebellious" behavior (Sura 4.34). Again, this is his right, for as one hadith puts it, "A man will not be asked as to why he beat his wife."[115]

Perhaps the most shocking Sharia privilege granted to men is that they are allowed to enjoy sexual intimacy with young children. Muhammad, the man whose behavior serves as an inspiration for all Muslims, had intercourse with his child bride Aisha when she was nine and was married to her when she was a mere six years old. Sharia law dictates that there is no legal minimum age for marriage (beyond puberty), an opinion upheld by Ayatollah Khomeini. Khomeini lowered the marriage age to 13 for girls but permitted girls as young as 7 to be married, if a physician signed a certificate agreeing to their sexual maturity.[116] The Ayatollah also stated that a Muslim man could "quench his sexual lusts with a child as young as a baby" provided he did not "penetrate."[117] It is legally sanctioned pedophilia.

Millions of Muslim women are also forced to undergo the practice of female genital mutilation each year. FGM involves the total or partial removal of the female genitalia, often without anesthetic, and its long-term health consequences can include psychological trauma, urinary infections, bleeding, infertility and septicemia. Finally, it should not be forgotten that the vast majority of honor killings around the world affect women in Muslim countries.

Specific examples of discrimination are rife in the Middle East. In Saudi Arabia women are subject to various forms of domestic violence and rape, and the opportunities for legal redress are very limited. Women also cannot travel or drive a car without their husband's permission, and women must sit at the rear of buses, evoking the spirit of the Jim Crow laws in the American South. Women who are not dressed modestly enough are also harassed by the *mutaween*, Saudi Arabia's "virtue" police.

Women suffer discrimination in Jordan, where inheritance and divorce laws favor men. Until its recent overhaul, article 308 of the Jordanian Penal Code allowed charges against a rapist to be dropped if the victim agreed to marry the rapist, even though this decision may have been forced on the victim. Under Article 98 of Jordan's penal code, a murderer can receive a short sentence of as little as six months for a murder committed in anger, something often used in cases of honor killing. These laws come against a background in which patriarchal customs and male dominance persist.

In Syria, despite constitutional guarantees of equality, women suffer badly too. According to Human Rights Watch: "Personal status laws and the penal code contain provisions that discriminate against women and girls, particularly in marriage, divorce, child custody, and inheritance. While the penal code no longer fully exonerates perpetrators of so-called honor crimes, it still gives judges options for reduced sentences if a crime was committed with 'honorable' intent. The nationality law of 1969 prevents Syrian women married to foreign spouses the right to pass on their citizenship to their children or spouses."[118]

According to Hanaa Edwar, the head of the charity Al-Amal, Iraqi women suffer "marginalisation and all kinds of violence, including forced marriages, divorces and harassment, as well as restrictions on their liberty, their education, their choice of clothing, and their social life."[119]

Sadly, these problems are not confined just to Arab countries. In Iran, the strict application of Sharia law means that when a woman is in a court of law, her testimony is worth only half of a man's. Women suffer from inequitable inheritance rights, and they are generally not granted guardianship rights for their children.

According to the World Economic Forum's 2010 Gender Gap report, which compared disparity between men and women on economic participation, access to education, health, and political empowerment, Iran ranked very low at 123 out of 134 countries.[120] An Iranian study of domestic violence from 2004 by sociologist Dr. Ghazi Tabatabaei found extremely high levels of emotional, physical, educational and sexual abuse, the latter including rape within marriage, forced pregnancies and abortions and restrictions of access to birth control. Though laws to prevent women from violence have been put before the Iranian parliament, they are unlikely to be enforced without changes at the cultural level.

THE MISTREATMENT OF SEXUAL MINORITIES

Attitudes towards homosexuality in the Arab and Muslim world vary from country to country, but intolerance towards sexual "deviance" is rife across the region. Gay and lesbian relationships are heavily frowned upon, to put it mildly, with huge anecdotal evidence of persecution, arrest, torture and intimidation. Gay sons are seen to bring shame and dishonor on the family name. Arab society remains heavily male-dominated with young sons being expected to marry and produce offspring of their own. It is even worse for young girls who become pregnant before they are married. This brings an even greater stain on the family's reputation, with the tragic result that the girl is killed to restore "tribal honor."

In post–Saddam Iraq, hardline Sharia judges have handed down death sentences to gay people. Hundreds of gay people have been killed and kidnapped by militias. Homosexuality is illegal in Iran, and many homosexuals have been lashed or killed. Homosexuality is also illegal in Saudi Arabia, and if a married man is found to be engaging in homosexual acts, he can be subject to the death penalty. No protection exists for gays and lesbians, who are frequently arrested and imprisoned for their "crimes." Yemen is one of nine or ten countries around the world (almost all are Muslim countries) where the death penalty can be applied for people engaging in homosexual sex. Punishments range from flogging to death. In Egypt under Mubarak, gays were routinely harassed, arrested and tortured in a country where homosexuality remained illegal.

Even in the more tolerant parts of the Middle East, laws exist to prosecute homosexuality, even if they are rarely applied. Thus article 534 of the Lebanese Penal Code prohibits having sexual relations that contradict "the laws of nature." Those arrested face up to a year in prison, though it is not always applied.[121] In pro–Western Jordan, homosexuality behind closed doors has been legal since 1951. However, under the prevailing codes of Islamic morality, homosexuality is condemned across society and there is no legal protection from harassment on the grounds of sexual orientation.[122]

Such rampant bigotry does not arise in a vacuum. It reflects the fact that Muslim majority populations across the region subscribe to traditional Islamic law, which regards homosexuality as a grave sin. One of the most influential Web sites in the Muslim world is IslamOnline. The Web site, which is supervised by Sheikh Qaradawi, is quite unsparing in its rejection of homosexuality. It is described as "the most heinous sin" in the faith, a "perverted act" that can only lead to a "devilish lifestyle" and acts deserving of the most severe punishment. Muslims are advised to shun those of a homosexual disposition and ensure that their children do not mix with gay people. Gays themselves are advised to seek a cure for their "illness." IslamOnline is no fringe phenomenon in the blogosphere. It is accessed by tens of millions of Muslims in many parts of the Islamic world. The site's authors merely "tap into a populist vein, harnessing existing prejudices for a supposedly Islamic cause."[123]

In the past, Muslim states have played a leading role in blocking global recognition of homophobia. In 2003, Brazil put forward a motion expressing "deep concern at the occurrence of violations of human rights in the world against persons on the grounds of their sexual orientation." The resolution, a landmark in recognizing sexual discrimination, was defeated by opposition from five Muslim countries—Saudi Arabia, Egypt, Libya, Malaysia and Pakistan. They achieved this by the use of a filibuster that resulted in the commission's halting the debate.[124]

In 2012 Pakistani diplomat Zamir Akram, who was a coordinator of the Organization of Islamic Cooperation on human rights, wrote that the OIC states were "deeply concerned by the introduction in the Human Rights Council of controversial notions like "sexual orientation and gender identity" and added that the OIC countries had been "consistent in their opposition to the consideration of these controversial notions." Further: "We are even more disturbed at the attempt to focus on certain persons on the grounds of their abnormal sexual behaviour."[125] In the very same month, Libya's permanent representative at the UN, Ibrahim Dabbashi, delivered a homophobic outburst at the Human Rights Council when he declared that the discussion of LGBT issues "affect religion and the continuation and reproduction of the human race."[126]

But that was as nothing compared to the shocking hate speech from Yahya Jammeh, Gambia's Sunni Muslim president. In 2008, he vowed to "cut off the head" of any gay person in the country and demanded that they leave Gambia. At the UN he described homosexuality as "very evil, antihuman as well as anti–Allah," and added, "Those who promote homosexuality want to put an end to human existence."[127] A year later he declared: "We will fight these vermins called homosexuals or gays the same way we are fighting malaria-causing mosquitoes, if not more aggressively."[128] These attitudes enjoy widespread social approval, which is one reason they are so rarely challenged.

In many parts of the Arab and Muslim world, then, sexual minorities struggle to be free and to live lives based on dignity and respect. Yet the one country that offers the greatest legal protection for gay, lesbian and transgender individuals is accused of sexual apartheid.

Religious Apartheid in the Arab and Islamic World

As Arab and Islamist academic elites rush to attack the West and Israel over the perceived mistreatment of Muslims, they turn a blind eye to how Arab states deny religious minorities the most basic freedom of religious conscience. Across the Middle East, minorities face persecution, discrimination and second-class treatment. Many live in fear of their lives. Christians, who have lived in the Middle East for two millennia, today face a slow and silent genocide. This is a violation of the most basic principles of human rights, including Article 18 of the UN Declaration of Human Rights, which states, "Everyone has the right to freedom of thought, conscience and religion."

Assyrians of Iraq

The Assyrian International News Agency's report "Incipient Genocide: The Ethnic Cleansing of the Assyrians of Iraq" makes for grim reading. In 2003, Assyrians constituted 8 percent of the Iraqi population and formed an indigenous group with a 7,000-year history in the region. In the last decade alone, nearly half the population has fled Iraq after a tidal wave of repression, intimidation and violence at the hands of (mainly) Sunni Muslim jihadists. More than 300 have been murdered since 1995; several members of the clergy have been kidnapped, beheaded and dismembered; and over 70 churches have been firebombed.

Their connection to the U.S. occupation forces has struck a particularly lethal blow to the community. Assyrian students at Iraqi universities have been beaten and harassed for not wearing sufficiently Islamic dress. Women have been kidnapped and forced to marry men after their compulsory conversion. Christian women have been attacked, raped and suffered horrific acid attacks for not having their heads covered. In October 2006, a 14-year-old boy was even crucified in Basra. There are also cases where Assyrians living under al-Qaeda rule were forced to pay the *jizya*, the discriminatory poll tax, in order to survive. Assyrian businesses, too, have been attacked, particularly liquor stores and music shops, which have been burned and looted. Vast numbers of Assyrians have been forced into exile in neighboring Jordan and Syria just to avoid extermination.[129] The Assyrians, unlike the Israeli Arabs, are a fast-disappearing community facing the relentless onslaught of Islamism.

In 2014–15, ethnic communities across Iraq were being slaughtered, expelled or forced to convert by the newly formed Islamic State (ISIL) or Daish. The Yazidis have been forced to flee for their lives to the Iraqi mountains after thousands of their members were systematically slaughtered. People have been dying there daily, despite Western humanitarian assistance.

Bahai in Iran

Approximately 90 percent of Iran's population is Shia Muslim. Non-Shia Muslims and a number of other religious minorities regularly suffer various forms of discrimination, intimidation and harassment. But probably no group has suffered more than the followers of the Bahai faith, whose headquarters are in Israel. More than 200 have been killed by the government since the Islamic Revolution of 1979, a government that accuses them of apostasy and of "espionage on behalf of Zionism."

According to a State Department report, members of the Bahai faith have suffered "arbitrary arrest and prolonged detention, expulsions from universities, and confiscation of property." They are barred from all leadership positions in the government and military and are also denied compensation for injury and criminal victimization as well as the right to inherit property. Children in schools have faced attempts at conversion, and they can only enroll in schools if they are not identified as Bahai. They cannot "teach or practise their religious beliefs" or "maintain links with coreligionists abroad." Their cemeteries and holy places have also been subject to vandalism by unknown assailants.[130] This persecution is very much state policy. According to a recent report, "Inciting Hatred: Iran's Media Campaign to Demonize Baha'is," the community is subject to "slanders and falsehoods" that are "disseminated in state-controlled and state-sanctioned media, through pamphlets and tracts, from pulpits, and at public exhibitions and events."[131]

Kurds

The Kurds have long suffered political repression in a number of countries. Since the 1950s, the Arab nationalist regimes in Syria have treated them as a marginalized minority, revoking the citizenship of some 120,000 people and rendering some 300,000 stateless. Successive governments, particularly under the Ba'ath regime, have repressed Kurdish identity by restricting the "use of Kurdish language in public, in schools, and in the workplace, banning Kurdish-language publications, and prohibiting celebrations of Kurdish festivities." School geography texts have even denied that there is a Kurdish minority in the country.[132]

In Turkey, the Kurds, who comprise nearly one-fifth of the population, have suffered a wide range of human rights violations over many decades. Tens of thousands have been killed, with thousands of villages forcibly depopulated, leaving over 300,000 Kurds homeless. Today, Kurdish political parties have been banned under the pretext that they are linked to the PKK, and the expression of Kurdish identity in the cultural sphere is severely curtailed. Dozens of journalists have also been arrested for merely criticizing government policy relating to the Kurds.[133] Under the rule of the Islamic Republic, the Kurds have suffered ill treatment and the most severe forms of discrimination. Viewing the idea of ethnic minorities as a threat to Islamic doctrine, the Ayatollah's forces destroyed scores of villages after 1979, killing some 10,000 people.

According to a recent Amnesty report, Iran's Kurds have suffered "deep rooted discrimination," the repression of their "social, political and cultural rights ... resulting in entrenched poverty," as well as "forced evictions and destruction of homes" that have left Kurds with "restricted access to adequate housing." The use of the Kurdish language in education "is frequently thwarted." Kurds are also denied equality in employment and political participation due to the discriminatory "gozinesh" system, which "requires prospective state officials and employees to demonstrate allegiance to Islam and the Islamic Republic of Iran." Human rights activists have found themselves in jail for highlighting these and other abuses.[134]

But by far the worst persecution of Kurdish people occurred in Iraq under the regime of Saddam Hussein. During the Anfal campaigns in the late 1980s, it is estimated that tens of thousands of Kurdish civilians were systematically massacred, including women and children. In one attack on the village of Halabja in 1988, several thousand Kurds were exterminated by poison gas in what a Dutch court later described as genocide. During the campaign the Iraqi forces destroyed some 2,000 Kurdish villages, together with a vast number of Kurdish schools, mosques and hospitals.[135]

Those who fixate on Israel's treatment of Palestinians ignore the far greater issue of the denial of Kurdish rights by many nations. Amid the clamor for an independent Palestine, there is a far greater case today for an independent, democratic Kurdistan living in peace with neighboring states.

Copts of Egypt

Egypt's Copts, an indigenous Christian community, have faced persecution for many decades from their Muslim neighbors. Throughout the 1980s and 1990s, there was a spate of violent attacks on Coptic communities, resulting in the deaths of many hundreds of people. These murders were accompanied by the looting of property, the burning of churches and the destruction of businesses. In some cases, Copts were murdered after they refused to pay protection money or renounce their faith, and it is notable that, on occasion, the police turned up only after the violence had abated. Often this murderous orgy of violence was triggered by vicious sermons during Friday prayers, where crowds were whipped up into a frenzy of hatred against the Copts, and where young men were reminded of their jihadist duty to murder "infidels." In post–Mubarak Egypt, the number of attacks has increased and up to 200,000 Copts are believed to have fled in fear of their lives. One of Egypt's Coptic communities was threatened with mass execution following the release by an American Copt of the 13-minute amateur production "The Innocence of Islam."[136] There has also been a surge in the disappearance of young Coptic girls who are reportedly coerced into converting to Islam. For most, this conversion is almost impossible to reverse under current jihadi rule.[137] Again, much of this violence is justified by Islamists with references to scripture: "Then go to the persons who do not join the congregational prayer and order their homes to be burnt."[138]

Christians Under PA Rule

Since 1995, 98 percent of the population centers in the West Bank have come under the rule of the Palestinian Authority. During much of that time, the PA and various armed groups under its control have shown a brazen disregard for Christian interests while paying lip service to the idea of religious tolerance. When Yasser Arafat took over Bethlehem as part of the Oslo II agreement, he engaged in a process of political gerrymandering. He changed the city's municipal boundaries, incorporating 30,000 Muslims from neighboring areas and encouraging Muslim immigration from Hebron and other towns. This, together with a higher Muslim birth rate, tipped the demographic scales in the town, so that the once Christian majority of 60 percent in 1990 became a small and beleaguered Christian minority in 2005. Arafat also fired the Bethlehem City Council (with nine Christians and two Muslims) and replaced it with a 50–50 council. Bethlehem Christian women have been intimidated, by PLO/PA personnel, since Arafat's takeover in 1995. Rapes of Christian women have occurred frequently (especially in Beit Sakhur) as was the case in Lebanon.[139]

There have been grave incidents affecting Christian holy sites. Thus in 1997 PLO militias seized Hebron's Abraham's Oak Russian Holy Trinity Monastery, evicting its monks and nuns by force. After the outbreak of Palestinian violence in September 2000, the PA's Tanzim militia positioned themselves near Christian homes, hotels and churches in the Christian town of Beit Jala to shoot at Jerusalem. The most notable example was in 2002 when more than 100 Palestinian gunmen, including armed militias from Arafat's Tanzim, took over the Church of the Nativity in Bethlehem and held more than 40 Christian clergy and nuns hostage. They seized stockpiles of food, drank vast quantities of alcohol, tore up Bibles to create toilet paper, and stole prayer books, gold and crucifixes. According to one of the monks, those inside "opened the doors one by one and stole everything.... They stole our prayer books and four crosses ... they didn't leave anything."[140]

At PLO rallies, the chant "After we do away with the Saturday People, we shall take care of the Sunday People" has been heard frequently. Such incitement had led to attacks on cemeteries, churches and Christian youth centers. Theft of Palestinian land has occurred and money has been extorted. Many Christian women have been raped, abused and abducted. Christian graves have also been dug up and cemeteries and statues defaced.

In Gaza, the plight of Palestinian Christians is also perilous. Following the Hamas takeover in 2007, Christian schools and shops were firebombed and the owner of Gaza's only bookstore was abducted and murdered.[141] Women have been forced to wear the veil or face violent reprisals, while there are allegations of forced conversions. Amid the climate of fear and intimidation accompanying Hamas rule, the Christian population in Gaza has fallen considerably from 2007 to 2015. The experience of Christians living in the West Bank and Gaza reminds us that, when given the accouterments of statehood, the Palestinians have failed to build a democratic model of governance that respects the rights of minorities.

These are by no means the only minorities who suffer persecution within the Middle East and wider Islamic world. The Taliban were well known for their intolerance towards other faiths, destroying the ancient Buddhist statues in the Bamiyan Valley in 2001. The Islamist regime in Khartoum imposed Sharia law throughout Sudan in the 1980s, resulting in a civil war that has killed nearly two million people to date, mainly Christians. The tragedy of Darfur is a stirring reminder of the genocidal intentions of Islamists towards their enemies.

In the Wahhabi state of Saudi Arabia, no other religious groups can legally practice their faith. It is illegal to build a church or engage in non–Islamic public prayer, and there are harsh sentences for proselytizing or saying something that is deemed an insult to the faith. Non–Muslim religious materials are also prohibited.[142] Among Muslim groups who suffer from this intolerant atmosphere are the country's Shia communities, who face varying forms of harassment and discrimination. They have been labeled as "Islamic apostates" and heretics, with *fatwas* being issued to denounce the community. Shias have been completely marginalized in public life. As Vali Nasr points out, "There have been no Shia Cabinet ministers. Shias are kept out of critical jobs in the armed forces and the security services.... There are no Shia mayors or police chiefs." The government has even restricted the names that Shia can use for their children.[143]

The overall picture is fairly clear. Vulnerable minorities have suffered persecution, discrimination and harassment at the hands of intolerant Arab and Islamic regimes. These are cases where there is true religious and ethnic apartheid in the Middle East, unlike in Israel. Yet these regimes are given a free pass when they disseminate the falsehood that Israel's treatment of Palestinians is the greatest human rights issue of our age. Where cases of maltreatment in Israel dominate global attention to the exclusion of vastly worse human rights abuses, there is something corrupt about public discourse.

Like the Copts, the Bahai, the Kurds and the Iraqi Assyrians, Jews are a minority in a Muslim/Arab-dominated Middle East. Just as those religious groups have been persecuted for not conforming to Islamist ideals, so too Israeli Jews have found themselves under attack for being non–Arab and non–Muslim. They have found the region just as inhospitable as their Christian counterparts. The crucial difference is that Israelis have a powerful state to defend their interests.

Conclusion

In his survey of the "contested histories" of Israel and Palestine, Neil Caplan says that each side "with dreadful predictability ... will interpret all the facts of its historical experience as reinforcing its own deep sense of grievance and victimhood at the hands of the other." Each side "sincerely and righteously believes that it is the victim of the other side's aggression and evil intentions." He goes on to say that "scholars on both sides of this debate seldom rise above the widespread myopic tendency of the partisans and the populations they represent to believe that 'Our narrative tells the facts: their narrative is propaganda.'"[1] He goes on to suggest that the true cause of this conflict is that "Jews and Arabs are locked into an unavoidable clash of two national groups competing for mastery over the same territory" and that there is an "unbridgeable gap between the declared nationalist aspirations of Palestinian Arabs and Zionists/Israelis."[2] Both sides see themselves, in the words of Benny Morris, as "righteous victims" of the other.

Caplan is right on some points. First, clearly, neither side has a *monopoly* of right or victimhood in this conflict, and we can agree that there are "righteous victims" on both sides. Not every Palestinian or Arab grievance can be dismissed as propaganda, while not every Israeli justification is the truth. This book's overriding assumption is that one side (Israel) has a *preponderance* of right in the conflict. To quote King Lear, she has been "more sinned against than sinning."

Second, Caplan is right to argue that there is an unbridgeable divide between the current narratives of most Israelis and Palestinians. It is extremely difficult to foresee this changing, at least in the short term. One can agree with Caplan that official histories of the conflict, where governments dictate the narrative of the past for propaganda purposes, leave little room for nuance and complexity.

But the idea that both sides are locked into the same closed-minded mentality ignores some crucial differences. Only one side (Israel) has independently minded professional historians who openly challenge their side's official history. In the 1980s, the New Historians offered altered perspectives on their country's past, including the prehistory of Israel and the 1948 war.

To take one example, it used to be assumed among Israelis that no Palestinian Arabs were expelled in 1948, whereas Morris' vital research has shown that this was not the case. He added a much-needed critical perspective on the past and offered the kind of independent analysis that was vital if genuine national myths were to be laid to rest. (Sadly, he sullied his reputation by making spurious claims about the early Zionist leaders.) Indeed, there is evidence that the revisionist accounts of the 1948 war have influenced official documentaries as well as the country's history curriculum.³ Today, Israel hosts a vast number of academics who actively challenge officialdom on a wide array of public issues.

Yet there has been no such undertaking among Palestinian historians. As Neil Caplan observes, "The Western tradition of open public archives is not generally replicated in the Arab world." Yet he goes on to argue, rather unconvincingly, that this is also partly related to the "asymmetrical power relationship between the two parties."⁴ This merely parrots the Palestinian line that victim status confers a different set of obligations and moral standards, including the right not to be open about one's past. This is a highly dubious argument. To feel victimized is psychologically damaging and naturally unfortunate, but it hardly means that one's viewpoint is beyond reproach. Ultimately, historical truth does not depend on the identity of historians or on whose side one is on; it rests on the quality of evidence left by the past, and such evidence is easily accessible to all, regardless of nationality.

As in every conflict around the world, both sides must be honest about their past crimes and misdemeanors rather than engage in willful blindness. If the closed and authoritarian society in the territories gives way to transparency, openness and pluralism, it is entirely possible for a Palestinian Benny Morris or Tom Segev to emerge. Indeed, a simple willingness to access Western archives is enough to challenge long-established beliefs.

More crucially, the mainstream Zionist and Israeli nationalism has accommodated a pragmatic endorsement of compromise, including the acceptance of the principle of partition in 1937 and 1947, the offers of peace after 1967 and the bargaining that could have resulted in Palestinian statehood in 2000–1 and 2008. The Jewish people's unassailable right to all the land was set aside for longer-term interests. Some Arab states have shown a similar statesmanlike formula, most notably Egypt's Anwar Sadat and Jordan's King Hussein. There remains a deep recognition within Israel, and among moderate Palestinian voices, that in the battle for this small strip of land, compromise is essential. But mainstream "Palestine" holds out for what they see as "total justice." Though there is no longer talk of destroying Israel, at least to a Western audience, there is a demand for the right of return, which is tantamount to the same thing.

Thus it should be clear that the occupation of the West Bank, the status of Gaza and the proliferation of settlements are not the defining causes of today's Israeli-Palestinian/Arab conflict. Nor is this dispute a simple argument over territory, water, borders or refugees, though these issues are vital for any long-term resolution. At the heart of this dispute is a simple but maddening refusal by Arab and Muslim forces to recognize Jewish national rights to their own sovereign land. Palestinian leaders, backed by their allies around the world, refuse to recognize Israel's legitimacy as a state, preferring to view this national "infidel" as a state born in sin. To even talk of Israel as a Jewish state is to engage in an act of national treason. Steps towards normalization, such as joint Israeli-Palestinian ventures, are often derided and rejected by the PA. If this is a clash of nationalisms, as some claim, then the Arab nationalist claim is to the whole of the land, effectively eradicating the Jewish claim.

The problem for most Palestinians is that they believe their tragedy is anything other than self-imposed. They see themselves as the victims of a great Zionist-imperialist conspiracy to rob them of what is rightfully theirs, to forcefully dispossess them of land, money, houses and heritage. In this view, Israel is an illegal aggressor and to compromise with such a state is tantamount to bargaining with a thief. David Suissa sums up the resulting problem admirably. If you are seen as a thief, "the other side has no reason to negotiate—all they want is for you to return their stolen property."⁵ Worse, by compromising with this "thief," they are effectively legitimizing a historical crime carried out at their expense.

Worse still for the Palestinians is the nature of the enemy who has "robbed" them. Those who inflicted successive defeats on the Arab world were not, as Bernard Lewis points out, the "armies of a mighty imperial power" but a people who, historically speaking, were "few, scattered and powerless."⁶ For much of the Muslim world, the Jews had a divinely ordained position as a dhimmi people and their resurgence as a national sovereign in Israel has undermined the natural order of things. Their deliberate reversal of status is an outrageous act of subversion in Islamic thinking. Not for nothing did President Sadat, in a speech at the el-Hussein mosque in 1972, promise to send the Jews "back to their former status."⁷

Moreover, Palestinians believe that they are being made to suffer for the sins of a post–Holocaust world. Israel, they argue, was given to the Zionists as recompense for Jewish suffering during the Second World War. The Palestinians ask why they, rather than other European countries, were forced to pay the price for mass murder. Acknowledging the Holocaust is therefore doubly hard for the Palestinian leadership. On the one hand, they believe it strengthens Jewish claims to the land, while on the other, it reminds people that Jews have been victims too.

To understand the Palestinian position, one must also appreciate the cardinal importance of honor in Arab societies. In his book *The Arab Mind*, the famed anthropologist Raphael Patai notes various characteristics of the Bedouin mentality that have left their mark within Arab culture. He writes: "Honor in the Arab world is a generic concept which embraces many different forms." Some of these pertain to sexual virility, including having many sons of pure Arab blood. Other forms of honor concern martial behavior, such as participating in a raid and exhibiting a "strong sense of kin group adherence." Maintaining the dignity of one's public image and avenging oneself on those who dishonor it is of crucial significance. As Patai points out, "The honor concept is easily extended from the individual, the family, and the tribe to the nation as a whole."⁸ Margaret Nydell, a leading Arabist writer, makes a very similar point in her influential book *Understanding Arabs*: "Honour (or shame) is often viewed as collective, pertaining to the entire family or group."⁹ For the Palestinians, safeguarding their past has become a matter of national honor, a sacred task for future generations. But this is a distorted past and the future has been abandoned.

To really grasp, then, why the Palestinians have refused a sensible compromise for years, one must understand what is at stake. It is not primarily about resolving complex territorial and economic issues. Instead it is more about redeeming national honor in a conflict that has increasingly become suffused with religious demands. Compromises with the "dhimmi" Jews are tantamount to an attack on this sense of honor.

Thus one can understand, though not sympathize with, the Palestinians' maddening intransigence during peace talks. They feel they are being asked to negotiate away their birthright. The only way to ensure that this birthright (the whole of the land of Palestine) is not forever removed from their grasp is to insist on the right of return and control of the Old City of Jerusalem. This way, there would be an eventual Arab majority in the land and, promises to the contrary, Israel would cease to exist as the sovereign power. Instead, a new land of Palestine would be added to the list of Arab states that proliferate throughout the Middle East. Honor would be restored, pride returned and the struggle would have been worthwhile all along.

Compromise is very much a Western construct that various leaders have tried to foist on an unbending Palestinian leadership, but it is to gravely misrepresent the Arab (and Palestinian) mindset. Such a mindset is prepared to feign compromise and moderation as a ruse for extracting goodwill and concessions from the West. Thus as Faisal al-Husseini has put it: "If we agree to declare our state over what is now 22 per cent of Palestine, meaning the West Bank and Gaza, our ultimate goal is the liberation of all historic Palestine from the River to the Sea. We distinguish the strategic, long-term goals from the political phased goals, which we are compelled to temporarily accept due to international pressure."[10] Such obduracy makes sense in light of what Palestinians believe has happened to them. Thus until their narrative and mindset is transformed, it is hard to envision an end to this conflict.

Of course the alternative, namely a smaller Palestinian state in the West Bank and Gaza, would be an admission that the 90-year struggle against the Jews, and their Western backers, was ultimately futile. The Palestinians would be forced to admit that they could have got a much better deal, not just in 2008 under Olmert, or 2000–1 under Barak, but in 1947 under the UN Partition Plan and in 1937 when they might have had six-sevenths of the land. All the deaths and injuries, all those years in the refugee camps, all the suffering could have been avoided by the simplest of compromises.

The Palestinians, as well as their supporters throughout the West, must stop harboring illusions. They must be allowed to question their narrative. The people primarily responsible for the Palestinian tragedy are those who have led them for the last century, and the Arab states that have feigned concern but showed little interest in their material improvement. A number of policy recommendations now follow:

1. Western policy elites should continue to encourage Israeli and Palestinian moderates in their quest for a just resolution to the conflict. The standard formula has been two states for two peoples. However, they must appreciate that the principal stumbling block to achieving this outcome has been an ongoing refusal by Palestinian leaders, supported increasingly by Western leftists and Islamists, to accept a Jewish state in the Middle East. Western leaders must demand an end to Palestinian rejectionism if peace is ever to be achieved. They must be told to recognize that Israel is here to stay, that it is a permanent fixture in the Middle East and that it must be recognized as the "Jewish state." The PLO must be told to abrogate its charter and teach the Palestinians in both Arabic and English that Israel will not be replaced with another Arab state. In other words, while the West can support a Palestinian bid for independence, they will do this on condition that their movement is willing to normalize relations with Israel. "Two states for two peoples" cannot be implemented while one side harbors dreams of destroying the other.

2. However, paying lip service to these mantras is not enough. The West, which provides significant quantities of aid to the PA, must insist on an end to the glorification of violence if such funding is to continue. Funding must be conditional on eradicating anti–Semitism from textbooks, radio shows and television programs with harsh penalties for turning suicide bombers into heroes and martyrs. They must insist that laws against incitement are introduced and vigorously upheld. Neither should the West provide money for the PA to fund terrorists' salaries. Such complicity with terror is a moral outrage.

3. Consistent with this position, the Palestinians need to be told that the right of return will only ever be to a future Palestinian state. Any insistence on more than a token number of Palestinians returning to Israel must be met with a firm rebuke. The misery of many Palestinians living in refugee camps outside Israel (and the territories) must also be alleviated. This is best done by changing the entire culture of UNRWA, which has fostered false notions of refugee status and an impossible return to Israel. The descendants of refugees must be allowed to assimilate freely in neighboring countries and given full citizenship rights, their continuing statelessness being a blot on the Arab world. UNRWA should be exposed as being complicit in terrorism, most notably in the 2014 Gaza conflict when their schools were found to be storing weapons, which were then promptly returned to Hamas. The EU and United States, who together provide nearly half of UNRWA's funds, must stop funding this organization.[11]

4. The Palestinians in both the West Bank and Gaza clearly deserve a better future. Life in both areas should be improved through economic investment and the building of infrastructure, as well as improved trade. The West should tell the Palestinians that their lives would be enhanced further without measures such as the border controls, the security barrier and the West Bank checkpoints. However, there should be no pressure to alleviate these measures without a corresponding improvement in the overall security situation, including an end to all incitement and a continuing crackdown on terror. Any fundamental change in the relations between Israel and Gaza must rely on the demilitarization of the enclave and the long-term removal of Hamas' threat to Israel. It should be recognized that the fundamental cause of Gazans' misery is the tyrannical and despotic rule of Hamas, which has stifled its people's chance of peace and prosperity.

5. In the absence of a sudden breakthrough between Israel and the Palestinians, peace should be built on the ground. Projects that aim to bring both parties together should be encouraged. These include but are not limited to joint musical ventures, such as the East-West Divan orchestra, joint sporting events, educational initiatives that aim to teach each side about the other's history and culture, and visits to Holocaust sites. In other words, coexistence projects should be encouraged and facilitated. For the time being, the model should be one of conflict management, rather than conflict resolution.

6. Israel's government will need to clarify its position in regard to settlements. It will need to consider exactly where settlement expansion should occur, which presumably is in those areas that will be formally part of Israel after any peace agreement. It may want to consider whether to put in place a settlement freeze in areas that are likely to be part of a future Palestinian state. Democratic Israel may well ask whether there should be an incentivized evacuation of all those who live in areas that will become part of a Palestinian state. It is possible that a consensus will emerge in favor of this option. In addition, Israel has an obligation to continue improving the prospects for Israel's Arab minority, ensuring the integration of the community, perhaps through national service, and continuing to crack down on incitement and racism within society.

7. It must be stressed constantly that Israel is a stable ally of the West that embodies its core values: it is a haven of science and technology; it aids the West in fighting common enemies; it is a stable democracy upholding the rule of law, and it has long sought peace but been frustrated by the intransigence of its enemies. For all its flaws, it

is one of us. Despite occasional policy differences, the West should continue to nurture the many economic, technological, diplomatic, scientific and medical links with the Jewish state.

8. By the same token, the United States and other Western countries should start to reevaluate their long-term relationships with Arab states. They should question the value of alliances with regimes that do not share their values and that are heavily engaged in funding anti–Western jihadism. Two prime examples are Saudi Arabia and Qatar. Both nations are involved in supporting and funding the most radical Sunni extremism yet seen in the region, the greatest direct threat (apart from Iran) to U.S. and Western interests. Nations such as Saudi Arabia must be prevented from funding yet more extremism on Western soil in the form of jihadist schools, mosques and madrassahs. There should be close monitoring of all such institutions, with arrests of any imam or scholar who incites hatred on Western soil. Above all, long-term alternatives to the purchase of Arab oil are a critical matter for national security. The more oil that the West buys from these regimes, the more they are funding extremism.

9. In the absence of peace, Israel will continue to face a prolonged terrorist threat on all her borders. Like every Western nation, Israel faces an ongoing dilemma in how to reconcile human rights with security. Thus Israel will need to pursue a vigorous counterterrorist policy, involving direct military force, air strikes against terror targets, extrajudicial killings and intelligence-led operations against her enemies. It is essential that the West stop giving succor to terrorist groups in order to hasten their defeat. The West should identify and denounce the media strategy used by both Hamas and Hezbullah whereby they use civilians as human shields prior to launching indiscriminate attacks on Israeli civilians. Media outlets should act responsibly when covering events in the territories. This will ensure that groups such as Hamas, the true enemies of the peace process, do not gain a public relations dividend from the wars they initiate.

10. The pro–Israel narrative can be subtly altered too. The Israeli-Palestinian conflict can be conceived as part of a broader struggle between non–Arab and non–Muslim minorities and the tyrannical forces of Arab and Islamist imperialism. The rejection of Jewish self-determination by generations of Arab and Muslim leaders, together with so much of the Middle Eastern "street," is not *sui generis*. It mirrors the frequently hostile treatment meted out to the Middle East's other minorities over half a century. Recent decades have seen the relentless persecution of Christians in Iraq, Egypt and the Palestinian territories, the forced exodus of the Bahai and discrimination against Shia Muslims. In 2014–15, the plight of the Yazidi Christians was highlighted vividly during their persecution by the Islamic State. Half of Israel's population consists of Jews who were forced to flee from Arab countries after 1948, together with their descendants. The overall picture is of a region dominated by the hegemonic demands of Arabism and Islamism, and one where hostile and intolerant attitudes towards minorities are the norm. This point cannot be overstated. Unless regional attitudes improve towards vulnerable communities, there can be no true and lasting peace. Israel is one such vulnerable community, which, despite its military prowess, is forced to live among hostile and intolerant neighbors.

11. Israel, too, needs to fundamentally improve its messaging to the world. For many years, its lack of sound public relations has been an embarrassment and a hin-

drance to those outside the country who wish to speak on its behalf. To rectify this, Israel must invest resources in confronting and countering the twisted Western narrative on the conflict. Israel must produce a coherent narrative of its own that it can propound to the world. It must send out a vast plethora of speakers and advocates who can argue Israel's case with conviction. They should seek to make alliances with other dissidents from the region who can make the link between their own plight and that of the Israelis. And it should nurture these people at every opportunity. The view that hostility to Israel is a permanent fixture of the European mindset is much too defeatist. It must give way to a more constructive approach using the tried and tested principles of public relations.

12. As parts of this book have hopefully made clear, one of the prime culprits in the global demonization of Israel is the international media, or significant sections of it. It is vital to explain how photographers, journalists and broadcasters help create a distorted picture of Israel's conflict with the Palestinians. Among the many problems afflicting mainstream media coverage are the following:

a. "Conflict bias": the automatic assumption of Israeli guilt and Palestinian innocence, based in part on the belief that Israel is a colonialist aggressor illegally denying Palestinians their right to a state. Experienced AP journalist Matti Friedman says, "One of the central elements of the 'progressive' Western zeitgeist, spreading from the European left to American college campuses and intellectuals, including journalists," is a core belief that "to some extent the Jews of Israel are a symbol of the world's ills, particularly those connected to nationalism, militarism, colonialism, and racism." Naturally, this creates distortion because describing "the uglier characteristics of Palestinian politics and society" would "disrupt the Israel story, which is a story of Jewish moral failure."[12]

The fact that Palestinians form the overwhelming majority of casualties in wars with Israel cements the impression that they are the morally superior party. This creates an aggressor-vs.-victim mentality that shapes perceptions of the conflict among the journalists who cover it. It also means that too often, the evidence of Palestinian incitement, terrorism and rejectionism is ignored, downplayed or excused. This has been true for the *New York Times*, one of the world's most influential papers. Its opinion editor has said that Palestinian racism and incitement will be covered as "soon as they have [a] sovereign state to discriminate with."[13] CNN, too, was dismissive of Israeli claims of Palestinian incitement during the second intifada.[14]

b. The "selective credibility gap": the willingness of media outlets to accept Palestinian victimhood as the gospel truth but to take a skeptical approach to every Israeli denial. The classic example was in Jenin during Operation Defensive Shield when (spurious) Palestinian claims of a massacre were widely believed. Another example was the willingness to blame Israel for the death of Muhammed Al-Dura in 2000. By contrast, there seems to be no such suspension of disbelief when Israel provides a counter narrative. As Colonel Miri Eisen says of the BBC, "Everything we say they have to 'check'; everything the Palestinians say they take as fact."[15]

c. The "censorship gap": Whereas Israel is a free and open society where journalists operate with relatively little hindrance, the same is not true for the Palestinian territories, where terrifying forms of censorship have taken hold. This is especially true of Gaza under Hamas rule. After the 2014 Gaza war, the Foreign Press Association condemned the "blatant, incessant, forceful and unorthodox methods employed by the Hamas authorities and their representatives against visiting international journalists in Gaza over the past month." Foreign reporters, according to the FPA, were "harassed, threatened or questioned" over the stories they produced. The net result was that viewers were denied "an objective picture from the ground." Furthermore, there was evidence of Hamas trying to use a "vetting" procedure that would, in effect, allow for the blacklisting of specific journalists. Almost as soon as the conflict finished, reporters confirmed the reasons why they had kept silent about Hamas war crimes. According to one Spanish reporter: "We saw the Hamas men. But had we dared point the cameras at them, they would have opened fire at us and killed us." According to another journalist: "There's a conspiracy of silence rooted in fear—no one wants to report in real-time."[16] As Tom Friedman, reflecting on his time as a reporter in Beirut, put it: "Any reporter who tells you he wasn't intimidated or affected by this environment is either crazy or a liar."[17]

But similar problems exist in the West Bank under Fatah. When an AP photographer/reporter took footage of Palestinians celebrating the 9/11 attacks in Nablus, the film had to be destroyed after the cameraman was captured and threatened with death if the film was released.[18] A British photographer, Mark Seager, witnessed the horrific aftermath of the 2000 Ramallah lynching as he saw the body of an Israeli soldier being dragged through the streets. As he reached for his camera, he was forced to hand over his film and his camera was smashed. Fortunately, an Italian film crew captured some of the scenes.[19] One obvious remedy is to inform viewers that journalists are reporting from areas that are subject to reporting restrictions, allowing the audience a more balanced perspective on what they are seeing. Yet this is precisely what has been absent from reports in recent Israeli-Palestinian wars.

d. "The language gap problem": Quite simply, many Western journalists arrive in Israel and the territories without any advanced knowledge of the Arabic language. The language barrier means that bureaus are unable to translate Arabic materials and rely instead on Palestinian editors who effectively vet copy in line with the PA's rules of censorship. In addition, the Palestinian fixers used by Western press agencies are able to control what journalists see and report. Given that these fixers live in a society that is used to a culture of censorship, they cannot risk disseminating views that are at odds with the regime. Western journalists also have frequent recourse to the employees of NGOs in Gaza and the West Bank. These NGOs will usually have their own highly politicized agendas because, as Stephanie Gutmann points out, they "have a material stake in a continued sense of crisis."[20]

e. Simple "political correctness": An abject refusal by news agencies to use words such as "terrorist," preferring instead a more neutral and non-value-laden term such as "militant." There is a similar reluctance to identify that the perpetrators of terror attacks might hail from a certain ethnic or religious background; i.e., that the majority are Muslim or Arab. Political correctness leads journalists to talk of a "cycle of violence" in the region, again so as to avoid making value judgments about the manner in which Israelis and Palestinians are being killed.

All these problems mean that, as Matti Friedman puts it, "The Western press has become less an observer of this conflict than an actor in it."[21] To confront this, we need a new generation of more honest and transparent reporters and editors. They must identify the various cultural, political and linguistic constraints on their reporting, especially in war zones, which they should then share with their audiences. Above all, they should provide informed context to their reports that would allow the more multifaceted nature of this conflict to emerge.

In the long term, one can only hope that true moderates can emerge from within mainstream Palestinian society—people who are animated not by a desire for revenge but by a belief in prosperity, liberty and democracy. They will care more about building their people's future than trying to resurrect a mythical past. When this day arrives, we may start to hope that there can finally be a better future in the Middle East, for Israelis and Palestinians alike.

Chapter Notes

Preface

1. Damien Thompson, *Counterknowledge* (London: Atlantic), 2008, 1.
2. Turning away from more political issues, one could add to this list the growing belief in astrology, homeopathy, Satanic cults, alien visitations and quack medicine.

Introduction

1. Peace Index, http://www.peaceindex.org/index MonthEng.aspx?num=56.
2. Anthony King, "The countries that we love and hate," *Daily Telegraph* 3rd January 2005.
3. Manfred Gerstenfeld, *Demonizing Israel and the Jews* (New York: RVP, 2014), 11.
4. Michael Prior (ed.), *Speaking the Truth: Zionism, Israel and Occupation* (Northampton: Olive Branch, 2005), 14.
5. "Bloomberg: Shekel Strongest Currency in First Quarter," *Globes*, 9 April 2013.
6. Caroline Glick, *The Israeli Solution: A One State Plan for Peace in the Middle East* (New York: Crown, 2014), 230.
7. Since 2009, reservoirs of natural gas have been discovered off the coast of Israel that have the potential to make it a gas exporter. The first major gas field (Tamar) began production in March 2013; with its estimated capacity of 8 trillion cubic feet, it is capable of supplying the domestic market with gas for decades. Another gas field in Israeli maritime waters (Leviathan) has an estimated capacity of 16 trillion cubic feet.
8. "Central Bureau of Statistics, figures for 2015, http://www1.cbs.gov.il/reader/?MIval=cw_usr_view_SHTML&ID=417.
9. "CERN to Admit Israel as First New Member State Since 1999," CERN, http://press.web.cern.ch/press-releases/2014/01/cern-admit-israel-first-new-member-state-1999.
10. Shai Oseran and Stephane Cohen, "Don't Be Fooled: Hezbollah Is Bigger and Badder Than Ever," *The Tower*, no. 12 (March 2014).
11. Tamim Elyan, "Insight: In Sinai, Militant Islam Flourishes, Quietly," *Reuters*, 1 April 2012.
12. Hence Levi Eshkol's comment to his defense minister, Ever Weizmann, that in asking the U.S. for help in 1967 he should describe Israel as "Samson the nebuchdicker." The word "nebbish" means a timid or ineffectual person. The Samson reference means that, like the Biblical hero Samson, Israel has famed strength. Thus Israel is militarily and economically strong while also politically isolated and vulnerable.
13. Ahron Bregman, *Cursed Victory* (London: Allen Lane, 2014), xxvii.
14. Ephraim Karsh, *Fabricating Israeli History* (New York: Frank Cass, 2000), xxii.
15. Michael Widlanski, *Battle for Our Minds: Western Elites and the Terror Threat* (New York: Simon and Schuster, 2012), 29.
16. Irving Howe and Carl Gershman (eds.), *Israel, the Arabs and the Middle East* (New York: Bantam, 1972), 158.
17. David Muravchik, *Making David into Goliath* (New York: Encounter, 2014), 123.
18. Daniel Gordis, *The Promise of Israel* (Hoboken: John Wiley, 2012), 49.
19. Barry Rubin, *The Tragedy of the Middle East* (Cambridge: Cambridge University Press, 2002), 44.
20. Khaled Abu Toameh, "What About the Arab Apartheid? Part II," *Gatestone Institute*, 23 March 2010, http://www.gatestoneinstitute.org/1120/what-about-the-arab-apartheid-part-ii.
21. Barry Rubin, *The Tragedy of the Middle East* (Cambridge: Cambridge University Press, 2002), 205.
22. Efraim Cohen, "Price Tag Attacks Are Terror," *Jerusalem Post*, 17 February 2014.
23. *Commission of Inquiry into the Clashes between the Trenches' Security and Israeli Citizens Set Up in October 2000.*
24. These figures were obtained from the Israeli Central Bureau of Statistics for 2012.
25. Yaron Kelner, "Mortality Rates Still Higher Among Arab Infants in Israel," *Ynetnews*, 29 November 2014.
26. For example, according to WHO figures for 2012, life expectancy in Jordan was 75 for women, 72 for men. In Iraq, the corresponding figures are 74 and 66 and Saudi Arabia, 78 and 74 ("Global Health Observatory Data Repository," World Health Organization, http://apps.who.int/gho/data/view.main.680?lang=en).
27. Yaron Kelner, "Mortality Rates Still Higher Among Arab Infants in Israel," *Ynetnews*, 29 November 2014.
28. The Bedouin are an Arabian ethnic group spread across many countries who often dwell in the desert. Some 115,000 live in Israel.
29. Alan Johnson, *The Apartheid Smear* (London: BICOM, 13 February 2014), 13.
30. Dav Even, "How Jews and Arabs Respond Differently to the Same Israeli Health Basket," *Ha'Aretz*, 5 December 2012.

31. U.S. State Department, "Country Reports on Human Rights Practices for 2013: Israel and the Occupied Territories.
32. Joshua Muravchik, "Why the Left Should Stop Carping and Love the Jewish State, Again," *The Tower* no. 11 (February 2014).
33. Amnon Rubinstein, "The Curious Case of Jewish Democracy," *Azure Online* no. 41 (Summer 2010), http://azure.org.il/article.php?id=545.
34. Joshua Muravchik, "Israel's Arab Citizens and the Struggle for Equality," *Fathom* (BICOM), Winter 2014.
35. Moti Bassok, "Israel's Unemployment Rate Declined in 2014, Fourth Quarter," *Ha'Aretz*, 30 January 2015.
36. U.S. State Department, "Country Reports on Human Rights Practices for 2013: Israel and the Occupied Territories.
37. David Regev, "Study: Arabs Discriminated Against in Prestigious Professions," *Ynetnews*, 16 November 2009.
38. Alan Johnson, *The Apartheid Smear* (BICOM, 2014. 18.
39. "Out of Work: Israel's Arab Labour Force," *The Economist*, 5 February 2014.
40. Ariel Magnezi, "Rise in Arab National Service Volunteers," *Ynetnews*, 25 October 2010.
41. Steven Plaut, "The Myth of Ethnic Inequality," *Middle East Quarterly* 21, no. 3 (Summer 2014).
42. Amy Kaslow, "Israeli Arab Women: Stuck in Economic Purgatory, Without a Paddle," *Fortune*, 22 September 2014.
43. Plaut, "Myth of Ethnic Inequality."
44. Joshua Muravchik, "Why the Left Should Stop Carping and Love the Jewish State, Again," *The Tower*, no. 11, February 2014.
45. Steven L Pease, *The Golden Age of Jewish Achievement: The Compendium of a Culture, a People, and Their Stunning Performance* (Deucalion, 2009).
46. Muravchik, "Why the Left Should Stop Carping."
47. Jack Khoury and Yuval Yoav, "Civil Rights Group: Israel Has Reached New Heights of Racism," *Ha'Aretz*, 8 December 2007.
48. Amir Mizroch, "Survey: Israel's Arabs Harden to Jews; Jews Soften to Arabs," *Israel Hayom*, 25 June 2013.
49. Marcy Oster, "Sephardi Leader Yosef: Non-Jews Exist to Serve Jews," *Jewish Telegraphic Agency*, 18 October 2010.
50. Eli Ashkenazi, "Safed Rabbis Urge Jews to Refrain from Renting Apartments to Arabs," *Ha'Aretz*, 20 October 2010.
51. Jonah Mandel, "Author of 'Torat Hamelech' Speaks Out, *Jerusalem Post*, 4 July 2011.
52. Alexander Safian, "Can Arabs Buy Land in Israel?," *Middle East Quarterly*, December 1997, 11–16.

Chapter 1

1. Henry Siegman, "Israeli Withdrawal Is the Precondition for Peace," *Le Monde diplomatique*, http://mondediplo.com/2001/02/05mideast.
2. Among the voices were former Mossad director Ephraim Halevy, Israeli ambassador to the U.S. Michael Oren, and Matthew Gould, British ambassador to Israel.
3. Harriet Sherwood, "Merkel Rebukes Israeli PM Netanyahu for Failing to Advance Peace," *The Guardian*, 25 February 2011.
4. David Remnick, "A Man, a Plan," *The New Yorker*, 21 March 2011.
5. Michael Gove, *Celsius 7/7* (London: Weidenfield and Nicholson, 2006), 52.
6. Amnesty International: "Document—Israel/Occupied Palestinian Territories: The Conflict in Gaza: A Briefing on Applicable Law, Investigations and Accountability."
7. Human Rights Watch: Human Rights Council Special Session on the Occupied Palestinian Territories, 6 July 2006.
8. "Irish FM Urges EU to Pressure Israel to End Gaza Blockade," *Ha'Aretz*, 5 March 2010.
9. Statement to the Commons, 2 June 2010.
10. Ronen Medzini, "EU Official: No Restrictions—No Gaza Crisis," *Ynetnews*, 18 May 2011.
11. Harriet Sherwood, "Chris Patten Urges Bolder EU Approach over Middle East Conflict," *The Guardian*, 18 July 2010.
12. Declaration adopted at the Third European Union-League of Arab States, 11 June 2014.
13. War on Want, statement on 2009 Gaza assault.
14. Johann Hari, "The True Story Behind This War Is Not the One Israel Is Telling," *The Independent*, 29 December 2008.
15. Nicholas Watt and Harriet Sherwood, "David Cameron: Israeli Blockade Has Turned Gaza Strip into a 'Prison Camp,'" *The Guardian*, 27 July 2010.
16. "Vatican Justice Minister Calls Gaza Strip a 'Big Concentration Camp,'" *Daily Telegraph*, 7 January 2009.
17. "Kerry Blames Israeli Settlements for Peace Talks Stalemate," *Japan Times News*, 9 April 2014.
18. Jill Dougherty and Elise Labott, "Clinton Presses Israelis, Palestinians to Make Tough Choices for Peace," *CNN*, 11 December 2010.
19. "Powell: Israeli Settlements on Agenda," *Associated Agenda*, 5 May 2002.
20. Thomas L Friedman, "Baker Cites Israel for Settlements," *The New York Times*, 23 May 1991.
21. Letter to president of the European Council, 2 December 2010.
22. Azriel Bermant, "Margaret Thatcher and Israel," *Ha'Aretz*, 10 February 2012.
23. "The Clashes That Divided Thatcher and Israel," *Political Dove: Freeing Politics*, n.d., http://politicaldove.tumblr.com/post/16471804439/the-clashes-that-divided-thatcher-and-israel.
24. Andrew Sparrow, "Israeli Settlements Are Blockage to Middle East Peace, Says Gordon Brown," *The Guardian*, 15 December 2008.
25. "Time Running Out for a Two State Solution," *Ynetnews*, 16 January 2012.
26. Melanie Phillips, "Cameron and Clegg Give a Free Pass to Racism," *Daily Mail*, 23 January 2012.
27. David Blair, "Now or Never for a Two-State Solution," *Daily Telegraph*, 21 July 2013.
28. Jeremy Bowen, "How 1967 Defined the Middle East," *BBC Online*, 4 June 1967.
29. Jeremy Bowen, "A Year of Mid East Disappointment," *BBC Online*, 21 December 2006.
30. Blair, "Now or Never," n.p.
31. Peter Oborne, "The Cowardice at the Heart of Our Relationship with Israel," *Daily Telegraph*, 12 December 2012.

32. Spencer Ho, "UN Human Rights Chief Decries Settlements," *Times of Israel*, 25 March 2014.
33. Roane Carey, *The New Intifada: Resisting Israel's Apartheid* (New York: Verso, 2001), 139.
34. William Hague, "We Should Not Be Afraid to Criticize Israel," *Daily Telegraph*, 23 July 2006.
35. This was a bizarre comment. The country was under fire in 2006 too.
36. Joshua Muravchik, *Making David into Goliath* (New York: Encounter, 2014), 215.
37. Robin Shepherd, *A State Beyond the Pale* (London: Weidenfeld and Nicholson, 2009), 73.
38. http://www.europarl.europa.eu/sides/getDoc.do?type=MOTION&reference=B6-2009-0058&language=EN.
39. "Turkish premier says Israel caused humanity tragedy by using excessive force" *Today's Zaman*, 5th January 2009.
40. http://www.un.org/sg/statements/index.asp?nid=3635.
41. Quoted in: "Legitimacy and Legality in International Law: An Interactional Account" Jutta Brunnée, Stephen J. Toop, p. 298, n. 113.
42. "Communiqué on Today's Events in Gaza," Ministry of Foreign Affairs and Cooperation, Spain, 27 December 2008.
43. Sarkozy quote: "France's Sarkozy Wants Probe into Gaza Flotilla Incident," *Agence France Presse*, May 31, 2010.
44. Portuguese Foreign ministry quote: "Portugal calls for greater input in Korea, Mid-East crises," *Portugal News Online*, 5 June 2010.
45. Cameron: Jennifer Lipman, "Cameron criticises Israel's 'unacceptable' behaviour" The Jewish Chronicle, 2 June 2010.
46. "India slams 'disproportionate use of force' in Gaza," *Hindustan Times*, November 21, 2012.
47. Owen Jones, "'Israel Under Renewed Hamas Attack,' says the BBC. More balance is needed," *The Guardian*, 9 July 2014.
48. The cartoon was produced in the edition of 9 July 2014.
49. Michelle Nichols, "Palestinians Flex Legal Rights; U.N. Condemns Rockets, Civilian Deaths," Reuters, 10 July 2014.
50. Johann Hari, "The True Story Behind This War Is Not the One Israel Is Telling," *The Independent*, 29 December 2008.
51. Shepherd, *State Beyond the Pale*, 69.
52. Richard Millett, "War Horse Writer Michael Morpurgo: Israel Shoots Palestinian Children 'Like a Video Game,'" RichardMillett's Blog, http://richardmillett.wordpress.com/2012/01/16/war-horse-writer-michael-morpurgo-israel-shoots-palestinian-children-like-video-game/.
53. All the quotes above are taken from Stephanie Gutmann, *The Other War: Israelis, Palestinians and the Struggle for Media Supremacy* (San Francisco: Encounter, 2005), 48–50.
54. Michael Widlanski, *Battle for Our Minds: Western Elites and the Terror Threat* (New York: Simon and Schuster, 2012), 91.
55. "Qana Bombs an Israeli 'War Crime,'" *BBC News*, 31 July 2006.
56. "Report on the UN Fact Finding Mission on the Gaza Conflict," A/HRC/12/48 25 September 2009, 408.
57. War on Want, "War on Want Statement on 2009 Gaza Assault."
58. "Breaking the Cycle," *The Economist*, 2 November 2001.
59. John Irish and Emmanuel Jarry, "France's Sarkozy Proposes 1 Year Mid East Peace Map," *Reuters*, 21 September 2011.
60. "The Impact of the Arab-Israeli Conflict on Palestinian and Israeli Children," BBC, 16 March 2006, http://www.bbc.co.uk/learningzone/clips/the-arab-israeli-war-impact-on-palestinian-and-israeli-children/3224.html.
61. "Violence Escalates in Mideast with More Victims," *CNN*, 6 March 2002.
62. "Israeli Girl Killed, Fuelling Cycle of Violence," *Reuters*, 18 June 2003.
63. David Matas, *Aftershock* (Toronto: Dundrun, 2005), 145.
64. Stephanie Gutmann, *The Other War: Israelis, Palestinians and the Struggle for Media Supremacy* (San Francisco: Encounter, 2005), 88.
65. "In Pictures: Israelis and Palestinians End Days of Tit for Tat," *The Week*, 13 March 2012.
66. Ishaan Tharoor, "The Problem of Gaza: An Endless Cycle of Violence," *Time Magazine*, 21 November 2012.
67. "Editorial: A Fatal Israeli-Palestinian Flaw," *Los Angeles Times*, 14 March 2011.
68. Global Policy Forum, "Israel, Palestine and the Occupied Territories," https://www.globalpolicy.org/component/content/article/189-israel-palestine/38375-israel-palestine-and-the-occupied-territories.html.
69. Christian Aid, "Locked Out: Palestinian Refugees and the Key to Peace," June 2011.
70. Article 42, "Annex to the Laws and Customs of War on Land" (Hague IV); October 18, 1907.
71. Yoram Dinstein, *The International Law of Belligerent Occupation* (Cambridge: Cambridge University Press, 2009), 42–4.
72. Ibid., 17.
73. Ibid., 58.
74. *Mara'abe v. The Prime Minister of Israel* (2004) and *Jamait Askan et al. v. IDF Commander of Judea and Samaria* et al.
75. Avinoam Sharon, "Why Is Israel's Presence in the Territories Still Called 'Occupation'?," *Jerusalem Centre for Public Affairs*, 2009.
76. Dinstein, *The International Law of Belligerent Occupation* (Cambridge: Cambridge University Press, 2009), 24.
77. This suggestion appears in Robin Shepherd's book *A State Beyond the Pale*.
78. Dinstein, *The International Law of Belligerent Occupation*, 2 (it should be noted that laws of occupation are still applicable, regardless of whether an occupation is legal or not).
79. Ibid., 144.
80. Ibid., 47.
81. "Israel-OPT: Relentless Rocket Attacks Take Psychological Toll on Children in Sderot," *Irin News*, 27 January 2008.
82. James Bennet, "Seized Arms Would Have Vastly Extended Arafat Arsenal," *New York Times*, January 12 2002.
83. Jeffrey Heller, "Israel Seizes Ship with Iran Arms for Gaza-Netanyahu," *Reuters*, 15 March 2011.

84. United Nations, and Geoffrey Palmer, "Report of the Secretary-General's Panel of Inquiry on the 31 May 2010 Flotilla Incident," (New York: United Nations, 2011).
85. The Golan Heights, which were seized in 1967, are not discussed here, though their status remains as an occupied territory despite their annexation by Israel.
86. Timothy Shanahan, "The Morality of Palestinian Terrorism," in *Israel, Palestine and Terror*, ed. Stephen Law (London: Continuum, 2008), 37.
87. Alan Dershowitz, *The Case for Israel* (Hoboken: John Wiley, 2003), 92.
88. Muravchik, *Making David into Goliath*, 11.
89. Michael Oren, "Who Started It?," *Washington Post*, 10 June 2007.
90. William H. Taft IV, "The Legal Case for Pre-Emption," Council on Foreign Relations, 18 November 2002.
91. Malcolm Brailey, "Pre-Emption and Prevention: An Ethical and Legal Critique of the Bush Doctrine and Anticipatory Use of Force in Defense of the State," *Institute of Defense and Strategic Studies*, November 2003.
92. U.S. Department of State, "U.S. National Security Strategy: Prevent Our Enemies from Threatening Us, Our Allies, and Our Friends with Weapons of Mass Destruction," http://2001-2009.state.gov/r/pa/ei/wh/15425.htm.
93. Henry Shue and David Rodin (eds.), *Preemption* (Oxford: Oxford University Press, 2007), 3.
94. Examples include the Cuban Missile Crisis and Israel's pre-emptive strikes in 1967. It was also invoked after the Israeli attack on Iraq's Osiraq nuclear reactor in 1981. Even though the latter case was condemned widely and deemed illegal at the UN, it was not accepted because it did not meet the *Caroline* test.
95. Michael Walzer, *Just and Unjust Wars*, p. 81 (Basic Books 2015).
96. Ted Honderich, "Terrorisms in Palestine," in *Israel, Palestine and Terror*, ed. S. Law (London: Continuum, 2008), 6.
97. Professor Ruth Lapidot, "Security Council Resolution 242: An Analysis of Its Main Provisions," *Jerusalem Centre for Public Affairs*, 4 June 2007.
98. This does not mean that Chapter VI resolutions can be ignored, and there may be consequences for Israel in the event of a decisive breach with the resolution.
99. Lyndon B. Johnson, "272—Address at the State Department's Foreign Policy Conference for Educators," 19 June 1967, The American Presidency Project, http://www.presidency.ucsb.edu/ws/index.php?pid=28308.
100. Rosalyn Higgins, "The Place of International Law in the Settlement of Disputes by the Security Council," 64 *Am. J. Int'l L.* 1 (1970).
101. *The Jerusalem Post*, January 23, 1970.
102. Shepherd, *State Beyond the Pale*, 127.
103. This suggestion is regularly made by David Horovitz, editor of *The Times of Israel*.
104. Alan Baker, "The Settlements Issue: Distorting the Geneva Convention and the Oslo Accords," *Jerusalem Centre for Public Affairs*, 5 January 2011.
105. Matas, *Aftershock*, 75.
106. I am particularly grateful to lawyer Sebastian Shinefeld for his comments on article 49 of the 4th Geneva Protocol.
107. Eugene Kontorovich, "Non-Recognition and Economic Dealings with Occupied Territories," *Columbia Journal of Transnational Law* (working draft) (2015).

108. Article 51 (5) (b) of Protocol I, restated in Article 8 (2) (b) (iv) of the Rome Statute of the International Criminal Court.
109. Yoram Dinstein, *The Conduct of Hostilities Under the Law of International Armed Conflict* (Cambridge: Cambridge University Press, 2004), 121.
110. Ibid., 123.
111. Alan Dershowitz, *The Case Against Israel's Enemies* (New Jersey: John Wiley & Sons, 2008), 156.
112. Article 48 of Protocol I.
113. https://www.idfblog.com/about-the-idf/idf-code-of-ethics/.
114. David Horovitz, "The Moralist," *The Jerusalem Post*, 22 April 2011.
115. OHCA, "Occupied Palestinian Territory: Hostilities in Gaza and Israel," 9 July 2014, http://www.ochaopt.org/documents/ocha_opt_sitrep_09_07_2014.pdf.
116. Matthew Kalman, "New Missile Offers Strafe Minus Strife," *New York Daily News*, 3 December 2006.
117. Colonel Richard Kemp, "A Salute to the IDF," *The Jerusalem Post*, 15 June 2011.
118. In 2011, Goldstone backed away from the allegations that Israel had committed war crimes by saying: "If I had known then what I know now, the Goldstone Report would have been a different document." But as his conclusions were not shared by the other authors, the UN report remains unaltered.
119. Muravchik, *Making David into Goliath*, 217.
120. "Hamas Using Palestinians as Human Shields: We Desire Death as You Desire Life," http://www.youtube.com/watch?v=RTu-AUE9ycs.
121. "Afghanistan Taliban Using Human Shields," *BBC News*, 11 February 2010.
122. "Probe: Taliban Used Civilians as Human Shields," *NBC News*, 9 May 2009.
123. Widlanski, *Battle for Our Minds*, 86.
124. Thomas Hunter, *Targeted Killing: Self Defence, Preemption, and the War on Terrorism* (Charleston: Booksurge, 2009), 2.
125. Ibid., 67.
126. Ibid., 38.
127. Daniel Statman, "Can Just War Theory Justify Targeted Killing? An Investigation into Three Models," 26 August 2011, SSRN, http://ssrn.com/abstract=1917154 or http://dx.doi.org/10.2139/ssrn.1917154.
128. Michael Walzer, *Arguing About War* (New Haven: Yale University Press, 2004), 130.
129. Tamar Meisels, "Territory and Terrorism in Israel," in *Israel, Palestine and Terror*, ed. Stephen Law (London: Continuum, 2008), 182.
130. David Whitaker (ed.), *The Terrorism Reader*, 3rd ed. (Oxon: Routledge, 2007), 10.
131. Shanahan, "Morality of Palestinian Terrorism," 38.
132. Susan M. Akram, Michael Dumper, Michael Lynk and Iain Scobbie (eds.), *International Law and the Israeli-Palestinian Conflict* (London: Routledge, 2012), 18.
133. "1951 Convention and Protocol Relating to the Status of Refugees.
134. Don Peretz, *Palestinians, Refugees, and the Middle East Peace Process* (Washington: United States Institute of Peace Press, 1993), 11–12.
135. Sol Stern, *A Century of Palestinian Rejectionism and Jew Hatred* (New York: Encounter, 2011).

136. Matas, *Aftershock*, 100.
137. "Resolution 194," United Nations Relief and Works Agency for Palestine Refugees in the Near East, http://www.unrwa.org/content/resolution-194.
138. *Al-Misri*, Egypt, 11 October 1949, quoted in Harris O. Schoenberg, *A Mandate for Terror: The United Nations and the PLO* (New York: SPI, 1989), 239.
139. Cynthia Wallace, *Foundations of the International Legal Rights of the Jewish People and the State of Israel: Implications for a New Palestinian State* (Lake Mary: Creation House, 2012), 30.
140. Terence Prittie, quoted by Michael Curtis in *The Palestinians: People, History, Politics* (New Brunswick, New Jersey: Transaction, 2011), 71.
141. Susan Akram, "Myths and Realities of the Palestinian Refugee Problem: Reframing the Right of Return," in *International Law and the Israeli-Palestinian Conflict*, ed. Susan M. Akram, Michael Dumper, Michael Lynk and Iain Scobbie, (London: Routledge, 2012), 30.
142. Jose Ingles, *Study of Discrimination in Respect of the Right of Everyone to Leave Any Country, Including His Own, and to Return to His Country*, UN Doc E/CN.4/Sub.2/220/Rev.1, 1963.
143. Matas, *Aftershock*, 109.
144. Louis Henkin, "The Freedom of Movement," in *The International Bill of Rights* (New York: Columbia University Press, 1981), 180.
145. Neil Caplan, *The Israel-Palestine Conflict* (Chichester, U.K.: John Wiley, 2010), 160.

Chapter 2

1. See chapter 10 of Robert Wistrich, *Hitler's Apocalypse* (London: Weidenfeld and Nicholson, 1985).
2. Wistrich, *Hitler's Apocalypse*, 241–42.
3. Dershowitz, *The Case for Peace*, 153.
4. Yasmin Alibhai Brown, "Israel's Friends Cannot Justify This Slaughter?," *The Independent*, 19 January 2009.
5. Ronnie Kasrils, "Who Said Nearly 50 Years Ago That Israel Was an Apartheid State?," *Links: International Journal of Socialist Renewal*, 17 March 2009.
6. John Pilger, "Holocaust Denial," *New Statesman*, 8 January 2009.
7. Noam Chomsky, *The Fateful Triangle* (London: Pluto, 1983), 217.
8. Noam Chomsky, "Exterminate All the Brutes," January 19 2009, http://www.chomsky.info/articles/20090119.htm.
9. Tom Paulin, "Killed in Crossfire," *The Observer*, 18 February 2001.
10. Omayma Abdel-Latif, "That Weasel Word," *Al-Ahram*, 4–10 April 2002.
11. Slavoj Žižek, "What Goes On When Nothing Goes On?," in *The Case for Sanctions Against Israel*, ed. Audrea Lim (London: Verso, 2012), 19.
12. Shepherd, *A State Beyond the Pale*, 56.
13. "UN Human Rights Official: Gaza Evokes Memories of Warsaw Ghetto," *Ha'Aretz*, 23 January 2009.
14. Oona King, "Israel Can Halt This Now," *The Guardian*, 12 June 2003.
15. John Prescott, "Israel's Bombardment of Gaza Is a War Crime—and It Must End," *Daily Mirror*, 26 July 2014.
16. "Lib Dems Condemn MPs Criticism of Israel Ahead of Holocaust Memorial Day," *BBC News*, 25 January 2013.
17. Jennifer Lipman, "Lee Jasper Shows No Respect for Israel or HMD," *Jewish Chronicle*, January 24, 2013.
18. George Galloway, "Dark Echoes of the Holocaust," *Scottish Daily Record*, 28 December 2009.
19. Daniel McGowan, "Why We Must Remember Deir Yassin," in *Speaking the Truth: Zionism, Israel and Occupation*, ed. Michael Prior (Northampton: Olive Branch, 2005), 92 and 95.
20. Anthony Loewenstein, "Why Aren't Jews Outraged by Israeli Occupation?," *Ha'Aretz*, 17 June 2009.
21. Mitchell Bard, *The Arab Lobby: The Invisible Alliance That Undermines America's Interests in the Middle East* (New York: Broadside, 2011), 314.
22. Afif Safieh, *The Peace Process: From Breakthrough to Breakdown* (London: Saqi, 2010), 14.
23. "Parliament Business: 15 Jan 2009: Column 402," UK Parliament, http://www.publications.parliament.uk/pa/cm200809/cmhansrd/cm090115/debtext/90115-0013.htm.
24. Andre Vornik, "Is There a Holocaust Industry?," *BBC News*, 26 January 2000.
25. Gilad Atzmon, "Truth, History and Integrity, 13 March 2010, http://www.gilad.co.uk/writings/truth-history-and-integrity-by-gilad-atzmon.html.
26. Ben White, "Is Israel a Democracy or an Ethnocracy?," *New Statesman*, 5 February 2002.
27. Ken Livingstone, "This Is About Israel, Not Antisemitism," *The Guardian*, 4 March 2005.
28. John Pilger, "Denying the Israeli Past," 3 June 2002, http://johnpilger.com/articles/denying-the-israeli-past.
29. Noam Chomsky, *Peace in the Middle East: Reflections on Justice and Nationhood* (New York: Pantheon, 1974), 119.
30. Ibid., 17.
31. Jennifer Bleyer, "Noam Chomsky Interview," The New York City Independent Media Center, 24 October 2004, http://nyc.indymedia.org/en/2004/10/46362.html.
32. Ben White, "Is Israel a Democracy or an Ethnocracy?," *New Statesman*, 5 February 2012.
33. Ilan Pappe, "Israeli Jewish Myths and the Prospect of American War," 13 September 2002, http://www.labournet.net/world/0209/pappe1.html.
34. Judith Butler, *Parting Ways: Jewishness and the Critique of Zionism* (New York: Columbia University Press, 2013), 4, 18, 117–8.
35. Actually it is not a complete guarantee, for some Jews can and are barred if their presence is deemed unwelcome.
36. Ben White, "Is Israel a Democracy or an Ethnocracy?," *New Statesman*, 5 February 2002.
37. Butler, *Parting Ways*, 118.
38. Seumas Milne, "This Slur of Antisemitism Is Used to Defend Repression," *The Guardian*, 8 May 2002.
39. Michael Neumann, *The Case Against Israel* (Petrolia, Cal.: Counterpunch, 2006), 16–20.
40. Tony Judt, "'Jewish State' Has Become Anachronism," *Los Angeles Times*, 10 October 2003.
41. Joel Kovel, "On Left Antisemitism and the Special Status of Israel," 15 February 2013, http://joelkovel.com/on-left-antisemitism-and-the-special-status-of-israel/, accessed 10 January 2014.
42. Ken Livingstone, *You Can't Say That* (London: Faber and Faber, 2012), 512.

43. Naomi Klein, "Victim to Victimizer," *The Varsity* (University of Toronto), 29 November 1990, 5–6.
44. Jostein Gaardner, "God's Chosen People," *Aftenposten*, 5 August 2006.
45. Deborah Orr, "Is an Israeli Life Really More Important Than a Palestinian's?," *The Guardian*, 19 October 2011.
46. Tariq Ali, "A Protracted Colonial War," *The Guardian*, 20 July 2006.
47. Yasmin Alibhai-Brown, "Israel's Friends Cannot Justify This Slaughter," *The Independent*, 19 January 2009.
48. Jose Saramago, *El Pais*, 21 April 2002.
49. Marcelo Svirsky, "A Statement," in *After Israel: Towards Cultural Transformation* (London: Zed, 2014).
50. Naim Ateek, "2001 Easter Message," Sabeel, http://www.sabeel.org/res-archives.php?eventid=126.
51. Missy Beatie, "How Israel's Eye for an Eye Terrorism in Gaza Will Make Everyone Blind," *Stop the War*, 4 July 2014.
52. Michael Neumann, "What's So Bad About Israel," *Counterpunch*, July 6–8 2002.
53. Chris Moore, "Sadist, Sociopath Jewish State Fears Palestinian Statehood Because Its Captive Prey Would Then Have Police Recourse," Judeofascism.com, 3 September 2011, http://www.judeofascism.com/2011/09/sadist-sociopath-jewish-state-fears.html.
54. Paul Woodward, "Israel's Emerging State of Psychosis," War in Context, 23 May 2010, http://warincontext.org/2010/05/23/israels-emerging-state-of-psychosis/.
55. Muravchik, *Making David into Goliath*, 193.
56. Alexei Sayle, "Israel Is the Jimmy Saville of Nation States," *Belfast Telegraph*, 16 July 2014.
57. "Gaza: From Blockade to Bloodshed," *The Guardian*, 1 June 2010.
58. Johann Hari, "Israel Is Suppressing a Secret It Must Face," *The Independent*, 27 April 2008.
59. Quoted in Charles Glass, "Balfour, Weizmann and the Creation of Israel," *London Review of Books*, Vol. 23 No. 11, 7 June 2001.
60. Resolution 3151 (XXVIII), 14 December 1973.
61. Ronnie Kasrils, "South Africa's Israel Boycott," *The Guardian*, 29 September 2010.
62. Tony Judt, "Israel: The Alternative," *The New York Review of Books*, 23 October 2003.
63. Rafael Reuveny, "The Last Colonialist: Israel in the Occupied Territories Since 1967," *The Independent Review*, Winter 2008.
64. Nir Rosen, "Gaza: The Logic of Colonial Power," *The Guardian*, 29 December 2008.
65. Lisa Taraki and Mark LeVine, "Why Boycott Israel?," in *The Case for Sanctions Against Israel*, ed. A. Lim (London: Verso, 2012), 166.
66. "Ilan Pappe on How Israel Was Founded on Ethnic Cleansing," *Socialist Worker*, 29 July 2006.
67. Chomsky, *Fateful Triangle*, 161.
68. Ibid., 455, 467–9.
69. Ronnie Kasrils, "Sour Oranges and the Sweet Taste of Freedom," in *The Case for Sanctions Against Israel*, ed. A. Lim (London: Verso, 2012), 109.
70. Meron Benvenisti, "Bantustan Plan for an Apartheid Israel," *The Guardian*, 26 April 2004.
71. Desmond Tutu, "Realizing God's Dream for the Holy Land," *The Boston Globe*, 26 October 2007.
72. Desmond Tutu, "Apartheid in the Holy Land," *The Guardian*, 29 April 2002.
73. Ronnie Kasrils, "Apartheid in Duplicate," *Middle East Monitor*, 1 July 2011.
74. Jimmy Carter, "Israel, Palestine, Peace and Apartheid," *The Guardian*, 12 December 2006.
75. Max Blumenthal, *Goliath: Life and Loathing in Greater Israel* (New York: Nation, 2014), 17.
76. Anthony Loewenstein (ed.), *After Zionism: One State for Israel and Palestine* (London: Saqi, 2012), 135.
77. The term genocide was coined by a Polish Jew, Raphael Lemkin, who lost most of his family in the Holocaust.
78. "Convention on the Prevention and Punishment of the Crime of Genocide," Organization of American States, http://www.oas.org/dil/1948_Convention_on_the_Prevention_and_Punishment_of_the_Crime_of_Genocide.pdf.
79. Bregman, *Cursed Victory*, xxvii.
80. Ephaim Karsh, "What Occupation?," *Commentary*, July–August 2002.
81. Israel Ministry of Foreign Affairs, "The Activities of the Civil Administration in the Territories," 16 June 1994.
82. Karsh, "What Occupation?," *Commentary*, July–August 2002.
83. Colin Shindler, *What Do Zionists Believe?* (London: Granta, 2007), 4.
84. http://www2.ohchr.org/english/law/ccpr.htm.
85. Gordis, *Promise of Israel*, 89.
86. Neumann, *Case Against Israel*, 18.
87. Christian Joppke, *Immigration and the Nation-State: The United States, Germany and Great Britain* (Oxford, Oxford University Press, 1999), 110.
88. Dan Cohn-Sherbok, *The Palestinian State: A Jewish Justification* (Exeter, UK: Impress, 2012), 19.
89. Michael Prior, "Zionism and the Challenge of Historical Truth and Morality," in *Speaking the Truth*, 36.
90. https://treaties.un.org/doc/Publication/UNTS/Volume%201015/volume-1015-I-14861-English.pdf.
91. Majalli Whbee (sometimes spelled Wahabi), an Israeli Druze politician born in 1954.
92. The Prohibition of Discrimination in Products, Services and Entry into Places of Entertainment and Public Places Law.
93. Ariel Ben Solomon, "National Service in Arab Sector up 76% over Past Year," *The Jerusalem Post*, 20 June 2013.
94. Johnson, *Apartheid Smear*, 10.
95. This follows from section 15 of the Basic Law (Judicature), according to which all state and local officials (including those in the territories) are subject to judicial review by the High Court of Justice.
96. Dinstein, *The International Law of Belligerent Occupation*, 26.

Chapter 3

1. Dennis Sewell, "A Kosher Conspiracy," *New Statesman*, 14 January 2002.
2. Richard Ingrams, "Who Will Dare Damn Israel?," *The Guardian*, 16 September 2001.
3. John Pilger, "Why My Film Is Under Fire," *The Guardian*, 23 September 2002.
4. Cnann Lipshshiz, "Dutch Pro-Palestinian Socialite: Jewish Lobby Plays on Holocaust," *Ha'Aretz*, 31 January 2010.

5. Shepherd, *State Beyond the Pale*, 74.
6. David Hirsh, "Revenge of the Jewish Lobby?," *The Guardian*, 5 May 2006.
7. Hagit Kleinman, "UK Politician: Pro-Israel Politician Controls West," *Ynetnews*, 21 September 2006, n.p.
8. Nicholas Watt, "Lib Dem MP: Why I Would Consider Being a Suicide Bomber," *The Guardian*, 23 January 2004.
9. Martin Bright and Robyn Rosen, "MP: Israel's Tentacles Will Steal the Election," *The Jewish Chronicle*, 29 March 2010.
10. Martin Bright, "Jeremy Corbyn Calls for Inquiry on 'Pro-Israel Lobby,'" *The Jewish Chronicle*, 19 April 2012.
11. Marcus Dysch, "Storm over Jack Straw's 'Hate' Remarks," *Jewish Chronicle*, 31 October 2013.
12. Jerry Lewis, "British MP Condemned for Anti-Israel Comments," *The Jerusalem Post*, 19 October 2014.
13. Peter Oborne and James Jones, "The Pro-Israel Lobby in Britain," *Our Kingdom*, 13 November 2009, https://www.opendemocracy.net/ourkingdom/peter-oborne-james-jones/pro-israel-lobby-in-britain-full-text.
14. Ibid.
15. Richard Millett, "Former BBC Middle East correspondent Tim Llewellyn: 'Zionists are scattered at strategic points throughout British business,'" Richard Millett's Blog, 19 October 2012, http://richardmillett.wordpress.com/2012/10/.
16. John Mearsheimer and Stephen Walt, "The Israel Lobby," *The London Review of Books* 28, no. 6 (23 March 2006).
17. Ibid.
18. Abe Foxman, *The Deadliest Lies: The Israel Lobby and the Myth of Jewish Control* (New York: Palgrave Macmillan, 2007), 36.
19. Doug Bandow, "The Case for Ending Aid to Israel," *The National Interest*, 5 June 2012.
20. Peter Oborne, "The Cowardice at the Heart of Our Relationship with Israel," *Daily Telegraph*, 12 December 2012.
21. Conservative Friends of Israel, www2.cfoi.co.uk.
22. Nadav Safran, *Israel: The Embattled Ally* (Cambridge, Mass.: Harvard University Press, 1981), 577.
23. Goldberg, *Jewish Power: Inside the American Jewish Establishment* (New York: Basic, 1997), 158.
24. Organski, Abramo, *$36 Billion Bargain: Strategy and Politics in U.S. Assistance to Israel* (New York: Columbia University Press, 1990), ch 5.
25. Safran, *Israel*, 578.
26. Ibid., 583–4.
27. Ibid., 586–7.
28. Abramo Organski, *$36 Billion Bargain* (New York: Columbia University Press, 1990), 25.
29. Bard, *The Arab lobby*, 142.
30. Gareth Porter, "Israel Warned Us Not to Invade Iraq After 9/11," *IPS*, 28 August 2007.
31. Gerald Posner, "How Obama Flubbed His Missile Message," *The Daily Beast*, 17 September 2009.
32. Bard, *Myths and Facts: A Guide to the Arab-Israeli Conflict*, 122.
33. Howard Blitzer, *Between Washington and Jerusalem: A Reporter's Notebook* (Oxford: Oxford University Press, 1985), 21.
34. Goldberg, *Jewish Power*, 13.
35. Ibid., 31–2.
36. It is true that Reagan won more of the Jewish vote in 1980.
37. Organski, *$36 Billion Bargain*, 67–8. The results of the study can be found on 234–39.
38. Whether similar patterns pertain in the last two decades is a subject for extensive research.
39. Organski, *$36 Billion Bargain*, 73.
40. Mitchell Bard, *Will Israel Survive?* (New York: Palgrave Macmillan, 2007), 217.
41. I benefited from conversations with a former MP, Professor Eric Moonman, in writing about Britain's pro-Israel lobby.
42. Ali Gharib, "What Kind of Friend to Israel Was Thatcher?," *The Daily Beast*, 8 April 2013.
43. "British Prime Minister Gordon Brown Demands 'Freeze on Israel's Settlement Expansion,'" AP, 20 July 2008.
44. "Fairness: Israel Palestine," The Guardian, http://www.theguardian.com/values/socialaudit/story/0,,1931205,00.html.
45. Jemima Khan, "Tell the Truth About Israel," *The Guardian*, 1 November 2000.
46. Faisal Bodi, "Israel Simply Has No Right to Exist," *The Guardian*, 3 January 2001.
47. "2012 Dates for Your Diary," BBC, 2 January 2012, http://www.bbc.co.uk/sport/olympics/2012/countries/israel.
48. "BBC Bias," *Jerusalem Post*, 26 July 2012.
49. Alex Singleton, "Why Won't the BBC Come Clean over Its Bias Against Israel—a Moral Country That Deserves Our Support?," *Daily Mail*, 26 August 2012.
50. Peter Sissons, "Left-Wing Bias? It's Written Through the BBC's Very DNA," *Daily Mail*, 22 January 2011.
51. Ibid.

Chapter 4

1. The article, which is unavailable on the *Telegraph's* Web site, was published in December 2001 and caused a storm of controversy. Ambassador Bernard did not deny making the comments, though he claimed they had been taken out of context.
2. Bernard later refused to apologize, claiming that his remarks had been "distorted."
3. Polly Tonybee, "Say It Loud: No More Support Until Israel Agrees to Pull Out," *The Guardian*, 24 October 2001.
4. http://www.engageonline.org.uk/blog/article.php?id=2244.
5. Robert Fisk, "If You Want the Roots of Terror, Try Here," *The Independent*, 12 August 2006.
6. Dore Gold, "After the London Bombings: Blair's Israeli-Palestinian Detour from the Real Root Causes of Terrorism," *Jerusalem Centre for Public Affairs*, 1 September 2005.
7. Elad Benari, "British MP Says Israel Is 'Cause of Terrorism,'" *Arutz Sheva*, 23 November 2010.
8. Madeleine Bunting, "Throwing Mud at Muslims," *The Guardian*, 22 August 2006.
9. "UK in New Mid-East Row," *BBC News*, 24 September 2001.
10. Suzanne Goldenberg, "Blair Defuses Israel's Anger After Straw Remark Threatens Talks," *The Guardian*, 26 September 2001.

11. "Blair Meets Arafat in London," CNN.com, 15 October 2001.
12. "Draft Report on Young Muslims and Extremism," GlobalSecurity.org, April 2004, http://www.globalsecurity.org/security/library/report/2004/muslimext-uk.htm.
13. John Pilger, "The Source of Terror in Palestine," 22 March 2004, http://johnpilger.com.
14. Ken Livingstone, "This Is About Israel, Not Anti-semitism," *The Guardian*, 4 March 2005.
15. Gutmann, *The Other War*, 4.
16. 9/11 Commission testimony, June 16, 2004.
17. Counterpunch, 18 September 2001, http://www.counterpunch.org/chomskyintv.html.
18. Bard, *Arab Lobby*, 277.
19. Michael Ignatieff, "The Burden," *New York Times*, 5 January 2003.
20. Susan Sontag, "Talk of the Town," *The New Yorker*, 24 September 2001.
21. Matthias Kuntzel, *Jihad and Jew-Hatred: Islamism, Nazism and the Roots of 9/11* (New York: Telos, 2007), 124.
22. Elizabeth Barlow, "Waking the Sleeping Giant," in *Speaking the Truth*, ed. Michael Prior (Northampton: Olive Branch, 2005), 243.
23. John Mearsheimer and Stephen Walt, "The Israel Lobby," *The London Review of Books* 28, no. 6 (23 March 2006).
24. John Kerry, "Remarks at a Reception in Honor of Eid Al-Adha," U.S. Department of State, 14 October 2014, http://www.state.gov/secretary/remarks/2014/10/233058.htm.
25. Walid Phares, *The War of Ideas: Jihadism Against Democracy.* (New York: Palgrave Macmillan, 2007), 1.
26. Speech delivered by President George W. Bush to Congress, 20 September 2001.
27. The White House, http://www.whitehouse.gov/news/releases/2001/09/20010917-11.html.
28. Daniel Pipes, "Not Calling Islamism the Enemy," 12 September 2001, http://www.danielpipes.org/blog/2001/09/not-calling-islamism-the-enemy.
29. "Deputy Secretary Wolfowitz with the German Foreign Minister," Department of Defense, http://www.defenselink.mil/news/Sep2001/t09202001_t919wolf.html.
30. Charles Krauthammer, "A Terrorist War Obama Has Denied," *Washington Post*, 1 January 2010.
31. Andrew C. McCarthy, "Will the Senate Confirm a CIA Director Who Denies the Existence of What the Secretary of State Called 'the Global Jihadist Threat'?," National Review, 6 February 2013, http://www.nationalreview.com/corner/340012/will-senate-confirm-cia-director-who-denies-existence-what-secretary-state-called.
32. Yitzhak Benhorin, "US Spy Chief: Muslim Brotherhood Secular," *Y Net News*, 11 February 2011.
33. Widlanski, *Battle for Our Minds*, 273.
34. David J. Rusin, "Problems in the U.S. Military Denying Islam's Role in Terror," *Middle East Quarterly*, Spring 2013.
35. Melanie Phillips, *Londonistan* (London: Gibson Square, 2006), 101.
36. Ibid., 212.
37. "Woolwich Murder 'a Betrayal of Islam,' Says David Cameron," *Daily Telegraph*, 3 June 2013.
38. Boris Johnson, video interview, in "Boris Johnson: 'Fault lies with wholly with attackers,'" BBC, 23 May 2013, http://www.bbc.co.uk/news/uk-22639958.
39. Melanie McDonagh, "Why Does David Cameron Refuse to Admit That the Terrorist Attack in Nairobi Is Linked to Islam?," *The Spectator*, 23 September 2013.
40. Alan Johnson, "After the Pakistan School Attack, We Need to Talk About Islam," *Daily Telegraph*, 17 December 2014.
41. "Ban Offers Condolences to French Government in Wake of 'Charlie Hebdo' Attack," UN News Center, 9 January 2015, http://www.un.org/apps/news/story.asp?NewsID=49768.
42. Piers Morgan, "I Can Accept That the Paris Murderers Aren't Real Muslims Why Won't the MUSLIM World Say So Too?," *Daily Mirror*, 9 January 2015.
43. Phares, *War of Ideas*, 61.
44. Fraser Egerton, *Jihad in the West: The Rise of Militant Salafism* (Cambridge: Cambridge University Press, 2011), 8.
45. David Aaronovitch, "Nursing a Grievance, Blinded by Narcissism," *The Times*, 19 July 2005.
46. Egerton, *Jihad in the West*, 93.
47. Ibid., 95.
48. Bernard Lewis, *The Crisis of Islam: Holy War and Unholy Terror* (London: Weidenfeld and Nicholson, 2004), 28.
49. Ibid., 32.
50. Widlanski, *Battle for Our Minds*, 212.
51. Charles Allen, *God's Terrorists: The Wahhabi Cult and Hidden Roots of Modern Jihad* (London: Little, Brown, 2006), 46.
52. Ibid., 57.
53. Dore Gold, *Hatred's Kingdom: How Saudi Arabia Supports the New Global Terrorism* (Washington, D.C.: Regnery, 2003), 63.
54. Mary Habeck, *Knowing the Enemy: Jihadist Ideology and the War on Terror* (New Haven: Yale University Press, 2006), 11.
55. Loretta Napoleon, *The Islamist Phoenix* (New York: Seven Stories, 2014), 81–2.
56. Bernard Lewis, "The Roots of Muslim Rage," *The Atlantic*, 1 September 1990.
57. Michael J. Mazarr, *Unmodern Men in the Modern World: Radical Islam, Terrorism and the War on Modernity* (Cambridge: Cambridge University Press, 2007), 13.
58. Ibid., 66.
59. Lia Brynjar, *The Society of the Muslim Brothers in Egypt: The Rise of an Islamic Mass Movement, 1928–1942* (Reading, England: Ithaca, 1998), 28.
60. Ibid., 33, 58.
61. Mazarr, *Unmodern Men*, 225.
62. Jamie Glazov, *United in Hate: The Left's Romance with Tyranny and Terror* (Los Angeles: WND, 2009), 140.
63. Gilles Kepel, *The Roots of Radical Islam* (London: Saqi, 2005), 46.
64. Bruce Lawrence (ed.), *Messages to the World: The Statements of Osama Bin Laden* (London: Verso, 2005), 15, 17.
65. Ibid., 25, 28, 45.
66. Ibid., 183, 188, 215.
67. Ibid., 61, 171, 121, 227.
68. Mazarr, *Unmodern Men*, ix.
69. Lawrence (ed.), *Messages to the World*, 166–68.
70. Vali Nasr, *The Shia Revival* (New York: W.W. Norton, 2003), 136–37.

71. Daniel Pipes, *Militant Islam Reaches America* (New York, W.W. Norton, 2003), 39–42, 64–65.
72. Phares, *War of Ideas*, 13.
73. Sayyid Qutb, *Milestones* (New Delhi: Islamic Book Service, 2001), 88.
74. Lawrence (ed.), *Messages to the World*, 92.
75. Habeck, *Knowing the Enemy*, 43.
76. Ibid., 58.
77. Lee Harris, *The Suicide of Reason: Radical Islam's Threat to the West* (New York: Basic, 2007), 8.
78. Phares, *War of Ideas*, 70.
79. Habeck, *Knowing the Enemy*, 62.
80. Kim Ezra Shienbaum and Jamal Hasan (eds.), *Beyond Jihad: Critical Voices from Inside Islam* (Palo Alto, Cal.: Academica, 2006), 118.
81. Habeck, *Knowing the Enemy*, 60.
82. Syed Abul 'Ala Maudoodi, *Political Theory of Islam* (Lahore: Islamic Publications, 1976), 20.
83. Lawrence (ed.), *Messages to the World*, 228.
84. Caroline Cox and John Marks, *The West, Islam and Islamism* (London: Civitas, 2006), 35.
85. Phares, *War of Ideas*, 74.
86. Qutb, *Milestones*, 9, 60.
87. Habeck, *Knowing the Enemy*, 64.
88. Gove, *Celsius 7/7*, 9.
89. Kepel, *Roots of Radical Islam*, 55.
90. Habeck, *Knowing the Enemy*, 48.
91. Ibid., 119.
92. Qutb, *Milestones*, 58–59.
93. Habeck, *Knowing the Enemy*, 78.
94. Maudoodi, *Political Theory of Islam*, 27–30.
95. Qutb, *Milestones*, 94.
96. Kuntzel, *Jihad and Jew-Hatred*, 32.
97. Habeck, *Knowing the Enemy*, 80.
98. Bernard Lewis, *The Political Language of Islam* (Chicago: University of Chicago Press, 1988) 84–85.
99. Cox and Marks, *The West, Islam and Islamism*, 35.
100. Qutb, *Milestones*, 130.
101. Ibid., 87. This is more fully discussed in the section "Jihad Against the Jews."
102. Phares, *The War of Ideas*, 63.
103. William E. Shepherd, *Sayyid Qutb and Islamic Activism* (New York: E.J. Brill, 1996), 282–83.
104. Habeck, *Knowing the Enemy*, 95.
105. Qutb, *Milestones*, 160.
106. Paul Berman, *Terror and Liberalism* (New York: W.W. Norton, 2003), 91.
107. Roger Scruton, *The West and the Rest* (London: Continuum, 2002), 131.
108. Phares, *War of Ideas*, 33.
109. "Osama Bin Laden: Palestinian Cause Prompted 9/11," CBS News, 16 May 2008.
110. Bernard Lewis, *Semites and Anti-Semites* (London: Phoenix, 1997), 129.
111. Andrew Bostom (ed.), *Legacy of Islamic Antisemitism: From Sacred Texts to Solemn History* (New York: Promotheus, 2008), 166.
112. Nonie Darwish, *Cruel and Usual Punishment* (Nashville: Thomas Nelson, 2008), 155.
113. Lewis, *Semites and Anti-Semites*, 122.
114. Daniel Benjamin and Steven Simon, *The Age of Sacred Terror* (New York: Random House, 2002), 67–68.
115. Gold, *Hatred's Kingdom*, 25.
116. Syed Abul 'Ala Maudoodi, *Towards Understanding the Qur'an*, vol. 3, (Markfield, Leicester, UK: Islamic Foundation, 1990), 201–02.
117. Ibid., vol. 1, 78–80.
118. Schoenfeld, *Return of Antisemitism*, 41.
119. Robert Wistrich, *Antisemitism* (London: Methuen, 1991), 226.
120. Sayyid Qutb, *Milestones* (Islamic Book Service, New Delhi, 2007), 82.
121. Sayyid Qutb, *In the Shade of the Qur'an*, vol. 1 (Leicester, UK: Islamic Foundation, 1999), 17.
122. Schoenfeld, *Return of Antisemitism*, 43.
123. Kuntzel, *Jihad and Jew-Hatred*, 21.
124. Ibid., 23.
125. Ibid., 28.
126. Wistrich, *Hitler's Apocalypse*, 177.
127. Daniel Pipes, *Militant Islam Reaches America*, 205.
128. Walter Laqueur, *The Changing Face of Antisemitism* (Oxford, UK: Oxford University Press, 2003), 199.
129. Wistrich, *Antisemitism*, 227–28.
130. Ibid., 228–9.
131. Kuntzel, *Jihad and Jew-Hatred*, 108.
132. Information Division, Israel Foreign Ministry, "The Covenant of the Hamas—Main Points," http://fas.org/irp/world/para/docs/880818a.htm.
133. Dr. Yussuf Al-Sharafi, Hamas representative, 12 April 2007, as reported by Palestinian Media Watch (PMW), 23 April 2007.
134. Hamas communiqué, 5 October 1988, translated and distributed in the U.S. by the Islamic Association for Palestine.
135. Sheikh Dr. Ahmad Bahar, acting Speaker of the Palestinian Legislative Council, 20 (23) April 2007; reported by Palestinian Media Watch.
136. Cox and Marks, *The West, Islam and Islamism*, 93.
137. Gold, *Hatred's Kingdom*, 174–5, 163.
138. Lawrence (ed.) *Messages to the World*, 189–90.
139. Ibid., 123.
140. Ibid., 67, 167.
141. Ibid., 9.
142. Kuntzel, *Jihad and Jew-Hatred*, 129–30.
143. Schoenfeld, *Return of Antisemitism*, 52.
144. Ibid., 50.
145. Robert Wistrich, *Anti-Semitism: The Longest Hatred* (London: Methuen: 1991), 218.
146. Schoenfeld, *Return of Antisemitism*, 43.
147. Ruhollah Khomeini, *Islam and Revolution* (Berkeley: Mizan, 1981), 127.
148. Ibid, 27.
149. Wistrich, *Hitler's Apocalypse*, 180.
150. Schoenfeld, *Return of Antisemitism*, 10.
151. Alex Spillius, "Iran's Supreme Leader Vows to Confront 'Cancerous Tumour' of Israel," *Daily Telegraph*, 3 February 2012.
152. "UN Chief: Ahmadinejad's Verbal Attacks on Israel Intolerable," *Ha'Aretz*, 21 February 2008.
153. Emanuele Ottolenghi, *Under a Mushroom Cloud: Europe, Iran and the Bomb* (London: Profile, 2009), 92.
154. Ibid., 91.
155. Ibid., 90.
156. Jonathan Spyer, *The Transforming Fire* (New York: Continuum, 2011), 107.
157. *As Safir*, 16 February 1985.
158. *Lebanon Daily Star*, 23 October 2002.
159. Steven Stalinsky, "Hezbollah's Nazi Tactics," *The New York Sun*, 26 July 2006.

160. Michael Rubin, "Hezbollah Is Neither Reformed nor Moderate," *Commentary Magazine*, 18 January 2015.
161. Schoenfeld, *Return of Antisemitism*, 13.
162. Ibid., 12.
163. Tarek Fatah, *The Jew Is Not My Enemy: Unveiling the Myths That Fuel Muslim Antisemitism* (Toronto: McClelland and Stewart, 2010), 11, 18.
164. Schoenfeld, *Return of Antisemitism*, 9.
165. "Dr. Mahathir Mohamad—'Jews rule the world by proxy,'" uploaded by Tajdid Agama dan Politik, You Tube, https://www.youtube.com/watch?v=-PJ9u8h3Gzw.
166. The Coordination Forum for Countering Antisemitism, http://antisemitism.org.il/article/74691/dr-m-says-glad-be-called-"antisemitic".
167. Lewis, *Semites and Anti-Semites*, 194.
168. Raphael Israeli, *War, Peace and Terror in the Middle East* (London: Frank Cass, 2003), 64.
169. Wistrich, *Hitler's Apocalypse*, 192.
170. Gove, *Celsius 7/7*, 59.
171. Dore Gold, "After the London Bombings: Blair's Israeli-Palestinian Detour from the Real Root Causes of Terrorism," *Jerusalem Centre for Public Affairs*, no. 534, 1 September 2005.
172. Gove, *Celsius 7/7*, 52.
173. Harris, *Suicide of Reason*, 27, 35.

Chapter 5

1. Dan Cohen-Sherbok and Douad El-Alami, *The Palestine-Israel Conflict: A Beginner's Guide* (Oxford, UK: Oneworld, 2002), 118.
2. Doreen Ingrams, *Palestine Papers 1917–1922: Seeds of Conflict* (London: John Murray, 1972), 177.
3. Daniel Pipes, "The Muslim Claim to Jerusalem," *Middle East Monitor*, September 2001.
4. Dore Gold, *The Fight for Jerusalem* (Washington, D.C.: Regnery, 2007), 39–40.
5. Charles Smith, *Palestine and the Arab-Israeli Conflict* (Boston: Bedford/St. Martin's, 2007), 5.
6. Martin Gilbert, *Exile and Return: The Emergence of Jewish Statehood* (London: Weidenfeld and Nicholson, 1978), 19.
7. Ibid., 21.
8. Samuel Katz, *Battleground: Fact and Fantasy in Palestine* (London: W.H. Allen, 1973), 95.
9. Cohen-Sherbok and El Alami, *The Palestine-Israeli Conflict*, 206.
10. Julius Stone, *Israel and Palestine: Assault on the Law of Nations* (Baltimore: Johns Hopkins University Press, 181), 15.
11. Bernard Lewis: "Palestine: On the History and Geography of a Name," *The International History Review* 11 (1 January 1980).
12. Bernard Lewis, "The Palestinians and the PLO, A Historical Approach," *Commentary*, January 1975, 32.
13. Stone, *Israel and Palestine*, 10.
14. Smith, *Palestine and the Arab-Israeli Conflict*, 41.
15. Ephraim Karsh, *Palestine Betrayed* (New Haven: Yale University Press, 2009), 9–10.
16. Benny Morris, *1948: A History of the First Arab-Israeli War* (New Haven: Yale University Press, 2008), 13.
17. Arieh Avneri, *The Claim of Dispossession: Jewish Land-Settlement and the Arabs, 1878–1948* (New York: Transaction Publishers, 1982), 13–14.
18. Ibid., 16–17.
19. Quoted by Joan Peters in *From Time Immemorial* (Chicago: JKAP, 1993), 155–57.
20. E. Mills, *Census of Palestine 1931*, vol. 1, *Palestine* (Alexandria: Printed for the Govt. of Palestine by Whitehead Morris, 1933), 148–51 and 170–71.
21. Tzvi Ben Gedalyahu, "Factbox: In 1919, 'Palestine Part of Arab Syria,'" *Arutz Sheva*, 20 December 2011.
22. Smith, *Palestine and the Arab-Israeli Conflict*, 31.
23. Benny Morris, *One State, Two States: Resolving the Israel/Palestine Conflict* (New Haven: Yale University Press, 2010), 30.
24. Daniel Pipes, "The Year the Arabs Discovered Palestine," *Middle East Review*, Summer 1989.
25. Alan Dershowitz, *The Case for Israel* (Hoboken: John Wiley, 2003), 7.
26. Karsh, *Palestine Betrayed*, 232.
27. Ibid., 248.
28. Stone, *Israel and Palestine*, 11.
29. Ibid., 16.
30. Wallace, *Foundations*, 16.
31. Stone, *Israel and Palestine*, 24. (This is not an argument for denying Palestinian self-determination outside of Jordan. It is merely to state a valid historical point.)
32. Tom Segev, *One Palestine Complete: Jews and Arabs Under the British Mandate* (London: Little, Brown, 2000), 273.
33. Interestingly, Palestine's malaria was eradicated by the pioneering work of Israel Kligler, a biologist whose work remains little known today.
34. Martin Gilbert, *The Routledge Atlas of the Arab-Israeli Conflict* (London: Routledge, 2002), 3.
35. Segev, *One Palestine Complete*, 275.
36. Avneri, *Claim of Dispossession*, 158.
37. Morris, *1948*, 83.
38. Shabtai Teveth, *Ben-Gurion and the Palestinian Arabs: From Peace to War* (Oxford: Oxford University Press, 1985), 31–32.
39. Kenneth Stein, *The Land Question in Palestine, 1917–1939* (Chapel Hill: University of North Carolina Press, 1984), chapter 6.
40. Colin Schindler, *A History of Modern Israel* (Cambridge: Cambridge University Press, 2013), 32.
41. Martin Gilbert, *In Ishmael's House: A History of Jews in Muslim Lands* (New Haven, Con.: Yale University Press, 2010), 175.
42. Palestine Royal Commission, *Report Presented to the Secretary of State for the Colonies in Parliament by Command of His Majesty, July 1937* (London: HMSO 1946), 93.
43. Martin Gilbert, *Winston S Churchill: Volume 5*, (London: Heinemann, 1976), 847.
44. Morris, *1948*, 15.
45. Karsh, *Palestine Betrayed*, 13.
46. Alexei Sayle, "I have got what it takes to lead the PLO: Jewish good looks," *Independent*, 2 December 2000.
47. Michael Curtis, *Jews, Antisemitism and the Middle East* (New Jersey: Transaction, 2013), 50.
48. Shlomo Avineri, *Herzl: Theodore Herzl and the Foundation of the Jewish State* (London: Weidenfeld and Nicholson, 2013), 132–33.
49. Avineri, *Herzl*, 178–79.
50. Ahad Ha'Am, "Truth from Eretz Yisrael," in *The Origins of Israel 1882–1948: A Documentary History*, ed. Eran Kaplan and Derek J. Penslar (Madison: University of Wisconsin Press, 2011), 30, 36–37.

51. Mark Tessler, *A History of the Israeli-Palestinian Conflict* (Indiana University Press, 2009), 135.
52. A Hebrew journalist, also known as Rabbi Binyomin.
53. Walter Lacqueur, *A History of Zionism* (New York: Schocken, 2003), 228.
54. David J. Goldberg, *To the Promised Land* (London: Penguin, 1996), 169.
55. Lacqueur, *A History of Zionism*, 236.
56. Ibid., 241.
57. Teveth, *Ben-Gurion*, 37.
58. Karsh, *Palestine Betrayed*, 26.
59. Teveth, *Ben-Gurion*, 32.
60. David Ben-Gurion, *Us and Our Neighbours* (Tel Aviv: Davar, 1931), 31, quoted in Judea Pearl, "Early Zionists and Arabs," *Middle East Quarterly*, Fall 2008, 67–71.
61. Shimon Peres (in conversation with David Landau), *Ben Gurion: A Political Life* (New York: Shocken, 2011), 61.
62. Judea Pearl, "Early Zionists and Arabs," *Middle East Quarterly*, Fall 2008, 67–71.
63. Teveth, *Ben-Gurion*, 70.
64. Ibid., 97.
65. The term "yishuv" refers to the Jewish community that was living in Palestine before the state of Israel was created in 1948.
66. Teveth, *Ben-Gurion*, 70.
67. Ibid., 56–57.
68. Karsh, *Palestine Betrayed*, 26.
69. Teveth, *Ben-Gurion*, 117.
70. Ibid., 145.
71. Ibid., 198.
72. David Ben Gurion, "Outlines of Zionist Policy (1941)" in *The Origins of Israel 1882–1948: A Documentary History*, ed. Eran Kaplan and Derek J. Penslar (Madison: University of Wisconsin Press, 2011), 316–17.
73. Morris, *One State, Two States*, 43.
74. Vladimir Jabotinsky, "On the Iron Wall," in *The Origins of Israel*, ed. Kaplan and Penslar, 257–58.
75. Karsh, *Palestine Betrayed*, 24–25.
76. Benny Morris, *The Birth of the Palestinian Refugee Problem* (Cambridge: Cambridge University Press, 1988), 24.
77. Curtis, *Jews*, 48.
78. Teveth, *Ben-Gurion*, 182.
79. Avi Shlaim, *Israel and Palestine* (London: Verso, 2010), 57.
80. It is also worth noting that in modern times, the parties that supported transfer (Kach and Moledet) never polled more than one-fortieth of Knesset seats.
81. Quoted by Ephraim Karsh in *Fabricating Israeli History: The New Historians* (New York: Frank Cass, 2000), 67.
82. Shlaim, *Israel and Palestine*, 56.
83. Hersch Lauterpacht, *International Law 3: The Law of Peace* (Cambridge: Cambridge University Press, 1977), 541.
84. Howard Grief, *The Legal Foundations and Borders of Israel* (Jerusalem: Mazo, 2008), 73.
85. "Council of the League of Nations Mandate for Palestine, 24 July 1922," in *Israel in the Middle East: Documents and Readings on Society, Politics and Foreign Relations Pre-1948 to the Present*, ed. Itamar Rabinovich and Jehuda Reinharz (Waltham, Mass.: Brandeis University Press, 2007), 35–40.
86. Wallace, *Foundations*, 8.
87. Cecil Genese, *The Holocaust: Who Are the Guilty?* (Lewes: Book Guild, 1988), 160–61.
88. Bernard Wasserstein, *On the Eve: The Jews of Europe Before the Second World War* (London: Profile, 2013), 367.
89. Ibid., 404.
90. Walter Lacquer, *A History of Zionism* (Fine Communications, 1997)), 506.
91. H. H. Ben-Sasson (ed.), *A History of the Jewish People* (Cambridge: Harvard University Press, 1976), 982.
92. Kathryn Blaze Carlson, "'None is too many': Memorial for Jews turned away from Canada in 1939," National Post, 17 January 2011, http://news.nationalpost.com/2011/01/17/none-is-too-many-memorial-for-jews-turned-away-from-canada/.
93. Goldberg, *Jewish Power*, 111–12.
94. David S. Wyman and Rafael Medoff, *A Race Against Death: Peter Bergson, America and the Holocaust* (New York: New Press, 2002), 4.
95. Wasserstein, *On the Eve*, 369.
96. Ibid., 370.
97. Barnet Litvinoff, *Weizmann: Last of the Patriarchs* (London: Hodder and Stoughton, 1976), 240.
98. Gilbert, *Exile and Return*, 259.
99. Ibid., 264.
100. It should be noted that Churchill did not share the indifference of his cabinet colleagues towards Jewish suffering. For a fuller treatment of this issue, see Martin Gilbert's *Churchill and the Jews* (New York: Simon and Schuster, 2007).
101. Wyman and Medoff, *A Race Against Death*, 6.
102. Ibid., 12.
103. Genese, *The Holocaust*, 119.
104. Honderich, "Terrorisms in Palestine," 4.

Chapter 6

1. Elie Kedourie, *In the Anglo-Arab Labyrinth: The McMahon-Husayn Correspondence and Its Interpretations, 1914–1939* (Cambridge: Cambridge University Press), 21.
2. Smith, *Palestine and the Arab-Israeli Conflict*, 102–4. Faisal would later repudiate his support for Zionism.
3. Kuntzel, *Jihad and Jew-Hatred*, 6.
4. Ibid., 37.
5. Karsh, *Palestine Betrayed*, 19.
6. Joseph B. Schechtman, *The Mufti and the Fuehrer* (New York: A.S. Barnes, 1965), 22.
7. Ibid., 25.
8. Gilbert, *Exile and Return*, 136.
9. Ibid., 139.
10. Gilbert, *Exile and Return*, 141.
11. Martin Van Creveld, *Land of Blood and Honey: The Rise of Modern Israel* (New York: Thomas Dunne, 2010), 51.
12. Norman Rose, *A Senseless, Squalid War: Voices from Palestine 1890s–1948* (London: Pimlico, 2010), 35.
13. Schechtman, *The Mufti and the Fuehrer*, 34–35.
14. Ibid., 38.
15. Gilbert, *Exile and Return*, 152.
16. Smith, *Palestine and the Arab-Israeli Conflict*, 134.
17. Nicholas Bethell, *The Palestine Triangle: The Struggle Between the British, the Jews and the Arabs, 1935–48* (London: Andre Deutsch, 1979), 26.
18. Schechtman, *The Mufti and the Fuehrer*, 46.

19. Litvinoff, *Weizmann*, 196.
20. David Ben-Gurion, "The Partition of Palestine," in *The Origins of Israel*, ed. Kaplan and Penslar, 240–43.
21. Morris, *One State, Two States*, 100.
22. Ibid., 99.
23. Ibid., 101.
24. Kuntzel, *Jihad and Jew-Hatred*, 38.
25. Karsh, *Palestine Betrayed*, 47.
26. "White Paper May 17, 1939," in *The Israel-Arab Reader: A Documentary History of the Middle East Conflict*, ed. Walter Laqueur and Barry Rubin (London: Penguin, 2008), 44–50.
27. Rose, *A Senseless, Squalid War*, 51.
28. Martin Gilbert, *In Ishmael's House: A History of Jews in Muslim Lands* (New Haven, Conn.: Yale University Press, 2010), 174.
29. Bethell, *The Palestine Triangle*, 44.
30. Ibid., 61.
31. Lewis, *Semites and Anti-Semites*, 148–49.
32. Bethell, *The Palestine Triangle*, 58.
33. Muravchik, *Making David into Goliath*, 7.
34. Schechtman, *The Mufti and the Fuehrer*, 117.
35. Nonetheless, in 1944 the Cabinet voted in favor of partition and accepting a Jewish state in Palestine.
36. Schechtman, *The Mufti and the Fuehrer*, 106.
37. Ibid, 110–11.
38. Quoted by Sarah Honig in "Fiendish Hypocrisy II: The Man from Klopstock Street, *Jerusalem Post*, 6 April 2001.
39. Schechtman, *The Mufti and the Fuehrer*, 141–45.
40. Lewis, *Semites and Anti-Semites*, 156.
41. Schechtman, *The Mufti and the Fuehrer*, 159–160.
42. Ibid., 163.
43. It must also be stressed here that by indicting the mufti, I am not implying that the Palestinian Arabs as a whole were responsible for the Nazi genocide. It is also worth noting that a significant number of Muslims came to the aid of Jews during the war, particularly in Albania.
44. Mark Curtis, *Secret Affairs: Britain's Collusion with Radical Islam* (London: Serpent's Tail, 2010), 22.
45. Schechtman, *The Mufti and the Fuehrer*,176.
46. Kuntzel, *Jihad and Jew-Hatred*, 147.
47. Said Aburish, *Arafat: From Defender to Dictator* (London: Bloomsbury, 1999), 15.
48. Mitchell Bard (ed.), *The Founding of the State of Israel* (Farmington Hills: Thomson Gale, 2003), 71.
49. Karsh, *Palestine Betrayed*, 82–83.
50. These issues are fully discussed in chapter 5 of Ephraim Karsh's excellent study *Fabricating Israeli History*.
51. Rose, *A Senseless, Squalid War*, 109, 117, 139, 147, 149.
52. Bethell, *The Palestine Triangle*, 344.
53. Ibid., 283.
54. Karsh, *Palestine Betrayed*, 90.
55. Morris, *1948*, 61.
56. Kuntzel, *Jihad and Jew-Hatred*, 50.
57. Hillel Cohen, *Army of Shadows: Palestinian Collaboration with Zionism, 1917–1948* (Oakland: University of California Press, 2007).
58. Lehi's Chief of Military Operations, Yitzhak Shamir, would go on to become Israel's 7th prime minister.
59. Morris, *1948*, 29.
60. Creveld, *Land of Blood and Honey*, 57.
61. David Ben Gurion, *Ben Gurion Looks Back* (London: Weidenfeld and Nicolson, 1965), 67.
62. Ibid., 76–77.
63. Morris, *1948*, 30.
64. Rose, *A Senseless, Squalid War*, 149.
65. Ahron Bregman, *Israel's Wars 1947–93* (London: Routledge, 2000), 11.
66. Karsh, *Palestine Betrayed*, 235.
67. Morris, *1948*, 118–120.
68. Ibid., 127.
69. Ibid., 125–27.
70. "The Arab Refugees," *The Economist*, 2 October 1948.
71. Morris, *1948*, 127.
72. Karsh, *Palestine Betrayed*, 182–83.
73. Rose, *A Senseless, Squalid War*, 213–14.
74. "The Arab Refugees," *The Economist*, 2 October 1948.
75. Katz, *Battleground*, 14–16.
76. Karsh, *Palestine Betrayed*, 2.
77. Ephraim Karsh, *Arafat's War* (New York: Grove, 2003), 34.
78. Bregman, *Israel's Wars*, 20.
79. Katz, *Battleground*, 19.
80. See also Karsh, *Palestine Betrayed*, 136–7, 138–9, 140, and 142.
81. Rose, *A Senseless, Squalid War*, 204.
82. "The Arab League's Dilemma," *The Economist*, 15 May 1948.
83. Matas, *Aftershock*, 158.
84. Ibid., 159.
85. Gilbert, *In Ishmael's House*, 222.
86. Ibid., 258.
87. Ibid., 332.
88. Ibid., 236.
89. Bregman, *Israel's Wars*, 17.
90. Akhbar al-Yom, Egypt, October 11, 1947; quoted by David Barnett and Efraim Karsh in "Azzam's Genocidal Threat," *Middle East Quarterly*, Fall 2011.
91. Morris, *1948*, 187.
92. Karsh, *Palestine Betrayed*, 214.
93. Yaacov Lozowick, *Right to Exist: A Moral Defense of Israel's Wars* (New York: Anchor, 2004), 88–89.
94. Van Creveld, *Land of Blood and Honey*, 117.
95. Ibid., 119.
96. Muravchik, *Making David into Goliath*, 26.
97. Karsh, *Arafat's War*, 10–12.
98. Barry Rubin and Walter Lacquer (ed.), *The Israel-Arab Reader* (New York: Penguin, 2008), 117ff.
99. Ibid., 122.
100. Michael Oren, *Six Days of War: June 1967 and the Making of the Modern Middle East* (Oxford: Oxford University Press, 2002), 84.
101. Martin Gilbert, *Israel* (New York: William Morrow, 1998), 373, 377.
102. Ibid., 380.
103. Dore Gold, *Tower of Babble: How the United Nations Has Fueled Global Chaos* (New York: Three Rivers, 2005), 96.
104. Morris, *One State, Two States*, 86.
105. Van Creveld, *Land of Blood and Honey*, 202.
106. Muravchik, *Making David into Goliath*, 47.
107. Jason Burke, "Bonn 'faked' hijack to free killers," *The Guardian*, 26 March 2000.
108. "Black September: Tough Negotiations," BBC News, 1 January 2001 http://news.bbc.co.uk/1/hi/in_depth/uk/2000/uk_confidential/1089694.stm.

109. Widlanski, *Battle for Our Minds,* 170–71.
110. "No. 21931: Multilateral: International Convention Against the Taking of Hostages. Adopted by the General Assembly of the United Nations on 17 December 1979," United Nations, n.d., http://www.un.org/en/sc/ctc/docs/conventions/Conv5.pdf.
111. Glick, *Israeli Solution,* 61.
112. Arafat was quoted in the *Washington Post,* 29 March 1970.
113. It is an open question whether autonomy could ever have led to a functioning Palestinian state. Crucially, the Palestinians never put Begin's autonomy plan to the test. The PLO lamented Sadat's "treasonous visit to the Zionist entity" and came to align themselves with other radical Arab states, this at a time when settlements were barely making an imprint on the disputed territories (Shindler, *A History of Modern Israel* (Cambridge: Cambridge University Press, 2008), 159).
114. Glick, *Israeli Solution,* 56.
115. *The Washington Post,* 16 June 1982.
116. Caplan, *The Israel/Palestine Conflict,* 199.
117. Karsh, *Palestine Betrayed,* 325.
118. Morris, *One State, Two States,* 120.
119. Shindler, *History of Modern Israel,* 236.
120. Karsh, *Palestine Betrayed,* 249.
121. Karsh, *Arafat's War,* 57.
122. Ibid., 63.
123. Ibid., 67.
124. Lozowick, *The Promise of Israel,* 230–1.
125. Ibid., 234.
126. Karsh, *Arafat's War,* 94.
127. William K. Langfan, "The PLO Charter Amendment That Never Was," *Arutz Sheva,* 1 June 2012.
128. "Fatah Congress to Keep 'Armed Struggle' Option," Monday 3, August 2009, Reuters.
129. Spyer, *Transforming Fire,* 46.
130. Barry Rubin, *The Transformation of Palestinian Politics* (Cambridge, Mass.: Harvard University Press, 1999), 58–62.
131. Karsh, *Arafat's War,* 136.
132. Raphael Israeli, *The Oslo Idea: The Euphoria of Failure* (New Brunswick: Transaction, 2012), 53.
133. Ibid., 89.
134. Karsh, *Arafat's War,* 153–54.
135. Robert Malley and Hussein Agha, "Camp David: The Tragedy of Errors," *The New Yorker,* 9 August 2001.
136. *Al-Ayyam,* July 29, 2001, at Middle East Media Research Institute, http://www.memri.org/sd/SP25001.html.
137. Saul Singer, "Whose Fault Was the Failure at Camp David?," *Jerusalem Centre for Public Affairs,* 15 March 2002.
138. Karsh, *Arafat's War,* 168.
139. *Al-Hayat,* 23 November 2000.
140. Karsh, *Arafat's War,* 169.
141. Dennis Ross, Margaret Warner and Jim Hoagland, "From Oslo to Camp David to Taba: Setting the Record Straight," *The Washington Institute,* 14 August 2001.
142. Karsh, *Arafat's War,* 193.
143. Ibid., 195.
144. "Suha Arafat Admits Husband Premeditated Intifada," *The Jerusalem Post,* 29 December 2012.
145. Gutmann, *The Other War,* 34–35.
146. Israeli, *The Oslo Idea,* 78.
147. Bregman, *Cursed Victory,* 226.
148. Ibid., 234.
149. Honderich, "Terrorisms in Palestine," 11.
150. Rubin and Lacquer, *The Israel-Arab Reader,* 567–73.
151. "Dennis Ross on Fox News Sunday," Fox News, April 21, 2002 http://www.foxnews.com/story/0,2933,50830,00.html#ixzz24lH5qww8.
152. Karsh, *Arafat's War,* 207.
153. Morris, *One State, Two States,* 149.
154. Muravchik, *Making David into Goliath,* 225.
155. Jonathan Cook, "The Engineer," *Al-Ahram Weekly Online* no. 582 (18–24 April 2002).
156. Rubin and Lacquer, *The Israel-Arab Reader,* 584–87.
157. Ibid., 583–84.
158. "Scientists Say Yasser Arafat Was Not Poisoned," *The Guardian,* 26 December 2013.
159. This terrorist carried out the "Passover massacre" in 2002.
160. http://www.pewglobal.org/2011/05/17/chapter-4-views-of-extremist-groups-and-suicide-bombing/.
161. Ilan Ben Zion, "PA Spends 6% of Its Budget Paying Palestinians in Israeli Jails, Families of Suicide Bombers," *Times of Israel,* 3 September 2012.
162. Itamar Marcus, *Deception: Betraying the Peace Process* (Jerusalem: Palestinian Media Watch, 2011), chapter 7.
163. "Abbas Claims Link Between Nazis and Zionists," Jewish Telegraphic Agency, 22 January 2013, http://www.jta.org/2013/01/22/news-opinion/israel-middle-east/abbas-claims-link-between-nazis-and-zionists.
164. Ed Hussein, "Jews, Muslims, the Holocaust and Israel," *Council on Foreign Relations,* 24 July 2012.
165. Herb Keinon (et al.), "In Qatar, Abbas Calls on Arab World to Visit J'lem," *Jerusalem Post,* 26 February 2012.
166. Glick, *Israeli Solution,* 182–83.
167. Tzippe Barrow, "Abbas, Erekat: Arabs Here for 'Thousands' of Years," CBN News, 8 September 2014, http://www.cbn.com/cbnnews/insideisrael/2014/February/Abbas-Erekat-Arabs-Here-for-Thousands-of-Years/.
168. Agreement on Movement and Access between Israel and the PA," 15th November 2005, http://www.eubamrafah.eu/files/Agreement%20on%20Movement%20and%20Access.pdf.
169. Aluf Benn, "Olmert's Plan for Peace with Palestinians," *Ha'Aretz,* 17 December 2009.
170. Ethan Bronner, "Olmert's Memoir Cites Near Deal for Mideast Peace," *New York Times,* 27 January 2011.
171. Shiri Hadar, "Netanyahu Stands by 2-State Solution," *Ynetnews,* 11 February 2013.
172. "Fatah Political Program," *Al-Ayyam,* 11 August 2009.
173. Israel has even been prepared to release prisoners and terrorists in return for the dead bodies of soldiers.
174. Glick, *Israeli Solution,* 72.
175. Ben Birnbaum and Amir Tibon, "The Explosive, Inside Story of How John Kerry Built an Israel-Palestine Peace Plan—and Watched It Crumble," *New Republic,* 20 July 2014.
176. Ibid.
177. Jack Khoury and Reuters, "Arab League Backs Abbas' Refusal to Recognize Israel as Jewish State," *Ha'Aretz,* 9 March 2014.

178. Yolande Knell, "Row over Demand for Palestinians to Recognise Israel as 'Jewish State,'" BBC News, 2 February 2014.
179. Shepherd, *State Beyond the Pale*, 20-1; Karsh, *Palestine Betrayed*, 257.
180. *Al-Hayat Al-Jadida*, 4 May 2013.
181. Cohn-Sherbok, *Palestinian State*, 109.
182. Irwin Cotler, "The Fatal Flaws of the Schabas Inquiry," *Jerusalem Post*, 11 September 2014.

Chapter 7

1. Aaron David Miller, "The Politically Incorrect Guide to U.S. Interests to Middle East," *Foreign Policy*, 15 August 2012.
2. Avi Shlaim, "Israel, the Great Powers and the Middle East Crisis of 1958," *Journal of Imperial and Commonwealth History* 12, no. 2 (May 1999).
3. David Eisenstadt and David Pollock, "Asset Test: How the United States Benefits from Its Alliance with Israel," Washington Institute for Near Eastern Policy, 2013, http://www.washingtoninstitute.org/uploads/Documents/pubs/StrategicReport07.pdf, 10.
4. America's airlift of weapons during the 1973 war naturally helped too, though it is doubtful these would have been given to a weak regime.
5. Blitzer, *Between Washington and Jerusalem*, 72.
6. Michael Bar-Zohar and Nissim Mishal, *Mossad: The Great Operations of Israel's Secret Service* (London: Robson, 2012), 168.
7. Ronald Reagan, "Recognizing the Israeli Asset," *Washington Post*, 15 August 1979.
8. Eisenstadt and Pollock, *Asset Test*, 11.
9. Bar-Zohar and Mishal, *Mossad*, 23.
10. Ibid., xi.
11. Ibid., 25.
12. Ibid., 19.
13. Blitzer, *Between Washington and Jerusalem*, 89–90.
14. Jeffrey Goldberg, "Is Israel America's Ultimate Ally?," *The Atlantic*, 26 April 2011.
15. U.S. Department of Defense, http://www.defense.gov/news/newsarticle.aspx?id=58479.
16. Udi Etsion, "F-35s to Carry Israeli Developed Helmet Display," *Ynetnews*, 13 October 2013.
17. Eisenstadt and Pollock, *Asset Test*, xi.
18. Vasudvan Sridharan, "US and Israel Hold Anti-Missile Defence Drill Juniper Cobra," *International Business Times*, 18 May 2014.
19. Eisenstadt and Pollock, *Asset Test*, 15.
20. Ibid., 16.
21. Ibid., 14.
22. Ibid., 15.
23. David Horowitz, "The Guy with the Bandage," *The Jerusalem Post*, 29 April 2011.
24. Jeffrey Kluger, "Edna Foa," *Time* 100, 29 April 2010.
25. Daniel Wagner, "What Israeli Airport Security Can Teach the World," *Huffington Post*, 17 March 2014.
26. Eisenstadt and Pollock, *Asset Test*, 20.
27. Richard Kemp, "A Salute to the IDF," *Jerusalem Post*, 15 June 2011.
28. Con Coughlin, "Britain Cannot Afford a Diplomatic Rift with Israel," *Daily Telegraph*, 3 December 2012.
29. "Hermes 450 Reaches 70,000 hours in Afghanistan," UK Ministry of Defence, 19 September 2013.
30. *Report: Added Value: Israel's Strategic Worth to the EU and Its Member States*," Henry Jackson Society, 2014, 10.
31. "Israel—an Unmanned Air Systems (UAS) Super Power," *Defense Update*, 3 May 2013.
32. "The 2004 Olympics Israel to Take Leading Role in Securing Athens Games in Case of Terror Attack," Jewish Telegraphic Agency, 30 July 2004, http://www.jta.org/2004/07/30/archive/the-2004-olympics-israel-to-take-leading-role-in-securing-athens-games-in-case-of-terror-attack.
33. Yoav Zitun, "IAF Holds Distant Strike Exercise," *Ynetnews*, 11 February 2011.
34. Pollard was a former U.S. intelligence analyst who received a life sentence for providing classified intelligence material to Israel.
35. Jan Goodwin, *Price of Honour: Muslim Women Lift the Veil of Silence on the Islamic World* (London: Sphere, 2006), 20.
36. International Energy Agency, http://www.iea.org/newsroomandevents/pressreleases/2012/november/name,33015,en.html.
37. "Obama Policies Making US More Dependent on Persian Gulf Oil," Institute for Energy Research, 28 August 2012, http://www.instituteforenergyresearch.org/2012/08/28/u-s-oil-imports-from-the-persian-gulf-and-Saudi-arabia-grow-in-2012-and-administration-policies-may-be-to-blame/.
38. Bard, *Arab Lobby*, 351.
39. Erik Gartzke and Kristian Gleditsch, "Why Democracies May Actually Be Less Reliable Allies," *American Journal of Political Science* 48, no. 4 (October 2004): 775–95.
40. Lewis, *Semites and Anti-Semites*, 242.
41. https://ustr.gov/countries-regions/europe-middle-east/middle-east/north-africa/israel
42. Michael Oren, "The Ultimate Ally," *Foreign Policy*, 25 April 2011.
43. Spencer Weary, *Never at War: Why Democracies Will Not Fight One Another* (New Haven: Yale University Press, 1998), 293.
44. For a fuller overview, see Helen Davis and Douglas Davis, *Israel in the World: Changing Lives Through Innovation* (London: Weidenfeld and Nicolson, 2005), 24–67.
45. For more information on the ReWalk, see "ReWalk Makes Miracles Possible," CNN, n.d., http://money.cnn.com/2014/12/08/technology/innovationnation/rewalk/.
46. Emily Singer, "Brain Surgery Using Sound Waves," *MIT Technology Review*, 21 July 2009.
47. "2003 Tyler Laureates: Sir Richard Doll, Hans R. Herren, Ph.D., and Yoel Margalith, Ph.D.," Tyler Prize for Environmental Achievement, n.d., http://tylerprize.usc.edu/laureates/tyler2003.html#margalith.
48. Davis and Davis, *Israel in the World*, 124–27.
49. Dan Senor and Saul Singer, *Start Up Nation: The Story of Israel's Economic Miracle* (New York: Twelve), 202–03.
50. "Israeli Firm Develops Android Phone for People with Disabilities of the Hands and Arms," The News Minute, 22 February 2015, http://www.thenewsminute.com/technologies/519.
51. David Shamah, "Chief Scientist: Israeli Nanotech Set to Make Commercial Leap," *Times of Israel*, 25 March 2014.
52. Eisenstadt and Pollock, *Asset Test*, xiii.
53. Senor and Singer, *Start Up Nation*, 147.
54. Eisenstadt and Pollock, *Asset Test*, 5.

55. Ibid., 4.
56. "Mullen's Testimony Challenges Pakistani Leaders on Terror: View," *Bloomberg*, 22 September 2011.
57. Sean Nevins, "America Gives Aid to Pakistan, Pakistan Gives Terrorism to the World," *mintpressnews*, December 16, 2014.
58. Max Boot, "Hosni Mubarak: Troublesome Ally," *Wall Street Journal*, 1 February 2011.
59. David Blair and Richard Spencer, "How Qatar Is Funding the Rise of Islamist Extremists," *Daily Telegraph*, 20 September 2014.
60. Patrick Tyler, "Intelligence Break Led U.S. to Tie Envoy Killing to Iraqi Qaeda Cell," *International New York Times*, 6 February 2003.
61. Haviv Rettig, "Expert: Saudis Have Radicalised 80% of U.S. Mosques," *Jerusalem Post*, 5 December 2005.
62. Dore Gold, "Who's Right on the War on Terrorism? The 9/11 Commission, the U.S. Senate Assessment of Prewar Intelligence, and the British Butler Committee," *Jerusalem Centre for Public Affairs* 3, no. 29 (26 July 2004).
63. "The Guantanamo Docket: Citizens of Saudi Arabia," *New York Times*, http://projects.nytimes.com/guantanamo/country/Saudi-arabia.
64. Nasr, *Shia Revival*, 245.
65. Greg Pallast and David Pallister, "FBI Claims Bin Laden Inquiry Was Frustrated," *Guardian*, 7 November 2001.
66. "Terrorist Financing": Task Force Report, *Council on Foreign Relations*, October 2002, 1.
67. Quoted in "An Assessment of Current Efforts to Combat Terrorism Financing," U.S. Senate Committee on Governmental Affairs, 15 June 2004.
68. Bard, *Arab Lobby*, 182.
69. Ibid., 145.
70. Ibid., 167.
71. Daniel Pipes, "The Scandal of US–Saudi Relations," *National Interest*, Winter 2002/03.
72. Lawrence Wright, "The Twenty-Eight Pages," *The New Yorker*, 9 September 2014.
73. Philip Stephens, "Britain Buckles Before Saudi Threats," *The Financial Times*, 19 December 2006.
74. Joshua Rozenberg, "SFO Director Good Man in Bad World, Say Law Lords," *Daily Telegraph*, 31 July 2008.
75. All data is available on the tables of the Pew Research Center: http://www.pewglobal.org/.

Chapter 8

1. Simon Hattenstone, "Saddam and Me," *The Guardian*, 16 September 2002.
2. George Galloway, *I Am Not the Only One* (London: Penguin, 2005), 55.
3. Stephen T. Hosmer, "Viet Cong Repression and Its Implications for the Future," Rand Corporation, May 1970, http://www.rand.org/content/dam/rand/pubs/reports/2008/R475.1.pdf.
4. George Galloway, quoted in *The Times*, 20 January 1994.
5. "George Galloway Meets Uday Hussein," posted by "Moslem74275," 8 June 2012, YouTube, https://www.youtube.com/watch?v=B3VgQDULX84.
6. For a fuller account, one can read Latif Yahia, *I Was Saddam's Son: As Seen on 60 Minutes a Shocking Eye Witness Account by the Man Who Was Forced to Serve as the Double of Saddam Hussein's Son* (New York: Arcade, 1997).
7. Galloway, *I Am Not the Only One*, 76.
8. Ibid., 114.
9. Colin Brown, "Galloway Tells Arabs to Fight 'Crusaders,'" *Daily Telegraph*, 29 September 2002.
10. Gwyn Topham, "Interview with George Galloway," *The Guardian*, 15 March 2004.
11. Nick Cohen, *What's Left?* (London: Fourth Estate, 2007), 301.
12. Christopher Hitchens, "George Galloway Is Gruesome, Not Gorgeous," Slate.com, 13 September 2005, http://www.slate.com/articles/news_and_politics/fighting_words/2005/09/george_galloway_is_gruesome_not_gorgeous.html.
13. "Galloway Claims Iran Executes Sex Offenders, Not Gays," *Pink News*, 14 March 2008.
14. John Miller, "Siding with the Oppressor," *One Law for All*, 41–2.
15. Robert Wistrich, "Anti-Zionist Connections: Communism, Radical Islam and the Left," in *Resurgent Anti-Semitism: Global Perspectives*, ed. Alvin Rosenfield (Bloomington: Indiana University Press, 2009), 409.
16. George Galloway, *The Fidel Castro Handbook* (London: MQ, 2006), 9.
17. "Cuba's Repressive Machinery: Human Rights Forty Years After the Revolution: I. Summary and Recommendations," Human Rights Watch, http://www.hrw.org/legacy/reports/1999/cuba/Cuba996-01.htm#P348_12349.
18. Edmund Standing, "Tiananmen Denial," Harry's Place, 2 June 2011, http://hurryupharry.org/2011/06/02/tiananmen-denial/.
19. "Livingstone Invites Cleric Back," BBC News, 12 July 2004.
20. Madeleine Bunting, "Friendly Fire," *The Guardian*, 29 October 2005.
21. Miller, "Siding with the Oppressor," 21.
22. Charles Johnson, "Top Islamic Cleric Wishes for Another Holocaust at the Hands of Muslims," Little Green Footballs, 3 February 2009, http://littlegreenfootballs.com/article/32643_Top_Islamic_Cleric_Wishes_for_Another_Holocaust_at_the_Hands_of_Muslims.
23. "Sheik Yusuf al-Qaradawi: Theologian of Terror," Anti-Defamation League, 3 May 2013, http://www.adl.org/anti-semitism/muslim-arab-world/c/sheik-yusuf-al-qaradawi.html#.VlTlxmSrSiY.
24. Miller, "Siding with the Oppressor," 22.
25. Peter Tatchell, "Islamist Clerical Fascism Threatens Muslims, Jews, Women and Gay People," http://www.petertatchell.net/religion/qaradawi.htm.
26. Ken Livingstone, "The Interview Part II," *Socialist Unity*, 15 September 2008.
27. Ken Livingstone, "Not a Difficult Choice at All," *The Guardian*, 15 May 2006.
28. "Iachr Publishes Report on Venezuela," Inter-American Commission on Human Rights, 24 February 2010, http://www.cidh.oas.org/Comunicados/English/2010/20V-10eng.htm.
29. Livingstone, *You Can't Say That*, 672.
30. "Mayor Livingstone Readmitted to Labour Party," *The Independent*, 6 January 2004.
31. Hugh Muir, "The Guardian Profile: Ken Livingstone," *The Guardian*, 18 February 2005.
32. Galloway, *I Am Not the Only One*, 14.

33. Ibid., 17.
34. Noam Chomsky and Edward S. Herman, *The Political Economy of Human Rights, Volume I: The Washington Connection and Third World Fascism* (Boston: South End, 1979), 16.
35. Farah Reza (ed.), *Anti-Imperialism: A Guide for the Movement* (London: Bookmarks, 2003), 117–18.
36. Noam Chomsky, *La Jornada*, Mexico, September 15, 2001.
37. Noam Chomsky, *American Power and the New Mandarins* (New York: Pantheon, 1969), 17.
38. Cohen, *What's Left?*, 157.
39. Paul Bogdanor, "The Top 200 Chomsky Lies," 2013, http://www.paulbogdanor.com/chomsky/200chomskylies.pdf.
40. Noam Chomsky, *At War with Asia* (New York: Random House, 1970), 219.
41. Stephen J. Morris, "Whitewashing Dictatorship in Communist Vietnam and Cambodia," in *The Anti Chomsky Reader*, ed. Peter Collier and David Horowitz (San Francisco: Encounter, 2004).
42. Noam Chomsky and Edward Herman, *The Political Economy of Human Rights, Volume II: After the Cataclysm* (Boston: South End, 1979), 62.
43. "The Legitimacy of Violence as a Political Act?: Noam Chomsky debates with Hannah Arendt, Susan Sontag, et al.," 15 December 1967, Chomsky.info, http://www.chomsky.info/debates/19671215.htm.
44. Chomsky and Herman, *Political Economy of Human Rights* II, 139.
45. "Cambodian Genocide Program: The CGP, 1994–2015," Yale University, http://www.yale.edu/cgp/.
46. Chomsky and Herman, *Political Economy of Human Rights* I, 149–50.
47. David Horovitz and Ronald Radosh, "Noam Chomsky's Jihad Against America," FrontPagemag.com, 19 December 2001.
48. David Horovitz and Ronald Radosh, "Chomsky and 9/11," in *The Anti Chomsky Reader*, ed. Collier and Horowitz.
49. It was titled "Some Elementary Comments on the Rights of Freedom of Expression."
50. Quoted by Alan Dershowitz in *Beyond Chutzpah* (Touchstone, 1992), 176.
51. Noam Chomsky, "Anti-Zionism, Israel and the Palestinians," *Variant*, no. 16, http://www.variant.org.uk/16texts/Chomsky.html.
52. Norman Finkelstein, *The Holocaust Industry* (London: Verso, 2000), 6.
53. Ibid., 7.
54. Don Atapattu, "How to Lose Friends and Alienate People: A Conversation with Norman Finkelstein," *Counterpunch*, 13 December 2001.
55. Norman Finkelstein, "The Business of Death," *The Guardian*, 12 July 2000.
56. Brian Appleyard, "Stop in the Name of the Holocaust," *The Sunday Times*, 11 June 2000.
57. Finkelstein, *Holocaust Industry*, 3.
58. Norman Finkelstein, "Israel Is Committing a Holocaust in Gaza," *Sunday's Zaman*, 19 January 2009.
59. "A Conversation with Professor Norman Finkelstein: How to Lose Friends and Alienate People, with Don Atapattu," *Counterpunch*, 13 December 2001.
60. Viktor Frvlke, "Shoa Business," *Salon*, 30 August 2000.
61. Dershowitz, *Beyond Chutzpah*, 83.
62. Finkelstein, *The Holocaust Industry*, 71.
63. Frvlke, "Shoa Business."
64. David Ceserani, "Finkelstein's Final Solution," *Times Higher Education*, 4 August 2000.
65. Omer Bartov, "A Tale of Two Holocausts," *New York Times*, 6 August 2000.
66. Peter Novick, "Offene Fenster und Tueren. Ueber Norman Finkelsteins Kreuzzug," in *Die Finkelstein-Debatte 159*, ed. Petra Steinberger, quoted by Alan Dershowitz in "The Hazards of Making the Case for Israel," http://www.jbooks.com/interviews/index/IP_Dershowitz.html.
67. Paul Bogdanor, "Interview: 'Jews Are Immune from any Kind of Criticism' [Excerpts]," http://www.paulbogdanor.com/antisemitism/finkelstein/interview2.html.
68. "Ilan Pappe on How Israel Was Founded on Ethnic Cleansing," *Socialist Worker*, 29 July 2006.
69. Ilan Pappe, "State of Denial: The Nakba in Israeli History and Today," in *Speaking the Truth*, ed. Michael Prior, 71.
70. Antony Loewenstein and Ahmed Moor, *After Zionism* (London: Saqi, 2012), 23.
71. Ilan Pappe, "Ilan Pappé: The Boycott Will Work, an Israeli Perspective," Ceasefire, http://ceasefiremagazine.co.uk/ilan-pappe-boycott-work-israeli-perspective/.
72. Alan Dershowitz, *The Case Against Israel's Enemies* (Hoboken: John Wiley and Sons, 2008), 125.
73. Meyrav Wurmser, "Made Up Massacre: The Tantura Affair, in which Post-Zionist Israel Libels Its Own Past," *The Weekly Standard*, 10 September 2001.
74. Ricki Hollander, "The Academic Blacklisting of Israel, the Tantura Affair and Ilan Pappe," 13 October 2005, Committee for Accuracy in Middle East Reporting in America, http://www.camera.org/index.asp?x_context=7&x_issue=55&x_article=991#tantura.
75. Baudouin Loos, "An Interview of Ilan Pappé," *Le Soir* (Brussels), 29 November 1999.
76. Ilan Pappe, "'Benny Morris's Lies About My Book,' Response to Morris' Critique of Pappé's Book, *A History of Palestine*," *New Republic*, 22 March 2004, History News Network, 5 April 2004.
77. Caplan, *The Israel/Palestine Conflict*, 230.
78. John F. Burns, "London Protesters Disrupt Israeli Orchestra's Concert," *New York Times*, 2 September 2011.
79. Jennifer Lipman, "Anti-Israel Protests Fail to Silence Habima Globe Performance," *The Jewish Chronicle*, 28 May 2012.
80. Richard Millett, "Israel's Batsheva Dances On in Edinburgh Despite PSC Invasions," 4 September 2012, RichardMillett's Blog, http://richardmillett.wordpress.com/2012/09/04/the-pscs-sights-and-sounds-of-hate-as-israels-batsheva-dances-on-in-edinburgh/.
81. Hannah Ellis-Petersen, "Tricycle Theatre Refuses to Host UK Jewish Film Festival While It Has Israeli Embassy Funding," *The Guardian*, 6 August 2014.
82. Nick Hallett, "Edinburgh Fringe Bans Israeli Show," *Breitbart*, 1 August 2014.
83. Harriet Sherwood and Matthew Kalman, "Stephen Hawking Joins Academic Boycott of Israel," *The Guardian*, 8 May 2013.
84. "Over 100 Artists Announce a Cultural Boycott of Israel," Letter, *The Guardian*, 13 February 2015.
85. Eric Lee, "From 'Pro-Peace' to 'Pro-Palestinian'—the British TUC Switches Sides," *Times of Israel*, 11 September 2014.

86. Kenneth Stern, "The Case Against Academic Boycotts of Israel," *Jewish Journal*, 16 February 2015.
87. Joanna Williams, "The Boycott-Israel Brigade Undermines the University," *Spiked Online*, 14 November 2014.
88. Anthony Julius and Simon Schama, "John Berger Is Wrong," *The Guardian*, 22 December 2006.
89. "Palestine Apology to Kuwait," *The Telegraph*, 12 December 2004.
90. Josh Wood, "The Palestinians' Long Wait in Lebanon," *New York Times*, 2 March 2011.
91. "Amnesty International: Lebanon: Exiled and Suffering: Palestinian Refugees in Lebanon," 17 October 2007.
92. Louisa Loveluck, Magdy Samaan and Ruth Sherlock, "Inside the Living Hell of Yarmouk," *The Daily Telegraph*, 7 April 2015.
93. "United States: Statement by President Bush: United Nations General Assembly: UN Headquarters, New York, 12 September 2002," United Nations, http://www.un.org/webcast/ga/57/statements/020912usaE.htm.
94. Anne Bayefsky, "The UN and Terrorism: Moral Relativism at Its Worst," *Human Rights Voices*, 22 May 2006.
95. Eric Reeves, "The UN's Bloody Failure," *The Guardian*, 20 June 2007.
96. Louise Charbonneau, "U.N. Assembly Holds 'Minute' of Silence for Kim Jong-il," *Reuters*, 22 December 2011.
97. Michael Higgins, "'Like Putting Jack the Ripper in Charge of a Women's Shelter': Iran to Head UN Conference on Disarmament," 14 May 2013, National Post, http://www.nationalpost.com/m/wp/blog.html?b=news.nationalpost.com/2013/05/14/fo0514-rogue.
98. "Emergency special sessions," United Nations, http://www.un.org/en/ga/sessions/emergency.shtml.
99. Caplan, *The Israel/Palestine Conflict*, 169.
100. Muravchik, *Making David into Goliath*, 80.
101. Ido Aharoni, "How the United Nations Human Rights Council Unfairly Targets Israel," *Time*, 30 July 2014.
102. "Annan Calls on Human Rights Council to Strive for Unity, Avoid Familiar Fault Lines," UN News Centre, 29 November 2006, http://www.un.org/apps/news/story.asp?NewsID=20770#.Vly15WSrSiY.
103. Mitchell Bard, *Myths and Facts, A Guide to the Arab-Israeli Conflict* (Washington: American Israeli Cooperative Enterprise, 2002), 122.
104. UN Watch, http://www.unwatch.org/site/c.bdKKISNqEmG/b.1359197/k.6748/UN_Israel__AntiSemitism.htm.
105. Wistrich, *Antisemitism*, 256–57.
106. Speech Given by Saudi Delegate to UN Seminar on Religious Tolerance, 5 December 1984.
107. "Israel Blasts Palestinian Charge That It Infected Children with HIV," *JTA News Agency*, 19 March 1997.
108. Matas, *Aftershock*, 25.
109. Michael Jordan, "Jewish Activists Stunned by Hostility, Antisemitism at Durban Conference," *Jewish Telegraphic Agency*, 5 September 2001.
110. "U.S. Urges U.N. Sleuth Resign over Blog Cartoon," *Reuters*, 8 July 2011.
111. Richard Falk, "Ending the Death Dance," *The Nation*, 29 April 2002.
112. Eli Lake, "U.N. Official Calls for Study of Neocons' Role in 9/11," *New York The Sun*, 10 April 2008.
113. Darwish, *Cruel and Usual Punishment*, 34.
114. Ibid., 43.
115. Ibid., 49.
116. Goodwin, *Price of Honour*, 113.
117. Darwish, *Cruel and Usual Punishment*, 57.
118. "World Report 2012: Syria," Human Rights Watch, http://www.hrw.org/world-report-2012/world-report-2012-syria.
119. Salam Faraj, "Women Deplore Restrictions in Male Dominated Iraq," *AFP*, 8 March 2012.
120. Ricardo Hausmann, Laura D. Tyson, and Saadia Zahidi, "The Global Gender Gap Report," World Economic Forum, http://www3.weforum.org/docs/WEF_GenderGap_Report_2010.pdf.
121. "Islam and Homosexuality," *The Economist*, 4 February 2012.
122. Hossein Alizadeh, "Straight but Narrow," *The Economist*, 4 February 2012.
123. Brian Whitaker, *Unspeakable Love: Gay and Lesbian Life in the Middle East* (London: Saqi, 2011), 169.
124. Ibid., 123.
125. "Letter from UN's Islamic Group to UNHRC President Opposing Panel on Violence Against Gays," UN Watch, http://blog.unwatch.org/index.php/2012/02/17/letter-from-uns-islamic-group-to-unhrc-president-opposing-panel-on-violence-against-gays/.
126. Patrick Burke, "African Leaders Reject U.N. Call for Homosexual Equality," *CNS News*, 20 February 2012.
127. Michelle Nichols, "Gambian President Says Gays a Threat to Human Existence," *Reuters*, 27 September 2013.
128. "Gambia's Jammeh Calls Gays 'Vermin,' Says to Fight Like Mosquitoes," *Reuters*, 18 February 2014.
129. Peter BetBaso, *Incipient Genocide: The Ethnic Genocide of the Assyrians of Iraq*, Assyrian International News Agency, 12 June 2007.
130. "Bureau of Democracy, Human Rights, and Labor, July–December, 2010 International Religious Freedom Report," U.S. Department of State, 13 September 2011, http://www.state.gov/j/drl/rls/irf/2010_5/168264.htm.
131. Bahá'í International Community, http://www.bic.org/sites/default/files/pdf/inciting-hatred-book.pdf.
132. "Group Denial: Repression of Kurdish Political and Cultural Rights in Syria," Human Rights Watch, 26 November 2009, http://www.hrw.org/node/86735/section/4.
133. Fazel Hawramy, "Turkey Would Rather Jail Journalists Than Address the Kurdish Question," *The Guardian*, 14 September 2012.
134. Amnesty International, http://www.amnesty.org/en/library/asset/MDE13/088/2008/en/d140767b-5e45-11dd-a592-c739f9b70de8/mde130882008eng.pdf.
135. "Introduction," Human Rights Watch, http://www.hrw.org/reports/1993/iraqanfal/ANFALINT.htm.
136. Aaron David Klein, "Egypt's Christians Face Mass Slaughter by Islamists," *WND*, 14 September 2012.
137. Angela Shanahan, "No Going Back for Egyptian's Converted Copts," *The Australian*, 21 May 2011.
138. Darwish, *Cruel and Usual Punishment*, 213.
139. David Raab, "The Beleaguered Christians of the Palestinian Controlled Areas," *Jerusalem Centre for Public Affairs*, 1-15 January 2003.
140. Margot Dudkevitch, "Gunmen Stole Gold, Crucifixes, Escaped Monks Report," *Jerusalem Post*, 24 April 2002.

141. Daniel Schwammenthal, "The Forgotten Palestinian Refugees," *Wall Street Journal*, 28 December 2009.
142. Phares, *War of Ideas*, 79.
143. Nasr, *Shia Revival*, 236–37.

Conclusion

1. Caplan, *The Israel-Palestine Conflict*, 30, 48–9.
2. Ibid., 263–4.
3. Muravchik, *Making David into Goliath*, 157.
4. Caplan, *The Israel-Palestine Conflict*, 241.
5. David Suissa. "Love Em or Hate Em, Settlements Are Not Illegal," *Jewish Journal*, 14 March 2013.
6. Lewis, *Semites and Anti-Semites*, 239.
7. Wistrich, *Hitler's Apocalypse*, 186.
8. Raphael Patai, *The Arab Mind* (New York: Hatherleigh, 2002), 96.
9. Margaret K. Nydell, *Understanding Arabs: A Guide for Modern Time* (Boston: Intercultural, 2006), 15.
10. Bard, *Will Israel Survive?*, 112–13.
11. Alexander H. Joffe, and Asaf Romirowsky, "Stop Giving Money to the U.N.'s Relief Agency for Palestinians," *The New Republic*, 18 August 2014.
12. Matti Friedman, "What the Media Gets Wrong About Israel," *The Atlantic*, 30 November 2014.
13. Tamar Sternthal, "New York Times Editor Admits Holding Palestinians to a Lower Standard," *Times of Israel*, 29 October 2014.
14. Gutmann, *The Other War*, 126–29.
15. Ibid., 78.
16. Yitzhak Benhorin, "Foreign Reporters Condemn Hamas' Censorship Policy in Gaza," *Ynetnews*, 12 August 2014; Daniel Bettini, "Foreign Journalists Reveal Hamas' False Front," *Ynetnews*, 7 August 2014.
17. Widlanski, *Battle for Our Minds*, 70.
18. Gutmann, *The Other War*, 152.
19. Mark Seager, "I'll Have Nightmares for the Rest of My Life," *Electronic Telegraph*, 15 October 2000.
20. Widlanski, *Battle for Our Minds*, 186.
21. Friedman, "What the Media Gets Wrong About Israel," 30 November 2014.

Bibliography

Aaronovitch, David. "Moderate Muslims—It's Time to Be Outraged." *The Times*, 3 July 2014.

Abdel-Latif, Omayma. "That Weasel Word." *Al-Ahram Weekly*, 4–10 April 2002.

Aburish, Said. *Arafat: From Defender to Dictator*. London: Bloomsbury, 1999.

Akram, Susan M., Michael Dumper, Michael Lynk and Iain Scobbie (eds.). *International Law and the Israeli-Palestinian Conflict*. London: Routledge, 2012.

Ali, Rashad, and Hannah Stuart. *A Guide to Refuting Jihadism*. London: Henry Jackson Society, 2014.

Alibhai-Brown, Yasmin. "Israel's Friends Cannot Justify This Slaughter." *The Independent*, 19 January 2009.

Alizadeh, Hossein. "Straight but Narrow." *The Economist*, 4 February 2012.

Allen, Charles. *God's Terrorists: The Wahhabi Cult and Hidden Roots of Modern Jihad*. London: Little, Brown, 2006.

Allen, Kate. "Quantitative Eating: It's Time for the World to Refuse Israel's Easing Rhetoric." *The Middle East Channel*, 7 December 2010, http://mideast.foreignpolicy.com/posts/2010/12/07/quantitative_easing_its_time_for_the_world_to_refuse_israels_easing_rhetoric_on_the.

Atapattu, Don. "A Conversation with Professor Norman Finkelstein: How to Lose Friends and Alienate People." *Counterpunch*, 13 December 2001.

Avineri, Shlomo. *Herzl: Theodore Herzl and the Foundation of the Jewish State*. London: Weidenfeld and Nicholson, 2013.

Avneri, Arieh L. *The Claim of Dispossession: Jewish Land Settlement and the Arabs, 1878–1948*. New Brunswick: Transaction, 2002.

Baram, Daphna. *Disenchantment: The "Guardian" and Israel*. London: Guardian, 2004.

Bard, Mitchell. *The Arab Lobby: The Invisible Alliance That Undermines America's Interests in the Middle East*. New York: Broadside, 2011.

———. *Will Israel Survive?* New York: Palgrave Macmillan, 2007.

Barnett, David. "The Mounting Problem of Temple Denial." *Gloria Centre*, 29 August 2011, http://www.gloria-center.org/2011/08/the-mounting-problem-of-temple-denial/).

Bartal, Shaul. "Palestinians Erase Jewish History." *Middle East Quarterly*, Summer 2012, 31–41.

Bar-Zohar, Michael, and Nissim Mishal. *Mossad*. London: Robson, 2012.

Bayefsky, Anne. "The UN and Terrorism: Moral Relativism at Its Worst." *Human Rights Voices*, 22 May 2006.

Benvenisti, Meron. "Bantustan Plan for an Apartheid Israel." *The Guardian*, 26 April 2004.

Beres, Louis Rene. "Do Not Lump Israel with Terrorists in 'Cycle of Violence.'" *US News*, 11 August 2009.

Berman, Paul. *Terror and Liberalism*. New York: W.W. Norton, 2003.

Bermant, Azriel. "Margaret Thatcher and Israel." *Haaretz*, 10 February 2012.

Bethell, Nicholas. *The Palestine Triangle: The Struggle Between the British, the Jews and the Arabs, 1935–48*. London: Andre Deutsch, 1979.

Birnbaum, Ben, and Amir Tibon. "The Explosive, Inside Story of How John Kerry Built an Israel-Palestine Peace Plan—and Watched It Crumble." *New Republic*, 20 July 2014.

Blair, David. "Now or Never for a Two State Solution." *Daily Telegraph*, 21 July 2013.

Blitzer, Wolf. *Between Washington and Jerusalem: A Reporter's Notebook*. New York: Oxford University Press, 1985.

Blumenthal, Max. *Goliath: Life and Loathing in Greater Israel*. New York: Encounter, 2014.

Bodi, Faisal. "Israel Simply Has No Right to Exist." *The Guardian*, 3 January 2001.

Boot, Max. "Hosni Mubarak: Troublesome Ally." *Wall Street Journal*, 1 February 2011.

Bowen, Jeremy. "A Year of Mid East Disappointment." BBC, 21 December 2006, www.bbc.co.uk.

Bradley, John R. *After the Arab Spring: How Islamists Hijacked The Middle East*. New York: Palgrave Macmillan, 2012.

Brailey, Malcolm. "Pre-Emption and Prevention: An Ethical and Legal Critique of the Bush Doctrine and Anticipatory Use of Force in Defense of the State." *Institute of Defense and Strategic Studies*, November 2003.

Bregman, Ahron. *Israel's Wars, 1947–93*. London: Routledge, 2000.

Bronner, Ethan. "Olmert's Memoir Cites Near Deal for Mideast Peace," *New York Times*, 27 January 2011.

Brown, Colin. "Galloway Tells Arabs to Fight 'Crusaders.'" *Daily Telegraph*, 29 September 2002.
Bukay, David. "Founding National Myths: Fabricating Palestinian History." *Middle East Quarterly* 19, no. 3 (Summer 2012): 23–30.
Bunting, Madeleine. "Friendly Fire." *The Guardian*, 29 October 2005.
Burleigh, Michael. *Blood and Rage: A Cultural History of Terrorism*. London: Harper, 2008.
Butler, Judith. *Parting Ways: Jewishness and the Critique of Zionism*. New York: Columbia University Press, 2013.
Byers, Michael. *War Law: International Law and Armed Conflict*. London: Atlantic, 2005.
Caplan, Neil. *The Israel Palestine Conflict: Contested Histories*. Chichester: John Wiley, 2010.
Carter, Jimmy. "Israel, Palestine, Peace and Apartheid." *The Guardian*, 12 December 2006.
Chesler, Phyllis. "Worldwide Trends in Honor Killings." *Middle East Quarterly* 17, no. 2 (Spring 2010): 3–11.
Cohen, Hillel. *Army of Shadows: Palestinian Collaboration with Zionism, 1917–1948*. New Jersey: University of California Press, 2009.
Cohen, Nick. *What's Left?* London: Fourth Estate, 2007.
Cohn-Sherbok, Dan. *The Palestinian State: A Jewish Justification*. Exeter: Impress, 2012.
_____, and Dawoud el-Alami. *The Palestine-Israel Conflict: A Beginner's Guide*. Oxford: Oneworld, 2001.
Collier, Peter, and David Horowitz (eds.). *The Anti-Chomsky Reader*. San Francisco: Encounter, 2004.
Cooper, Douglas Anthony. "Murder by Numbers." *Huffington Post*, 28 December 2011.
Coughlin, Con. *Khomeini's Ghost*. London: Pan, 2010.
Cox, Caroline, and John Marks. *The West, Islam and Islamism*. London: Civitas, 2006.
Crilly, Rob. "Osama Bin Laden Report: Pakistan Accused of 'Gross Incompetence.'" *Daily Telegraph*, 8 July 2013.
Crossman, Richard. *Palestine Mission: A Personal Record*. London: Harper and Brothers, 1947.
Curtis, Michael. *Jews, Antisemitism and the Middle East*. New Jersey: Transaction, 2013.
Darwish, Nonie. *Cruel and Usual Punishment*. Nashville: Thomas Nelson, 2008.
Dershowitz, Alan. *The Case Against Israel's Enemies*. Hoboken: John Wiley and Sons, 2008.
_____. *The Case for Israel*. Hoboken: John Wiley and Sons, 2003.
_____. *Why Terrorism Works: Understanding the Threat, Responding to the Challenge*. New Haven: Yale University Press, 2002.
Dill, Janina. "Applying the Principle of Proportionality in Combat Operation." *Oxford Institute for Ethics, Law and Armed Conflict*, December 2010.
Dinstein, Yoram. *The Conduct of Hostilities Under the Law of International Armed Conflict*. Cambridge: Cambridge University Press, 2004.
_____. *The International Law of Belligerent Occupation*. Cambridge: Cambridge University Press, 2009.
Durie, Mark. "How Dissimulation About Islam Is Fuelling Genocide in the Middle East." *Middle East Forum*, 12 August 2014.
Egerton, Frazer. *Jihad in the West: The Rise of Militant Salafism*. Cambridge: Cambridge University Press, 2011.
Evans, Julian. "The Militant Magician." *The Guardian*, 28 December 2002.
Falk, Ophir. "Proportionality: Doing What It Takes." *Jerusalem Post*, 21 November 2012.
Falk, Richard. "Slouching Towards a Palestinian Holocaust." *Countercurrents*, 7 July 2007.
Farrell, Stephen, and Beverley Milton-Edwards. *Hamas: The Islamic Resistance Movement*. Cambridge: Polity, 2010.
Fatah, Tareq. *The Jew Is Not My Enemy: Unveiling the Myths That Fuel Muslim Antisemitism*. Toronto: McClelland and Stewart, 2010.
Feinstein, Barry. "Proportionality and the Flotilla Incident in Light of International Law." *Jurist*, 21 January 2011.
Finklestein, Norman. "The Business of Death." *The Guardian*, 12 July 2000.
_____. *The Holocaust Industry*. London: Verso, 2000.
Fletcher, Martin. "Natural Gas: Israel's Game Changer." *Moment*, Jan./Feb. 2014.
Foxman, Abraham. *The Deadliest Lies: The Israel Lobby and the Myth of Jewish Control*. New York: Palgrave Macmillan, 2007.
Gaardner, Jostein. "God's Chosen People." *Aftenposten*, 5 August 2006.
Galloway, George. "Dark Echoes of the Holocaust." *The Daily Record*, 28 December 2009.
_____. *I'm Not the Only One*. London: Penguin, 2005.
Gartzke, Erik, and Kristian Gleditsch. "Why Democracies May Actually Be Less Reliable Allies." *American Journal of Political Science* 48, no. 4 (October 2004): 775–95.
Genese, Cecil. *The Holocaust: Who Are the Guilty?* Lewes: Book Guild, 1988.
Giddens, Anthony. *Runaway World*. London: Profile, 1999.
Gilbert, Martin. *Churchill and the Jews*. New York: Simon and Schuster, 2007.
_____. *Exile and Return: The Struggle for a Jewish homeland*. London: Weidenfeld and Nicolson, 1978.
_____. *In Ishmael's House: A History of Jews in Muslim Lands*. New Haven: Yale University Press, 2010.
Glick, Caroline. *The Israeli Solution: A One State Plan for Peace in the Middle East*. New York: Crown, 2014.
Gold, Dore. "After the London Bombings: Tony Blair's Israeli-Palestinian Detour from the Real Root Causes of Terrorism." *Jerusalem Centre for Public Affairs*, 1 September 2005.
_____. *The Fight for Jerusalem*. Washington: Regnery, 2007.
_____. *Hatred's Kingdom: How Saudi Arabia Supports the New Global Terrorism*. Washington: Regnery, 2003.

_____. "Historical Fiction: Israel Is Not a Colonialist State." *The New Republic*, 7 August 2010, http://www.newrepublic.com/article/politics/77072/israel-not-imperialist-state-historical-fiction.

_____. *Tower of Babble: How the United Nations Has Fuelled Global Chaos*. New York: Three Rivers, 2004.

_____. "Who's Right on the War on Terrorism? The 9/11 Commission, the U.S. Senate Assessment of Prewar Intelligence, and the British Butler Committee." *Jerusalem Centre for Public Affairs* 3, no. 29 (26 July 2004).

Goldberg, J.J. *Jewish Power: Inside the American Jewish Establishment*. New York: Basic, 1997.

Goldhagen, Daniel. *Worse Than war: Genocide, Eliminationalism and the Ongoing Assault on Humanity*. London: Abacus, 2012.

Goldstone, Richard. "Israel and the Apartheid Slander." *New York Times*, 31 October 2011.

Goodwin, Jan. *Price of Honour: Muslim Women Lift the Veil of Silence on the Islamic World*. London: Sphere, 2006.

Gordis, Daniel. *The Promise of Israel*. Hoboken: John Wiley, 2012.

Gove, Michael. *Celsius 7-7*. London: Weidenfield and Nicholson, 2006.

Grass, Gunther. "Gunther Grass Israel Poem Provokes Outrage." *The Guardian*, 5 April 2012.

Gray, John. *Al Qaeda and What It Means to Be Modern*. London: Faber and Faber, 2003.

Grief, Howard. *The Foundations and Borders of Israel Under International Law*. Jerusalem: Mazo, 2008.

_____. "Legal Rights and Title of Sovereignty of the Jewish People to the Land of Israel and Palestine Under International Law." *Nativ Online* 2 (2004), http://www.acpr.org.il/english-nativ/02-issue/grief-2.htm.

Gutmann, Stephanie. *The Other War: Israelis, Palestinians and the Struggle for Media Supremacy*. San Francisco: Encounter, 2005.

Habeck, Mary. *Knowing the Enemy: Jihadist Ideology and the War on Terror*. New Haven: Yale University Press, 2006.

Habib, Shahanazz. "Waking People Up to Reality." *Star Online*, 5 June 2011, http://www.thestar.com.my/story/?file=%2f2011%2f6%2f5%2fnation%2f8841100&sec=nation.

Halkin, Hillel. *Jabotinsky: A Life*. New Haven: Yale University Press, 2014.

Hamilton, Jill. *God, Guns and Israel*. Stroud: Sutton, 2004.

Hari, Johann. "Israel Is Suppressing a Secret It Must Face." *The Independent*, 28 April 2008.

_____. "The True Story Behind This War Is Not the One Israel Is Telling." *The Independent*, 29 December 2008.

Hawramy, Fazel. "Turkey Would Rather Jail Journalists Than Address the Kurdish Question." *The Guardian*, 14 September 2012.

Heymann, Paul. *Terrorism and America: A Commonsense Strategy for a Democratic Society*. Cambridge, Mass.: MIT Press, 1998.

Horovitz, David. *Unholy Alliance: How Liberals Got It Wrong in the Cold War and Still Blame America First*. Washington: Regnery, 2003.

Howe, Irving, and Carl Geshman (eds.). *Israel, the Arabs and the Middle East*. New York: Bantam, 1972.

Hunter, Thomas. *Targeted Killing: Self Defense, Preemption, and the War on Terrorism*. Charleston: Booksurge, 2009.

Ingrams, Doreen (ed.). *Palestine Papers 1917-1922: Seeds of Conflict*. London: John Murray, 1972.

Israeli, Raphael. *The Oslo Idea: The Euphoria of Failure*. New Brunswick: Transaction, 2012.

Johnson, Alan. *The Apartheid Smear*. Britain Israel Communications and Research Centre, 2014.

_____. "The Ethical Dilemmas of Fighting Terrorism." *Daily Telegraph*, 12 July 2014.

_____. "It's Time to Stop Infantilising the Palestinians." *Daily Telegraph*, 21 June 2014.

Judt, Tony. "Israel: The Alternative." *The New York Review of Books*, 23 October 2003.

_____. "'Jewish' State Has Become an Anachronism." *Los Angeles Times*, 10 October 2003.

Kaplan, Eran, and Derek J. Penslar. *The Origins of Israel 1882-1948: A Documentary History*. Madison: University of Wisconsin Press, 2011.

Karmi, Khami. *Married to Another Man: Israel's Dilemma in Palestine*. New York: Pluto, 2007.

Karsh, Ephraim. *Arafat's War*. New York: Grove, 2003.

_____. *Fabricating Israeli History: The New Historians*. New York: Frank Cass, 2000.

_____. *Islamic Imperialism: A History*. New Haven: Yale University Press, 2006.

_____. "The Middle East's Real Apartheid." *Jerusalem Post*, 3 May 2012.

_____. *Palestine Betrayed*. New Haven: Yale University Press, 2009.

Kasrils, Ronnie. "South Africa's Israel Boycott." *The Guardian*, 29 September 2010.

_____. "Who Said Nearly 50 Years Ago That Israel Was an Apartheid State?" *International Journal of Socialist Renewal*, 17 March 2009.

Katz, Samuel. *Battleground: Fact and Fantasy in Palestine*. London: W.H. Allen, 1973.

Kemp, Richard (Col.). "A Salute to the IDF." *Jerusalem Post*, 15 June 2011.

Kepel, Giles. *The Roots of Radical Islam*. London: Saqi, 2005.

Kessle, Oren, and Alice Bexson. "Added Value: Israel's Strategic Worth to the EU and Its Member States." Henry Jackson Society. January 2014. http://henryjacksonsociety.org/2014/02/05/event-summary-added-value-israels-strategic-worth-to-the-eu-and-its-member-states/.

Khan, Jemima. "Tell the Truth About Israel." *The Guardian*, 1 November 2000.

Khomeini, Ruhollah. *Islam and Revolution*. Berkeley: Mizan, 1981.

King, Oona. "Israel Can Halt This Now." *The Guardian*, 12 June 2003.

Kuntzel, Matthias. *Jihad and Jew-Hatred: Islamism,*

Nazism and the Roots of 9/11. New York: Telos, 2007.

Kuperwasser, Yosef, and Shalom Lipner. "The Problem Is Palestinian Rejectionism: Why the PA Must Recognize a Jewish State." *Foreign Affairs*, November/December 2011.

Lapidoth, Ruth. "Security Council Resolution 242: An Analysis of Its Main Provisions." *Jerusalem Centre for Public Affairs*, 4 June 2007.

Laqueur, Walter. *The Changing Face of Antisemitism*. Oxford: Oxford University Press, 2003.

———. *A History of Zionism*. New York: Schocken, 2003.

———. *No End to War: Terrorism in the Twenty First Century*. New York: Continuum, 2003.

———, and Barry Rubin (ed.). *The Israel-Arab Reader*. New York: Penguin, 2008.

Lattimer, Mark. "In 20 Years, There Will Be No More Christians in Iraq." *The Guardian*, 6 October 2006.

Law, S. *Israel, Palestine and Terror*. London: Continuum, 2008.

Lawless, Michael. "Terrorism: An International Crime." *National Defence and the Canadian Armed Forces*. http://www.journal.forces.gc.ca/vo9/no2/05-lawless-eng.asp.

Lawrence, Bruce (ed.). *Messages to the World: The Statements of Osama Bin Laden*. London: Verso, 2005.

Levy, Gideon. "Israelis' Ideal State: A Country Without Criticism." *Ha'Aretz*, 23 May 2010.

Lewis, Lewis. "Palestine: On the History and Geography of a Name." *The International History Review* 2, no. 1 (January 1980).

———. "The Palestinians and the PLO: A Historical Approach." *Commentary*, January 1975, 32.

———. *Semites and Anti Semites*. London: Phoenix, 1997.

———. *What Went Wrong? Western Impact and Middle East Response*. London: Phoenix, 2002.

Lia, Brynjar. *The Society of the Muslim Brothers in Egypt: The Rise of an Islamic Mass Movement 1928–1942*. Reading: Ithaca, 1998.

Lim, A. (ed.). *The Case for Sanctions Against Israel*. London: Verso, 2012.

Livingstone, Ken. "Not a Difficult Choice at All." *The Guardian*, 15 May 2006.

———. "This Is About Israel, Not Antisemitism." *The Guardian*, 4 March 2005.

———. *You Can't Say That*. London: Faber and Faber, 2012.

Loewenstein, Anthony. "Why Aren't Jews Outraged by Israel's Occupation?" *Ha'Aretz*, 17 June 2009.

——— (ed.). *After Zionism: One State for Israel and Palestine*. London: Saqi, 2012.

Lozowick, Yaacov. *Right to Exist: A Moral Defense of Israel's Wars*. New York: Anchor, 2004.

Mansdorf, Irwin. "Is Israel a Colonial State? The Political Psychology of Palestinian Nomenclature." *Jerusalem Center for Public Affairs*, 7 March 2010.

Marcus, Itamar. *Deception*. Israel: Palestinian Media Watch, 2011.

Mardean, Isaac. "The Desperate Plight of Iraq's Assyrians and Other Minorities." *The Guardian*, 24 December 2011.

Matas, David. *Aftershock: Anti-Zionism and Anti-semitism*. Toronto: Dundurn, 2005.

McShane, Denis. *Globalising Hatred: The New Antisemitism*. London: Weidenfeld and Nicolson, 2008.

Meotti, Giulio. "PA Rewriting Jewish History." *Yediot Achranot*, 11 October 2011.

Meron, Ya'akov. "Why Jews Fled the Arab Countries." *Middle East Quarterly* 2, no. 3 (September 1995).

Miller, Aaron David. "The Politically Incorrect Guide to US interests in the Middle East." *Foreign Policy*, 15 August 2012.

Miller, John. *Siding with the Oppressor: The Pro-Islamist Left*. N.p.: One Law for All, 2013.

Milne, Seumas. "This Slur of Antisemitism Is Used to Defend Repression." *The Guardian*, 9 May 2002.

Morris, Benny. *1948: A History of the First Arab-Israeli War*. New Haven: Yale University Press, 2008.

———. *One State, Two States: Resolving the Israel/Palestine Conflict*. New Haven: Yale University Press, 2010.

Muravchik, Joshua. "Israel's Arab Citizens and the Struggle for Equality." *Fathom*, Winter 2014.

———. *Making David into Goliath*. New York: Encounter, 2014.

Napoleon, Loretta. *The Islamist Phoenix*. New York: Seven Stories, 2014.

Nasr, Vali. *The Shia Revival: How Conflicts Within Islam Will Shape the Future*. New York: W.W. Norton, 2003.

Nathan, Susan. *The Other Side of Israel: My Journey Across the Jewish-Arab Divide*. London: Harper Perennial, 2006.

Neumann, Michael. *The Case Against Israel*. Petrolia, Cal.: Counterpunch, 2006.

Oborne, Peter. "The Cowardice at the Heart of Our Relationship with Israel." *The Daily Telegraph*, 12 December 2012.

Oren, Michael. "The Ultimate Ally." *Foreign Policy*, April 25 2011.

Organski, Abramo. *$36 Billion Bargain: Strategy and Politics in U.S. Assistance to Israel*. New York: Columbia University Press, 1990.

Orr, Deborah. "Is an Israeli Life Really More Important Than a Palestinian's?" *The Independent*, 19 October 2011.

Pappe, Ilan. "Benny Morris' Lies About My Book: Response to Morris' Critique of Pappe's book, *A History of Palestine*." *New Republic*, 22 March 2004.

———. "The Boycott Will Work: An Israeli Perspective." *Ceasefire*, 16 May 2012.

———. *The Ethnic Cleansing of Palestine*. London: Oneworld, 2007.

Patai, Raphael. *The Arab Mind*. New York: Hatherleigh, 2002.

Paulin, Tom. "Killed in Crossfire." *The Observer*, 18 February 2001.

Pavlischek, Keith. "Proportionality in Warfare." *New Atlantis*, Spring 2010.

Pearl, Judea. "Early Zionists and Arabs." *Middle East Quarterly* 15, no. 4 (Fall 2008).
Phares, Walid. *The War of Ideas: Jihadism Against Democracy*. New York: Palgrave Macmillan, 2007.
Phillips, Melanie. "Cameron and Clegg Give a Free Pass to Racism." *Daily Mail*, 23 January 2012.
———. *Londonistan*. London: Gibson Square, 2006.
Pilger, John. "Children of the Dust." *New Statesman*, 28 May 2007.
———. "Bloodshed and Hope." *The Guardian*, 28 July 2006.
———. "Holocaust Denied: The Lying Silence of Those Who Know." *New Statesman*, 8 January 2009.
———. "How They Teach Our Children Lies, About Vietnam, Afghanistan, Iraq, Libya, Iran..." *New Statesman*, 8 March 2012.
———. *The New Rulers of the World*. London: Verso, 2002.
Plait, Steven. "The Myth of Ethnic Inequality." *Middle East Quarterly* 21, no. 3 (Summer 2014).
Porter, Gareth. "Politics: Israel Warned Us Not to Invade Iraq After 9/11." *Inter Press Service*, 28 August 2007.
Prior, Michael (ed.). *Speaking the Truth: Zionism, Israel and Occupation*. Northampton: Olive Branch, 2005.
Qutb, Sayd. *Milestones*. New Delhi: Islamic Book Service, 2001.
Reeves, Eric. "The UN's Bloody Failure." *The Guardian*, 20 June 2007.
Remnick, David. "A Man, a Plan." *New Yorker*, 21 March 2011.
Reuveny, Rafael. "The Last Colonialist: Israel in the Occupied Territories Since 1967." *The Independent Review*, March 2001.
Rose, Norman. *A Senseless, Squalid War: Voices from Palestine 1890s-1948*. London: Pimlico, 2010.
Rosen, Nir. "Gaza: The Logic of Colonial Power." *The Guardian*, 29 December 2008.
Rosenberg, Yair. "Mahmoud Abbas, Still a Holocaust Denier." Tablet, 27 April 2014. http://www.tabletmag.com/scroll/170686/mahmoud-abbas-still-a-holocaust-denier.
Rubin, Barry. *The Tragedy of the Middle East*. Cambridge: Cambridge University Press, 2002.
———. *The Transformation of Palestinian Politics: From Revolution to State Building*. Cambridge, Mass.: Harvard University Press, 1999.
——— (ed.). *The Muslim Brotherhood: The Organization and Policies of a Global Islamist Movement*. New York: Palgrave Macmillan, 2010.
Rubinstein, Amnon. "The Curious Case of Jewish Democracy." *Azure Online* no. 41 (Summer 2010). http://azure.org.il/article.php?id=545.
Safran, Nadav. *Israel: The Embattled Ally*. Cambridge, Mass.: Harvard University Press, 1981.
Sayle, Alexei. "I Have Got What It Takes to Lead the PLO: Jewish Good Looks." *The Independent*, 3 December 2000.
Schechtman, Joseph. *The Mufti and the Fuehrer*. New York: Thomas Yoseleff, 1965.
Schneer, Jonathan. *The Balfour Declaration: The Origins of the Arab-Israeli Conflict*. London: Bloomsbury, 2010.
Segev, Tom. *One Palestine Complete: Jews and Arabs Under the British Mandate*. London: Little, Brown, 2000.
Senor, Dan, and Saul Singer. *Start Up Nation: The Story of Israel's Economic Miracle*. New York: Twelve, 2009.
Sewell, Dennis. "A Kosher Conspiracy." *New Statesman*, 14 January 2002.
Shapira, Anita. "The Failure of Israel's 'New Historians' to Explain War and Peace." *The New Republic*, 12 January 2000.
Shepherd, Robin. *A State Beyond the Pale*. London: Weidenfeld and Nicholson, 2009.
Shindler, Colin. *A History of Modern Israel*. Cambridge: Cambridge University Press, 2008.
———. *What Do Zionists Believe?* London: Granta, 2007.
Shlaim, Avi. *Israel and Palestine: Reappraisals, Revisions, Refutations*. London: Verso, 2010.
Shue, Henry, and David Rodin (eds.). *Preemption*. Oxford: Oxford University Press, 2007.
Silke, Andrew. *Terrorism*. London: Hodder and Stoughton, 2014.
Singleton, Alex. "Why Won't the BBC Come Clean over Its Bias Against Israel—A Moral Country That Deserves Our Support?" *Daily Mail*, 26 August 2012.
Sissons, Peter. "Left-Wing Bias? It's Written Through the BBC's Very DNA." *Daily Mail*, 22 January 2011.
Smith, Charles. *Palestine and the Arab-Israeli Conflict*. Boston: Bedford/St. Martin's, 2007.
Spyer, Jonathan. *The Transforming Fire: The Rise of the Israel-Islamist Conflict*. New York: Continuum, 2011.
Stalinsky, Steven. "Hezbollah's Nazi Tactics." *NY Sun*, 26 July 2006.
Stone, Julius. *Israel and Palestine: Assault on the Law of Nations*. Baltimore: Johns Hopkins University Press, 1981.
Taft, William, IV. "The Legal Basis of Pre-emption." *Council on Foreign Relations*, 4 November 2002. http://www.cfr.org/international-law/legal-basis-preemption/p5250.
Teveth, Shabtai. *Ben Gurion and the Palestinian Arabs*. Oxford: Oxford University Press, 1985.
Toameh, Khaled Abu. "What About the Arab Apartheid? Part II." Gatestone Institute. 23 March 2010. http://www.gatestoneinstitute.org/1120/what-about-the-arab-apartheid-part-ii.
Topham, Gwyn. "Interview with George Galloway." *The Guardian*, 15 March 2004.
Tutu, Desmond. "Realizing God's Dream for the Holy Land." *The Boston Globe*, 26 October 2007.
United Nations, and Geoffrey Palmer. "Report of the Secretary-General's Panel of Inquiry on the 31 May 2010 Flotilla Incident." New York: United Nations, 2011.
Van Creveld, Martin. *The Land of Blood and Honey: The Rise of Modern Israel*. New York: Thomas Dunne, 2010.

Verbeeten, David. "How Important Is the Israel Lobby?" *Middle East Quarterly* 13, no. 4 (Fall 2006): 37–44.

Wallace, Cynthia. *Foundations of the International Legal Rights of the Jewish People and the State of Israel.* Lake Mary, Fla.: Creation House, 2012.

Walt, John, and Stephen Mearsheimer. "The Israel Lobby." *London Review of Books* 28, no. 6 (23 March 2006).

Walzer, Michael. *Arguing About War.* New Haven: Yale University Press, 2004.

Wasserstein, Bernard. *On the Eve.* London: Profile, 2013.

Weart, Spencer. *Never at War: Why Democracies Will Not Fight One Another.* New Haven: Yale University Press, 1998.

Whitaker, Brian. *Unspeakable Love: Gay and Lesbian Life in the Middle East.* London: Saqi, 2011.

———. *What's Really Wrong with the Middle East.* London: Saqi, 2011.

White, Ben. "Is Israel a Democracy or an Ethnocracy?" *New Statesman*, 5 February 2012.

Whittaker, David J. (ed.). *The Terrorism Reader.* London: Routledge, 2007.

Widlanski, Michael. *Battle for Our Minds: Western Elites and the Terror Threat.* New York: Simon and Schuster, 2012.

Wistrich, Robert. *Antisemitism.* London: Methuen, 1991.

———. *Hitler's Apocalypse.* London: Weidenfeld and Nicholson, 1985.

Wood, Josh. "The Palestinians' Long Wait in Lebanon." *New York Times*, 2 March 2011.

Woodward, Bob. *Plan of Attack.* London: Simon and Schuster, 2004.

Wurmser, David. "The Strategic Impact of Israel's Export of Natural Gas." *Focus Quarterly*, Spring 2013.

Wyman, David, and Rafael Mediff. *A Race Against Death: Peter Bergson, America and the Holocaust.* New York: New Press, 2002.

Zuckerman, Mort. "Debunking the Myth of the Israel Lobby." *Huffington Post*, 25 May 2011.

Index

Abbas, Mahmoud 20, 21, 22, 37, 178, 182–188
Abdullah, Crown Prince 204
Ahmadinejad, Mahmoud 115, 208, 215
AIPAC 74–76
Al Assad, Basar 205, 208
Al-Assad, Hafez 31, 128, 177, 192
Al-Banna, Hassan 97–98, 111
Al Dura, Mohammed 24–25
al-Hussayni, Jamal 163
Al-Husseini, Hajj Amin (Mufti) 112, 128, 148–151, 155
Ali, Tariq 58
Alibai-Brown, Yasmin 52, 58
Allon Plan (1970) 167
al-Mabhouh, Mahmoud 44
al-Natsheh, Rafiq 174
al-Rahman, Abd 174
al-Tilmisani, Umar 112
al-Yamamah arms deal 204
al-Zarqawi, Abu Musab 202
al-Zawahiri, Ayman 99, 114
Amir, Yigal 177
Amnesty International 20, 25, 59
Annan, Kofi 43, 221, 222
Annapolis peace conference 184
anticipatory self defense 32, 43
anti–Semitism: cause of anti-Zionism 10; in 19th century Europe 142–3; in 20th century America 143–144; at the UN 224–225
apartheid: accusation 60–62; in the Arab world 225–232; definition 70
appeasement of Palestinian terror: British authorities 150, 152, 153–154; European governments 168, 172; Israeli leaders 173, 176, 180, 184, 185; UN 166–167, 169–170, 180, 187, 222–223; US governments 169, 171, 180–181, 187
Arab acceptance of Israel 158, 170, 188
Arab attitudes to USA 204–205
Arab rejectionism of peace 152, 157–158, 164, 165, 166, 167, 170–174, 177, 178, 181, 185
Arab revolt (1936) 151
Arab Spring 12
Arab world: problems in 12

Arafat, Suha 179
Arafat, Yasser 88, 118, 157, 165–166, 168–170, 172–183, 188, 231
Arlosoroff, Chaim 133–134, 152
Ashrawi, Hannah 174
Ataturk, Kemal 96, 97, 106–107
Ateek, Naim 59
Attlee, Clement 145, 157, 158
Atzmon, Gilad 54
Aufhauser, David 203

Balen report 85
Balfour Declaration 138, 147, 149, 150
Barak, Ehud 177–178
Barghouti,, Marwan 179
Bar Natan, Bernard 194
Basic Laws (Israel) 67, 70, 71, 197
BBC 22, 26, 73, 75, 84–85, 87
Begin, Menachem 22, 83, 170, 188
Ben-Gurion, David 60, 131, 134–137, 152, 154, 158, 159, 164, 165
Benvenisti, Meron 61
Bernard, Daniel 59, 87, 189, 249
Bevin, Ernest 157
Bin Laden, Osama 46, 99–101, 102, 103, 105, 107, 114, 118–119, 201–202
Black Sabbath 158
Black September massacre (1970) 92
Blair, Frederick 144
Blair, Tony 25, 74, 83, 88, 118, 204
Blumenthal, Max 62
Bosnian genocide 221
boycott movement (BDS) 6, 217–220
Brandt, Willy 168
Brennan, John 90
Brit Habiryonim 152
Brith Shalom 133
Brown, George 34
Brown, Gordon 22, 83
B'tselem 23
Bull, Gerald 191
Bush, George W. 32, 43, 79, 80, 82, 88, 90, 182, 191, 197, 203–205, 207, 209, 220
Butler, Judith 55–56

caliphate: collapse 96–98; restoration 102

Cameron, David 21, 22, 24, 75, 83, 91
Caroline incident 32, 43
Carter, Jimmy 20, 62, 196
Castro, Fidel 209
Chancellor, Sir John 150
Charlie Hebdo attacks 91
Chavez, Hugo 210
Chirac, Jacques 23
Chomsky, Noam 52, 55, 60, 88–89, 211–214
chosen people: concept of 57–58, 67–68
Churchill, Sir Winston 131, 149, 155, 208
Clapper, Lt. Col. James 91
Clegg, Nick 22
Clinton, Bill 81, 82, 175, 178, 180–181, 220
Clinton, Hillary 22
colonialism: accusation of 59–60, 68–70
Congress, support for Israel 77
Conservative Friends of Israel 77
conspiracy theories 1
Corbyn, Jeremy 74
Cordesman, Anthony 42
Coughlin, Father Charles 144, 194
Cuban missile crisis 32, 246
cycle of violence 25, 44–46, 221, 223

Dagan, Meir 192
Dalyell, Tam 74
Dar al Islam and Dar al Harb 94, 106
Darfur 92
Deir Yassin, battle of 161
democracy, Israel as 197
Dershowitz, Alan 2, 69, 168, 215
dhimmitude 108–110, 118
Dinstein, Yoram 28, 38, 39, 72
disproportionate or excessive force: accusation of 23–25, 38–40
distinction, principle of 23, 24, 40, 43, 44
Dreyfus affair 142
Duisenberg, Gretta 73
Duncan, Sir Alan 74
Durban Conference (2001) 5, 55, 61, 217, 224

267

Eban, Abba 145, 167
Egypt: anti-Semitism in 116; role in war on terror 201–202
Eisenhower, Ike 78
Entebbe raid (1976) 142, 194
Epstein, Yitzhak 133
Erdogan, Tayyip 24
Erekat, Saib 181, 184, 185, 186, 187
Esposito, John 10
Evian conference 144

Falk, Richard 53, 61, 224–225
Farhud 154, 155
Farouk, King 154
Fatah 165, 166, 170, 176, 181, 185, 187, 240
Faurisson affair 213–214
Fayyad, Salaam 22, 183
Feith, Douglas 196
Finkelstein, Norman 54, 84, 214–215
Fisk, Robert 87
Foa, Edna 194
Foreign and Commonwealth Office 85–86, 88
Foucault, Michel 1
Fourth Geneva Convention 27, 36, 40, 42
Freeman, Chas 89

Gaardner, Jostein 57
Gaddafi, Muammar 9, 205, 224
Galloway, George 53, 207–209, 211
Gates, Robert 201
Gaza: blockade of 29, 30; legal status of 20–21, 28–30; support for terror in 35; withdrawal (2005) 13, 33–34, 184
genocide: accusations of 51–55, 62–65
Gerstenfeld, Manfred 6
Ginsburg, Asher 133
Golan Heights 21
Goldstein, Baruch 177
Goldstone report 24, 25, 41, 77
Gove, Michael 20, 104, 119
The Guardian 83–84
Gurney, Sir Henry 163

Hagel, Chuck 23
Hague, William 20, 22, 23
Haig, Alexander 192
Hama massacre (1982) 92
Hamas 8, 29, 39, 41, 42, 44, 85, 112–113, 119, 176–177, 179, 184, 187, 193, 216, 232, 238, 240
Hamas Charter 113
Hammami, Said 188
Hamza, Abu 102, 106
Haniyeh, Ismail 84
Hari, Johann 21, 24, 59
Harris, Arthur (Bomber) 40
Hawking, Stephen 218
Heath, Ted 83, 168
Herzl, Theodore 129–130, 132–133
Hess, Moses 142
Hezbollah 8, 39, 115, 193, 195
Himmler, Heinrich 156
history, Palestinian distortion of 184

Hitler, Adolf 119, 154, 155
Hollande, Francois 91
Holocaust 63, 144–145, 156; denial 115, 183; hijacking of 54
honor: importance of in Arab world 227, 235
Human Rights Watch 20, 23, 25
human shields: Palestinian use of 42–43, 181
Hussein, Abdullah (King of Jordan) 140, 158, 165
Hussein, Amir Faysal 147
Hussein, King 167, 188
Hussein, Saddam 191, 197, 207–208, 219, 221, 230
Husseini, Faisal 174

Ibn Saud 154
ICCPR 49
IDF Code 40
Ignatieff, Michael 89
Immigration, British policy (Palestine) 149
incitement, Palestinian 17, 174–175, 179–180, 182–183, 236
Ingrams, Richard 73
International Covenant on Civil and Political Rights 49, 66
Intifada: first 65, 172; second 23, 26, 72, 179
Iraq war (2003) 79–80, 208
Irgun 54, 122, 152, 159, 161
Irving, David 116, 215
ISIL 8, 90, 92, 202, 220
Islamic Republic of Iran: anti-Semitism in 115; as theocracy 101; as threat to Israel 8, 192
Islamism: anti-Semitism of 107–117, 210; core tenets of ideology 102; different from Islam 93–94; rejection of democracy 103–104; rejection of freedom 105–106; western denial of 90–91
Israel lobby 73–86
Israeli Arabs: prospects for 14–17, 70–71
Iyad, Abu 172

Jabotinsky, Vladimir 136
Jasper, Lee 53
Jenin "massacre" (2002), 25
Jerusalem: false rumours of Jewish plotting 150, 179–180, 183–184; history of Jewish presence in 123–124
Jewish refugees from Arab world 163–164
jihad 94
Johnson, Boris 91
Johnson, Lyndon 34
Jones, Owen 21, 24
Jordan, as *de facto* Palestinian state 129
Judt, Tony 56, 60

Kach 177
Karsh, Ephraim 9
Kasrils, Ronnie 52, 59–62

Kaufman, Gerald 54, 74
Keegan, Maj. Gen. George F. 192
Kemp, Richard 41, 194
Kennedy, John F 32, 78–79
Kerry, John 21, 89–90, 186, 187
Khaled, Leila 168
Khamenei, Ali 115
Khartoum resolution 167
Khmer Rouge 212–213
Khomeini, Ruhollah 101, 115, 226
Ki-moon, Ban 24, 91
King, Oona, MP 53
King-Crane commission (1919) 128
Kirkpatrick, Jeanne 223
Klein, Naomi 57
Koran: anti-Semitism in 108–109
Kovel, Joel 56–57

Lang, Archbishop Cosmo 145
laws of return 66, 67
Lebanon War: (1982) 52, 171, 173, 191; (2006) 23
leftist apologies for terror 207–213
Lehi 122, 152, 159
Levy, Gideon 59, 219
Lewis, Bernard 94, 110, 126, 198, 235
Linton, Martin MP 74
Livingstone, Ken 55, 57, 88, 209–211
Llewellyn, Tim 75
Long, Breckinridge 145
Lucas, Caroline 87

MacDonald white paper 140–141
Malaysia: anti-Semitism in 117
mandate for Palestine (League) 69, 123, 129, 138–141, 149, 151
Martin, Michael 20
Mashaal, Khaled 202
Mavi Marmara, seizure 24, 59
Mawdudi, Abul Ala 99, 103, 105, 110
McDonald, Malcolm 153
Mearsheimer, John 62, 75, 79, 80, 89, 189, 205
media bias against Israel 239–241
Meir, Golda 144, 166, 188, 197
Merkel, Angela 20, 24
minorities persecuted in Middle East: Assyrians 229; Baha'is 197, 229–230; Christians under PA 231–232; Copts 231; Kurds 230–231; Yazidis 229
Mohammad, Umar Bakri 103
Mondale, Walter 191
Morgan, Piers 91
Morris, Benny 131, 136, 159, 161, 233–234
Mossad 44, 191–193
Mubarak, Hosni 170, 199, 201–202, 227
Mugniyeh, Imad 193
Muhammad (Prophet) 94, 95, 108–109, 111, 226
Muhammad, Khalid Sheikh 202
Muhammad V (Morocco) 164
Muhammed, Mahathir 117
Mullen, Mike (Admiral) 201
Mumbai terror attacks 87, 117, 203

Munich Olympics massacre 168
Muravchik, Joshua 16
Muslim Brotherhood 8, 97–99, 104, 111–112
Mussolini, Benito 153

Nasser, Col. Gamal 31, 79, 99, 165–167, 190
national self-determination 66, 138
Nazism: support for in Arab world 154–155
Netanyahu, Benjamin 20, 23, 37, 177, 185–188
Neumann, Michael 56, 59, 67
Nixon, Richard 78–79
Noel, Cleo A. (ambassador) 169
Nottebohm case 49
Nuremberg trial 156
Nuseibah, Hazem 224

Obama, Barack 20, 80, 82, 90, 185–186
Oborne, Peter 23, 74–75, 83–84
occupation of West Bank 17, 19–20, 27–35, 64–65, 168
Olmert, Ehud 36, 184–185
Operation Cast Lead 23–24, 41, 52
Operation Diamond (1965) 191
Operation Protective Edge (2014) 24, 26, 39, 42, 53, 187
Operation Solomon (1984) 142
Or commission (2000) 13
Organization of Islamic Conference 8
Organski, Abramo 77–78, 82
Orr, Deborah 57, 59
Osiraq attack 79, 83, 191
Oslo accords 28, 36, 173

Paddick, Brian 91
Pahlavi, Reza Shah 154
Pakistan: anti-Semitism in 117; role in jihadism 201
Palestine: as a backwater 126; birth of refugee problem 160–161; Jewish historical connection to 123–125; lack of Arab national identity 127–128; land purchase by Zionists 130; origin of name 126; population 126–127
Pappe, Ilan 55, 60, 215–217
Pasha, Ahmad Ziwar 147
Pasha, Azzam 164
Pasha, Heykal 163
Pasha, Nuqrashi 98
Passfield White Paper 150
Patten, Chris 20
Paulin, Tom 52
peace: offers made by Zionists/Israel 152, 158, 178, 181, 185, 234
Peel commission (1937) 125, 131, 137, 151–152
phased plan 172, 174
Pilger, John 52, 55, 73, 88
Pinsker, Leon 142
Plan Dalet (D) 160, 216
PLO 11, 31, 128, 165–166

PLO Charter 16, 175, 236
Pollard, Jonathan 80, 256
Powell, Colin 22, 90
Prescott, Lord John 53
price tag attacks 13
proportionality 38

Qaradawi, Sheikh al 103, 112, 202, 209–210, 228
Qatar, role in jihadism 202
Qibya raid 165
Qutb, Sayyid 98–99, 103–107, 110–111

Rabbo, Yasser Abd 174, 181, 187
Rabin, Yitzhak 175–177
Rafsanjani, Akbar 115
Reagan, Ronald 79, 82, 171, 172, 191
received wisdom about conflict 121–123
refugee: definitions 46
resolution 194 (1949) 47–48
resolution 242 (1967) 19, 33–34, 50
resolution 3379 (1975) 55
Reuveny, Raphael 60
right of Return: Israeli 56; Palestinian 26–27, 46–50, 178
Rodinson, Maxime 59
Ross, Dennis 178, 181
Rothschild, Matthew 60
Rubin, Barry 12
Rusbridger, Alan 84
Rwandan genocide 63–64

Sabeel 59
Sacher, Harry 133
Sadat, Anwar 170, 188
Said, Edward 10
saison, 159
Samuel, Sir Herbert 148–149
San Remo resolution 139–140
Saramago, Jose 52, 58
Sarkozy, Nicholas 19, 24, 26
Saudi Arabia: role in jihadism 202–204
Saudi peace plan (2002) 182
Sayle, Alexei 59
Schabas, William 187–188
Schalit, Gilad 57, 77, 185
scientific achievements, Israel's 199–200
separation barrier 72
September 11 attacks 25, 43, 73, 80, 118
settlements 13, 21–23, 35–38, 69, 237
7/7 attacks 194, 210
Sevres, treaty of 139
Sewell, Denis 73
sexual minorities in the Middle East 227–228
Shaath, Nabil 187
Shapira, Rabbi Yitzhak 17
Sharon, Ariel 165, 171, 179–180, 184
Shlaim, Avi 137
Shuckburgh, Sir John 149

Shuqiary, Ahmed 11
six days war 30–31-34, 166–167, 190
Sokolow, Nahum 133
Sontag, Susan 89
Stop the War 59
Straw, Jack 74, 88
Stuxnet 192
Suleiman, Muhammad 191
Supreme Court of Israel 28, 70, 71, 72, 197

Taliban 42
Tantura affair 216–217
taqiyya 93
targeted killings 43–44
Tatchell, Peter 210
tawhid 103
Taymiyyah, Ibn 94–95, 110
terror against Jews/Israelis 8, 148–149, 150–151, 159, 168, 170, 172, 175–177, 179, 181, 184
terrorism: definition of 45
Thatcher, Margaret 22, 83
Third Worldism 10–11
Thompson, Damien 1
Toameh, Khaled Abu 12
Tonge, Jenny 74, 87–88
Toynbee, Polly 87
transfer policy 137
Tuomioja, Erkki 53
Tutu, Desmond 61

United Nations: failures in peace-keeping 31, 220–221
United Nations Apartheid Convention (1973) 70
United Nations Genocide Convention (1948) 62
United Nations Human Rights Council 8, 187, 228
United Nations Partition Resolution (1947) 138, 158
United Nations Relief and Works Agency 47, 224, 237
United States: aid to Israel 78; Jewish electoral politics 81–83; pro-Israel veto at United Nations 80
Universal Declaration of Human Rights 48
unmanned aerial drone (UAV) 43, 193

Van Rompuy, Herman 22
Vietminh 207, 212
Von Clausewitz, Carl 11

Wahhab, Muhammad bin Abdul 95–96, 110
Wahhabism 10, 95–96, 113–114, 202, 232
Walt, Stephen 62, 75, 79, 80, 89, 189, 205
Walzer, Michael 32, 45
War Refugee Board 145
Ward, David, MP 53
war on terror: Israeli contributions to 193–195

War on Want 20
Weizmann, Chaim 133, 144, 147, 150, 152, 153
western ally, Israel as 11, 189–200, 237–238
White, Ben 54–56
White Paper (1939) 153
Wilhelm, Kaiser 129
Wilson, Sir Arnold 131
Wilson, Woodrow 138, 139
Wolfowitz, Paul 196
women's rights in Middle East 225–227

Ya Salam program 71
Yergin, Daniel 195

Yom Kippur War (1973) 196
Yosef, Ovadiah 16

Zaim, Hosni 165
Zangwill, Israel 136–137
Zionism: definition of 65–66
Žižek, Slavoj 53

www.ingramcontent.com/pod-product-compliance
Lightning Source LLC
Chambersburg PA
CBHW081546300426
44116CB00015B/2767